Forts Henry and Donelson

THE KEY TO THE
CONFEDERATE HEARTLAND

Forts Henry and Donelson

THE KEY TO THE
CONFEDERATE HEARTLAND

Benjamin Franklin Cooling

The University of Tennessee Press
KNOXVILLE

Copyright © 1987 by The University of Tennessee Press / Knoxville.
All Rights Reserved. Manufactured in the United States of America.
Second printing, 1988.

The paper in this book meets the minimum requirements of the
American National Standard for Permanence of Paper for Printed
Library Materials.
∞
The binding materials have been chosen
for strength and durability.

Library of Congress Cataloging-in-Publication Data

Cooling, B. Franklin.
    Forts Henry and Donelson—the key to the
Confederate heartland.

    Bibliography: p.
    Includes index.
    1. Henry, Fort, Battle of, 1862.   2. Donelson,
Fort, Battle of, 1862.   I. Title.
E472.96.c66   1987   973.7'31   87-5910
ISBN 0-87049-538-0 (alk. paper)

Contents

Illustrations and Maps

MAPS

*To John O. Littleton, Francis Wilshin, Ralph Happel,
Albert Dilahaunty, and Carlon Sills — National Park
Service historians — who first started me on the trail of
the Civil War; to Mrs. Lewis Feltner and her daughter
Peggy, of Dover and Nashville, Tennessee, who introduced
me to the ambience of the twin rivers; and to my mother,
who loved the little red mushrooms and cheery Tennessee
hickories on her visits to the hillsides at Fort Donelson.*

ACKNOWLEDGMENTS

It is never easy to thank all of the people who help in a project that has consumed over twenty-five years in conception. Certainly E.J. Pratt, R.G. Hopper, John W. Stockert, Carlon Sills, Carol Slaughter, and James Jobe of Fort Donelson National Military Park head the list. R.K. Haerle, Frank G. Rankin, and W.H. Dorris shared materials from their private collections. Professors Roy P. Stonesifer, Charles P. Roland, Jay Luvaas, and E.M. Coffman offered constructive comments. John Y. Simon (*Grant Papers*); Leona T. Alig (Indiana Historical Society Library); Archie Motley (Chicago Historical Society); Rodger D. Bridges (Illinois State Historical Library); Linda V. Bauch (Tennessee State Library and Archives); Patricia M. Hodges and Elaine M. Harrison (Western Kentucky University Library); Robert L. Byrd (Duke University Library); Richard A. Shrader (University of North Carolina Library); Peter J. Parker (Historical Society of Pennsylvania); Chester Kielman (University of Texas Library); Dale Floyd (Corps of Engineers Historical Office); Michael Musick (National Archives); and Louisa Arnold, John Slonaker, Dennis Vetock, Richard Sommers, David Keough, Michael Winey, and Randy Hackenberg (U.S. Army Military History Institute) stand out among librarians and archivists providing assistance. Working with the University of Tennessee Press staff has been a distinct pleasure. For the interested reader, research files gathered for this project have been deposited in the Library at the Fort Donelson National Military Park, Dover, Tennessee, and may be consulted there.

Preface

TWENTY YEARS HAVE PASSED SINCE Professor Thomas L. Connelly first referred to a Confederate "Heartland." He admitted that no Confederate official had bestowed that title upon the region encompassed by Tennessee, north-central Alabama, north-central Georgia, and northeast Mississippi. Yet he felt the name was appropriate for geographical as well as logistical and communication reasons. He also suggested applying the term to the principal Rebel army defending the locale. Connelly then proceeded to write an insightful, two-volume study of what another gifted author, Stanley Horn, had earlier called the Army of Tennessee.[1]

Perhaps Connelly is too modest about the extent of the Heartland. Possibly Horn's title is misleading. Geographically, the area stretches on a north-south axis across the plane of the Ohio River. If taken past the political limits of a civil war, it surely embraces what historians term "the Old Northwest," and "the Old Southwest." Militarily, various armies on both sides became involved with this area during the war. Indeed the whole story is more one of Mid-America — and of the men and women both north and south who extended the dream of a New World beyond the mere Atlantic slope, and then fought over it for four bloody years. To them belongs a lion's share of our national epic, our Civil War Iliad. From them flowed the human tide that fought the battles of the Heartland — from Henry-Donelson to Vicksburg; from Perryville to Nashville. They provided the main actors for the first battle of this Heartland drama: the campaign for those twin river forts called Henry and Donelson that yielded the key to unlocking the Confederate portion of the fabled region.

From the Henry-Donelson campaign rose the star of Ulysses S. Grant, a son of the Middle Border, whose leadership style very much reflected the qualities of the region. The tenacity and valor displayed by the participants on both sides reflected the self-reliance and pride of the trans-Appalachian west. Rural values and loyalty to kinsmen, as well as locale, led these men to this battleground. Most of them saw the fight as one for section or state, or even neighborhood. Yet before the saga of the

forts ended, northern and southern soldiers, politicians, and citizens discovered a wider, national implication that transcended their actions on
the Tennessee and Cumberland rivers.

What should have been understood by everyone at the time was the
central feature of rivers to the way of life in the Heartland. Waterways,
not roads or railroads, conditioned how people communicated, traded,
and survived in the Great Valley of Mid-America. Tributary streams,
such as the Tennessee and Cumberland, fed the mighty Ohio and Mississippi economically and politically as much as they did geographically
or naturally. Cotton was not king in this section, but rather bowed to
grain, tobacco, pork, timber, and iron. Carried by steamboat and traded
in the North for goods and services beneficial to the South's agrarian
system, these commodities forged linkages between sections of the Heartland. Because of the rivers and trade, Tennesseans and Kentuckians
had more cultural, economic, and even blood ties with people north
of the Ohio than they did with those of the Deep South. Forts Henry
and Donelson were constructed to guard the water passages but ironically became roadblocks to the one potential avenue for compromise
or reconciliation.

Much of this may be difficult to reconstruct after the passage of over
one and a quarter centuries. We can comprehend more easily the martial side of Forts Henry and Donelson, for we have become a people in-
ured to war. Back then it was a story of contrasts in command as well
as mobilization, logistics, technology, and human endurance superim-
posed upon nineteenth-century battle tactics. Unexpectedly smooth army-
navy cooperation and the fight between gunboats and earthen forts have
provided the traditional centerpiece of the tale; yet the story also embraces competition for power and control at higher command levels, and
the utter collapse of local Confederate ethics and leadership during the
battle. The shattered myth of Albert Sidney Johnston's invincibility as
the preeminent military man of the age stands in stark relief. The mar-
vel of frozen Confederate generalship injects a note of Greek tragedy
into the proceedings, but this seems counterbalanced by comic over-
tones of generals passing command and responsibility for surrendering
their army on the battlefield at the moment of victory. In so many ways,
Henry-Donelson was a brilliantly missed opportunity for the Confederacy to smash an uncertain Union strategic thrust by an untested Yankee
general.

On the other hand, Henry-Donelson was the scene of tactical bold-
ness by Ulysses S. Grant that snatched victory from defeat. Present were
the elements of professionalism versus amateurism which form a central

thread in America's martial past. The campaign reflected an organizational surge by a powerful North against the heroic but inadequate elan of the Confederacy. The operation also contrasted the strengths of tactical unity of command under Grant with the disarray of segmented leadership of the Confederates. As British military theorist J.F.C. Fuller once noted, no body of armed men could be considered an army unless it reacted to the will of one man, for a "multi-headed army is clearly a monster." The Confederate force at Henry-Donelson was no monster, but it was ill-served by its amateur leaders. In fact, Forts Henry and Donelson provide a study in command by West Pointers such as Grant, C.F. Smith, Henry Halleck, D.C. Buell, Sidney Johnston, P.G.T. Beauregard, Leonidus Polk, Simon B. Buckner, and Bushrod Johnson compared to citizen soldiers such as John B. Floyd, Gideon Pillow, John McClernand, Lewis Wallace, and Nathan Bedford Forrest. This West Point versus amateur leadership question reflects Arthur Mockler's suggestion that military history is pleasurable not because of maneuvers or campaigns or even reconstruction of battle details on maps or the actual ground, but because of seeing how men reacted to the sort of stress that could bring out the best or the worst in them.[2]

Nowhere was this impact of stress more apparent at Henry-Donelson than with the men in the ranks. Topography and weather affected the human will at Henry-Donelson as much as tactics or stratagems of generals. This stress conditioned the memories of veterans for years thereafter—memories of fighting and dying in the snow and cold and memories of the subsequent six months in Yankee prison camps for the unlucky. Aside from such remembrances, however, Henry-Donelson never gained the pantheon of great battles on either side, and we may wonder why. Did the stigma of shame and surrender so taint the mythic shield of southern valor that ex-Confederates blotted out such images of defeat from their Lost Cause? Perhaps the more memorable, hence honorable, "missed opportunities" of Shiloh or Chickamauga appealed more to aging men in gray. The Federals proved no better, for their reminiscences looked to Vicksburg and Chattanooga. Historians perpetuated the amnesia about the meaning of Henry-Donelson by protraying these battles as minor affairs, a mere prelude to Shiloh and beyond. Yet Bruce Catton observed at the height of the war's centennial: "Fort Donelson was not only a beginning; it was one of the most decisive engagements of the entire war, and out of it came the slow, inexorable progression that led to Appomattox."[3]

Henry Halleck, Grant's superior and senior Federal leader in the West, told Washington superiors on the eve of the battle that Fort Donelson was the turning point of the war,[4] but he promptly violated the opportunity to exploit the battle once Grant had presented him with victory. What followed were not only three more years of carnage, but a long and tedious "shadow war" behind the lines of advancing Federal power. The guerrilla war in the twin rivers section after the fall of Donelson has also been a forgotten legacy of the campaign. It provided a taste of Union occupation and reconstruction that left a bitter taste for decades.

Ultimately, a military event commands attention only if set against the role it plays as a force for modernization. A continuum exists in which the twin rivers and Forts Henry and Donelson provide a legacy from antebellum river culture to modern natural resources and recreational activities of the South. While Fort Henry lies beneath the waters of man-made Kentucky Lake, its outworks have been preserved by the very agency, the Tennessee Valley Authority, which ensured its demise. Fortunately, Fort Donelson became part of the National Park Service System in the 1920s as the automobile and tourist opened the region to a new generation determined to preserve natural and historical elements of its heritage.

In the end, the story of Henry-Donelson belongs to the Illinois plowboys, the Nebraska teamsters, the German and Irish tradesmen from upriver Nashville, and others like them who fought there. Today their descendants visit the park with picnic basket and happier hearts than did their ancestors. Yet few venture to the site on the anniversary of the battle when snow and cold can still provide a glimpse of what it must have been like in 1862. The visitor, standing beneath the pines in the national cemetery at Fort Donelson in any season, will feel the twinge of heart for those buried there, far from homes and youth.

Washington, D.C.   B. Franklin Cooling

CHAPTER I

Rivers and the Heartland in Crisis

BY THE FLOW OF THE INLAND RIVER, whence the fleets of iron have fled," begins a Civil War poem.[1] The people of that era are long dead, yet their poetic expression provides a theme for understanding this chapter in American history. The young nation depended upon its waterways to connect vast inland distances. Keelboats, flatboats, and then steamboats offered a way to tap the wealth of the hinterland by conveying goods and people. The steamboat was a "world in itself," says writer Francis Grierson, where friends and foes, gamblers and saints all rubbed elbows on shallow draught boats capable of carrying twenty tons of goods and thirty people across the shallow bars of the West's navigable rivers. Historian E. Merton Coulter states that the great Mississippi Valley streams always played a central role in the economic and political life of middle America.[2]

Trade centers from Pittsburgh and St. Louis to New Orleans, with Cincinnati, Louisville, Nashville, Memphis, and Natchez in between, all spring to life because of the waterways carrying cotton, iron, tobacco, foodstuffs, and manufactured goods. By the late 1850s, long-distance traffic between the Great Lakes and the Gulf had shifted to an east-west axis via canal and railroad to the Atlantic. But in its place came a profitable intravalley trade and a conscious development of political and cultural linkages. Northbound riverboats carried staple commodities such as molasses, sugar, tobacco, tropical fruits, and furniture, and exotic products, including apple brandy, tallow, and chestnuts, from the upper Cumberland and Tennessee valleys. In a sense, this economic interdependence blurred political contention between sections.[3]

The youthful railroads at this time complemented the river traffic. The railroads were beginning to draw off business, especially in the Midwest, but simply lacked carrying capacity, organization, and developmental capital south of the Ohio to compete with steamboats. Trunk-line railroads were few, and diversity of track gauge rendered long-distance travel difficult. Still, lines such as the Illinois Central, Louisville and Nashville, Mobile and Ohio, and Memphis and Charleston provided connecting links between the river arteries and the more remote local markets and farms. Several of the railroads paralleled the Mississippi down to the Gulf Coast. Yet at this point, rivermen who plied the western streams welcomed railroads as partners in commercial development of interior America.[4]

A "Golden Age" of steamboating continued as a rapidly changing political situation exploded upon the nation in 1860. Tension between North and South had been present for decades, but Abraham Lincoln's presidential election ignited the inflammatory environment of sectional politics and slavery. This election severed the alliance between free West and slave South, spelling the demise of the Democratic party as a unifying element in the country. Economic ties based upon western river trade remained unbroken, however. Most citizens of Heartland America saw the rivers and the north-south trade as unifying, not divisive elements. Yet, the tranquil days of packet whistles sounding around the bend and waters gently lapping against soft clay banks were numbered. Civil war descended in earnest upon the great rivers of the Heartland by the winter of 1860–61.[5]

The secession of the Deep South states left the question of free river navigation and the status of western states in doubt. The people of that section had several options: they could re-define the Union by forming a Northwest Confederacy, or join moderate slave states below the Ohio River to compensate for economic and familial ties. Instead, the Free West as well as Kentucky, Tennessee, Missouri, and Arkansas adopted an attitude of wait-and-see. As Kentucky governor Beriah Magoffin claimed on the eve of South Carolina's secession in December, the geography of the Heartland simply would not admit division, for the mouth and sources of the mighty Mississippi could not be separated without the horrors of civil strife. Middle Americans had long judged freedom of the rivers to be an inalienable right. Henry Clay, the "Great Compromiser," had said so on the floor of Congress in 1850. A decade later, western governors such as William Dennison of Ohio, Richard Yates of Illinois, and Oliver P. Morton of Indiana; legislators from Senators John Sherman of Ohio and Andrew Johnson of Tennessee to Ohio Congressman S.S. Cox; and private businessmen such as W.H. Osborn, George B. McClellan, and Nathaniel Banks of the Illinois Central railroad as well as James Guthrie of the Louisville and Nashville railroad echoed the call for free passage. Politicians and businessmen were less concerned

Steamboats on a Western River: government steamers *J. Donald Cameron* and *General McClellan*. National Archives.

with obstruction of the mouth of the Mississippi than with closure of the lucrative intravalley trade.[6]

Powerful commercial interests in upper river cities proved quite influential that winter. Unheeded in the East, where there was less sense of urgency about conditions in the Mississippi Valley, these commercial voices of the Midwest commanded attention in their own state capitals. Many midwesterners profited handsomely from the first surge in purchase of war materiel. Yet, the trade was with the South, and as the *Nashville Banner* noted on February 8, "The amount of flour, corn, and bacon which has passed through this city en route for the Republics of Georgia, Alabama, Mississippi and South Carolina is unprecedented." No wonder that Cincinnati voters elected a strong southern rights mayor in April; they followed the dictates of their purse strings, not the emotional propaganda of politicians.[7]

Of course a few leaders blundered. Governor James Pettus of Mississippi emplaced an artillery battery, designed to command navigation of the Mississippi River, at Vicksburg on January 12. A chill of foreboding swept across commercial interests north of the Ohio. Congressman John A. Logan of Illinois led the chorus of patriots in proclaiming that sons of the Northwest would cleave their way to the Gulf if the river remained blocked. As Pettus feigned innocence, the offending artillerists were withdrawn, but important lines had been drawn; people were upset by the action. A new Confederate Congress in Montgomery, Alabama, rushed legislation through to seduce the Old Northwest. By comparison, however, the United States government did little at this time for fear of disrupting the delicate balance of power pending Lincoln's inauguration.[8]

Midwestern governors and newspaper editors served as agents for the Lincoln administration, pressing for free navigation, yet carefully deferring to moderate state neutrality. After Lincoln took office in March, it appeared that even Kentucky legislators, upset earlier about Deep South control of the Mississippi, had lapsed into a comfortable "armed neutrality" so as to enjoy what Louisville and Nashville president James Guthrie counseled as "peace and harmony and attendant prosperity." The Fort Sumter affair in April and subsequent call by the federal government for volunteers to quell rebellion abruptly changed the situation. As Major Campbell Brown of Spring Hill, Tennessee, discovered, Unionism in his neighborhood evaporated into secessionism. Even defeated presidential hopeful John Bell despaired of conciliation with the Republicans in Washington. Moderation slipped from the grasp of leaders on both sides. By early summer, much of the Upper South including Tennessee, Arkansas, and Virginia also had left the Union.[9]

Lincoln's call for money and men to suppress rebellion brought quick response in states west of the Alleghenies. "Our people burn with patriotism and all parties show the same alacrity to stand by the Government and the laws of the country," wired Governor Richard Yates of Illinois. But, south of the Ohio, Beriah Magoffin countered that Kentucky emphatically refused to furnish troops for the "wicked purpose" of subduing fellow southern states. Isham Harris of Tennessee concurred that his state would not furnish a single man for coercion, but 50,000 if necessary for the defense of "our rights and those of our Southern brethern." In Arkansas, Governor H.M. Rector answered Lincoln with the observation, "The people of this Commonwealth are freemen, not slaves, and will defend their honor, lives, and property against Northern mendacity and usurpation." The lines became quickly drawn in the West, with high blown rhetoric of commercial freedom, abolition of slavery, and even sectional self-determination giving way to stern military necessity.[10]

Events moved swiftly as Cincinnatians began to monitor their city's trade with Louisiana, while Ohio and Indiana governors clamped restrictions on rail and telegraph traffic to the south. On April 24, Yates sent a Chicago militia contingent to seize control of the vital Cairo area where the Ohio and Mississippi converged. Terminus for the Illinois Central railroad, this dingy river town provided a choke point for river trade in the entire valley. It also stood at the tip of "Little Egypt," a southern-sympathizing tinderbox in that part of the state. Influential Illinois politicians such as Logan and John A. McClernand advised Lincoln against alienating this area, and they received army commissions largely for their success at keeping it in the Union. Arrival of the militia underscored its importance since Yates had tacit approval from Washington for the move.[11]

The militia soon intercepted the *C.E. Hillman,* out of St. Louis with 100 tons of lead, consigned to the state of Tennessee. The Volunteer State legislature protested loudly, and even Federal authorities directed that the militia commander stop harassing trade for fear of "extending the spirit of secession." This incident inflamed the region. Within weeks, a mini-war broke out between rivermen and various uniformed and irregular bands along the waterways. Soon, however, the Federals reversed course on using Cairo as a convenient checkpoint for monitoring traffic in war material passing southward. Customs officials in western river towns received conflicting instructions from Washington and were left to decide what comprised "contraband" and just what areas were "under insurrectionary control."[12]

The situation at Cairo, together with continued Federal and Confederate toleration of Kentucky neutrality, caused trading patterns to shift upstream to Louisville. Routes led south via rail and turnpike from the city, and despite renewed instructions and detailed regulations from the Treasury department, local customs officials proved powerless to stop the north-south trade through central Kentucky. Louisville merchants grew rich on such trade, although later that summer political conditions in the Bluegrass allowed the Lincoln government to prohibit "all commercial intercourse with the insurrectionary states." By this time, river travel had become extremely hazardous. When U.S. Navy Commander R.N. Stembel seized the *W.B. Terry* at Paducah on August 21, because of her role in the Confederate trade, her owners and their friends retaliated by seizing an Indiana-owned boat, *Stephen Orr;* then both sides retaliated with raids across the Ohio to tear down Unionist or Secessionist banners. Tennessee governor Harris put agents aboard Louisville and Nashville trains to intercept northbound cotton, rice, sugar, tobacco, molasses, and naval stores; and, when that did not work, he simply seized the portion of the road traversing his state. Ironically, Confederate authorities now relaxed duties on bacon, wheat, flour, and corn to woo midwestern farmers to their cause. It was too late; the individual actions of men like Harris prevented hopes of reconciliation.[13]

This turbulence had an impact north of the Ohio, also. Illinois Central managers bemoaned the drop in freight traffic at Cairo in April. Yet, as Ohioan E.D. Mansfield wrote his cousin, the U.S. Army's chief engineer in Washington, on June 7: "The interruption of Southern commerce affects business in Cincinnati very much, but failures are few, and generally, few people [are] in want." As the year moved to mid-point, thoughts turned more to marshaling fighting forces. Coercion, not conciliation, based on the river linkage, became apparent in pronouncements of men such as Mansfield, who touted the "Central West, which is enough to overwhelm the Gulf States, if it must be done."[14] Recruiters did not refer to free navigation or states rights to entice enrollees. Patriotism and thoughts of a short, easy war rallied young and old to Union and Confederate standards that spring and summer. None of the nostalgia associated with the departing recruit came through in official government proclamations, and mobilization was often a bungled affair. Few leaders knew the real strength of their militia organizations. Tennessee's 1840 statistic of 71,252 white males on the rolls and the 53,913 cited on Indiana's 1832 return (the latest information available for those states) poorly served War department officials either in Richmond or Washington. Still, the flower of the nation's youth marched off to war.[15]

Telegrams and newspapers during much of 1861 implied that everybody was threatened by somebody else — Missourians by Illinoisans, Hoosiers by Kentuckians (and vice versa), and Ohio's eastern counties by Confederates from western Virginia. Isham Harris contended that "moral power alone" could not keep rebellious East Tennessee Unionists from seeking separation from Confederate control. Harris wanted support from the central government in Richmond, just as a "loyal governors" meeting in Cleveland asked Lincoln to establish a military department for the West, set rules for stopping trade with the South, and emphasize military operations in the Mississippi Valley above other theaters of war. Governor Alexander W. Randall of Wisconsin suggested that a holy crusade might sweep down the Mississippi, across the Gulf states, and lay waste to the seedbed of secession at Charleston until "not one stone is left upon another, until there is no place for the owl to hoot or the bittern to mourn."[16]

At this stage of the conflict, Union authorities counted some 55,000 men under arms in the West. Illinois alone had 20,000 in the field. The Confederates could muster possibly 50,000 in this section. On July 2, Tennessee tendered to the Confederacy twenty-two regiments of infantry and two of cavalry, ten artillery companies, an engineer corps, and an ordnance bureau. State military leaders, such as Tennessee's senior general Gideon Pillow and Indiana Adjutant General Lewis Wallace, reflected political power, knowledge of the law, and Mexican War service as well as militia work among their credentials. Each man yearned for the glories of battlefield, not administrative housekeeping chores of mobilization. Few state soldiers seemed as proficient as Kentucky State Guard commander, Simon Bolivar Buckner, and his units numbered among the finest militia contingents in the country. Surrounding governors and their generals stood coveys of aides, clerks, and staff officers, and behind them came ranks of politicians and civilians seeking commissions, war contracts, and other favors. Mobilization consumed much time and effort during that summer and autumn of 1861.[17]

Regiments had to be recruited, equipped, armed, and trained before anyone could think about strategy and battle. Citizens delighted in plying loved ones in uniform with delicacies, extra clothing, and useless impedimenta for camp and field; but arms and equipment proved harder to find. State arsenals from Ohio to Mississippi contained rusty old firearms, and authorities in Washington and Richmond had little to provide in the way of munitions. Ohio quartermaster D.L. Wood went east to secure weapons, but to no avail. Yates of Illinois received Federal permission to tap the St. Louis arsenal. Most officials simply resorted to three devices: alter and repair existing munitions no matter the vintage or condition, improvise home manufacture, or procure where possible on the open market. Tennessee's team of Harris and Pillow led other states in developing a large munitions industry. Nevertheless, Kentucky flintlocks, converted smoothbore muskets, Austrian, Belgian, and English firearms, and a few newer Harpers Ferry and Springfield muskets passed into the hands of the troops. These were typical problems faced by Pillow, Wallace, Buckner, and others long before any thought was given to how to fight the war.[18]

Approximately 125 infantry, artillery, and cavalry units from sixteen Union and Confederate states were eventually committed to the first major western campaign for conquest of the Tennessee and Cumberland rivers of early 1862. The story for their early months in uniform and preparation of their first battle remains as crucial to understanding their role in operations as the actions of generals and politicians in formulating strategy and mobilizing armies. Many of the soldiers reflected the recruiting drives of spring 1861 — for instance, men from Lew Wallace's 11th Indiana Zouaves and Adolphus Heiman's German-Irish regiment, the 10th Tennessee. Some of these early arrivals literally hacked from the brush training camps Boone, Cheatham, and Trousdale in the Volunteer State; and Douglas, Morton, and others north of the Ohio. But exotic sobriquets (for example, "Light Infantry Blues" and "Gate City Guards") and multihued militia garb mostly melted away by the time units became components of state regiments. The initiation period was captured emotionally by William Felts of Company C, 18th Tennessee when he wrote his sweetheart from Camp Trousdale in Sumner County on June 23: "the Confinements of a Camp life and the grievances of those whom I hav left behind render me unhappy and the only Conciliation that I hav is this my friends has not forgottan [sic] me yet and I hope you hav not."[19]

Much has been made of the famous 21st Illinois, whipped into shape by a "very, very plain" ex-regular, failed farmer, and reputed drunk, Ulysses S. ("Sam") Grant. Undoubtedly, "Governor Yates' Hellions," as they were called, typified not only these eastern Illinois farmboys, but other units in both armies, including Colonel Benjamin F. Terry's 8th Texas Rangers and Captain John H. Guy's gentry-laced Goochland Artillery from Virginia; all would see action in the coming twin rivers campaign. Grant did just what every other volunteer colonel was doing at this time — judiciously applying old army discipline tempered by appreciation that to sharpen them for battle American citizen soldiers needed alternatives to chasing local belles and raiding barnyards for chickens. Grant admitted that his first few days with the 21st Illinois were tiring. Nathan Bedford Forrest began his war service as a private in J.S. White's Tennessee Mounted Rifles before friendship with Governor Harris secured authority for him to recruit his own battalion.[20]

Most of the main characters in the Forts Henry-Donelson campaign were spread across the country that summer and fall of 1861. George B. McClellan, who would command all of the Union armies at the time of the campaign, led the Department of the Ohio at this point. Henry W. Halleck, future departmental commander of the Missouri at St. Louis, was still a civilian as was Grant's aide, John A. Rawlins, and future colonels such as W.H.L. Wallace, John McArthur, James Tuttle, and William T. Shaw for the Federal forces. James B. McPherson, Grant's future engineer on the twin rivers, had been promoted to captain and sent to

Boston to take charge of harbor forts and to recruit miners, sappers, and engineers for a shrunken U.S. regular army. Lew Wallace had taken his Hoosier Zouaves to western Virginia for their first combat experience, and before John Logan trained and led his 31st Illinois, he spent the summer in Congress and then donned frock coat and musket to fight in the ranks at First Bull Run. Elderly naval Captain Andrew Hull Foote languished at the New York Navy Yard awaiting another assignment. Even that seasoned old regular and Grant's former teacher at West Point, C.F. Smith, was consigned to innocuous recruiting duty in New York City.[21]

Similar dispersion could be found among future Confederate actors in the Henry-Donelson drama. The soon deified Albert Sidney Johnston prepared to resign his U.S. Army commission to race eastward from Los Angeles to the side of his old friend and Confederate president, Jefferson Davis. In Virginia, Johnston's future second-in-command, the Louisianan hero of Fort Sumter and of First Bull Run (or so he claimed), P.G.T. Beauregard, faced Union forces protecting Washington. Leonidus Polk, giving up the robes of an Episcopal bishop for Confederate gray, was now in Memphis to forge the western frontier defenses along the Mississippi. Of the five Confederate generals involved with the twin rivers, John Bell Floyd (like the Yankee Wallace) first bloodied his Virginians in battles in the western part of that state. Gideon Pillow seemed to be everywhere, galvanizing a Tennessee army that numbered among the best in the South, despite a dearth of field artillery contingents. His unsung colleague Bushrod Rust Johnson (an Ohio Quaker by background) finished teaching chores at the Western Military Institute in Nashville and donned the uniform of his adopted state. Kentuckians Buckner and Lloyd Tilghman of Paducah focused upon perfecting their State Guard's southern-leaning members for any contingency. Still another Nashvillian, the colorful architect and German emigré Adolphus Heiman, and his subordinate Randal McGavock worked hard training their 10th Tennessee. They had also commenced the first rudimentary earthworks at a remote site some seventy miles northwest of the state capital on the Tennessee River. The position would soon be styled Fort Henry.

Nobody talked much about western river trade anymore. They now referred to the waterways in terms of military strategy. Some Tennesseans recognized their state's vulnerability via the rivers, but looked to Kentucky neutrality to protect them. Governor Harris sent some Tennessee troops to the defense of the Mississippi as the Federals made threatening moves in that direction. Major General John C. Fremont had arrived in St. Louis with orders both to hold Missouri for the Union and to prepare an expedition to move down the Mississippi and capture New Orleans. He soon dispatched reinforcements to Cairo, where Colonel Benjamin Prentiss' command languished because of inadequate provisions, the malarial climate, and general stagnation of garrison duty. Less than a month later, an impetuous Pillow and his Tennesseans relegated such stagnation to the dust bin of history. On September 4, Pillow led his men into neutral Kentucky and seized the strategic bluffs at Columbus on the Mississippi. The Great River had passed from symbol of nationalism and unity in the West, to a feature of regional concern, and finally to the axis of military invasion of the South.[22]

CHAPTER 2

Changing Plowshares into Swords

A<small>N UNLIKELY TEAM, A FORMER</small> bishop and a lawyer-planter, now changed the course of the war in the West. Incidents between Unionists and Secessionists in the Great Valley increasingly disturbed Leonidus Polk and Gideon Pillow. Federal naval authorities harassed Southern steamboats, and pro-Unionist militia tried to rally support throughout Kentucky. Polk, hardly a month on the job as Confederate commander in the region, also worried about Federal probes in southeastern Missouri. Destruction of the ferryboat and the presence of a small Federal force across the Mississippi from Columbus at Belmont provided a pretext for action. Not realizing that John C. Fremont had told his Cairo district commander, Ulysses S. Grant, to orchestrate such movements with a view "to occupy Columbus in Kentucky as soon as possible," Polk acted on his own. He wired Kentucky governor Beriah Magoffin that it was time to steal a march on the Unionists "in occupying Columbus and Paducah."[1]

By September 4, the repeated urgings of the ambitious and vainglorious Pillow had worked, as Polk ordered the invasion of neutral Kentucky and the Confederate defense line surged forward in an attempt to control what was perceived as the major invasion route into the Southern Heartland. Polk and Pillow spent the next three weeks explaining their action to Richmond authorities and the governors of Kentucky and Tennessee. Sharp protests rose on all sides, although as Tennessee senator Gustavus A. Henry noted shrewdly, "Whether it was altogether politic to take possession I need not say, but it will be ruinous to order [Polk] back." Therefore, said Henry, "let him advance his columns into Kentucky to Bowling Green and Muldraugh's Hill if necessary, and I predict he will not leave an enemy behind him south of that place in two weeks." In reality, the actions of Polk and Pillow reflected almost six months of frustration over Kentucky's vacillation and the unsettled conditions in Missouri. The weakness of Kentucky policy could be seen in the training camps for Unionists north of the Ohio, or those across the Tennessee line where Secessionists from the Bluegrass rendezvoused and trained. The fracturing of the Kentucky militia into Secessionist State Guard and Unionist Home Guard, as well as victimization of dedicated neutralists and businessmen soon became evident. Meanwhile, the strategic importance of the Columbus move acquired other dimensions.[2]

The Polk-Pillow invasion played to the worst fears of the river-oriented Upper Midwest. No matter that Confederate batteries downriver at Memphis or even further south at Vicksburg and New Orleans could effectively close the river; the Columbus bluffs were much closer to Illinois, Indiana, Ohio, and other Union states. Publicity on both sides focused on the Columbus issue, obscuring other vital approaches to the Southern Heartland. Actually, the Columbus occupation coincided with Federal moves to occupy equally useful positions at the mouths of the Tennessee and Cumberland rivers. Fremont had planned to take the Kentucky towns of Paducah and Smithland at those junctures; Columbus merely expanded Union options as far upriver as Louisville. From there, the Federal army could extend aid to East Tennessee Unionists and interdict the overland route to Nashville. Of course, the twin rivers of the Tennessee and Cumberland offered the most logical avenues for invasion not only to the Tennessee capital and rich agricultural area of Middle Tennessee, but far into the deeper recesses of northern Mississippi and Alabama. Some southerners could already see this threat. Local officials at Tuscumbia, Alabama, wrote the Davis government about the unprotected Tennessee River in late spring, but Confederate authorities could do little until the Volunteer State left the Union. Even then, competing priorities of states rights, military mobilization, and the war in Virginia usurped attention from the western front.[3]

Instigators behind the Columbus action seemed to be a handful of impatient Tennesseans. Still, Governor Harris expressed shock at the violation to Kentucky neutrality, if only because the incident dislocated his own plans. Like most shrewd politicians, Harris sought to fight Tennessee's battles beyond its soil—preferably in Missouri or Kentucky. The Columbus episode cost Harris valuable time to perfect his state's defense preparations. After successfully carrying the state out of the Union, Harris worked to develop a provisional army to transfer to Confederate control. He labored to suppress East Tennessee dissent, to build a munitions complex, and to insure his own reelection in August. He was just emerging from this extremely busy and vexing period when Polk and Pillow disrupted affairs by their invasion.[4]

Harris worked closely with the state's Military and Financial Board,

Map by Louis S. Wall

MAP I. The Western Theater, 1861–62.

a group of prominent Middle Tennessee Secessionists who played a major role in recruiting, subsisting, and equipping the state army. The board also recognized the potential invasion routes from the North. Its first piece of business on April 27, 1861, was to send a telegram to Adna Anderson, prominent engineer of the Edgefield and Kentucky railroad, whose offices stood near the state capitol. The board implored Anderson to "immediately" examine the most glaring gap in the state's defenses — the Cumberland and Tennessee rivers. But, for the moment, the board felt even more pressure from the Memphis business community, the Richmond government, and Gideon Pillow concerning the Mississippi River defense problem. As Pillow wrote Anderson on June 14, "no present danger on Tennessee River — nothing of military importance to be gained by ascending Tennessee River." Pillow failed to realize that Federal forces could outflank the river forts on the Mississippi, disembark from steamboats, or march overland into western Kentucky. The handful of citizens in northern Mississippi and Alabama worried the most about the wider ramifications of Federal invasion via the Tennessee River.[5]

Whatever Pillow's motives — response to the influential Mississippi River clique, or his own urge to undertake an offensive against Cairo — Governor Harris recognized the potential problem on the twin rivers. Despite the shield of Kentucky neutrality, the governor sent surveyors to the twin rivers in the early summer. Just how strenuous these efforts might have been with a more immediate Union threat remains unclear. Harris refused to violate Kentucky neutrality to get the best sites for fortifications, and so work had to be done on Tennessee soil, thus committing state and Confederate defense in this sector to certain peculiarities of politics and topography. Still, work began that summer on Fort Henry (the Tennessee post named for Gustavus A. Henry, the senior Confederate senator and native of nearby Montgomery County), as well as Fort Donelson (located twelve miles away on the Cumberland and named for the state's attorney general, Daniel S. Donelson, who participated in the survey). At the very least, Harris planned to use these positions for traffic check points on the rivers.[6]

The end of Kentucky neutrality meant the end of "no present danger" for western Confederates. As Federal forces poured into Kentucky, Confederate attention was partly diverted from the Columbus-Cairo sector. On September 6, Grant unilaterally seized Paducah, controlling egress both from the Tennessee and Cumberland rivers into the Ohio and Mississippi. At that moment, Grant was little more than just another West Pointer with a somewhat tarnished military and civilian record of mediocrity. He had secured his regimental command through political pull. But Fremont, sensing Grant to be "a man of great activity and of promptness in obeying orders without question or hesitation," sent him to handle affairs in southeast Missouri and southern Illinois. After arriving at Cairo, however, Grant immersed himself in Bluegrass matters. He was now challenged by one of those great opportunities of time and place in a war generally being conducted by rank amateurs.[7]

Grant sent messages to the Kentucky House of Representatives about the Rebel occupation of Columbus (promptly drawing Fremont's rebuke for meddling in political matters) and enjoined his command to refrain from marauding, insulting citizens, and searching houses. He constructed Fort Holt on the Kentucky shore opposite Cairo and patched together sufficient rivermen and their boats to send the 1,800–2,000 men

General Gideon J. Pillow. National Archives.

General Leonidus Polk.
National Archives.

upriver to seize Paducah. The town's Secessionist element fled before the blueclad host, and Grant settled his old friend and mentor C.F. Smith into command of the town. Smith slapped an ironclad rule on the locale, constructed defensive works, and then moved to garrison neighboring Smithland, at the mouth of the Cumberland. The Confederates did nothing to retaliate, although many southerners voiced concern over the Yankee threat to Columbus and to the L&N railroad at Bowling Green. Simon B. Buckner and a few others now in Confederate uniform sensed that Grant's occupation of Paducah and Smithland had neutralized both the successful seizure of Columbus and any southern hopes of using the Ohio River for the western frontier of their young Confederacy.[8]

War correspondent Franc B. Wilkie of the *Dubuque* (Iowa) *Herald* recalled later that he and his colleagues spent the autumn "chasing up rumors" that a Rebel force was advancing on Cairo or that guerrillas were threatening trouble in Missouri — noting, "there were endless expeditions going everywhere, but catching nothing." Dispatches to and from Grant's headquarters confirmed this. To no real avail, Federals and Confederates spent those months maneuvering over the area. Their actions seemed to signal some big push, which never came. Both sides learned the business side of war — civil-military relations, internal administration, and development of bases for future operations. Grant gathered his staff: young William S. Hillyer, a St. Louis lawyer; Clark Lagow, a

Crawford County resident and former subaltern in the 21st Illinois; and John A. Rawlins, another friend and lawyer from Grant's hometown of Galena. Rawlins had just lost his wife after a long illness, and complete dedication to Grant and the Union provided personal therapy. An old regular army surgeon, Dr. James Simons, became Grant's chief medic. Grant also encountered the harsh and ubiquitous world of brother officers — at one and the same time colleagues but also competitors. Counteracting C.F. Smith was the scheming McClernand, and other Illinois generals such as Prentiss and Eleazar A. Paine. Yet Grant, enjoying the patronage of Congressman Elihu B. Washburne in Washington, soon gained other trustworthy subordinates including Colonels Richard Oglesby and W.H.L. Wallace of the 8th and 11th Illinois, respectively. Grant alternately worried about his young troops and the needs of his family back home. He repeatedly told his wife, Julia, that he wished she could visit him at Cairo ("not half so unpleasant a place as I supposed it would be," he claimed), but that it would cost too much, and he might be called away "on army business."[9]

This "army business" seemed prosaic but also vital to future development of any army. Steamboat procurement and protection of loyal Union citizens in Kentucky, Missouri, and southern Illinois, as well as suppression of "demon rum," constituted some of this business. Grant and his generals attacked the drinking problem to the delight of chaplains such as Henry Hibben of the 11th Indiana at Paducah. Hibben wrote home that closing down the liquor traffic "is a blessed thing," for drunkenness was a great soldierly vice leading to more venal sins. He was aghast at what he found in the army, for while soldier life was hard, he reported, it was also demoralizing. Profanity abounded, and "it seems to me that men give way to all their passions and are worse than when they are at home," he sighed. Between the bothersome corps of newsmen snooping for stories at headquarters, increasing numbers of civilians in camp (from Western Sanitary Commission members to politicians), and the unceasing battle to keep the restless soldiers from stealing livestock and produce at will from suspected Secessionists, the dockets of the army's leaders proved quite full. Tirelessly, Grant and his staff kept the troops drilling, constructing fortifications and bridges, and occasionally scouting Confederate outposts. Grant wrote his sister Mary on September 11 that it was a rarity that he ever got to bed before two or three o'clock in the morning and was usually awakened later "before getting up in a natural way."[10]

Federal leaders never forgot their principal mission to develop a fighting force. By mid-October, Grant had brigaded his command under Mc-

Clernand, Oglesby, W.H.L. Wallace, and John Cook (all Illinoisans), as well as another ex-regular, Joseph B. Plummer. Regiments destined for future fame included the 7th, 8th, 10th, 11th, and 22nd Illinois infantry and 2nd Illinois cavalry; 7th and 10th Iowa, 11th Missouri, as well as Schwartz's, Taylor's, and MacAllister's batteries. Like Confederate Adolphus Heiman, Captain Adolph Schwartz was an emigré whose service with the Baden artillery quickly earned him respect. All of these units needed quarters, supplies, equipment, and training. Shoddy goods and rations had already posed problems for Grant, and in some cases the cost of constructing winter quarters at Cairo had risen above $23,000. Colonel Logan's 31st Illinois still lacked 920 muskets, and the cavalry remained virtually devoid of pistols as late as Christmas. McClernand and Colonel Michael Lawler of the 18th Illinois were furious about the state of their units' firearms; McClernand informed Grant that his brigade had "old altered U.S., and English Four muskets, fit, perhaps, for drill, but not for service." In turn, Grant informed the House Select Committee on Government Contracts in late October that when it came to the Austrian muskets in his command, the "men would hold them very tight, shut their eyes, and brace themselves to prepare for the shock." Yet, he rejected the vaunted new European "needle" gun, recommended by the committee, for such an "outlandish" weapon would only further compound his problems with different cartridges and primers as well as weight and reliability. As late as January 1862, the Cairo district commander complained about new units arriving with improper arms and equipment. Replacement of such equipment took time, as President Lincoln pointed out to his friend McClernand (who never tired of going around Grant to Washington political contacts).[11]

In November, Grant took his men by boat to attack the Confederate camp at Belmont, Missouri, an affair which hardly added luster either to the general's reputation or that of his troops who plundered the camp and wasted a tactical success. Grant wrote unabashedly to Washburne that as time passed, Belmont proved more successful than either he or McClernand had thought at first. Grant told his sister that his whole course had received "marked approbation" from soldiers and citizens, and Washburne mentioned to Secretary of the Treasury Chase that Grant and McClernand were two of the best soldiers in the West if only they had more money and better arms. Nevertheless, the stigma of failure clung to Grant and the ill-disciplined troops under his command. Their unpreparedness at Belmont hardly endeared either general or army to the new departmental chief at St. Louis, Major General Henry Halleck, who superseded Fremont. Halleck kept Grant in check, denied him any audience at headquarters, and the war in the West seemed stymied with the onset of early winter.[12]

Now, Grant began to see the need for closer collaboration with the U.S. Navy on western waters. The onset of war had closed down legitimate river trade, but not clandestine commerce, and Grant turned to suppressing it. The naval leader in the West, Commander John Rodgers, continued to seize steamboats and skiffs plying the waterways with illegal goods, in violation of Treasury department regulations. Grant told port officials in his jurisdiction to clamp down, and he sent various expeditions into the interior to stop the trade and ordered McClernand to place armed men aboard steamboats to ensure that the boat captains complied with their signed affidavits not to transport "contraband" materials. Some of the boats actually engaged regularly in runs from St. Louis to Columbus despite blockade and embargo, and Rodgers' Western Flotilla seized the steamers *John Gault* and *Jefferson* that were plying the Cumberland and Tennessee rivers in violation of trade restrictions. Unfortunately, the navy lacked men and ships to handle the problem properly. To hardened saltwater sailors, little glamour attended muddy river duty. The path to rank and glory was on the live-oak decks of blockading squadrons off southern coasts. Rodgers and his successor, Captain Andrew Hull Foote, experienced great problems in recruiting officers and men to perform river duty. Moreover, they had as much trouble as Grant in convincing superiors that the way to suppress armed rebellion was to confront main forces of the enemy, not engaging in search-and-destroy missions against elusive, clandestine traders.[13]

Either way, the United States Navy teamed with the army to mount a formidable threat to the Confederacy in the West. Birth of a so-called "brown-water navy" preceded Rodgers' appearance on the Ohio River in mid-May. Higher military and civilian authorities already entertained elaborate ideas about dispatching a great expedition of gunboats, transports, and 80,000 men to New Orleans via the Mississippi. Rodgers was sent west, however, to set up a smaller riverine force of gunboats or "naval armament" for "blockading or interdicting communication and interchanges with the States that are now in insurrection." He was to advise army leadership in this matter and to act in a secondary manner to the land forces in all operations. His first mission was to purchase three river boats and arm them. He quickly experienced opposition and antagonism from various private interests on the twin rivers.[14]

Rodgers came from a well-known Maryland nautical family, and he had earned a reputation for blue-and-gold professionalism that soon antagonized many steamboat owners on the rivers. He rejected their extor-

General Ulysses S. Grant. National Archives.

Flag Officer Andrew Hull Foote. National Archives.

tionist fees for use of their boats, and he worked closely with his brother-in-law, Union Quartermaster General Montgomery C. Meigs and the War Department to find and purchase the required craft. Eventually he purchased three passenger-freight boats totaling 1,167 tons for $62,000. After discovering their inadequacy for war, Rodgers engaged Daniel Morgan's Marine Railway and Drydock Company in Cincinnati to reconstruct the boats by adding oak bulwarks, lowering boilers below the deck, and cutting gun ports in the sides. Rodgers enjoyed the support of the Department of the Ohio commander, Major General George B. McClellan, but his detractors were many, and he experienced countless battles with the constructors about the defects to the boats. His closest aide was Lieutenant S.L. Phelps, destined for fame as a fighting sailor on the rivers, and the pair even managed to have ten 8-inch and six 32-pounder smoothbore naval cannon shipped to them from the Erie, Pennsylvania, depot. Eventually, these side-wheel steamers, *A.O. Tyler, Lexington,* and *Conestoga,* would become the renowned "timberclad" nucleus for an expanded Western Flotilla.[15]

By August, Rodgers learned that his greatest problem would be transporting the boats across shoal water in the Ohio, and he sought help from the local pilots' association. The pilots, however, whose indispensability to river commerce had led to banding against business exploitation, now equated the navy with just such exploitation. The navy required their services with high demands for patriotism but low wage scales. The pilots preferred more lucrative contract work as civilians with the army, leading Phelps to complain: "I find that people have an idea that there is a chance for a contract—upon which our country has gone mad and about which it is worse than dishonest—to get the vessels over the bars; anyone of these river men is ready to enter into contract to do it, even if there is not a particle of chance to succeed, knowing well that it is an easy matter to get relief from Congress to two or three times the amount of their outlay whether successful or not, as the Govt. is liberal and only needs the show of having undertaken to serve it for a good basis to recover largely." Get the contract, make a shot of carrying it out, and a speculation follows of course, noted Phelps. Rodgers eventually accommodated the pilots and signed on other rivermen at ranks lower than line naval officers, but never could enlist sufficient seamen despite recruiting stations in all the major river cities of the West. Those who did join were a seamy, ill-disciplined lot who caused Rodgers to write Washington anxiously about the need for saltwater sailors to stiffen the ranks of the river Tars. Even eventual passage downriver was not smooth: the people of Paducah threatened to take the gunboats should they pass unarmed, and all manners of devices were required to mount the cannon and small arms necessary for the trip. Nevertheless, by August 12, Rodgers had his timberclads tied up at Cairo, and "our estimated value and efficiency rose every hour," he reported. In a few days, Union authorities in the West regarded each boat as worth 5,000 soldiers, he claimed, "and no service is thought too arduous for our zeal or too dangerous for our powers."[16]

Paralleling Rodgers' activity with the timberclads came construction of another part of the new riverine flotilla. This resulted from Union General-in-Chief Winfield Scott's desire to commence operations down the Mississippi in support of his famous Anaconda plan. He directed Meigs to construct a fleet of ironclads and urged Congress to appropriate $1 million for this purpose. The boats would be manned by sailors and army volunteers, and officered by the navy. A product of the navy's best designers — including John Lenthall, chief of the Bureau of Construction and Repair, naval constructor Samuel A. Pook, and contract civilian A. Thomas Merritt, an experienced steam engineer from Cincinnati — the craft would eventually emerge as broad beamed, turtle-like boats with sloping armor-plated sides, blackened gunports, and silhouettes broken only by center-wheel housing aft, ubiquitous smokestacks, and a small pilot house forward. Twin engines propelled the single paddlewheel by steam and ten cannon — ranging in caliber from six traditional smoothbore 32-pounders, four old cannon reworked to fire rifled 42-pounder ammunition, and three new 8-inch rifles designed by naval ordnance expert John A. Dahlgren — were positioned to fire over the bow and stern as well as in traditional broadside. Fabricating and equipping the craft would be a joint army-navy venture, and one which would provide a Civil War prototype for latter military-industrial linkages in modern America. The question was who would actually construct these vessels. This building process proved more arduous than the timberclads for John Rodgers, and it eventually culminated in his replacement as naval commander in the West and in delays in mounting operations.[17]

Boat builders from the Midwest, the Great Lakes, and the East answered the War department solicitation for bids on the ironclads. Only inventor-engineer James B. Eads of St. Louis had the inside track on the contracts. With prominent friends such as Lincoln's attorney general Edward Bates, the influential Missouri political chieftains of the Blair clan, and the favor of Western Department commander John C. Fremont, Eads also profited from an extremely unsettled economic and political climate in Missouri. The gunboat project would aid financially depressed St. Louis and stimulate Unionism in the border state. Moreover, Eads, an experienced snagboat and salvage operator and amateur strategist as well as businessman, advocated military operations to reopen the Mississippi to the Gulf. Among the bidders he alone promised to complete the job in sixty-three days, at a cost of $89,000 per boat, and to forfeit $250 per day if he failed to meet the deadline. While critics accused him of inability to construct gunboats, Eads enjoyed an uncanny knack for erecting a network of subcontractors and suppliers throughout the Midwest to do his work. While the gunboats themselves were laid down on construction ways at Carondelet, Missouri, near St. Louis, and Mound City, Illinois, near Cairo, Eads coordinated separate piece work at St. Louis, Cincinnati, and Pittsburgh by telegraph, and his own fleet of barges and supply craft. He drove 800 construction workers day and night, utilized materials procured by special agents and purchasers all over the valley, with "nearly all the largest machine-shops and foundries in St. Louis, and many small ones" supplying the required twenty-one steam engines and thirty-five boilers for the craft. Rolling mills of Thomas G. Gaylor Son and Company of Portsmouth, Ohio; Swift and Company of Newport, Kentucky; and Harrison, Chouteau and Valle at St. Louis rolled the required armor plating, which Eads then tested by firing army cannon at them. While it was a team effort, Eads stood out for his indefatigable pace in attending to details, including predictable alterations during construction.[18]

Unfortunately, Rodgers proved an impediment. Fremont resented his links with Meigs (whose department had discovered corrupt supply practices in the West) and felt that Rodgers' greater interest in riverine operations had actually delayed completion of the gunboats. Rodgers had also vetoed purchase of an Eads' snagboat for conversion to military use. Fremont reversed this decision and awarded his friend Eads with a handsome profit of $66,850. This boat would become the USS *Benton,* and Fremont also circumvented Rodgers in buying an additional craft, a St. Louis ferryboat which became the powerful ironclad *Essex* after conversion. The general also became fascinated with mounting 17,500-pound seacoast mortars on rafts for use against Confederate shore batteries, and he gave Theodore Adams of St. Louis a lucrative contract for such work. Finally, Fremont engineered Rodgers' replacement from a compliant Navy department.[19]

Captain Andrew Hull Foote succeeded Rodgers in the West. He was a taciturn, old-line sailor from Connecticut, and cut from the same patriotic cloth as the Marylander. Equating country with service to God, Foote arrived at the very moment that Rodgers was busy convoying some of Grant's men to occupy Paducah. The niceties of proper change-of-command ceremonies were forgotten. Foote's takeover resembled Grant's action several days before when the general simply walked into Cairo district headquarters and announced that he had orders to straighten the place out. Rodgers "behaved well, officer-like and gentlemanly," reported Foote. Rodgers, in turn, wrote Washington, declaring that he had "naturally misunderstood in not asking more advice, in not suggesting more difficulties, and not more frequently reporting progress." Foote invited him to stay on, but the arrival of other senior officers such as Commander Henry Walke caused Rodgers to return east. Although Rodgers would go on to higher command in blockading squadrons, he never had the chance to lead the flotilla he had helped construct. Yet his four months on western waters in 1861 may well have been his most important contribution to eventual Union victory. At the time, however, he merely became one of the first casualties of bureaucratic infighting and necessary shakedown prior to establishment of joint cooperation for operations in the West.[20]

Foote had no real desire for a muddy river assignment either. This staunch Yankee, whose father had served in the Senate, had been reared to duty, honor, and service, just like Rodgers. Foote's Bible-backed advocacy of temperance not only cleared ships of demon rum, but earned Foote a reputation for brimstone sermons and devout prayer. He felt that rebellions should be suppressed quickly and harshly. Welles told Foote to "cooperate fully and freely" with Fremont, without subordination to the army. Fremont deferred to this naval officer, for he was too pressed with other duties, and relied on Foote to "spare no effort to accomplish the object in view with the least possible delay." Foote's own well-placed friends in Washington aided him; Lieutenant Henry A. Wise of the Ordnance bureau and Assistant Secretary Gustavus Fox opened doors even to the White House. President Lincoln himself developed an interest in the Western Flotilla, and particularly in the mortar boats. Foote lost no time in letting Washington know he could prove just as persistent as Rodgers. Rodgers "deserves great credit for what he has done, and his labors have been hard," Foote wrote Fox on September 8, yet "he has been so much confined to his boats, and for want of officers, that he could not be here as I am, for a few days, to push forward this work." Foote would not denigrate the efforts of a brother officer for the sake of currying political favor in the capital.[21]

The Navy department appreciated Foote's desire to stay close to army headquarters and Eads's construction yards. Foote sent Walke to direct timberclad deployment at Cairo and soon acquired help from other able

naval officers. Controversial but colorful William D. "Dirty Bill" Porter
(son of old Commodore David Porter of War of 1812 fame), John A.
Winslow (later commander of the famous *Kearsarge*), James W. Shirk
(whose yeoman service led virtually to permanent assignment on the
rivers), Leonard Paulding (son of Admiral Hiram Paulding who had
captured Walker's filibustering crew in 1857) — all joined Phelps and Stembel, holdovers from Rodgers' watch. Foote's friend Lieutenant J.P. Sanford persuaded Washington to let him direct an advisory team of ordnance, master carpenter, rigger, and engineering experts sent from the
New York Navy Yard to aid the Western Flotilla. Foote told superiors
that they were needed desperately in "this wilderness of naval wants"
where no one knew anything about naval matters. Indeed the autumn
proved nettlesome to Foote as both army and navy supply channels
clogged with his requests for material and midwestern governors proved
uncooperative. He worried about losing younger officers such as Shirk
and Sanford because of inequities of rank and assignment in this back-
wash of river duty. Foote's own disparity in rank contrasted with army
officers around him, and he wrote the department to suggest his promotion to flag officer since "now, when afloat, there is nothing to distinguish
my vessel from the others. Hence, I am embarrassed on all sides for want
of rank." Finally someone in Washington sensed the problem; Foote
received his promotion on November 13.[22]

By this time, Andrew Foote presided over America's first ironclad
squadron. He named the first vessel *St. Louis,* and within days the hulls
of the so-called "City Series"—*Carondelet, Cincinnati, Louisville, Mound City,
Cairo,* and *Pittsburg*—slid into the brown waters. Problems did not end
with their launching, however, as Foote discovered when he persuaded
Eads (who technically owned the craft until final commissioning) to move
them downriver to improve flotilla coordination and to overawe the residue of Secessionist sympathy in the area. Everyone was embarrassed
when the *Pittsburg* and *Benton* ran aground and a transport rammed and
damaged the first gunboat — the brown-water navy had not yet mastered
river navigation. On top of that, experts discovered that Merritt's steam
drums and boilers would not fit the boats, and four more weeks of alterations left Foote quite perplexed. The naval officer thought the boats drew
too much water ("a mistake was made by Pook," he claimed) and underpowered for maneuvering in swift currents. "I say they must do after a
fashion," reported Foote to Fox at the end of the year; "I only wish that
you could have spent one day here, for the last six weeks, as no imagina-
tion can fancy what it is to collect materials and fit out Western Gun

Boats with Eastern men, without a Navy yard — in the West, where no stores are to be had.[23]

The crux of Foote's frustration lay in one sentence he penned to the assistant secretary in early November: "We want money and men, and to get hold of the Gun boats." The problem lay with Meigs's quartermaster clerks. Congress had appropriated $1 million expressly for flotilla construction; no money flowed to Eads and the contractors. Congress appropriated a similar amount in December, but both the navy and the contractors saw very little of it until the following year. Eads came away from a meeting in December at Washington to write Foote distastefully: "After waiting four days I have had an interview with Meigs presenting accounts for more than three hundred thousand dollars[;] I can obtain no assurance of receiving a dollar and must return as I came." Money problems also hampered recruiting. Fox promised to send eastern sailors (remembered after the war by Walke as stalwart "Maine lumbermen, New Bedford whalers, New York liners, and Philadelphia sea-lawyers"), and he discovered some 500 sailors languishing on garrison duty at Fort Ellsworth, one of the capital's protective forts, and shipped them west. Foote had wanted 1,700 new recruits, but he could not pay either the ones he had or the pilots, and everyone in naval circles blamed the army system that handled accounting for the Western Flotilla effort. A tired Foote wrote his wife in November: "Still God reigns, and I can now and then see light aloft, tho it is darkness ahead." Because of such problems for both army and navy in the West, Federal authorities would mount no river offensive in 1861.[24]

CHAPTER 3

An Army for the Heartland

ALBERT SIDNEY JOHNSTON, DECLARED by his friend Jefferson Davis to be the greatest soldier and ablest man on either side, offered his services to the Confederacy on September 5. Johnston was a man of action; a debonair, robust six-footer of commanding presence; and the very epitome of a fifty-eight-year-old professional soldier. Soft spoken, known for gentle humor, his daunting mystique received support from a personal 2,000-mile anabasis that summer across the hot southwestern desert so that he could follow his beloved Texas out of the Union. The Lincoln administration had proposed promotion to the rank of major general to retain his loyalty, but the offer never reached him prior to his departure from the West Coast.[1]

Even Johnston's northward journey from New Orleans to Richmond resembled some triumphal processional of an ancient Caesar. As new commander of the Western Department, he ranked second only to elderly Samuel Cooper, the Confederacy's adjutant general. By mid-September, Johnston had gone to Tennessee to sort out the dilemmas of his new assignment. He agonized little over the Columbus move (after all, it had been sanctioned by his deputy and old West Point roommate Leonidus Polk), even though it forced his hand. Felix Zollicoffer, the Nashville newspaperman-turned-soldier, had also crossed the Kentucky line to suppress Unionism in the eastern part of the department. A third band of zealots plumbed for an advance into central Kentucky via rail and turnpike to Bowling Green. This group, led by Kentuckians Blanton Duncan and Simon B. Buckner as well as Tennesseans of the Military and Financial Board, secured Richmond's favor and took the action away from Johnston. Still, the Bluegrass State was Johnston's birthplace, and by September 18 he had directed Buckner to gather Kentucky and other units from training camps along the state boundary and advance to Bowling Green. By 10:00 A.M. that morning, Buckner had 4,500 men in the town, and another 500 pushing forward to the Green River at Munfordville. Despite the Confederates' lack of arms and training, everyone seemed enthusiastic, according to the *Memphis Appeal*'s editor who declared that Johnston's initiative would give new impetus to military movements in the Mississippi Valley, with "tangible results at once brilliant, scientific, and satisfactory."[2]

People expected too much of Sidney Johnston. He had commanded the 2d U.S. Cavalry before the war, led a punitive expedition against the Mormons in 1857, and administered the Department of the Pacific just before his resignation. Yet, in a fashion, all of this was deceptive. Large in geographical extent, the department, for example, contained only 210 officers and 3,885 enlisted men spread over twenty-nine separate posts. This was a peacetime garrison force, with Johnston's fifty-one separate companies positioned for control, not war. Today there seems absolutely no rational reason to think that this officer was any better prepared than his peers for the high Confederate command thrust upon him in September 1861. He, like everyone else, carried French military theorist Baron Antoine Henri de Jomini's *Art of War* in his knapsack. His Mexican War experience fifteen years before and his antebellum frontier duty hardly suggested the wider vistas required of leaders in this rapidly expanding civil conflict.[3]

Johnston found scarcely 23,000 ill-equipped troops available for his mission in the Confederate West. Lateral communications were weak; localism in strategic focus was rife; and intelligence, administration, and logistics proved amateurish at best. Five major invasion routes east of the Mississippi alone rendered Johnston's task quite formidable, and his command responsibilities extended to the trans-Mississippi sector as well. If the western South held the key to ultimate Confederate success for economic even more than political reasons, little remains in Johnston's record to indicate anything more than cursory appreciation of that fact. His orientation remained devotedly military. He concentrated upon raising and organizing an army to hold a cordon defense from fixed strongholds, while placing reliance upon the judgment and discretion of key subordinates to carry out the tactics of such defense. Johnston devoted his life to this cause until his untimely death at Shiloh the following April. Few questions would linger after his passing about the difficulty of his mission, but many doubts would continue about the quality of his performance.[4]

Johnston's mission entailed protection of the South's Heartland. This 150,000-square-mile swath of territory provided a veritable cornucopia of resources invaluable to an emerging nation. Notwithstanding an invertebrate society decentralized for war, and an undernourished communication system, Johnston's Heartland bustled with war production that autumn. State and private entrepreneurs had joined hands in the

spring and summer to provide enough percussion caps and other munitions to help win the eastern battle at Manassas. Clothing mills, tent
factories, and ordnance plants turned out the finished products necessary for winning independence. The fact that concerns such as the Nashville Plow Works had shifted from using its locally mined Cumberland
Valley ore for farm implements to munitions work had profound implications not only for citizens in Johnston's theater, but also for those east
of the Appalachians. If slaveowners in Middle Tennessee could no longer
get food for their workers from north of the Ohio due to the war, their
own rich farmland quickly took up the slack both for civil and army pop-
ulations. Economic conditions seemed quite favorable when Johnston
appeared at harvest time. All he had to do was to look around him to
realize the value and vitality of his region.[5]

Johnston had no acquaintance with the economics of his theater, and
few could advise him of its true importance. Local boosters projected
a "hominy and hog" theme, but Johnston probably listened half-heartedly
to the politician's recitals of 1 million bushels of corn, 2.5 million bushels of wheat, thousands of horses and mules and cattle, and an unsur-
passed tobacco crop from Middle Tennessee alone. More importantly,
Johnston should have been made aware of the "Great Western Iron Belt"
that stretched across thirteen counties and especially dominated the narrow strip of land between the Cumberland and Tennessee rivers on the
Kentucky-Tennessee border. Billed as the South's greatest iron production center at that time, white and black laborers manned blast furnaces,
trip-hammer forges, and foundries. The 1860 census showed that Tennessee investors had $284,835 in capital tied up with thirty-five ironmak-
ing facilities, where 344 employees turned out 5,144 tons of bar iron annually. Nine other establishments in Kentucky, Alabama, and Missouri
added an additional 18,711 tons of bar, sheet, and boiler plate metal to
this total. As did the cotton planters in the Memphis Delta and the
proud denizens of Franklin Pike mansions below Nashville, the owners,
operators, and workers of the Great Western Iron Belt worried about
prices and markets. Shut off from lucrative Yankee markets, the pro-
ducers of the 1 million pounds of raw iron "between the rivers" turned
to a Confederacy at war for their succor, notwithstanding their own political or patriotic preference.[6]

Men now looked to local markets where buyers for the army and mu-
nitions plants might be located. Provincial towns from Union City and
Jackson in West Tennessee and Columbia, Clarksville, McMinnville,
Murfreesboro, and Sparta in mid-state to Hopkinsville and Bowling
Green in Kentucky gained favor. Despite the loss of the intersectional

General Albert Sidney Johnston.
National Archives.

cotton trade, Memphis boomed on war profiteering. Second only to Nashville as the Confederacy's transmontane supply and production center, no wonder that Polk, Pillow, and other generals proved so anxious to do the bidding of local prominent citizens. River defenses stretched northward to Columbus as autumn leaves turned in the Mississippi Valley, and a fixation with that city's protection faded only with eventual Federal capture and occupation in the spring of 1862.[7]

Johnston's attention riveted on defense of Nashville. The city stood as "the Athens of the South" because of its 17,000 prosperous and urbane citizens, its prominent position where north-south rail and river routes bisected, its state capital, and its center as the Middle Tennessee marketplace. The city boasted a flourishing theater, gas-light company, steam-driven fire apparatus, a medical college, military college, and large mansions of a slavocracy. Preeminently it was presided over by the state capitol designed by the famous architect William Strickland. Five daily newspapers, an iron suspension bridge across the Cumberland to Edgefield, newly strung telegraph wires, and first families with names from Fogg, Robertson, Cheatham, and Overton to McGavock and Heiman (reflecting ethnic newcomers) added to the scene. Just outside the city lay the Hermitage lands of Andrew and Rachel Jackson, and their kinsmen bearing the name Donelson still could be found among the leading coun-

Ruins of Bowling Green, Kentucky, after Johnston's Evacuation. Sketch by McComas, *Frank Leslie's Illustrated Newspaper*, March 22, 1862.

try folk. If the people of the city projected luxury (and they annually imported 3,500 tons of Illinois ice for juleps and food preservation), they also felt strongly about adding to their prosperity. Allegiance to the Confederacy scarcely cloaked a preoccupation with the mounting profits from the war. They simply had no time to worry about their own defense — besides, that was Johnston's task.[8]

Nashville's war boom made it a miniature military-industrial complex. Cannon and caissons, muskets and swords, revolvers, belts, clothing, powder, and percussion caps poured from city factories run by T.M. Brennan, and Ellis and Moore, with even the state penitentiary called upon to do its share. Moreover, the warehouses bulged with tons of war material. Coupled to the transportation arteries and the political significance of the city, Nashville became a beacon for Federal war planners. Johnston realized this fact, and he was particularly enamoured with the railroad lines running into the city. Alongside the tracks were indispensable telegraph wires, as the New Orleans-based Southwestern Telegraph Company controlled the communication links in Johnston's theater. Governor Harris endorsed their service, and the "merchants and businessmen of New Orleans will bear testimony to the efficiency of our lines, which for construction and reliability are not excelled by any on the continent," claimed company spokesmen. But what might be true in peacetime remained to be proven in war. The same could be said for the railroads, with their non-standard gauge, unballasted roadbed, and timber trestles inviting enemy mischief. And all this was but the tip of the problem.[9]

Southern industrial facilities making railroad equipment had converted to munitions work. Buckner commandeered L&N locomotives and rolling stock during his move to Bowling Green amidst howls from the road's president that the Confederates "have destroyed the road and its business." In truth, by early 1862 Colonel Robert Woolley, one of Johnston's aides, could declare grimly: "The railroad was almost bare of transportation. The locomotives had not been repaired for six months, and many of them lay disabled in depots. They could not be repaired at Bowling Green, for there is but one place in the South where a driving-wheel can be made, and not one where a whole locomotive can be constructed." Confederate officers throughout the theater constantly interfered with railroad traffic; they shifted cars and locomotives without authority, altered schedules to suit their own needs, and confiscated trains to ship particular units to a camp or station as they saw fit. Railroad officials barraged Johnston's headquarters rather than going through the War Department traffic coordinator, Colonel V.K. Stevenson, at Nashville. Stevenson, the

State Capitol, Nashville. National Archives.

prewar president of the Nashville and Chattanooga line, should have had the power to unsnarl the railroads, but he conflicted with Johnston's own representative, M.R. Fleece, and the presence of Memphis and Charleston president Sam Tate as a "voluntary aid" colonel on Johnston's staff did not help. In sum, Johnston's land mobility was severely constrained by railroad problems on the eve of Federal invasion.[10]

Yet Johnston, like other Civil War commanders, was mesmerized by the potential of the "Iron Horse" and warfare. In some sense, he had no choice in the West. The rivers ran in the wrong direction for interior line shifting of men and supplies. Where they could be used for logistical purposes, the withdrawal of steamboats by northern owners left

Johnston with few craft to do the work. Some 281 regular and transient packet boats had worked the prewar Cumberland River, for example, but scarcely a dozen remained available for Johnston's use; probably only three or four boats existed at the end of the year. The remainder of the boats in 1861 were tied up in semiretirement at Edgefield, their machinery silent, boilers shut down, and paint chipping away, while most of their captains and crews had long since departed for army service. People generally suspected that the government intended to convert all of these craft to gunboat, not transport service, in 1862. So a viable means of resupply via the rivers simply did not exist for Johnston when he most needed it.[11]

Actually, the theater commander worked hard to coordinate rail, turnpike, rivers, and telegraph so as to effect command and control over widely dispersed strongpoints on the western defense line that autumn, but manpower and equipment remained Johnston's abiding concern. Colonel E.W. Munford told a Memphis group after the war, "to those who ask why so able a man lost Kentucky, Tennessee, and *seemed* to fail, four words will answer, namely — *he had no army*." His orders stated that for men he could draw upon all the western states of the Confederacy and even upon the naval service, but he learned that everybody was indispensable, and that was why Leonidus Polk simply raised a local defense corps from "married men of business that cannot leave home" and thus free others for front-line duty. Johnston wrote Richmond: "We have not over half the *armed* forces that are now likely to be required for our security against disaster." When he requisitioned 30,000 muskets, he received 1,000; when he appealed to southern governors such as Joseph Brown of Georgia, A.P. Moore of Alabama, Pettus of Mississippi, and Rector of Arkansas, he received repeated rebuffs. Major General Braxton Bragg at Pensacola agreed with Johnston's need, but said that "it is in my power to do but little for you" because the exposed coastline, inadequate arms and ammunition, and lack of manpower plagued his own efforts. Richmond leaders, including the new Secretary of War Judah P. Benjamin, chided Johnston about calling on others when the Upper South had not filled manpower quotas. Benjamin criticized Johnston for accepting brigade-size units from Mississippi in violation of Confederate law, and on October 25 pointedly told him to disband all unarmed twelve-month units in the West. The secretary claimed that long service, armed units lost men to these short-term outfits and that the treasury could not afford winter encampments for unarmed men. Even Governor Harris told Johnston that Tennesseans had no desire to sit in winter encampments without arms or equipment to fight the enemy. No wonder that Johnston wrote his friend Munford: "Our people seem to have suffered from violent political fever which has left them exhausted."[12]

It was obvious to everyone that Tennessee would shoulder the burden of the Upper South defense of the hinterland. Both Johnston and Harris wrote Richmond urging a shift of forces from less threatened zones to the Kentucky-Tennessee border. Johnston even battled the War department about priorities for production in his department. Confederate ordnance officers Captain Moses H. Wright and Major William R. Hunt supervised shops at Nashville, Memphis, and Chattanooga, but they shifted munitions shipments away from Johnston's forces under War department orders. Johnston complained bitterly about sending 150 barrels of powder to Mobile and New Orleans when Wright's only supply "consists of 15 or 20 barrels which I ordered for the use of Buckner in Kentucky." Nashville powder mills were Johnston's sole supply source for this commodity, although production rose constantly from about 400 to 2,800 pounds per day by November. When the Nashville ordnance shops burned in a mysterious fire shortly before Christmas, the losses were catastrophic — 400 to 600 sets of artillery harness, 8,000 to 14,000 sets of accoutrements and equipment, 300 cavalry saddles, 2 million percussion caps, 5,000 friction primers, plus all of Wright's office files. Expediency became the watchword in Johnston's department.[13]

Polk complained privately to President Davis about lack of powder at Columbus and vowed to supply his army with firearms directly from Cuba. Terry's crack Texas Rangers came equipped with twenty different kinds of firearms, while another mounted outfit reported only two rounds of ammunition per man and no winter clothing for patrolling the Kentucky countryside. Colonel John Gregg's 7th Texas arrived in the department with different arms in each of nine companies, and the irate Texan told headquarters on November 7 that Captain John Brown's company alone contained 32 rifles, 12 double-barreled shotguns, 3 Mississippi rifles, and 2 "Yager" rifles. Unit commanders quickly realized the seriousness of the problem when their men began target practice. Young James T. Mackey of Columbia and his mates in the 48th Tennessee declared that their guns were more appropriate for squirrel hunting. Ordered to guard the 100-yard long iron railroad bridge across the Elk River in Todd County, Kentucky, Mackey wrote home that while some of his friends came close to a target with their old flintlocks, few could hold up the heavy pieces and that it was quite dangerous to stand anywhere but behind them. A Knoxville ordnance officer complained that 200 firearms procured from local citizens came without bayonet fittings, rammers, or workable locks, and were all of different calibers. Repairs would require shipment to Memphis, 400 miles away. Captain Wright in Nashville reported on November 23 that 3,560 new Enfield muskets and 112,000 rounds of ammunition had run the blockade, but everyone still wondered what they should do about the old weapons on hand. Johnston pointedly told them not to stop making new firearms just to convert the old weapons.[14]

Sidney Johnston's army was a logistician's nightmare; yet Richmond officials dismissed his repeated calls for help, and Governor Harris counseled patience. Harris reminded the general that Tennessee had lacked a prewar arsenal to draw upon. What incensed the western generals was the presence of Confederate warehouses at Nashville, only seventy miles behind the front, but with supplies earmarked for Virginia. Things got so bad with food rations that Johnston, Polk, and Pillow took matters into their own hands. At one point, Johnston banned shipment of anything from Nashville to Virginia. Polk and Pillow imposed an embargo on Kentucky foodstuffs passing south to distant markets. They claimed a greater need for hay and corn in their own army, but their action only enraged Bluegrass farmers, their agricultural associations, and their market representatives in West Tennessee. The farmers wanted U.S. gold or Kentucky scrip, not Confederate notes, and the Memphis Chamber of Commerce protested military interference with "freedom of trade." Finally the generals simply backed down and lifted their embargo.[15]

The autumn and winter tested the troops as much as it did their leaders. Louisianans, Arkansans, Mississippians, and Texans joined Tennessee and Kentucky soldiers in Johnston's department. Howell Carter remembered moving northward with the 1st Louisiana cavalry by steamboat and train before breaking in their horses on the turnpike between Nashville and Bowling Green. Along the way, they learned to outsmart local farmers to gain free food and shelter. The sight of the army commander and their idol, Sidney Johnston, quickened pulses as they settled into permanent posting at Russellville. Englishman Henry Morton Stanley (later famous for "finding" lost explorer David Livingstone) was there, decked out with the "Dixie Grays" from Arkansas. His company officers boasted of their Virginia ancestry, and one lieutenant claimed kinship with Robert E. Lee. The privates, thought Stanley, were all young men of fortune, overseers of plantations, small cotton-planters, professional men, clerks, a few merchants, "and a rustic lout or two." Some brought black personal servants with them. After they strutted before local belles at Little Rock fairgrounds, in the August heat their colonel marched them with full packs and equipment all the way to the army at Columbus. By the time they reached Kentucky, even Stanley admitted his folly "in devoting myself to be food for powder." He also decided that the most singular characteristic of his comrades was their readiness to take offense at any reflection of their "veracity or personal honor," this being unmatched by anything other than their inability to take individual care of themselves.[16]

Stanley objected to pitching tents for officers and other demeaning chores, although more liberal officers such as Lieutenant William P. Davis of the 14th Mississippi mixed freely with his men and shared some of their duties. A former U.S. senator, vice president, and now a Confederate general, John C. Breckenridge chastised one of his junior officers for demanding that his privates do personal tasks for him by roaring, "they are all gentlemen." But there was little inclination for democratization in most units, and officers kept the men drilling, mounting guard, and building fortifications. Still the restless, ingenious soldiery found the grog parlors, houses of ill-repute, card games, fist-fights, and knifings that always attend an army in garrison. Davis completed one tour as guard officer during a cold, sleety November evening by incarcerating some liquor dealers and turning their wares over to the quartermaster with the self-satisfaction of "making that much for the Southern Confed-[eracy]." One Unionist lady of the Bowling Green neighborhood found the Rebels generally well-behaved except for a few Texas Rangers and Irishmen. Terry's people were there to stiffen the backbone of the easterners, in Johnston's mind, and they fared well in early brushes with the enemy despite their commander's death in a rash attack at Woodsonville on the Green River. Ironically he had been born at nearby Russellville. Honor and glory attended Terry even in death, for his body lay in state at the Tennessee capitol, with wounded members of his command clustered around the bier. The South needed heroes even at this stage of the war.[17]

The army encamped at Bowling Green reflected the linkages between southerners. Private George Quincy Turner wrote his father back home in Lavaca County that his company commander had moved his family up from Texas to winter with him outside town. The captain's wife came originally from Columbia, Tennessee, and her uncle, Colonel William Milton Voorhies, commanded the 48th Tennessee elsewhere in Johnston's army. Another Texan, the Reverend R.F. Bunting, dutifully sent "dispatches" to the *San Antonio Herald* recounting army life at Camp Terry, near Cave City. He praised the lovely countryside and balmy Indian summer days of November but longed for his West Texas home. The chilly nights and damp living atmosphere "of the States" bothered him, and he noted over 1,500 sick in the army with measles and fever. Bunting served as voluntary chaplain to the rangers, and strong interest in religion swept across Confederate camps to vie with the lustier desires of the flesh. Young William Felts of the 18th Tennessee at Camp Trousdale pleaded with his mother to visit him and bring a parson "prepared to preach with a Song in his Mouth even praises to God." Some clergymen, such as the bantam ninety-five pound Thomas Hopkins Deavenport of the 3d Tennessee, arrived in camp in late September feeling "like a stranger in a strange land." Everything was new to him and by no means inviting, he recalled, but he bravely shouldered musket, haversack, knapsack, and canteen, and endured grueling marches, ash cake, green corn, and blanketless sleeping to be with the ranks of his regiment.[18]

Johnston's soldiers wrote home about poorly managed commissariats, the eternal rain and mud, the chills and dampness of ill-chosen campsites, and the deplorable inaction of their generals. I.W. Mason of the 2d Kentucky spoke for most on Christmas Eve when he admitted from his Cave City hut that he would gladly go home. Surgeon David W. Yandell, staff doctor at Bowling Green headquarters and eldest son of a prominent Louisville physician (now serving the Confederacy in a Memphis military hospital) wrote his father that he was well fixed with two good horses, medical instruments, books, and the favor of his generals. Indeed it would be Yandell that Johnston would dispatch to tend wounded Yankees at Shiloh the next April—at the very moment that his own leg wound went unnoticed and untreated. It would be Yandell's absence which contributed to the general's death and loss to the Confederate hope of victory. But, all that lay in the future. Yandell's thoughts at Yuletide were of comfort and garrison life, not bloody operating tables of the battlefield.[19]

David Yandell's brother, Lunsford "Lunny" Jr., was assistant surgeon of the 4th Tennessee at Columbus, but he wanted to be a fighter, not an army doctor. His letters to their father mentioned flamboyant violations of dress regulations, quarters replete with andironed fireplace, bookshelves, washstands, and comforts of home. The Federals posed no threat, he assured his father, but pneumonia, measles, dysentery, and jaundice did. In fact, sickness and melancholia plagued Confederate forces all over Johnston's department in late 1861. Whatever the regiment, the men had enlisted to fight, and inaction sapped physical and mental stamina. The army's greatest enemy at this point was disease. Typhus and meningitis carried off the Rebels in droves, irrespective of rank, age, or place of origin. Deep South units suffered the most, it seemed, since their men were ill-prepared for the damp chill of a Kentucky winter. "They had come out to fight the enemies of their country in human shape, but not in the form of fever and pestilence," observed a surgeon in the 22d Mississippi.[20]

Climate, inadequate diet, and half-primitive medicine not Yankee bullets reduced Johnston's army. "Corn partially roasted, partially burnt, and principally raw," drinking water from "green scum" standing pools, shallow wells, or camp-polluted creeks produced major health problems. Army leadership lacked appreciation of sanitary engineering, and Henry Stanley summed up conditions in his memoirs by noting that just as regimental doctors and assistants were needed to cure sickness, so too a regimental chef to manage the company cooks would have prevented illness in 50 percent of the cases that winter. But he added, "the age was not advanced enough to recognize this." He castigated the generals who devoted themselves solely to strategy and operations, or searching for supplies but seldom or never to "the kindly science of health-preservation." The outspoken Englishman suggested that the officers knew how to keep their horses in better condition than their men, and he could not recall having seen any of them examining messes or taking interest in the rankers. True, admitted Stanley, should a soldier take sick, he could go on report. But it never occurred to any officer, from general to lieutenant, he claimed, "that it might be possible to reduce the number of invalids by principal attention to the soldier's joys and comforts." Such omission would cost the Confederate command dearly when the campaigns of 1862 demanded large numbers of healthy soldiers.[21]

Most of the men wondered why their general had not carried them north to winter on the banks of the Ohio. Johnston obviously worked hard at strategy, organization, and logistics. He spent the fall trying to forge one army from the separate contingents guarding Columbus and the Mississippi, the middle routes to Nashville, and East Tennessee. His goal was an effective strength of 50,000 men, for if he planned to remain on the defensive, he needed only a 1 to 2 or even 1 to 3 ratio of men to his enemies. His actual numbers exceeded 68,368 on paper on December 31, with an additional 23,620 carried on the rolls as absent for various reasons, and some of his commands had not even reported. Clearly Johnston did not lack manpower, but his main problem was that of properly positioning those present. While there is reason to believe that the general still retained a certain flexibility of focus regarding various threatened points along his front in early autumn, all that would change as the year wound down. Johnston would revert to his earlier contention — which he conveyed to Davis on September 16 — that distinct indications led to the conclusion that "the enemy design to advance on the Nashville Railroad, and will immediately occupy Bowling Green, if not anticipated."[22]

As soon as Johnston learned that Buckner had consolidated the Bowling Green position, he took a train to inspect Polk's position at Columbus. Arriving on September 18, the two men rode among the camps and forts, inspiring the men, restoring discipline and elan, and discerning the best disposition of resources at hand. Above all, Johnston's mystique shone forth brightly. One young man approached the general about enlisting. Johnston put him at ease, literally magnetizing the prospective recruit so that "to this hour, his splendid person stands out in my thought as the incarnation of that 'Confederacy' to which my heart yielded its utmost love and loyalty." Johnston was "as royal Arthur to England's brave romance" in this fellow's mind. During Johnston's stay, it helped that a Yankee gunboat chanced to come down from Cairo and heaved a few shells at the Confederates. One 64-pounder landed near Johnston and Polk, but the departmental commander "merely looked back over his shoulder at it and resumed his spyglass." Such a noble gesture could not help but impress naive country boys experiencing their first taste of enemy fire. Even the Confederate governor-in-exile of Missouri, Thomas C. Reynolds, felt the general's allure. After the war he told William Preston Johnston (the general's son and biographer) that "the entire army, as by some instinct, soon conceived the greatest admiration of and confidence in him." Such a legend was born during Sidney Johnston's singular visit of three weeks to the "Gibraltar of the Confederacy."[23]

Polk remained sensitive to departmental criticism about his work and asked for more men and munitions. Johnston reassured him to be patient, said that he appreciated his contribution, and promised support. On September 21, Johnston assigned Polk responsibility for the "First Division," and, in the words of William Preston Johnston, "henceforth General Polk became the right arm of his commander." More specifically, Polk's area of responsibility became clearly defined as:

> Beginning at the point on the State line crossed by the Memphis and Louisville Railroad, and running along the Henderson and Central Alabama (excluding the city of Nashville); thence west along said boundary and the northern boundary of Mississippi to the Mississippi River; thence northwardly along the western bank of the river. On the north side the division will extend so far into the State of Kentucky, west of the Cumberland River, as the major-general may find it advisable to cover by his army.[24]

The wording of the directive was clear; Polk's choice for emphasis remained less so. Seriously contemplating leaving army service, Polk remained reluctant to divert attention and resources from Columbus. As Federal naval and land activity increased that autumn from the Cairo area, Polk's focus became even more riveted upon this one position. Then, suddenly, events on the Louisville-Nashville land axis effected similar result upon Johnston. An urgent telegram, dated October 4 from Buckner at Bowling Green, reached the department commander at Columbus and warned about 14,000 Federals massed to cross Green River and strike the center of the Confederate defense line. Johnston telegraphed back to hold Bowling Green as reinforcements were on the way. These reinforcements included Brigadier General William J. Hardee's brigade from Arkansas. Reaching Bowling Green on October 11, Hardee conferred with Buckner, and the pair decided that Johnston really wanted to hold on the Green River rather than at Bowling Green. Finally, Hardee wired Johnston at Columbus: "The enemy is reported to be advancing from Elizabethtown. Your presence here much needed." The next night, the army's leader and his thirteen-man staff left the post on the Mississippi.[25]

Governor Reynolds remembered devotedly that he had helped resolve Johnston's problem of cold feet in an unheated railroad car leaving Columbus that night by wrapping the general's boots with socks. Johnston feigned ignorance of such an expedient, but Reynolds insisted, "of course, he was perfectly familiar with the atmospherical laws which elucidated it." Johnston seemed infallible to everyone. Rushing to the threatened sector of his command appeared quite correct and in character. Nobody questioned the panicky Bowling Green generals. Still here was a turning point, for Sidney Johnston had been sucked into the swirl of district, not theater command. Evidently Johnston could not control his impetuous subordinates. Part of this October crisis resulted from the Hardee-Buckner lurch northward beyond Bowling Green. Green River country, however, was Buckner's home ground, and he wanted no Yankee invader's heel treading upon its soil. Subsequent maneuvers by both sides kept the district unsettled throughout the rest of the autumn. Feint and parry became Johnston's hallmark, but in so doing he lost sight of overall theater strategy. He never convinced Polk to relieve pressure upon the center by offensive activity from Columbus. To enjoinders from Secretary Benjamin that he should also attend to trans-Mississippi affairs, Johnston merely responded with more calls for help "to meet the advance of what I assume now to be the overwhelming force of the enemy through the Mississippi valley." Just before Christmas, Benjamin wrote: "It has made me very uneasy, and the President and [Adjutant] General [Samuel] Cooper are equally at a loss to make out how the matter stands."[26]

Richmond had called Johnston's hand, but he responded on Christmas Day both to Benjamin and Tennessee governor Harris by noting that his chief opponent, on the Louisville-Nashville approach, had massed some 75,000 men against his own wholly inadequate force of 17,000 (his end-of-month report a week later showed considerably more men in his army). Johnston warned the Richmond officials that he needed additional help and that he had sent his chief engineer, Major Jeremy Gilmer, to prepare a second defense line directly before the Tennessee capital. "At present I can only conjecture whether they will make their attack here or turn my right, or, relying upon their superiority of numbers, attempt both at the same time," he wrote Benjamin. To Harris, Johnston merely reiterated the refrain which had pervaded all his dispatches that fall: "The vulnerable point is the line from Louisville towards Nashville, and the Northern generals are evidently aware of it." Locked to this overland threat, Johnston deemphasized the twin river defense of the Tennessee and Cumberland. While they clearly lay within Polk's area of responsibility, they would remain central to Johnston's overall, cordon defense plan for the Heartland, as well as his more immediate fascination with the Bowling Green situation. A Federal thrust via the twin rivers could outflank both Columbus and Bowling Green armies, thus shattering Confederate defenses in the West.[27]

CHAPTER 4

Land Between the Rivers

IT TOOK ONLY NINETY DAYS FOR Albert Sidney Johnston to descend from theater to district commander. His Christmas dispatches reflected an overwhelming preoccupation with the land threat to Nashville from Louisville. Yet, in his defense, he repeatedly warned subordinates to look out for their flanks. He especially told Polk to watch the seam between the Columbus and Bowling Green sectors. The importance of that seam was apparent on every map and was reflected by F.G. Norman (president of the Tuscumbia, Alabama military commission) the previous May when he pointedly told the young Confederate government: "In view of the defenseless condition of the Tennessee River, the facilities it offers for the transportation of troops to Northern Mississippi and North Alabama, and the want of arms and ammunition and organization in this valley, the undersigned respectfully suggests that the War Department take the matter into consideration." The War department passed the problem to state and local officials until the September 1861 push into Kentucky. Even then very little changed as Johnston's western line contained a dangerous weakness at the point where the Tennessee and Cumberland rivers led directly into the Heartland.[1]

This twin rivers region formed a triangle, with eastern base points at Bowling Green and Nashville, and its western corner turned on Columbus. The people of the locale paid little attention to the potential military significance of their area. The western boundary extended along flat croplands given to cotton, tobacco, and other produce as well as plantations closely resembling those of the Memphis Delta to the south. East of the Cumberland lay an equally well-disposed area of partly wooded, rolling, and fertile ground supporting livestock and agricultural products. More cosmopolitan than its western counterpart, the eastern boundary focused its culture upon towns such as Clarksville, Tennessee, and Hopkinsville, just across the state line in Kentucky. Clarksville rivaled Nashville with its 5,000 inhabitants, comfortable dwellings, large tobacco warehouses, prosperous businesses, two hotels, seven churches, police protection, and male and female academies. Served by 2,000 steamboat dockings each year, the new Memphis, Clarksville, and Louisville Railroad crossing of the Cumberland provided an important transfer point for a Louisville to Memphis run. This strongly Secessionist community projected exuberant optimism in the early Confederate period.[2] A third neighborhood nestled between the other two. Neither as wealthy nor as well known, it bore the simple appellation "land between the rivers" and generally retained the unkempt look of wilderness with heavy timber, deep gullies, and a sparse population. A flourishing iron industry, river hamlets such as Dover, Lineport, and Tobaccoport gave a thin veneer of habitation, and places from which to ship backwoods products of this area including grain, pork, beef, tobacco, and whiskey. Dover provided both the county seat for Stewart County, Tennessee and a tobacco shipping port, and would be destined for national fame far out of proportion to its local political and economic role.[3]

The iron industry gave this region importance to the Confederacy. The limonite or brown hematite ore, smelted in cottage industries fueled by locally produced charcoal, was shipped via creek and river to Clarksville, Nashville, or northward to the Ohio. Early entrepreneurs—from William "Pig Iron" Kelly to the famous Hillman family—employed white and black and imported Chinese laborers for works at the Suwanee furnace and Tennessee Rolling Mills near Eddyville, Kentucky; around tiny Dover, at furnaces such as the Great Western, Randolph, Peytona, Laura, Eclypse, Clark, Iron Mountain, Mammoth, and Bear Springs; and at the Cumberland Iron Works and rolling mills, operated by John Bell, one-time United States senator and the 1860 Unionist presidential candidate. Periodic drops in farm equipment prices, slave unrest, and the Panic of 1857 dislocated business somewhat by the eve of Secession, but iron making was still lucrative. Seventeen furnaces in Kentucky alone continued production in 1860, spewing 42,500 tons of iron per year, valued at almost $1,250,000. J.P. Lesley, secretary of the American Iron Association, enumerated some 39 furnaces, 13 forges, and 3 rolling mills along an axis stretching northwestward from Nashville in the lower Cumberland Valley.[4]

Here was an almost incalculable resource for the Confederate war effort, if properly developed, utilized, and protected. The Clarksville Iron Works produced small arms, and the foundry of Whitfield, Bradley, and Co. (also styled Whitfield, Bell and Co.), turned out cannon and shells. L. Weil and Brother tripled a ten-per-day cracker barrel production because of government contracts. All, including local farm equipment makers, various millers, and shoe and textile manufacturers, enjoyed windfall profits during the conflict. War relief solicitations netted thousands of dollars in support of the Confederate cause, and local volunteers formed Company I of the 10th and Company B of the 50th Tennessee. Still, trans-fixed as they were by states rights, laissez-faire capitalism when it came to war production, and Kentucky neutrality, both national and state leaders equivocated about defense of the section; they both failed to mobilize a coordinated and unified effort to restore iron production to full operation, and then neglected military protection for the facilities. The Confederate defense line bisected rather than shielded the area, and Johnston's concentration on the Louisville-Nashville axis left to oth-ers the vital task of constructing and manning fortifications for the twin rivers.[5]

Historians suggested later that the Confederates would have done bet-ter to construct their fortifications at the so-called Birmingham "nar-rows" in Kentucky where the twin rivers were only three miles apart. This however, was impossible in the spring of 1861 when civil engineer Adna Anderson and his assistant, Wilbur R. Foster, arrived from Nash-ville under orders form Governor Harris to lay out fortifications. Ana-lyzing all the topographic details, Anderson selected a site upon a steep hillside about one mile from Dover for the first water battery position of what would be called "Fort Donelson." The site seemed sound; it lay 11 miles south of neutral Kentucky and 60 miles from the mouth of the Cumberland, as well as 75 miles from Nashville. The hill—so often styled a bluff—rose 75 to 100 feet above the river, and its irregular shape encom-passed 100 acres. It was surrounded by deep gullies offering barriers to land assault. Several country lanes linked the fort site with Dover and eventually led to other Middle Tennessee hamlets on the river and rail-road. Similar roads ran to the Tennessee River crossings and northward into Kentucky. Anderson recruited "a large force of men" from the Cum-berland Rolling Mills to begin digging the earthworks, and then moved the survey party across to the Tennessee River.[6]

Here the team studied high-water marks for flood potential since all of the Tennessee bottomlands were considerably flatter than the Cum-berland site. Finally Anderson chose a location for this fort "shortly be-low the mouth of Standing Stone Creek and nearly opposite the mouth of Sandy." Lacking a labor force to break ground for this additional for-tification, Anderson's party returned to Nashville, where Anderson and Foster disbanded the survey team after briefing Harris on their work. The governor, however, wanting corroboration, selected one of his mili-tary authorities, a West Pointer and former militia veteran, Brigadier General Daniel S. Donelson, to retrace Anderson's survey. Donelson found the works already underway at Dover (albeit proceeding slug-

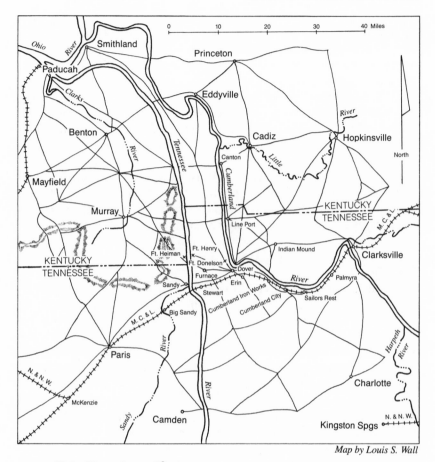

Map by Louis S. Wall

MAP 2. Twin Rivers Area, 1862.

gishly due to disinterest among the millhand laborers), and he approved Anderson's choice for that fort, which subsequently would bear Donelson's name. Upon reaching the Tennessee, Donelson decided that no suitable site existed on Volunteer soil for the second fort. Harris had vetoed any violation of Kentucky neutrality at this point. So, disliking Anderson's choice, Donelson found an alternate site — Kirkman's Old Landing, almost twelve miles due west of the Dover fort and on the east bank of the Tennessee River. No dirt was overturned here either, and a third site across the river at Pine Bluff attracted attention. Some work began on the latter, but the bluff seemed too high to permit proper cannon depression for interdiction of a river passage. The final siting for what became "Fort Henry" occurred on June 9, when Major Bushrod Rust Johnson arrived for another judgment on the position. He selected Donelson's original site at Kirkman's Old Landing over Anderson's alternative below Standing Rock Creek.[7]

Bushrod Johnson would subsequently bear the stigma for selecting the ill-fated Fort Henry position. An 1840 graduate of West Point with William Tecumseh Sherman and George H. Thomas, Johnson fought the Seminoles and Mexicans before being forced from the army on a charge of smuggling. An Ohio Quaker, he embraced the politics of Tennessee while associated with the Western Military Institute in Nashville. He became chief engineer of the Tennessee state forces in 1861. Always an enigma, Johnson rationalized his Fort Henry decision to Harris by noting that alternate sites were commanded by higher ground, and that "too much delay has already occurred." Notwithstanding the criticism, the position lay well forward of the railroad crossing south of Big Sandy.[8]

Very little construction actually took place on the twin rivers that summer. Local laborers preferred army enlistment, and eleven companies of Stewart County men departed for Virginia in mid-July with the 14th Tennessee, leaving work on the forts to millhands and slaves. Two water batteries (styled "upper" and "lower" according to river flow) began to take shape at Fort Donelson, and the first token garrison spent more time regulating river traffic than upon construction work. Most observers felt that any emergency could be handled by Confederate units training outside Clarksville, forty miles upriver. On the Tennessee River, Colonel Adolphus Heiman's 10th Tennessee (720 men armed with flintlocks) completed their organization and began work on Forts Henry and Heiman (across the river). Heiman was a German emigré whose father had supervised the Prussian king's Sans Souci summer palace, and Heiman himself had worked his way to the forefront of Nashville society by architectural skill as well as by valor in the Mexican War. He was joined by his second-in-command, Randal McGavock, to reflect the German-Irish flavor of the regiment. The pair provided stern drillmasters not only for their "Sons of Erin," but also for Captain Jesse Taylor's Company H, "Fixed Artillery" from the state artillery corps. The 10th Tennessee spent most of its time attacking an illegal liquor traffic with the Kentuckians but failing—one smuggler cleared $10,000 in the quinine trade alone.[9]

An upsurge in interest about the twin rivers came after Confederate moves into the Bluegrass State. Heiman telegraphed Nashville on

General Bushrod Rust Johnson.
National Archives.

September 8 that "one of Lincoln's gunboats ascended the Tennessee River and was seen 30 miles below Fort Henry." The state military board thought this merely coincidental with Federal occupation of Paducah and Smithland and indicative of a turning movement against Columbus, not a forerunner of invasion of the Heartland. Bushrod Johnson reported a week later that Fort Henry comprised a "good, inclosed work, with bastion fronts, mounting six 32-pounders and two 12-pounders," but would require 1,000 men as a garrison. When Sidney Johnston took over the department, he expressed great concern about lack of progress on the twin river forts but could find no time to visit the sites in person. On September 30, he ordered Lieutenant Joseph Dixon, an engineer at Columbus and former topographical engineer in the old army, to visit the twin rivers.[10]

Johnston's guidance to Dixon conflicted with similar direction from Heiman to a local state provisional army engineer, Lieutenant F.R.R. Smith. The presence of engineers suggested Johnston's concern that Polk might be neglecting the area between Columbus and the Tennessee River. The two engineers penned reports which provided the Confederate high command with its first specific information concerning this area of weakness. Actually Smith's account proved more influential because he spoke not only about roads, river crossings, and political sentiments of the area, but also raised the issue of obstructing the navigable streams with cable chains and anchors (similar to work being done at Columbus), and referred especially to a site on the Tennessee at Aurora, Kentucky. This barrier idea would surface continually over the next six months. In fact, a Nashville steamboat captain, H.H. Harrison, noted three places in Kentucky that could especially support sunken barges laden with stone covered by masked shore batteries. Smith's ideas captured Johnston's attention, but for the moment he relied on Dixon remaining on the twin rivers and supervising heavy ordnance installation at the Fort Donelson water battery, while he sent word to Polk to order Heiman to detail McGavock to cross to Dover and take command there.[11]

At this point, the Union navy obligingly reinforced Confederate concern about the twin rivers. Lieutenant S.L. Phelps and the *Conestoga* began their periodic incursions on the rivers in early October, tying up just downstream from Fort Henry on October 12 and watching the Rebel buildup. His detailed dispatch to Foote noted that "the fortification is quite an extensive work and armed with heavy guns, mounted en barbette, and garrisoned by a considerable force" and told of finding it necessary to use strong language to the citizens in regard to persecution of Union people. Phelps also said that most active Secessionists along the river fled at his approach.[12]

The next day Phelps took Paducah district commander C.F. Smith with him on a reconnaissance. For about a week thereafter the navy commander roamed the waterway capturing flatboats and skiffs laden with goods for Confederate troops nearby. Phelps reported enemy preparations for sinking barges at Line Island and mounting cannon at the Fort Donelson water batteries. Moreover, he suggested to Foote that the Confederates were constructing their own gunboat flotilla, using iron plating from the extensive ironworks on the rivers. "They have one of the finest and fastest steamers in the West—the *Eastman* [*Eastport*]," Smith noted. In fact the Confederates were quite active in attempting to procure gunboats, for Polk wrote Secretary of the Navy Stephen R. Mallory at midmonth asking permission to purchase a fine boat at $20,000 for the Mississippi and two additional craft at $12,000 each for the twin rivers. "They can be converted into armed gunboats," Polk suggested, for "they are indispensable to our defenses." Secretary of War Judah P. Benjamin agreed to purchasing the *Eastport*, "if you are confidant you can make good use of her," he wrote Polk. The soldier-bishop had already alerted

Captain E. Wood of Danville, Tennessee, and a Lieutenant Carter of the fledgling Confederate navy to begin their conversion. Speed, however, was not to be a hallmark of their efforts over succeeding months, and like so much Confederate activity in the West, the Rebel river navy proved to be more talk than action. Still the rumors bothered Union naval leaders like Phelps and Foote.[13]

Phelps and C.F. Smith reminded their navy and army superiors that they too could place sunken barges in the rivers to impede potential Confederate naval incursions. Nobody listened, so the rivers below Confederate positions remained free for passage that autumn, and the *Conestoga*'s harassing patrols constantly unnerved Heiman at Fort Henry. He ordered alerts and increased cavalry patrols along the river banks but refused to test fire his heavy guns lest they disclose the limited range of the 32-pounders. The gunboat produced such a stir that even local citizens began firing at her, and on one occasion, recalled a young Mississippi artillery instructor at Fort Henry, Lieutenant H.L. Bedford, when smoke was seen three miles downriver, the drums sounded an alert, and there was much scurrying to and fro, "companies were getting under arms and into line with the rapidity of zealots, though wanting in the precision of veterans." The excitement subsided only with the smoke's disappearance.[14]

This excitement did not subside so easily for men like Senator Gustavus Henry, local Clarksville denizen and the fort's namesake. He wrote both Polk and Johnston that "there is no part of the whole West so exposed as the Valley of the Cumberland." Could not a whole regiment instead of merely one artillery company be sent from Hopkinsville to the twin rivers, he asked. Since the streams were rising with autumn rains, the Yankee gunboats might soon range up the rivers and destroy local industries like the Cumberland Rolling Mills with its irreplaceable machinery, or the Clarksville railroad bridge, which would take $200,000 to repair. Citing Dixon's lethargy in not mounting the 32-pounders sent to Fort Donelson from Memphis with the senator's help, Henry suggested that "If the river keeps up Nashville itself is not safe" and added, "I am now more fully impressed with [the] danger, and cannot too urgently urge you to send prompt relief to us." Even McGavock wrote Polk from Dover that "we are in a defenseless condition, having only three companies of raw recruits, poorly armed and not one artillerist to manage what heavy guns we have." He "regretted" that only Taylor and Lieutenant Peter Stankiewicz of the Tennessee Artillery Corps knew anything about heavy ordnance. As if to reinforce the gloomy reports, Phelps staged another gunboat penetration up the Cumberland on October

26, as he convoyed a raiding party against a Confederate camp near Eddyville.[15]

Polk responded to all this by asking Heiman, as senior officer on the rivers, to render a full report. But the perfectionist Prussian emigré fired back a detailed commentary that was hardly reassuring. He described Fort Henry as a bastioned fort enclosing an area of about three acres, having an eighteen-foot dry moat surrounding earthen parapets, and mounting six 32-pounders, two 12-pounders, and one 6-pounder field gun. Heiman complained that the fort sat on low ground, prone to flooding, and was dominated by high ground behind and across from the position. "These hills I consider the really dangerous points, and proper batteries placed on them will certainly command the fort," he noted. He felt 820 men in the 10th Tennessee sufficed but wanted more artillerists and field guns for land defense. "Whether a gunboat can pass Fort Henry depends greatly upon the skill and efficiency of our gunners," he told Polk. Gunboats could take the position under fire one and one-half miles downstream, closing rapidly past the danger point of Confederate fire, and simply slip by the fort unscathed since none of the heavy ordnance could be turned to fire back upstream. Inferior powder and poorly made shells further weakened the defense, and if the Union gunboats got by the fort, a "two hours run will take them to Danville and there is nothing to prevent the destruction of the railroad bridge." Heiman cited the need for more cavalry to protect that bridge from enemy raids and to convey dispatches, and he sought another transport and freight boat for work on the river.[16]

Heiman was even less enthusiastic about Fort Donelson which had "so far been almost entirely overlooked." He noted that his men had constructed "a little fort" and had emplaced two 32-pounders in what was probably the upper water battery, but the "hemmed-in position of this work" made it quite useless, he claimed. Construction of earthworks on the hill behind the water batteries seemed necessary, but overall "this post was entirely abandoned until within the last few weeks," he claimed, when McGavock had organized three newly formed companies at the post. This was probably the nucleus of the 50th Tennessee from the state's reserve corps, and they were largely unarmed "except with such guns as they could furnish themselves — mostly shotguns." Heiman had also detached Lieutenant W.O. Watts of Taylor's battery at Fort Henry to instruct selected men of McGavock's new command in working the heavy cannon. McGavock had wanted more, but with the *Conestoga* posturing on both rivers, Heiman had demurred. Frankly, he had "no confidence in [Fort Donelson's] efficiency," Heiman told Polk.[17]

Heiman also held the barrier projects in low regard. One was planned for Ingram's Shoals, thirty-five miles below Dover on the Cumberland. Two steamboats and six barges with stone and wood waited under the guns of the water batteries at Fort Donelson for a decision. "This will be a fruitless operation," said Heiman, "in a river which rises from low-water mark at least 57 feet, and which I myself have often known to rise at least 10 feet in 24 hours." Still he offered no alternatives, and Polk told him to get on with it. Polk was so preoccupied at Columbus that he could only write Johnston on October 19: "I shall in two or three days be so well forward with my work that I shall be at liberty to look around me, if need be." He never found that need. He did contemplate sending two Mississippi regiments to the twin rivers, "but they can be relieved in a few days and return." Actually he dispatched only the 4th Mississippi and Major A.P. Stewart with four artillery instructors to train Fort Donelson's gunners. Polk knew that his superior wanted something done, but he procrastinated, failing to do an adequate job as district commander. He wrote Heiman: "Your report of dispositions for defense of Forts Donelson and Henry are satisfactory and I hope you will not relax your vigilance."[18]

Even Johnston may have overlooked the extent of Polk's negligence, but he specifically told Polk on October 17 to "hasten the armament of the works at Fort Donelson and the obstructions below the place at which a post was intended." He ordered Mississippi brigadier J.L. Alcorn to send 200 men to Dover from Hopkinsville, and then replaced Alcorn with western Kentuckian Lloyd Tilghman when the Mississippian balked at Confederate refusal to regularize his one-star rank. Johnston was most cheered, perhaps, by arrival of Major Jeremy Gilmer at mid-month to relieve the hard-pressed departmental engineer corps. Gilmer was not happy to learn that offensive plans had been shelved, but he dutifully set out with Senator Henry to inspect the situation on the twin rivers, including that at Clarksville and Nashville. A central figure in the drama now unfolding on the Confederacy's western frontier, Gilmer was a North Carolinian, a graduate of West Point, and, with his Georgia-bred wife, Loulie, had been a popular member of the San Francisco military community that also included Henry Halleck. Like Sidney Johnston, Gilmer had made his own circuitous way back east to join the Confederacy. Not until October, in fact, could he learn with certainty that Loulie and their son had arrived safely in Georgia. No wonder that his letters home during the initial weeks of duty with Johnston evidenced more familial concern than interest in his new assignment.[19]

Gradually, Gilmer became a major figure concerned with the defenses of the twin rivers. He and Henry claimed that Heiman's command was the best they had seen in the service, and the politician pronounced Fort Henry now to be "in fine condition for defense." But Fort Donelson was another matter. Henry declared bluntly that it was in poor shape "with no work of any account" done on it, and once again blamed engineer Dixon for the trouble. Meanwhile Gilmer in the company of Dixon braved autumn rains to inspect alternate battery sites downriver at Line Port and Ingram's Shoals, returning with the impression that since Fort Donelson had been started already, "our efforts for resisting gunboats should be concentrated there." These were Gilmer's words, and Senator Henry added that the hillside behind the water batteries afforded good protection against land attack. Johnston quickly wired back "to hasten forward the works at that point." So the team moved on to Clarksville and Nashville, leaving Dixon to work out the details. Before leaving, Gilmer decided that Fort Donelson's armament should be doubled from the four 32-pounders and two "naval guns" on hand, so that four additional 32-pounders and "two 8-inch Colombiads or long-range Parrott guns, all with garrison carriages" might make a reliable defense against a fleet of gunboats. He also wanted a single battery of bronze field pieces, plus two small iron guns made in Clarksville to be supplemented by "say 20 to 25 guns, mounted on siege carriages." They could be employed with field batteries brought up in an emergency. Gilmer also became fascinated with river obstructions and planned one for emplacement directly beneath the water batteries at Fort Donelson. He echoed Dixon that, "in all ordinary stages of water the obstructions render the river impassable for gunboats and for any other boats at this time." Neither man came from the area and knew less than Henry or Heiman about stream fluctuation.[20]

Gilmer moved on to Clarksville where he envisioned using the Red River, which emptied into the Cumberland just north or downstream from the city, as a defense line. Abatis would obstruct the fords and "cutting the banks so as to make them vertical" would impede crossings by the enemy. Field batteries and troop encampments would guard the railroad bridges from Bowling Green, while a water battery with three 32-pounders would cover the Cumberland approach. Moving rapidly, Gilmer reached Nashville by mid-November and began to sample the pleasantries of the country around the capital while ostensibly surveying fort sites. Still believing Johnston would advance rather than retreat, he proceeded rather leisurely about his mission, enjoying local planter hospitality and the lovely countryside more than his work. He rather casually informed his wife by letter that while citizens of Clarksville and Nash-

General Lloyd Tilghman.
National Archives.

ville had fears of the Union gunboats passing Fort Donelson and getting upriver, he had none. More concerned than Gilmer, Tilghman and Senator Henry continued to press Johnston with letters outlining the state of confusion, disorganization, and lethargic work attending efforts at Fort Donelson. As Tilghman noted on October 27, from Clarksville, "I fear our interests there are well-nigh beyond our control."[21]

Actually, Henry, Tilghman, Gilmer, and even Polk and Johnston may have been unaware of the extenuating circumstances affecting progress on the twin river defenses. Heiman, McGavock, and Dixon almost constantly battled sickness among the troops and work crews. The pressures and uncertainty of Union naval movements and seemingly rapid changes in priorities at headquarters all proved disturbing. Lack of labor plagued the construction work as there were insufficient slaves in the area, and reluctance of troop commanders to employ their soldiers on such work hampered the program. When the expedition left to construct the barrier at Ingram's Shoals, it drew off 115 cavalrymen of Major D.C. Kelly's contingent from Colonel Nathan Bedford Forrest's regiment stationed at Fort Henry, as well as three additional infantry companies and 40 artillerists with their four field guns from Fort Donelson. One participant later noted that the only remarkable thing about the expedition was that it cost the Confederate government nothing because generous Kentuckians fed and subsisted the expedition for two weeks (willingly or not). At least five barges of 1,200 tons of stone were dumped by early November, supposedly blocking the Cumberland (said Lieutenant Colonel Milton A. Haynes, chief of the Tennessee artillery corps, for "any rise less than about 12 feet over the present stage." Scarcely five days later, at flood stage, Haynes's words were contradicted as the *Conestoga* passed over the barrier without trouble. Dire predictions from Cumberland Valley residents proved true, and a very frustrated Sidney Johnston simply passed the news to Richmond without comment.[22]

Neither Johnston nor Governor Harris nor their engineers could ever raise enough laborers to build the complete defense system conceived for the Confederate West. None of the slaveowners wished to lose harvests by renting slaves to the government at this time. Some 1,500 laborers were needed at Nashville, a similar number at Clarksville, and an additional 2,000 were required for the twin river forts. Not one-tenth of that number came forward, and the raw soldiers who did the work merely prolonged the task, and in turn this work affected their own training, discipline, morale, and even health. Citizen groups such as Fisher A. Hannum's Clarksville Military Board and their counterparts in north Alabama provided well-intentioned advice and carping criticism to Johnston and his people, but gave little substantial help by way of labor gangs. In late November 1861, the Clarksville group promised to supply 200 family-bound local men for a local defense corps to help man the twin river posts, but nothing came of that scheme either. Johnston searched desperately for some element of unity and control over preparations in Middle Tennessee, yet never once did he go in person to inspect Forts Henry and Donelson.[23]

Johnston's method was to send subordinates to do this task. Tilghman became Johnston's representative on the rivers by early winter, and he was expected to absorb newly arriving contingents such as Gregg's 7th Texas, a 749-man unit described by its commander as having "more coughs and colds than I ever saw among the same number of men." To Tilghman and Gregg, Johnston noted: "The value of the railway from Clarksville to [Bowling Green] is too well known to you to need explanation, but it must not be lost sight of in the pressure of other business." This other business involved the forts, and Johnston ordered Polk to dispatch 5,000 men under Gideon Pillow from Columbus to Clarksville and to fortify those heights across from Fort Henry. Polk's response was typical. Telegraphing reluctant compliance with the order, he sent the troops marching overland rather than sending them more rapidly by railroad. Then Polk sidestepped the issue on November 4, catching Johnston off-guard.[24]

Polk wrote his chief expressing worry that the 5,000 men would seriously weaken his Columbus position. The best that he could offer would be to move laterally and occupy Mayfield to cover his right flank, per Johnston's earlier warning. But this would require use of the 5,000 men under Pillow. Without them, he said, "the utmost that could be done would be to offer the best resistance possible, with the assurance that from the disparity of numbers isolation would be inevitable." Wringing his hands, Polk concluded, "We shall, of course, endeavor to do our duty, but I think it proper respectfully to submit these views as those which weigh upon my mind." Two days later Polk sent a letter of resignation to President Davis, but neither Davis nor Johnston accommodated the general. The president persuaded Polk to remain at Columbus by assuring him, "You are master of the subject involved in the defense of the Mississippi and its continguous territory." Johnston proved less diplomatic, telling his subordinate flatly, "that order [sending Pillow and the 5,000 to the twin rivers] will be executed." Johnston realized that Polk was not pulling his weight on the western team, especially when the thought was widespread in his army and cogently captured by Randal McGavock in his private journal: "The people in the counties of Trigg and Lyon, in Kentucky, are calling on us every day for protection, and I think we are losing ground in that region simply because they are over-awed by gunboats and small parties that come out from Smithland and steal everything that they can lay their hands upon." Still Johnston remained ever the gentleman, choosing to defer to subordinates on how they would manage their duties and responsibilities.[25]

At that point a sudden series of events dislocated Johnston's plans for increasing the defense posture on the twin rivers. Ulysses S. Grant's vaguely conceived and poorly executed Belmont operation still managed to frighten Polk's people further, and then Polk himself was knocked out of action for several weeks by an artillery accident at Columbus. At first Johnston remained adamant about Pillow's transfer, writing Polk that, "you had reported no imperious necessity for suspension of the order, and your decisive victory [at Belmont] has doubled your forces [psychologically]." Then, sensing the increasing pressure upon his incapacitated subordinate, Johnston backtracked, and by mid-November, the departmental commander's dispatches reflected complete bafflement as to course of action. Should he risk the loss of Columbus merely to counter what appeared to be a Federal feint toward the Tennessee and Cumberland? Should he overlook the possibility that such a feint might be a prelude to something more, just to keep Polk strong on the Mississippi? He wrote Richmond on November 8, "I have risked the latter," and promised offensive action himself very soon. Meanwhile Harris and Henry kept the pressure on Johnston about the Cumberland defenses, both agreeing "fully as to the importance — indispensable necessity, indeed — of effectual defenses and obstruction below the iron establishments on that river." Harris particularly cited the "absolute national necessity" of these facilities, and Johnston repeatedly assured the War department that Fort Donelson was in a state of defense to protect them. Actually none of the reports reaching Bowling Green headquarters from the twin rivers indicated anything of the kind, and neither Fort Henry nor Fort Donelson lay far enough downriver to protect all of the iron facilities in Johnston's department. But by sending Tilghman to the twin rivers on November 17, Johnston possibly thought that he had resolved the problem.[26]

All too little is known about the man sent by Johnston to bolster flagging defense efforts on the Tennessee and Cumberland in the late fall. Contemporary photographs show him as dapper, even cavalier in carriage and style, and his reputation as a strict disciplinarian preceded him. Lloyd Tilghman was born to the Maryland portion of his clan at Rich Neck Manor, near Claiborne in Talbot County about 1816. He graduated only thirty-sixth in a class of forty-nine cadets at West Point in 1836, and he resigned his commission in the Dragoons within the year. He worked as a civil engineer on railroads in the East and South, as well as Panama, and served both as staff and company grade officer in the Maryland and District of Columbia volunteer battalion during the Mexican War. Finally settling in Paducah, Kentucky, in 1852, he rose to some prominence in Buckner's Kentucky State Guard. Tilghman took command of the Confederate 3d Kentucky, and Buckner's patronage combined with Polk's affinity for West Pointers as well as Tilghman's own familiarity with western Kentucky produced the twin rivers assignment. Tilghman attracted Johnston's attention also by using his Hopkinsville base to protect and requisition quantities of beef and hogs from the area for the army, as well as passing intelligence reports about Union gunboat activity quickly up the chain of command. Still, whatever other professional qualities possessed by this officer, few of them surfaced in his new position. Indeed a note of controversy erupted with his move to the twin rivers.[27]

Overlapping authority, unclear command channels, and conflicting orders all proved as troublesome to Lloyd Tilghman as lack of ordnance, manpower, and fortifications. He interfered with Gilmer's engineering duties by telling the local construction superintendent, T.J. Glenn, to cease work on the timber obstacle under Fort Donelson's guns. Gilmer circumvented Tilghman and simply instructed Glenn to proceed with this tree and stone barrier, to be located about 1,000 to 1,200 yards downstream from the water batteries. Of course Tilghman was not the only problem, for Gilmer soon had to contend with Gideon Pillow's meddling also. The Tennessean had taken temporary command at Columbus during Polk's convalescence, and he immediately talked of an offensive. Ever bombastic and ambitious, Pillow caught the attention of Johnston and Harris with pronouncements about a Federal buildup, the need for more soldiers, and the pitiful state of the Columbus defenses. He instructed Sam Weakley's north Alabama defense committee on what they should do to help with the Tennessee River defenses by telling them bluntly, "If Alabama will furnish the means of constructing them, with arms, &c., the troops from that State will be placed in them for the purpose of defending them, thus allowing her to hold the keys of the gateway into her territory." On November 20, Pillow ordered Dixon to move from Fort Donelson to Fort Henry and survey a fort on "Stewart's Hill" across from the latter post. Gilmer exploded indignantly to Johnston when he learned of such interference with his work, and the notion that Alabama slaves and whites should work together on construction gangs except in "imminent danger." The department commander agreed that Captain Charles Hayden, a civil engineer, could do the work at Fort Henry, leaving Dixon to chores on the Cumberland, but he allowed the slave-white labor plan to stand.[28]

By this time Dixon had assured Gilmer that the lower water battery at Fort Donelson was ready for ordnance and that he had constructed a small earthwork atop the hill behind the batteries to protect the troop encampment in the natural bowl adjacent. He had surrounded the camp with abatis, although no more than 200 men were ever present for duty there due to leave and sickness. When Polk returned to duty, he showed sudden interest in the twin rivers situation. On December 4, he ordered Tilghman to exempt the black and white laborers at the Cumberland Iron Works from all military related duties involving the fortifications and to concentrate on war production because "these works being the only ones that can now supply the requisite material for the manufacture of small-arms and other munitions of war." Polk suggested that Tilghman expand the district limits for labor impressment, and he advanced the notion of building a gunboat for the Cumberland like the *Eastport* on the Tennessee. Various individuals from Johnston to Nashville mayor R.B. Cheatham favored the scheme, although engineer Gilmer did not.[29]

Gilmer felt that his land engineering efforts would be threatened by dispersal of effort and resources to gunboat construction. He told Johnston that he doubted that a common steamboat could be converted into a efficient gunboat, and cited the lack of suitable timber in the twin rivers area, and that "there is not plate iron in the whole Confederacy sufficient to protect the hundredth part of the surface of one boat." Even the draught of such craft would be too much for the Cumberland except in winter and spring. In sum, Gilmer told his chief, "I am forced to the opinion that the best reliance for defense will be batteries ashore, in combination with such obstructions as may be devised in the channel under the guns of the works." Others in Richmond disagreed, and Johnston decided to go ahead, but then lapsed into preoccupation with the overland approach from Louisville once more and lost touch. Cheatham meanwhile joined Governor Harris in working to whip up enthusiasm among local slaveowners outside the capital to provide labor for Gilmer's fortifications for that city. By December 7, Gilmer would write his old friend and Johnston's chief of staff, William Mackall, that all the slaves had been hired out until year's end and that militia calls had drained the white labor supply. Ironically, the docking of a steamer from Louisville, the *Pink Marble,* which had somehow made it past Union naval patrols with its cotton machinery for McMinnville, mocked both the enemy gunboats and the Confederate's own fort and barrier construction on the Cumberland.[30]

Weather uncertainties kept Confederate plans unsettled. One day spring-like temperatures and dry roads prompted fears as to an imminent Yankee advance. Then ominous winter storm clouds blew in from the Mississippi Valley, suggesting the shutting down of all active campaigning for that year. Johnston planned to supplement the meager twin rivers and Hopkinsville garrisons with fresh levies from Alabama and Mississippi and Tennessee militia and from the Virginia brigade of John Bell Floyd fresh from their autumn success in the western part of their home state. Johnston now looked upon any Federal thrust at Polk's flank as merely diversionary. The one Confederate who began to perceive reality was Gideon Pillow, as he predicted to Mackall on December 11, "my opinion is that the enemy are preparing to move up the Tennessee river in force," for the Federals "will use their large water power to capture Fort Henry and pass up and take possession of Tennessee bridge and separate your command and General Polk's and will then advance down the railroad on Memphis." But who would listen to so troublesome a fellow as Gideon Pillow?[31]

Tilghman shared Pillow's fears as he, too, told Mackall, "I am not secure at either Henry or Donelson," noting only 1,500 unarmed men and that his requests for two companies of heavy artillery had gone unanswered. He added: "Think movements at Cairo look to Cumberland and Tennessee certain." When he failed to receive a satisfactory reply from headquarters, he defied protocol and wrote directly to President Davis in Richmond. He needed arms, Tilghman told the chief executive, and the exposed position of the twin rivers and the impossibility of securing those arms in Tennessee had induced his indiscretion in writing. Everyone needed aid, he realized, but, "I am deeply solicitous about our condition on the Tennessee and Cumberland, and believe that no one point in the Southern Confederacy needs more aid of the Government than these points." By early January, Tilghman seemed somewhat more positive telling Bowling Green that men were returning from holiday leave, and that while he could still only man 50 percent of his works, he was ready to mount all the guns as quickly as they arrived and that the whole Fort Henry command was in a "most admirable state of efficiency."[32]

For the men under Tilghman's command, the autumn had passed pleasantly enough. "We lived, all of us, luxuriously in comfortable tents," recalled the Reverend James H. M'Neilly after the war. In addition to government rations of flour, fresh and cured meats, sugar, and coffee, every boat brought great boxes from home filled with all the good things that farm or store could provide, "or mother love suggest for our comfort," he said. A "bucket of lard" went down by boat to Lieutenant Thomas W. Beaumont from his wealthy Clarksville father, while neighborhood lads like John Nolin, David Sills, and Christopher Columbus Stewart hunted and fished off duty in the same locations they had frequented not six months before as civilians. Over at Fort Henry, Smith Crutcher and his friends socialized with their old neighbor from the Rushing Creek community who now had a flourishing blacksmith and general repair facility at that post. "It was just a big picnic," thought M'Neilly, and what a contrast to two or three years later, when rags hardly covered their bodies and when "the little corn dodger and the scant slice of fat bacon" only emphasized the emptiness of stomachs. By Christmas 1861, the weather had turned wet, gloomy, and disagreeable. The soldiers and some 150 slaves from the area busily built 400 log huts at Fort Donelson, and a telegraph line now linked the twin river forts with Nashville and Bowling Green via Cumberland City. Yuletide cheer swept over the garrisons as families and friends from the locale arrived with food and presents for their kinfolk.[33]

The youths in gray passed the final days of the year inscribing diary entries and in letter writing. On December 22, Captain James E. Bailey, commanding newly arrived Company A of the 49th Tennessee, wrote home to Clarksville about how encouraged he was with news of a probable conflict between the United States and Great Britain, "and of a speedy return to the pursuits of civil life." A lawyer in peacetime, he had served both in the state legislature and on the state military board. He felt that if England entered the war, it would quickly "settle all our troubles in a short time." Fellow townsman, Hugh Beaumont, responded to his son's confident prediction that Fort Donelson was ready to give the enemy a warm reception with a warning, "you are not yet 'out of the woods.'" He had already told his son in November, "the North is *now* making their death struggle and should they succeed the war will be a long and bloody one, but if *we* drive them back both by Land and Water, the war will soon terminate." Everyone looked anxiously at the bleak wintry sky and hoped for the best in the new year.[34]

CHAPTER 5

The Federals Discover the Key

IT SEEMED LIKE THE YEAR 1861 WOULD NEVER end for the Lincoln administration. December alone produced its share of disasters. Corruption and cost overruns plagued the War department. An impetuous naval officer removed Confederate diplomats from a neutral British vessel on the high seas, triggering an international incident. Secretary of War Simon Cameron's ill-timed advocacy not merely of slave emancipation, but outright arming of the freedmen to fight for the Union caused a major domestic uproar. Federal armies seemed stymied everywhere, and correspondence between the administration and its principal field commanders in the West particularly reflected such inertia. Don Carlos Buell (the Ohio departmental leader) and Henry W. Halleck (the Missouri leader) exasperated Washington officials by displaying a tiresome lack of cooperation and insensitivity to political urgency. Preoccupation with administrative and organizational problems, local graft, and chasing rumors about enemy operations could be found throughout the army. The problem for President Lincoln was how to make stubborn generals get on with the task of suppressing the rebellion. As the harried chief executive scribbled on one letter, "as everywhere else, nothing can be done."[1]

The reason why the great armies and flotillas of the United States could not move forward on schedule may be found in a simple declaration of an unknown brigadier general at Cairo. Chiding hometown newspaper readers about seeking only the headlines of battles, Ulysses S. Grant wrote his father in late November that the citizenry failed to understand that men had to be disciplined, arms fabricated, and transport and provisions procured before armies could move to battle. It mattered little whether Jesse Grant knew what his son was talking about; the general and the soldiers did. War at their level concerned army housekeeping, including mail inspection to guard against spies, hassles about commissary matters, establishment of uniformed medical procedures and facilities, and the fugitive slave question. Grant informed his superiors that his command was poor in every particular except discipline; he reeled off a list of inferior clothing, arms, equipment, lack of ambulances and wagons, and his dissatisfaction with the progress of gunboat construction. Foote echoed the latter complaint, telling Quartermaster General Meigs, "our difficulties have been legion, and it is now almost doubtful . . . of having gun and mortar boats in efficient condition for going down the river in December." But down the Mississippi he went from St. Louis to Cairo, with some of his boats finding every sandbar in the stream, much to the consternation of the salt water sailor. Nobody, it appeared, was ready for any invasion of the South at the end of 1861.[2]

The world of Grant, Foote, and their subordinates remained too unsettled. Men were still learning to work with one another. Surgeon John Brinton, a snobbish Philadelphia physician destined to become one of Grant's inner circle (his red and gray dressing gown provided Julia Dent Grant with a model for her less flamboyant husband), admitted that his first contact with fellow midwestern doctors convinced him that many were rough, but "I think that I at first underrated them," for "their hearts were good, and they were professionally zealous." Brinton succeeded in starting a weekly meeting of an "Army Medical and Surgical Society of Cairo" to share professional knowledge and experiences. Colonel Michael Lawler was less successful when he attempted to curb his rowdy 18th Illinois by appointing a Roman Catholic chaplain for this predominantly Protestant regiment. Cooperation did not always work in the army. Cases of rape, plunder, and intoxication passed constantly across every officer's desk, and even Grant braved bread and lumber frauds (the latter made difficult by the fact that one contractor was Lincoln's personal friend). Grant had taken unruly volunteers to Belmont, Missouri (across from Columbus) in November and might have emerged victorious from a little scrap with Gideon Pillow had not the youthful Federals stopped to plunder the Rebel camp. They lost the battle and were pushed back to their transports in disarray. So, everyone learned invaluable lessons from such forays, although Grant began to display an alarming tendency to underestimate the enemy's ability to counterattack at the moment of defeat. But, generally, affairs settled back into a routine after Belmont, enabling people to pursue other activities.[3]

Colonel "Black Jack" Logan of the 31st Illinois took leave to visit New York and Washington to seek guns for his men. Susan Wallace, wife of Hoosier colonel Lew Wallace, and Sam Fletcher of the 2d Indiana cavalry experienced their first glimpse of slavery as Federal forces fanned out into the Kentucky countryside beyond Paducah and Smithland. Increasing numbers of Unionist refugees returned almost daily to Federal lines with Phelps's river patrols, and the naval commander complained not only about Secessionist violence against such people, but about the opportunists profiting from the illegal commercial trade across the battle lines. Some of this activity benefited the Federal soldiery, especially brightening the Yuletide season. Surgeon Brinton, for example, feted the holiday with a dinner of wild game washed down with burgundy and some "old 'Constitution madeira' which its donor said had made the voyage around the world in that old warship." Less exotic was Sylvester C. Bishop's Christmas dinner of boiled beef, boiled potatoes, soft bread, and a cup of water, and he noted that New Year's Day was "about as dull as Christmas" because the weather was so warm that his Illinois comrades scarcely left their tents. Others like P.O. Avery in the 4th Illinois cavalry spent the holiday practicing with his carbine against a target labeled "Jeff Davis." Union troops in the West were going soft by year's end. It was time to move them out of stagnant camps. The men were willing to go south; their generals were not.[4]

Halleck and Buell quite simply could not either cooperate or commit their two armies to action. The stolid Buell possessed a mistaken notion of his own mandate form General-in-Chief George B. McClellan, and he stood torn between fulfilling Lincoln's desires for a move to aid East Tennessee Unionists and to cut the vital railroad to Virginia and a more alluring military objective of bulling his way southward through Bowling Green to Nashville. Halleck, meanwhile, viewed Columbus as his major impediment to conquering the Mississippi Valley, but he also needed to clean up strife-torn Missouri (which made sense, given his view from a St. Louis headquarters). To a textbook general like Halleck (and he had written several of them in the old army), commencement of two separate movements simultaneously on what professionals termed "exterior lines" defied the best military teachings of the age. He could not spare troops to help Buell, he told Washington, and Buell responded in kind about aiding Halleck. It was during this impasse that the germ of an idea for conquering the forts at twin rivers began to take shape.[5]

Students of the war have long argued about the sequence of events that led to the twin rivers campaign. The question of authorship of the campaign plan has led most commentators to suggest that the whole thing was patently obvious to anyone looking at a map in 1861. But merely gazing at a map or advancing some pet scheme have never meant acceptance in military circles. Prescient individuals abounded in the autumn and winter of 1861–62. As Grant told his patron Congressman E.B. Washburne when the campaign was over, it accomplished little to credit any particular general with first proposing the idea, since Union

gunboats had been scouting Confederate fort-building on the twin rivers for months before the campaign. Other clairvoyants included St.
Louis steamboatman Charles M. Scott; Fremont's sometime spy, Captain Charles D'arnaud; Buell's Paducah Unionist candidate, John Lellyett; Charles Whittlesey, principal army engineer at Cincinnati; and
Anna Ella Carroll of Maryland, who claimed to have advised Lincoln
and Stanton on the matter. Grant and McClernand advanced variants
of the twin rivers approach to Washburn and Lincoln, while Buell noted
it for McClellan. Attorney General Bates, as well as an anonymous retired naval officer (passing the information through an unidentified Nashville Unionist), also suggested the plausibility of the river invasion route
some months before. East Tennessee loyalist senator Andrew Johnson
spiced his letters freely with the thought, and C.F. Smith at Paducah provided feasibility reports on the idea. Therefore it is apparent that the
rivers approach for breaching the Rebel defense line in the West was
common knowledge in the West at the end of 1861.[6]

Key individuals on the Union frontlines fueled everyone's enthusiasm
by the turn of the year. Porter constantly pressured C.F. Smith and Foote
to dash up the Tennessee and reduce Fort Henry. Porter particularly
chided higher authorities about finding "all of the United States troops
lying inactive behind intrenchments, while the enemy are active in every
direction with a force not more than half the number of the United
States forces." Smith refused to act, fretting continuously about Confederate offensive intentions, until about Christmas when it became apparent to all that Rebel troop movements were intended to reinforce Bowling Green and other threatened points, not for an offensive. Phelps had
taken the *Conestoga* back to the Cumberland on December 8, and he returned with the most detailed information yet available on the situation
in Middle Tennessee. He reported Confederate impressment of Kentucky whites for military duty and of blacks and Unionists for work on
the twin rivers forts. "Virulent fevers" supposedly ravaged these forts,
while additional heavy guns and completion of the chain and stone obstructions at Fort Donelson had been accomplished. Moreover, Phelps
repeated rumors of gunboat construction at Clarksville and Nashville
and detailed the type of work being done aboard the *Eastport* on the Tennessee. He closed his report with information supplied by old river pilots
that the twin rivers seldom froze over in winter like the Ohio. "If any
movement is contemplated up the Cumberland," he suggested, "I am
confidant it should not be delayed longer than is necessary."[7]

Ironically, one winter evening while chatting over cigars with William
T. Sherman and G.W. Cullum, Halleck turned deftly to a map and cir-

cled the Confederate forts on the twin rivers. "That's the true line of operations," he proclaimed. Yet he could not act upon mere impulse. Foote warned that the gunboats were not ready, and Buell fluctuated on cooperation because their respective departmental boundaries ended on the Cumberland. Washington officials might communicate administration wishes and gratuitous advice, but Lincoln basically deferred to his professional military advisers, and his own personal style of self-effacement and persuasion failed to resolve fundamental differences in organization, management, and leadership of the armies in the West. It helped little that McClellan took ill and failed to clarify how government desires to aid Appalachian Unionists from Tennessee to Alabama meshed with his generals' desires to forge ahead with advances against Nashville and the lower Mississippi Valley. Attractive as Nashville might seem to Louisville interests, McClellan wrote Buell on January 6, that city's possession seemed distinctly subordinate to administration desires to aid southern loyalists. His viewpoint failed to persuade a stubborn Buell, and while the Ohioan was perfectly willing, at one point, to use the twin rivers to force Johnston out of Bowling Green, he could never quite coordinate things with Halleck, although Lincoln himself wrote directly to both generals to do just that. For his part, "Old Brains" (as Halleck was known) snapped back to his commander-in-chief, "I am satisfied that the authorities at Washington do not appreciate the difficulties with which we have to contend here."[8]

Top military and civilian officials of the Union hammered back and forth at one another on strategic matters as a new year dawned on the divided nation. Halleck lectured the administration about the proper way to conduct military movements (by not operating on separate exterior lines, he said), and Lincoln and McClellan belabored the point with Buell that "delay is ruining us, please name as early a day as you safely can or before which you can be ready to move southward in concert with Major General Halleck." Halleck finally admitted that a late January date seemed reasonable for some measurable, active cooperation with his Louisville colleague. By that time the Missouri situation would be finished, although a mere demonstration supporting Buell might be all that he could contribute for the gunboats were not ready and he could spare only 15,000 to 20,000 men for "an expedition up the Cumberland." At the same time, he told his Cairo district commander, Ulysses S. Grant, to prepare for limited movement into western Kentucky. Only one purpose could cause such a demonstration, and that was to pin down Johnston's forces from reinforcing one another, as the separate prongs of the Halleck-Buell advance took place the following month.

General Henry Halleck,
Commanding, Department of the
Missouri. National Archives.

Nobody really explained this to anyone else, however. Halleck was stubborn and unfathomable at times. If nothing more, the western generals, and even more, their subordinates began a moderate cooperation by mid-January. What would start as a simple, limited, and minor demonstration in force became the first stage of a more serious advance.[9]

Halleck's instructions to Grant were specific: he was to advance in two columns, converging at Mayfield, Kentucky, and then move on and threaten Camp Beauregard and Murray. McClernand from Fort Holt (opposite Cairo) and C.F. Smith from Paducah were to let it be "understood that Dover is the object of your attack," Halleck told Grant. Grant was to leak word of the expedition through the newspapers to the effect that with 20,000 to 30,000 reinforcements coming from Missouri, he was merely the vanguard of a mighty force. This deception would pin the Rebels to Columbus, thought Halleck. Grant was to tell nobody that it was merely a demonstration to "give your men a little experience in skirmishing" and to test Foote's flotilla, which would drop downriver and throw some shells at Columbus. The time seemed ripe for scaring Polk anyway since scouts brought news that "sixty-day" men had been transferred from the citadel to Camp Beauregard on the New Orleans and Ohio railroad nearby, and that Gideon Pillow had retired in a snit to his Columbia, Tennessee home because of the orders sending him to help Johnston rather than allowing him to attack Cairo. So Grant alerted his subordinates to push off at noon on January 9, with five days' rations, full cartridge boxes, and twenty additional rounds of ammuni-

General Don Carlos Buell, Commanding, Department of the
Ohio. National Archives.

tion per man in the accompanying wagons. The young soldiers were to stay in orderly formation, to refrain from firing their weapons or mixing with other units, and most certainly not to plunder the neighborhood, even though the directive declared that "every stranger met is our enemy."[10]

By noon on that date, Cairo had been turned into a quagmire by marching feet, a blanket of fog prevented departure, and the expedition waited until the next day to get moving. Anything and anywhere to get out of camp, remembered John B. Connelly of the 31st Indiana in his diary, so that his unit was ready in one half the allotted time. Muddy roads and undisciplined troops, however, hampered progress. Foote beat back a sharp little counterattack by the Confederate's minuscule flotilla from Columbus, and Grant gave short shrift to the whole affair in his memoirs. He noted simply that the weather was bad, roads intolerable, and the whole force sloshed through mud and snow for about a week, "the men suffering very much." On one occasion Grant himself rode forty or fifty miles behind Columbus—"the day dreadful with snow and sleet and cold," noted Dr. Brinton—and got back late at night leaving all of his escort and staff, save Rawlins and a young surgeon, "to struggle in as best they might." Grant never forgot the harrowing ride and determined against winter campaigning on western Kentucky roadways, but, he added tartly, the enemy "did not send reinforcements to Bowling Green."[11]

Grant realized precisely how treacherous the climate could be for both movement and soldier morale. Many of McClernand's men left their blankets and overcoats in Cairo. Wet feet, soggy uniforms, and poor discipline about rationing food all tempered the volunteers' enthusiasm, leaving a sullen crowd milling around in the countryside east of Columbus. Fortunately the Confederates did not attack. Young Tom Miller of H company, 9th Illinois, complained to homefolks about packing fifty pounds of gear on the trek with little to eat but fat bacon and hard crackers "that is not particularly fit for a dog to eat." It was a hard sight, he noted, to see hundreds of stout young men sitting and lying along the roadside, many of them crying and weeping because they could not keep up with their comrades. On the whole, he declared, "it was the damndest time that I ever seen." Still, said Miller, the Federals had made the local Secessionists realize "we was a hard Set to deal with."[12]

In turn, the soldiers and accompanying reporters received their first close-up view of the Southern enemy and countryside. R.W. Overby noted for his *New York Herald* readers that "budding intellects and tobacco

seem to be the only crops raised in this part of the State" while the plain-
est food graced tables of both planter and laborers (black and white),
with "salt meat, and hominy, hoe cake and molasses, and rye coffee"
prevailing and with butter seldom seen, sugar found only occasionally,
wheat bread a rarity, and vegetables eaten only on Sundays and "on visit-
ing occasions." Women and children abounded, since the men of the
area had mostly joined the Confederate cause. Observers noted that
while everyone expressed southern sympathies they could be coerced to
declare for the Union. "They want mails and freedom to go to market,"
claimed Overby, and with those granted, they would be satisfied whether
attached to the Union or Confederacy. Mostly these people were "heartily sick of the war, the blockade, and the internal disruption," in the reporter's view, and little wonder, for, as one Illinois soldier on the expedition noted, "we ruined every farm we camped on," declaring that it was
hard for him to see a person's property all destroyed and broken up, but
that "we had to do it." Others proved less reluctant, for most of the men
had anticipated actually capturing Columbus or Bowling Green and
were bitterly disappointed with the mere demonstration. Spoiling for
a fight, especially to midwesterners when Columbus seemed to be second in importance only to Washington; Tom Miller spoke for hundreds
when he suggested that the citadel on the Mississippi was one of the keys
to the great Mississippi, "which we feel it is our business to use in unlocking the temporary blockade of the magnificent thoroughfare of such importance to the states of the Northwest." It must be free to all, he went
on, and doubtless no one in the North would rest until a citizen of any
state "may travel thereon without molestation and at will." This frustration of not capturing Columbus led to wanton Federal destruction by
Grant's force of everything viewed as "Secesh" in the backcountry east
of the fortress.[13]

McClernand, Smith, and their commands brought little back from
the expedition except chills and headcolds, and some of the inexperienced soldiers died from the effects of the march. Others returned to find
interlopers among new units encamped in their old quarters. Newcomers like Captain Luther Cowan of the 45th Illinois joined the veterans
in appreciating Cairo—"so famous for dirt, filth, mud, mean houses and
accommodations, and meaner men, verily a place of rascals and rascal-
ity." So Grant's whole force of old-timers and the novices settled once
more into the muddy camps, wintry landscape, and promise for the future. Secretly, the men who had marched into Kentucky smiled at their
accomplishments. Even Foote's sailors learned from convoying the soldiers and their equipment upriver and working together in a joint ven-

ture, but they also discovered the perils of Rebel bushwackers on shore and the submerged tree trunks and shoals in the rivers. Most of all, both junior and senior officers ashore and afloat received invaluable shake-down experience in preparation for more serious campaigning ahead.[14]

In truth, C.F. Smith's people probably produced the most useful re-sult of the demonstration. Together with a late December task force un-der Colonel Lewis Wallace that had discovered the shift of "sixty-day men to Camp Beauregard," Smith's subsequent work in western Ken-tucky taught him much about the roads, bridges, depths of streams, and loyalty of residents in the area. Moreover he became convinced by Janu-ary 21 "that a larger force accompanied by a train of supplies cannot be moved south from Paducah during the season of rain, which is expected to commence in the latter part of this month." While awaiting steamboat resupply during the January demonstration, Smith went upriver aboard the *Lexington* to examine Fort Henry. While the navy fired shells at the fort to draw hostile fire, Smith worked his binoculars to discern salient facts about the position. He saw many Rebels working ashore but no signs of gunboat construction. Incorporating what he saw with earlier scouting reports onto a sketch map for Grant, he added: "I think two iron clad gun-boats would make short work of Fort Henry." Not surpris-ingly, this sentiment soon found its way into newspapers, for newsmen were everywhere. Luckily, by that point, events had moved apace.[15]

Any number of Federal officials could see clearly the direction for a campaign by late January. Combined with restiveness among soldiers, newsmen, politicians, and citizens at home, the climate became electric for some type of action. Whitelaw Reid told his *Cincinnati Gazette* readers; "What is the truth about the great expedition from Cairo? Nothing, my inquiring friend, nothing. The great expedition is still only great expec-tations." If the blow is to be struck at all, added a New York reporter, "it can be struck at no more favorable time than the present." But a cross-town rival at the *New York Times* debunked the rumors, declaring, "the whole thing looks like an immense humbug." It was not humbug, however, to Grant, Foote, C.F. Smith, McClernand—even St. Louis headquarters. These people knew Sidney Johnston's line was spongy in western Kentucky. The twin rivers offered a way to avoid assault on both the forts at Bowling Green and the iron-brimmed bluffs at Columbus. An end run around Columbus manifested great potential even to those who wanted a head-on confrontation with the Rebels on the battlefield. The problem for Union subordinates in the West was to convince higher authority to order the mission before the Confederates moved to block it.[16]

Technically, the Confederate defense line in the West was breached at the very moment Grant's demonstration ploughed around in the mud of western Kentucky. Far to the east, near Somerset, Kentucky, on the road to East Tennessee, a Federal force from Buell's command sharply defeated Sidney Johnston's right wing at Mill Springs. Confederate Major General George B. Crittenden and Brigadier General Felix Zollicoffer attempted to surprise and destroy Brigadier General George H. Thomas' advancing Federals, only to be destroyed in turn. The Yankees now had a golden opportunity to bring off Lincoln's dream of freeing East Tennessee, except that Thomas decided the absence of an enemy in that quarter negated the need for continuing the advance, and he turned to take a position at Burkesville on the upper Cumberland above Nashville and thus threaten Johnston's Bowling Green position. The North cheered Mill Springs, with Colonel William Lyon of the 13th Wisconsin writing his wife, "it shows how western men fight."[17]

Buell now thought Halleck's gunboats could simply strike up the Cumberland, race past Fort Donelson (destroying the Clarksville railroad bridge), and unite with Thomas above Nashville. Halleck argued for a concentration of the better part of both departmental armies for a grand push through the center of Johnston's line via the Tennessee, thus negating any need to move directly against Bowling Green, Nashville, or Columbus. McClellan preferred the deep strike into the Heartland of the Confederacy (with a concentration against Stevenson, not the Decatur railroad junction in Alabama), but he remained acutely aware of Lincoln's imperative that Nashville be taken for political reasons — such as restoration of a loyal state administration in the Union. Once more the passage of communiques delayed the decision-making process. At the same time, Halleck had internal considerations within his departmental hierarchy that also held up action.[18]

Grant anxiously sought to explain the results of his January demonstration to Halleck in person. Rebuffed at first, he fumbled his chance to coherently discuss western Kentucky and the twin rivers. Halleck, in turn, failed to inform Grant that he, Buell, and McClellan already conceived the plan envisioned by Grant. He might have even told Grant about Paducah Unionist John Lellyett's latest observation concerning high water in the rivers since "the present stage of water, the snow which covered the country, and the heavy rain which has fallen for eighteen hours and is still falling renders it absolutely certain that a flood will for a week or two be running out of the Tennessee and Cumberland, great enough to allow your heaviest gunboats to run far above Nashville." Lellyett had also noted how sufficient water would enable even Foote's mortar boats to go above Muscle Shoals on the Tennessee and destroy the Nashville and Chattanooga railroad bridges as well as those of the Memphis and Charleston railroad beyond that point. Buell's army could advance to the Cumberland in eastern Kentucky, he claimed, and together with the gunboats cut off Johnston north of the river and prevent removal of military stores from Middle Tennessee. Less than 20,000 men would be required to capture and hold Nashville, while the Tennessee River force could roam inland and destroy other tunnels and bridges on the railroad from Nashville to Chattanooga. This brilliant scheme sounded good and would have attained virtually every objective that it would subsequently take Federal forces over a year to accomplish. Although it overlooked any countermeasures from the Confederates, Lellyett concluded that it struck him that "the door is now open where I have indicated, for the striking of a most crushing blow against the rebellion." He felt that the present freshet might be the last opportunity that season, while the Mississippi was nearly always open. Citing the enemy's hard work on the twin rivers forts—"every day is worth a great deal to the rebels"—Halleck might have informed his impatient subordinate about Lellyett and the other communications on such matters, but nothing in army protocol demanded that a departmental commander need tell a subordinate anything. Furthermore, Halleck had little confidence in Grant's abilities anyway.[19]

Halleck respected old army men like C.F. Smith more than Grant. In fact, in December, Halleck had requested that McClellan send him a general officer "capable of commanding a corps d'armee of three or four divisions" because he did not think Grant could be spared from his administrative chores at Cairo to take a force to the field. Of course he allowed Grant to undertake the January demonstration. A major operation was different, however, and Halleck may well have harbored continuing doubts about Grant's competence in light of his former drinking problems. At any rate Halleck had his own timetable for a major campaign — mid-February and not before. This would permit more time to collect gunboat crews, complete the mortar boats, muster more land units, and permit the ice-clogged rivers to open. Just as Grant sought to present his own plan to Halleck, the departmental commander directed C.F. Smith to report on the condition of roadways "from Smithland to Dover and Fort Henry; also of the road south of the Tennessee to Fort Henry, and the means of crossing at different points above Paducah." Halleck was certainly not procrastinating, but neither was he going to be stampeded into precipitous action by an eager Cairo subordinate. Anyway, he was just recovering from a bout with the measles that left him weak and unreceptive to sudden jolts such as Grant and his scheme.[20]

Much of Halleck's delay resulted from the navy's difficulties. Eads's gunboats had been completed and commissioned on January 16, but they still lacked proper crew complements. Foote searched everywhere for more men, causing testy Secretary of the Navy Gideon Welles to chide that the Atlantic blockading squadrons also needed able-bodied seamen. Halleck ordered volunteer regiments tapped for men, with particular attention given to culling out troublemakers such as the "Mechanics-Fusiliers" of the 56th Illinois encamped at Chicago. "Ship them to the gunboat service," he ordered. Many colonels balked at this loss of manpower, and much correspondence passed before Foote got his crews. Heavy ordnance also posed problems as many of the pieces shipped from the East proved defective. Halleck, McClellan, and Foote harbored doubts about the mortar boats, but Lieutenant Henry A. Wise, the flag officer's friend at the Navy department, passed the word that "with reference to the mortar boats, Uncle Abe, as you already know, has gone into that business with a will, making his first demonstration, *entre nous,* by pitching General Ripley out of his Ordnance Bureau. I have told him how the work can be done expeditiously, and take my word for it, my friend, that the wires have not ceased vibrating since, nor will they until the thing is done." The behind-the-scenes politics involving the western campaign was awesome.[21]

Then Foote himself confused the issue further by telling Halleck that, given the river currents, mortar boats would have to be towed up the Tennessee and Cumberland rather than floated down the Mississippi, and that since neither boats nor mortars had yet arrived at Cairo, he did not consider these craft "adapted to the proposed service." To the contrary, protested Phelps, who had studied Forts Henry and Donelson from a distance and now contended that high angle or arc fire from mortars would be precisely what was needed to silence them. He saw no reason why the gunboats could not tow the mortar craft, and he concluded: "I have faith to believe that the gunboats can reduce the works on both rivers; I think mortars would render the result more certain." Foote continued to dither about underpowered gunboats, the lack of manpower, and lack of appreciation at army headquarters. His subordinates were far more positive, as young "morally stalwart, vigorously patriotic" men such as Ohioans Symmes and Harry Browne joined the gunboat service and settled into a new and mysterious world below wooden decks, thus shaping the Western Flotilla in ways perhaps unnoticed by senior officers such as Foote.[22]

On shore, similar indecision and restiveness were evident as recruits and more seasoned men milled about in the winter camps. Political intrigue was rife among colonels and brigadier generals such as McClernand as they wrote friends in Washington for favors. McClernand especially plumbed for a new command in the West more responsive to Illinois' needs than "a *quasi* foreign pro consulate" (a thinly veiled barb about Halleck's focus on Missouri). Mary Logan, wife of the commander of the 31st Illinois, warned her husband about McClernand (his superior officer) as a "man of so little hard sense and so aristocratic and over bearing and suspicious of you." Prewar political competition had carried over into the army, and Mary Logan thought that her husband and his regiment would never get "merited credit." The enlisted ranks were much more concerned about families at home and health in camp. The wonder is that they did not all die, thought Luther Cowan of the 45th Illinois, as "they are so careless of their health." Cairo had become a veritable stinkhole, somewhat vaudevillian in scene with the St. Charles Hotel constantly jammed by officers, contractors, speculators, "Hebrew dealers," river men, northern visitors, the press, and, undoubtedly, spies. Every room "was a vile atmosphere, impregnated with whiskey, stale tobacco-smoke, unwashed stockings, and perspiring feet," noted Franc B. Wilkie of the *Dubuque Herald*. It was an era of whiskey, he declared, "one day there was no whiskey, no Grant; the next day there were both whiskey and Grant in unlimited quantities." Brawls, continuous games of euchre and poker, much idleness, and much mischief pervaded the scene. The newsmen chased every rumor—Rebels coming up from Columbus and guerrilla Jeff Thompson rampaging in Missouri, with "endless expeditions going everywhere, but catching nothing." Then suddenly everything changed. John B. Connelly of the 31st Illinois recorded in his diary at Carrollton, Kentucky: "From the way the air feels, and movements about headquarters, it is evident a movement is not far off, but when and where we can not tell."[23]

At first Grant could not tell either. He had returned from his unsatisfactory interview with Halleck to face rising flood waters at Cairo, the machinations of McClernand and others, and a quagmire of encampments groaning with bored, sick, and poorly supplied soldiers. Grant seemed high-spirited when he sat next to Dr. Brinton at "a rather low theater" and said, "Oh, Doctor, Doctor, if you only knew how it grieves me to find you in such a low place, and in such company." Upon his return to base, Grant grew morose from Halleck's rebuff. The one bright spot seemed to be C.F. Smith's detailed reports as well as Foote's proximity to discuss prospects for a joint operation. The soldier and sailor

General Ethan Allen Hitchcock. National Archives.

studied Smith's information, compared their own findings, and decided that it was time to act. On January 28, they sent two telegrams to St. Louis. The one from Grant merely stated, "with permission, I will take Fort Henry, on the Tennessee, and establish and hold a large camp there." Foote's cable respectfully stated that he and Grant thought that Fort Henry could be subdued by four gunboats and a land force and permanently occupied, and he asked Halleck's permission to act in such a way as to force the issue: "Have we your authority to move for that purpose when ready." Then Foote added a curious little afterthought: "I made the proposition to move on Fort Henry first to General Grant." This may have been Foote's method for overcoming Halleck's evident disdain for Grant.[24]

Foote's afterthought may have won Grant a temporary reprieve. Just four days before, Halleck had urged McClellan to appoint the venerable old warrior Ethan Allen Hitchcock as a major general of Volunteers. Halleck may have felt a senior regular could overcome the petty squabbling among his corps of brigadier generals—Grant, Sherman, John Pope, Samuel Curtis, Stephen Hurlburt, Franz Sigel, Benjamin Prentiss, and John McClernand (some of them were Illinois appointees who had been feuding over seniority for some months),—or Halleck may have simply wanted Hitchcock as his "corps d'armee" commander. But he did not push the matter since the campaign lay some weeks in the future, according to his plans. Apparently McClellan, retired senior commanding general Winfield Scott, and others approved Hitchcock for the task, but the man's health precluded appointment. The idea would not go away, however. Then other events intervened coincidentally to arrival of the telegrams from Foote and Grant. Defying tidy lines of civil and military protocol, President Lincoln (spurred on by the war and navy secretaries) issued his famous War Order Number 1, on January 27. The weary chief executive prodded his generals to action; they must all commence their forward movements on George Washington's birthday, February 22, 1862. Impossible to enforce, illogical to impose, and ill-advised to issue, perhaps, here was a spark of impetus provided by the White House. The date fit Halleck's schedule anyway, but McClellan added his own enjoinder just to keep things militarily proper. That same day, he sent a shorter, possibly more meaningful telegram to Halleck.[25]

"A deserter just in from the rebels says that Beauregard had not left Centreville [Virginia] four days ago, but that as he was going on picket he heard officers say that Beauregard was under orders to go to Kentucky with fifteen regiments from the Army of the Potomac [CSA]," read McClellan's missive. Halleck might overlook Lincoln's war order, and he might reply to Foote's telegram (he never replied directly to Grant) that he was simply awaiting Smith's report on the state of the Smithland-Fort Henry road, but this Beauregard business galvanized "Old Brains" to action. He sent a readiness order to Foote and advised Grant to organize his command into brigades, divisions, or columns as he thought feasible. Grant and Foote both urged speed in follow-up letters sent to headquarters on January 29. The two subordinates had tired of Halleck's evasiveness. This could be found in Grant's final terse comment: "The advantages of this move are as perceptible to the general commanding as to myself, therefore further statements are unnecessary." Of course Halleck knew this also. Bowing to the inevitable, he sent the simple order to Grant that same day to "make your preparations to take and hold Fort Henry. I will send you written instructions by mail."[26]

These written instructions proved highly informative. The expedition would be waterborne because the roads "are almost impassable for large forces." Sufficient garrisons and the gunboat *Benton* would remain behind to guard against a Confederate thrust from Columbus. Then Halleck told his subordinate precisely how to attack a fort which neither had seen personally. Grant's forces would disembark north of Fort Henry, move to trap the Confederates from the land side, while cavalry would move to destroy the railroad above the fort. Halleck wanted the railroad bridge across the Tennessee preserved for future Federal use. He promised to erect a telegraph line down the east side of the river from Paducah to Fort Henry, and he added a new name to Grant's roster, that of Lieutenant Colonel James B. McPherson, as principal engineer for the expedition. Finally, showing a complete misreading of McClellan's information about Beauregard but betraying why he had suddenly agreed to an advance ahead of his own timetable, Halleck added: "A telegram from Washington says that Beauregard left Manassas four days ago with fifteen regiments for the line of Columbus and Bowling Green. It is therefore of the greatest importance that we cut that line before he arrives. You will move with the least delay possible."[27]

Halleck was now the man in a hurry. He wired McClellan that same day about the expedition, adding that the mortar boats would not be taken along, "and I doubt if they will ever be of much use in the Mississippi." As for cooperation with Buell, Henry Halleck had little to say, but he informed the Ohioan separately that he had ordered an advance— "it will be made immediately"— and that he would "telegraph the day of investment or attack." Buell was aghast at Halleck's haste. He replied that it would be several days before he could help or seriously engage the enemy, since he was still discussing plans with both Halleck and McClellan and perceived no agreed-upon design for cooperation. This failed to deter Halleck, for his secret agenda held something more than sharing honors with Buell. In an aside to McClellan, he hinted, "as Fort Henry, Dover, &c. are in Tennessee, I respectfully suggest that the State be added to this department." Few people in Cairo or Paducah knew of such scheming. A reporter for the *Missouri Democrat* telegraphed his home office from Cairo that "affairs are exceedingly quiet," and filled his dispatch with minor tidbits about impending unit arrivals, receipt of the mortars, and the muster-out of Colonel David Stuart's 55th Illinois regi-

mental band. At Paducah, Sylvester G. Bishop of the 11th Indiana Zouaves wrote home that he and four companions had built a cabin at Camp
Macauley since it appeared unlikely that they would move very soon.
January 30, 1862, seemed just like any other day in camp, but it was the
lull before the storm.[28]

CHAPTER 6

On the Eve of Battle

G RANT'S JANUARY DEMONSTRATION MYSTIFIED WESTERN
Confederate leaders. Johnston thought that "the movements of the enemy indicate his intention to turn General Polk's right by the Memphis and Ohio Railroad, yet three days later reported to Richmond that the movement had as its "ultimate object the occupation of Nashville." He therefore shifted 8,000 infantry, cavalry, and artillery from Hardee's Central Army of Kentucky to Russellville to protect the Bowling Green-Memphis rail line. Polk, meanwhile, barraged the War department, southern governors, and Johnston with missives declaring his position to be under imminent threat of attack. Even he admitted to his chief on January 24: "What the particular object [of the demonstration] was has not clearly transpired," adding that the only thing made plain was that it "intended to make a demonstration on [the] Tennessee River."[1]

Polk also sent reserves to his threatened area, including Colonel James Gee's 15th Arkansas from Memphis, and some 1,000 cavalrymen to harass the Federals as they retired to Cairo and Paducah. Polk now realized that his flank lay open, and he pleaded with Johnston to rush 40,000 men to the region between Columbus and the Tennessee River. Of course Johnston had no such number available, and Polk refused to send troops from his fortress. The hour of decision had arrived in the West. Suddenly everyone realized that "to suppose within the facilities of movement by water which the well-fitted rivers of the Ohio, Cumberland, and Tennessee give for active operations, [the Federals] will suspend them in Tennessee and Kentucky during the winter months is a delusion." Johnston now demanded that all the resources of the young nation be placed at his disposal; the whole country had to be aroused "to make the greatest effort that they will be called upon to make during the contest," he proclaimed. He supplemented his pleas to President Davis by sending a personal envoy, Colonel St. John Liddell, to argue his case. But the chief executive cut the junior officer off with a curt, "why did General Johnston send you to me for arms and reinforcements, when he must know that I have neither." His tone softened, but his ultimate answer was the same: surely his friend had sufficient men and arms, and, even if not, then he must rely on local procurement for shotguns, rifles, even pikes, for "I can do nothing for him."[2]

By February 2, the harried Confederate government requisitioned long-service or "war regiments" with 11 demanded from Alabama, 12 from Georgia, 7 from Mississippi, and 32 from Tennessee. Some of these units would eventually pass to Johnston but not in time to meet the most immediate need. The best that Richmond could do was dispatch its victorious but controversial eastern general, Pierre Gustav Toutant Beauregard, to help Johnston (and possibly to remove his tempestuous presence from the Virginia front). As for more fighting men, only Floyd's seasoned brigade of Virginians could be spared for Kentucky. At least these men had smelled the smoke of battle at Cross Lanes and Carnifex Ferry, and understood the rigors of winter operations. Fully 20 percent of them straggled into Bowling Green after Christmas, nursing ill-effects from field exposure. Floyd and his staff spent most of January sorting out vouchers and sick rosters. Nonetheless, these veterans bolstered spirits of the westerners, and provided an experienced maneuver element for Hardee's army. They were the main contingent shifted to Russellville in late January.[3]

Mill Springs and Grant's January demonstration together increased Johnston's quandary. Withdrawal from central Kentucky offered greater freedom of action, but retirement from the strong, well-defended (even comfortable) environs of Bowling Green seemed politically and militarily difficult. Yet the reasons for staying in Kentucky and wooing her to the Confederacy seemed to diminish daily. Frank Batchelor of Terry's Texas Rangers wrote home from the picket line near Bell Station that he might be doing the Blue Grass an injustice, but from his viewpoint, "she is rotten to the core upon the slave question." He wanted to break up the Bowling Green army and undertake guerrilla operations, claiming that the Rangers alone had successfully harrassed 20,000 Federals for months. "When we find the Lion's skin too short, we must patch it with the Fox's and resort to cunning, or cruelty, to save ourselves from destruction," he observed. It was a life and death struggle, said Batchelor, and "where saltpetre is ineffectual, we should not hesitate at poison." These were the thoughts of the Texas frontier, but they were too unprofessional for the West Point-trained southern gentlemen such as Johnston. His advisers and subordinates pictured him preparing to fight the classic set-piece Napoleonic battle. As Jeremy Gilmer wrote his wife on January 22, the arrival of Colonel John Bowen's unit from Polk's army enabled Johnston to garrison Bowling Green as an anchor, while the rest of his force would move out to strike the advancing Federals.[4]

The onset of winter, the Bowling Green base, and Buell's snail-like advance transfixed Johnston's plans. He continued to feel outnumbered by the enemy, with January returns showing perhaps 30,781 (one citation mentioned only 24,574) effectives out of 39,548 on the rolls at Bowling Green. Polk's figures fluctuated weekly, but nearly 18,000 out of 22,000 to 25,000 men on the rolls at Columbus showed at month's end. Polk's so-called "Fourth Division" on the twin rivers numbered 5,000 present out of 7,000 on the rolls. Had Johnston known the truth, Buell reported but 46,150 "present for duty and fit for the field," while even Grant's Cairo district in Halleck's department counted scarcely 20,679 officers and men. The war in the West was a numbers game, a game of perceptions and bluff for the generals. Confederate perspective stretched no farther than their own log huts at Bowling Green and Columbus or the picket line along Green River, and what their scouts told them about the Federals. Medical directors, Dr. David Yandell for example, helped shape perceptions, as they noted that the transition from autumn hues to winter chill had done little to quell epidemics of small pox, measles, dysentery, typhoid, and influenza. J.K. Pope wrote home from Camp Weakley in late January: "most of us are sick with colds and measles, and several have gone home and there are more to send tomorrow." Neither the ministrations of Yandell and his staff nor the care of volunteer nurses such as Ella Newsom of Arkansas could cure the image of a sick army. The army was incapable of stopping a determined Union drive because of its health problems, and Sidney Johnston knew it.[5]

Then, too Johnston lacked the resources to change base quickly, other than in an emergency. His severely taxed railroad line was overworked with the "present demand . . . from the army alone, from Paris, 800,000 pounds; from Clarksville, 1,000,000 pounds; from Nashville, 1,500,000 pounds," noted his railroad advisers. Superintendent G.B. Fleece of the Louisville and Nashville told Johnston on January 2 that the entire road was crowded with business unprecedented in its history. He cited livestock and freight at every station, large numbers of passengers, and constant troop movements. To service this business, the L&N, as well as the Memphis, Clarksville and Louisville had but 10 locomotives, 120 box cars, and 55 flat cars to work 225 miles of track. This was less than half the normal peacetime ratio, said Fleece. All over Johnston's department, rail service was breaking down. Memphis branch superintendent J.J. Williams complained bitterly to Polk about his inability to retrieve trains sent up the line to Bowling Green, and how he had borrowed cars from other lines such as the Mississippi Central to offset such losses. Fleece established a schedule "best adapted for the speedy, safe, and certain final accomplishment of all work," but even then his equipment would permit but a single thirteen-car freight daily to Bowling Green, and a similar twelve-car daily on the Memphis branch, as well as a single passenger train each way each day on both lines. Johnston asked Richmond to recruit "a full corps of competent Engineers and Machinists" from Captain John S. Butler's "Railroad Boys" with the 1st Tennessee at Winchester, Virginia, but nothing came of it.[6]

In sum, Fleece's somber evaluation suggested that rapid reinforcement via Johnston's vaunted interior rail lines was quite out of the question. Small contingents up to brigade size might be shifted expeditiously by railroad, but not an entire army. Given such facts, Polk probably had it correct when he wrote Johnston on January 17 that, in view of the size of his force, "I see nothing left me but to strengthen my position and await [the enemy's] coming," while shifting the responsibility for dealing with such force "as we cannot defeat on the War Department and the people of the states around Columbus." He resolved to withstand a siege, and he looked to Richmond for such aid as bureaucrats and the country could afford him, declared a defiant Polk. Johnston could not have said it better; this was his very stance at Bowling Green.[7]

Despite their continuing fixation with Bowling Green and Columbus, both generals turned some of their attention to the twin rivers in January. Questions about expediting work on floating batteries, dispatch of galvanic mines (called "torpedoes"), heavy ordnance, and anchor chains for river obstacles dotted official dispatches. Polk requested $60,000 from the War department to complete purchase of the *Eastport*. Mackall wrote repeatedly to the Nashville ordnance chief, Captain M.H. Wright, about speeding ordnance fabrication and then forwarding heavy guns and equipment downriver to the forts, and he noted on January 20 that Johnston wanted 1,000 pikes made specifically for Fort Donelson. In turn Wright and his Memphis colleague, W.R. Hunt, communicated their own production problems to the Confederate ordnance chief, Josiah Gorgas, at Richmond. Gorgas worked to ship heavy guns westward from the Tredegar Iron Works, but would they reach the twin rivers in time? Then, late in January, Johnston further clogged the requisition process by demanding a rush order for over 100 heavy and light cannon for the planned Nashville and Clarksville fortifications, additions and replacements to other batteries, as well as carriages, chassis, and implements.

This sudden appetite for heavy ordnance must have confounded even the very best armory workers in the Confederacy.[8]

Meanwhile the carping criticism of Lloyd Tilghman stung everyone. The Kentuckian sounded cheery enough in his New Year's Day dispatch to headquarters, but when Mackall and Johnston evaluated the rest of his notes, they found disgruntled comments about everything from elevating screws and fixtures for a 32-pounder left at Columbus, a 10-inch Columbiad that consistently "jumps its carriage," inadequate seacoast gun ammunition to deficiencies across the spectrum of small arms, knapsacks, canteens, and even tarpaulins to cover ammunition dumps. That Tilghman had never surveyed the works across the Tennessee at Fort Heiman greatly irritated Johnston. "General Tilghman had not passed on the plan," complained north Alabama defense committeeman James Saunders on January 17, despite the large work force of slaves which he had taken down to Fort Henry for that purpose. Johnston immediately sent a terse telegram to Tilghman directing that he "occupy and *intrench* the heights opposite Fort Henry. Do not lose a moment. Work all night." A new telegraph line now linked the twin rivers with both Bowling Green and Columbus via the Cumberland, so that communications could be speeded up and better control could be executed by the distant departmental commander. Tilghman remained unperturbed by those Federal gunboat shellings in January, but that may have been mere bravado. More serious was his severe alienation of ordnance officials in Nashville and Memphis by his ill-tempered criticism of their support. Wright assured Johnston that the twin rivers commander had ample supply of cannon ammunition, lead, caps, powder, and "72,000 small arms" rounds and contended that troops at Forts Henry and Donelson had from twice to nine times more heavy ammunition as Confederates blockading the Potomac River below Washington, or at Pensacola, Florida. In his opinion, "According to the experience of the past war—you could not, in three days of unabated firing—consume the 100 rounds for that 10 in. Columbiad."[9]

Suddenly, Johnston, Polk, and even Governor Harris all attempted to find out what was wrong on the twin rivers. Johnston sent an inspector, Harris dispatched Colonel Bushrod Johnson, and Polk ordered his heavy artillery specialist, Lieutenant Colonel Milton A. Haynes, to take over gunnery instruction at the two forts. By the close of the month, even engineer Gilmer had returned to the area under orders to inspect the works, impress labor, and expedite all defense preparations from the twin forts to Nashville. Whether Gilmer accomplished much remains

suspect. His letters to his wife contained gossip about the army, his longing for Savannah, his aversion to duty at the remote forts, and his theory
that the Yankees would never attack before spring. In some ways the day
of the engineer had passed on the twin rivers. By late January, initiative
belonged to gunners like Haynes. Still, Gilmer did his duty, and his visits to Forts Henry and Donelson provided his superiors with alternative
views to those held by Tilghman.[10]

As January turned to February, Gilmer spent three days consulting
with the Kentuckian and inspecting on-site engineer Joseph Dixon's
work. Gilmer pronounced Fort Henry to be a fine bastioned work, ready
for defense, with 17 well-mounted guns, 12 of which fronted the river. Extensive lines of infantry trenches covered the rear of the position. Despite the long delays in commencing Fort Heiman across the river, Tilghman's energy had laid out a comparable earthwork, also supported by
infantry trenches, "requiring only a few days additional labor to put
them in a state of defense," noted the engineer. Yet, the greatest need
continued to be that of heavy ordnance. Tilghman relied upon field
guns and small arms—in Fort Heiman sufficient to contain a land assault, perhaps, but absolutely inadequate for helping Fort Henry cope
with a river attack. Gilmer conveyed Tilghman's fears "that it might
cause disaster if the place were vigorously attacked by the enemy gunboats," which was "his greatest danger." The engineer then rode the twelve
miles to Fort Donelson, spending February 3–4 in siting lines of infantry
cover on the commanding ground behind this fort. Gilmer thought the
Cumberland position needed more work than Fort Henry, and he was
especially concerned about raising the level of parapets for the water batteries by adding sandbags, as at Fort Henry.[11]

Moreover, Gilmer met with Haynes concerning the heavy artillerists
now training the gun crews at Fort Donelson. Haynes had reported to
Tilghman at Fort Henry on January 15 and had been sent immediately
to the Cumberland. A West Pointer, veteran of the 3d Artillery in campaigns against the Seminoles, Haynes had also served in the prewar Tennessee militia with Pillow, Zollicoffer, Heiman, and Bushrod Johnson.
Author of a state-sponsored training guide, *The Confederate Artillerist: Instructions in Artillery, Horse, and Foot,* Haynes must have been appalled to
find the situation at Dover far different from the tightly managed heavy
artillery organization at Columbus. Fort Donelson's garrison comprised
the 30th, 49th, and 50th Infantry, and Captain Frank Maney's light battery—all Tennesseans—and the force commander, Colonel John W. Head
of the 30th, could spare only Captain Bell G. Bidwell's Company A
of his regiment, and Captain Thomas W. Beaumont's company of the

50th for water battery duty. Beaumont's people had received some training on the guns before Haynes arrival, but Bidwell's people had none.
Haynes quickly enbraced the challenge at Fort Donelson, and developed
a corps of heavy artillerists on short notice.[12]

Haynes grouped infantry and artillery men into a provisional battalion, set them through strenuous and continuous gun drill, and employed them to strengthen the water batteries. He had them repair and
strengthen embrasures, platforms, and traverses with fascines made of
twigs and grapevines, and with cotton-seed and coffee sacks filled with
earth to substitute for sandbags. He wired Polk asking for instructors
from Columbus, and the arrival of two lieutenants together with an ex-
U.S. Navy officer, Captain J.P. Shuster, provided the cadre for training
the new gunners to target their cannon at 1,000, 1,500, and 2,000 yards
downriver. The trainees also learned how to properly measure the amount
of powder and shot for each setting and how to place implements and
ammunition within reach for rapid firing; they divided into fifteen-
man gun crews (with reserves) so as to work under designated gun captains appointed by Shuster. Fatigue parties constructed a 1,000-round
bombproof magazine and a covered way for access to the lower water
battery. All of this coincided with final receipt of the heavy cannon ordered for the fort. Ten 32-pounders (including two naval carronades in
the upper battery) were already in place. But on January 2, a 10-inch Columbiad and its iron chassis went by water from Nashville, and it took
three weeks to mount the huge piece by using blocks, tackles, and hoists
according to specifications in the manuals. Another large cannon of the
Columbiad type from Tredegar arrived without proper pintle and pintle
plates, and necessitated a delay until Haynes could send a lieutenant to
secure these parts for the rebored and rifled 6.5-inch piece.[13]

This flurry of activity created an air of expectation and excitement on
the twin rivers. New troops arrived daily with Colonel Thomas H. Abernathy's 53d Tennessee organizing at Fort Donelson on January 7, and
Major Stephen H. Colms arriving with an independent infantry battalion
several weeks later from Camp Weakley near Nashville. Tilghman's stiff-
necked discipline led the colonel of the 50th Tennessee to resign, and
even Colonel John W. Head had problems with the Kentuckian. A great
deal of dissatisfaction existed in the ranks, reported newly elected Colonel James E. Bailey of the 49th Tennessee, who also acted as a peace-
maker between Tilghman and his discordant subordinates. Sickness
was claiming too many lives and there seemed to be far too many parents trying to retrieve sick offspring "in disobedience of a positive order."
Bailey told his wife that the garrison seemed almost crazy to go home:

"It requires great exertion to get the different company officers to do their duty, and sometimes I have almost despaired of getting them to do so." Some men were indifferent, some idle, others ignorant, and zealous leaders such as Bailey expressed great uneasiness in the face of the impending Union attack. Young soldiers sounded more hopeful, as in the case of David Clark of the 49th Tennessee writing to his cousin Maggie Bell on January 18: "I hope the enemy will attack us at [Fort Henry] or this [place], I care not which," he wrote. "I feel confidant that we can whip three times our number here [and] if they attack us at either place, our company will enjoy the fun."[14]

Tilghman and his commanders had little time to worry about either the optimism or the uneasiness. Severe flooding threatened gun positions and magazines in Fort Henry as the Tennessee River crested thirty feet above normal. This high water also negated the vaunted torpedo or mine defense of the river. These sheet-iron cylinders, 5½ feet long by 1 foot in diameter, held seventy pounds of black powder and were anchored to the river bottom at normal flow level. A tipped rod from the top of the contraption activated a musket lock that fired the weapon when a vessel brushed the rod coming upriver. Some twenty of these torpedoes had been placed in the western channel or chute where Panther Island divided the river just below Forts Henry and Heiman. As the water rose, the torpedoes became useless, and slipshod attempts to float more mines from the hospital and supply boat *Samuel Orr* failed miserably. Any Yankee naval movement at high water could expect no trouble with this barrier.[15]

Tilghman watched the flood and tallied his effective strength: 3,033 officers and men fit for duty at Forts Henry and Heiman and about 1,956 available at Fort Donelson. He noted 926 absent on the Tennessee, and another 1,640 missing from the Cumberland post. Although strength figures had increased by 1,200 raw recruits in Abernathy's regiment, the governor's emissary, Bushrod Johnson, caught the measure of that unit when he wrote Nashville on January 26: "One more regiment of new troops will be as many of that description as will be desirable here. Should still be pleased to get one good regiment of old troops." Johnston wired Richmond that "Fort Donelson is now our weakest point." The *Memphis Appeal* boasted to readers (including Ulysses S. Grant at Cairo, who got the paper through the lines): "Fort Donelson with its 3,000 heroes will be held against all opposition. More solicitude is felt about Fort Henry." Grant determined to test both statements.[16]

Halleck's go-ahead telegram of January 30 hit Cairo headquarters like a bombshell. It was snowing outside and all movements were at a standstill. Grant's staff threw their hats into the air and kicked them with glee as they fell to the floor. Normally taciturn John Rawlins knocked over several chairs and pounded his fist against the wall. Grant watched with amusement and then observed drily that they really should be quieter for they might awaken the slumbering Bishop Polk at Columbus. Things settled down, for much had to be done before any expedition could leave the Cairo and Paducah levees. Upriver at St. Louis, George Cullum also got busy. On February 1, he told the local telegraph superintendant, George H. Smith, to proceed at once on constructing a telegraph line from Paducah to Smithland, and thence "south by the usual traveled route" between the Tennessee and Cumberland rivers as rapidly as protection could be provided by the army's advance. Communications would be the key to success, and Halleck wanted no expeditionary commander beyond the reach of his own personal command and control. He also sent McPherson along to report back on Grant's behavior.[17]

Actually Halleck and Grant were similar on some matters. The departmental chief wanted a taut, battle-ready strike force that would "move *rapidly* and *promptly* by steamers, and to reduce [Fort Henry] before any large reinforcements can arrive." Grant's instructions to subordinate generals C.F. Smith and McClernand were to take little cavalry or wagon transport, relying instead on the steamboats for re-supply. The soldiers would travel light—no more than three days rations and forty rounds of ammunition apiece. Grant instructed local quartermaster Captain P.T. Turnley to secure boats for 10,000 infantry, four artillery companies, equipment, rations, and so on. He fitted out the steamer *Uncle Sam* as a headquarters boat and ordered another 100,000 rations stockpiled for animals and 600,000 rounds of musket and rifle ammunition. Grant ordered McClernand to organize his "First Division" from two of the four brigades at Cairo. The other two (plus an additional regiment) would remain behind under Brigadier General E.A. Paine to dig levees against rising flood waters and to perfect fortifications against any possible counterthrust from Columbus. Similarly C.F. Smith would take his "Second Division" from among the Paducah and Smithland units. But Halleck's instructions for a taut column quickly evaporated as Grant's supply train included four wagons plus teams per infantry regiment, one per cavalry company, and three for each artillery battery. Fortunately most of McClernand's men had standard Enfield rifled muskets, but C.F. Smith's division included varying calibers and makes of weapons, thus complicating the ammunition re-supply picture.[18]

The ultimate problem proved to be water transportation. Grant's quartermasters could gather only thirteen steamers, including the *Aleck*

Scott, Minnehaha, City of Memphis, Chancellor, Fanny Bullett, Keystone, Lake Erie, Iatan, Illinois, D.A. January, Wilson, "W.A.B.," and *Uncle Sam*. This dearth of steamboats meant that the army would have to move forward in segments, with Foote's gunboats shielding one element at a time. This was dangerous, but neither Grant nor Foote anticipated Confederate attack on the twin rivers. By February 2, in fact, Grant seemed more concerned about his old nemesis, discipline, than the enemy. He ordered his troops not to fire weapons indiscriminately, not to wander from camp, and not to loot—all matters that had plagued the Belmont and western Kentucky expeditions. Foote, meanwhile, would try to instill similar discipline among his inexperienced boat crews.[19]

In fact Foote worked feverishly to prepare the naval element to the joint expedition. He searched for more men, pushed mortar boat construction, and told Commander A.H. Kilty of the *Mound City* to remain behind to work with Paine on defending Cairo. Kilty was also to strip every boat in the area to outfit the *Louisville,* the final ironclad coming on-line for the expedition. He studied Phelps's last minute reconaissance reports about torpedoes below Fort Henry. Foote was less concerned with these obstacles (ironclad construction and high water would obviate their threat, he decided) than he was with getting his boats in order. Finally casting off from Cairo at 9:00 P.M. on February 1, he ordered the ironclads *Essex, Carondelet, Cincinnati,* and *St. Louis* to rendezvous with timberclads *Conestoga* and *Lexington* at Paducah by noon the next day. Accompanied by the heavy sounds of steam engines and paddle wheels, Foote settled into his stateroom and plotted instructions to his boat captains for the coming action. The four ironclads of his "First Division" would advance against Fort Henry in parallel line, evenly spaced, taking their lead from signals of the flagship *Cincinnati*. The "Second Division" of timberclads would provide backup firepower from a reserve position. Ammunition should be conserved by firing only at the guns in the fort, he noted, not random bodies of Rebel troops. Ever vigilant to detail that might mean the difference between victory and defeat, Foote ordered anchor chains stowed to avoid interference with fire control of the guns, and the uncovering of hatch gratings, lest "great injury will result from the concussion of the guns in firing.[20]

Foote joined Grant at Paducah where the two anxiously awaited McClernand's arrival on February 3. The Ohio's floodwaters had delayed the general's transports, but late that night twinkling running lights off the levee suggested his arrival. Grant immediately directed him to push on into the Tennessee River and, escorted by *Essex* and *St. Louis,* to make for Pine Bluff, eight miles below Fort Henry, or about sixty-five miles above Paducah. The sooner McClernand's troops disembarked, the quicker the steamers could return for Smith's men. Then Grant telegraphed Halleck: "Will be off up the Tennessee at six (6) o'clock. Command twenty-three (23) regiments in all." Once the general and his staff were afloat, no restraining communiques from Halleck could reach them and thwart their departure. For the moment Grant hung back to insure proper loading of Smith's command, and he did not move upriver with McClernand's advance force.[21]

The young Federals were in high spirits despite crowded conditions aboard the transports. Just before their departure, one Illinois officer, John Wilcox, wrote his wife that as soon as they gained reinforcement, they would "float up the Cumberland and take the two forts before breakfast." Now they were underway. "Blackjack" Logan's boisterous 31st Illinois had jammed their haversacks with sausage, cheese, and tobacco from a local sutler, buying on credit before boarding their boat. The disgruntled sutler felt pangs of regret at his action as he watched his debtors steam off upriver. Unfortunately, the departure was marred by the loss of Colonel W.H.L. Wallace's younger brother Matthew, an officer in the 4th Illinois cavalry. Losing his footing on the slippery deck of the *D.A. January*, young Wallace plunged into the icy waters and drowned. "Poor Mat," wrote his grieving brother to his own wife back in Ottawa, Illinois, "had he fallen in action I should not have felt it so keenly, as that is the fate a soldier contemplates, but to be thus cut off in the flush of his youth, with a bright career just opening before him, is indeed sad." W.H.L. Wallace would fall in battle just two months later at Shiloh, and others on this first crusade in the West would suffer similar misfortune as Matthew when some heavily armed and equipped cavalry was swept into the Tennessee flood while disembarking with McClernand's men before Fort Henry. These would be but the vanguard of a host of young northern and southern youth whose rendezvous with death would leave vacant chairs and flowing tears back home before the end of the campaign.[22]

Others, besides the sutlers, felt the sting of frustration as Grant's boats pulled away from the levees. "Annoyance" was the word used by Acting Ensign Symmes Brown aboard *Mound City* at Evansville, Indiana, as many of his comrades were pulled off to flesh out other gunboat crews for the expedition. Colonel William F. Lyon, whose 13th Wisconsin remained behind at Cairo due to their gray militia uniforms, wrote his wife: "Our fear now is that the fight will come off at Bowling Green before we start, and if the rebels are defeated there they may retreat from Columbus without giving us battle. We really want a turn with them at Columbus." Much of this feeling subsided quickly as those left behind found other diversions. Enoch Colby and friends in the Chicago Light Artillery at Paducah went on a rampage in the "secesh" countryside only to encounter a formidable southern farmer wife "with a good farm, lots of poultry, honey, niggers, and everything that bespoke wealth." She blunted their thievery, "so after bidding them good day," noted Colby, "we left as empty as we came."[23]

Secrecy problems attended the expedition from the start. Halleck had decreed absolute silence, and not even Grant's staff, much less his army, knew that Fort Henry was the precise target. Lyon told his wife that "it is supposed they will go up the Cumberland River." Only after the boats turned into the Tennessee could McClernand, C.F. Smith, and the men in the ranks know for sure that Forts Henry and Heiman were the goal. *Chicago Tribune* reporter, Albert H. Bodman, scooped the story, however, by wiring home on February 4 that the transports had gone up the Tennessee. Whether Confederate scouts discovered the invasion force or their senior commanders read about it in Yankee newspapers, it behooved Grant and Foote to move fast to close their whole force quickly. Dropping the 4th Illinois cavalry at Patterson's Ferry, only thirteen miles from Paducah, where it would move overland probing for Confederate outposts between the rivers, the transports then landed McClernand's infantry at 4:30 A.M. on the fourth, at Itra Landing, on the east bank across from Pine Bluff. At some point, while the steamers dropped back to Paducah for the remainder of Smith's men, Grant boarded the *Essex* for a reconnaissance of Fort Henry.[24]

The general wanted to move his army beyond the flooded slough of Panther Creek to avoid crossing that stream in the face of the enemy, but such a landing would put the army within range of Fort Henry's guns, so he needed evidence of their range and accuracy before issuing the order. The *Essex* drew only desultory Confederate fire at first, confirming Grant's theory that he could move McClernand beyond the creek. Then, when the gunboat stood about two and one-half miles below the fort, a 24-pounder shell passed over the craft and shattered saplings along the bank. Grant changed his mind about landing McClernand, reinforced by a second shell which nearly killed Grant and Commander W.D. "Dirty Bill" Porter as it crashed through the stern deck, smashed into "officers country," and cleanly severed the feet from a pair of Porter's socks before dropping into the water astern. A visibly shaken Grant immediately ordered a retirement to Itra Landing, where he told McClernand to reembark and proceed to Bailey's Ferry, three miles from Fort

Henry but downstream from Panther Creek. The weary bluecoats dutifully trudged on and off the boats once more.[25]

The Confederates at Forts Henry and Heiman had little warning of the Union invasion: there was an absence of intelligence reports from Paducah spies and scouting reports from partisans, while a dark and wintry night cloaked Grant's movement. Milton's Rangers finally sent up a rocket alert only when McClernand's command was actually going ashore. Even then they transmitted erroneous information about gunboat strength, thereby sending Fort Henry's garrison scurrying to the cannon, but doing little to harass or actually prevent the landing. Part of the problem lay with the already divided command on the twin rivers. Tilghman and Gilmer were alternating supervision of construction work at the forts, and on that night they were at Dover, with Heiman in charge on the Tennessee River. The Nashvillian dispatched couriers to find Tilghman, but the first indication of trouble came only about noon the next day when the sound of Fort Henry's guns reached Dover. Finally a messenger did get through near dusk, indicating that the situation was far more serious than merely one of the Union navy's periodic visits. Tilghman and Gilmer immediately began the ride back to Fort Henry, but they never reached the fort until 11:30 P.M., and their cold, fatigued, and late arrival hardly permitted sound decision-making. The chance to catch Grant's army during debarkation eluded the Confederates.[26]

Meanwhile Heiman tried to prepare for the regular defense of his position. He sent steamboats to retrieve 400 men of the skeletal 48th and 51st Tennessee from Paris Landing (five miles away), and Danville (some fifteen miles further). Heiman counted less than 3,000 men in his command, including his own 10th Tennessee, Drake's 4th Mississippi, Hughes' 27th Alabama, Gee's 15th Arkansas, Garvin's Alabama battalion, several companies of Alabama cavalry as well as Nathan Bedford Forrest's Tennessee cavalry, Crain's light battery, and Captain Jesse Taylor's heavy artillery company. He positioned some of these units at Fort Heiman, along with a contingent of Kentucky scouts. Garvin was sent to block the ford across Panther Creek and the main road leading inland from Bailey's Ferry to Boyd's house. This road would enable the Federals to outflank the garrison and cut them off from their communication link with Fort Donelson. Heiman put most of his men to work strengthening the rifle pits, while his cavalry patroled the woodland roads and trails toward Itra Landing.[27]

Heiman's main trouble was that he and his men moved too cautiously. Garvin did not really control the creek crossing, and nobody actively

Landing of Federal Troops below Fort Henry, February 4, 1862. Sketch by
H. Lovie, *Frank Leslie's Illustrated Newspaper*, March 15, 1862.

Interior of Fort Henry, the Morning after its Capture, February 7, 1862. Sketch by H. Lovie, *Frank Leslie's Illustrated Newspaper*, March 15, 1862.

resisted the advancing Federals. Most of the Rebels remained skittish about the gunboats, and time worked against the defenders. Heiman wired Polk at Columbus about his predicament at 5:00 P.M. on February 4, but rushing reinforcements over rickety railroad lines from the Mississippi (seventy-five miles away) or even Bowling Green (ninety-five miles in the opposite direction) to the twin rivers was almost impossible. Tilghman and Heiman were on their own, and McClernand's skirmishers quickly probed weak spots near Boyd's house and the ford. The loss of self-confidence soon compounded Confederate tactical errors.[28]

The division of the Confederate position by the Tennessee River haunted everyone. Heiman claimed later that he had never had much confidence in the fort bearing his name. Deemed so vital earlier for holding the high ground commanding Fort Henry itself, the position lacked the heavy artillery necessary to interdict the river properly. Heiman worried that the Federals would trap his men across the river; why this had not occurred before to the Confederate leaders remains vague. When Tilghman arrived, he ordered a pull-out from Fort Heiman, rationalizing in his after-action report: "I deemed it proper to trust to the fact that the extremely bad roads leading to that point would prevent the movement of heavy guns by the enemy, by which I might be annoyed [at Fort Henry]." Leaving a single battalion of Alabama cavalry and a spy company to contain Federal movements on the Fort Heiman side of the stream, Tilghman and Heiman all too quickly relinquished a position upon which much time and effort had been expended, and which distinctly commanded the main fort which they declared ready to defend to the death. Rebel leadership became more concerned with concentrating their forces for the principal water defense of Fort Henry.[29]

Young Federals such as David Leib Ambrose of the 7th Illinois spent much of February 5 complaining about the mud at Camp Halleck (McClernand's encampment near Bailey's Ferry) and watching the "Stars and Bars" fluttering defiantly atop the Fort Henry flagstaff. Others such as Luther H. Cowan of the 45th Illinois could not understand why they were still aboard the steamers. Some of the men had gone ashore, had consumed their three day rations, and now were quite hungry. Over in Confederate lines, Randal McGavock recorded in his diary that Yankee regimental bands serenaded everyone with "Yankee Doodle," "Hail Columbia," "Star-Spangled Banner," and — in honor of his "Sons of Erin," he thought — "St. Patrick's Day in the Morning." It did not seem like war to most of these young Americans, and W.H.L. Wallace wrote his wife: "I am very tired . . . I haven't got used to my new responsibilities as commander of a brigade in the field and feel, of course, a great deal of anxiety about details."[30]

In fact, anxiety about details bothered both sides on the eve of the battle. It was a time "of unusual animation," said Jesse Taylor, with a never ending bustle of enemy transports downriver. His Confederate colleagues merely watched and waited. Grant ordered more reconnaissance, while Foote swept the river for torpedoes. Back in St. Louis, Halleck got word from Buell that he was gathering reinforcements to forward to the twin rivers. Halleck collared Assistant Secretary of War Thomas A. Scott from a midwestern inspection tour and asked him to press the governors of Michigan, Indiana, and Ohio to speed forward more recruits. At Columbus, General Polk finally stirred and telegraphed Tilghman to anticipate cavalry reinforcements. The perplexed Kentuckian responded sulkily, "thank you for the cavalry, but had rather have disciplined infantry." In turn, he wired Johnston at 11:00 A.M. on the fifth, "If you can re-enforce strongly and quickly we have a glorious chance to overwhelm the enemy."[31]

Of course this was not possible, although memories of Pillow's last-minute victory at Belmont must have crossed many minds. Tilghman promised to have his steamboats ready at the Danville railroad crossing for the arrival of troop trains. None were forthcoming. Johnston told the arriving Beauregard that very day at Bowling Green that he did not intend to support Fort Henry if it was attacked. Tilghman was on his own, and optimistically assured Polk that he would concentrate close-in at Fort Henry, warning, however, "don't trust to Johnston's re-enforcing me; we need all. I don't want raw troops who are just organized; they are in my way. Act promptly and don't trust any one." The best he could do was to organize his force at hand into two brigades under Heiman and Colonel Joseph Drake. Tilghman sent word to Head at Fort Donelson to move the 30th and 50th Tennessee regiments to Peytona Furnace, midway between the two forts. He unaccountably failed to increase the strength of the cavalry screen on Panther Creek and did not fire upon Foote's boats as they swept the river for torpedoes. Like Heiman, Tilghman practiced a reactionary, passive defense, awaiting Grant's move.[32]

The Federals trickled off the transport well into the evening on February 5, with some of the 45th Illinois staggering down the ramps drunk from the liquor they had discovered during a firewood stop coming upriver. Grant leisurely penned his attack order and readied the joint army-navy assault. McClernand's column, guided by engineer McPherson, would take the road from Bailey's Ferry to the Telegraph Road (which linked Henry and Donelson). His mission would be to cut this vital ar-

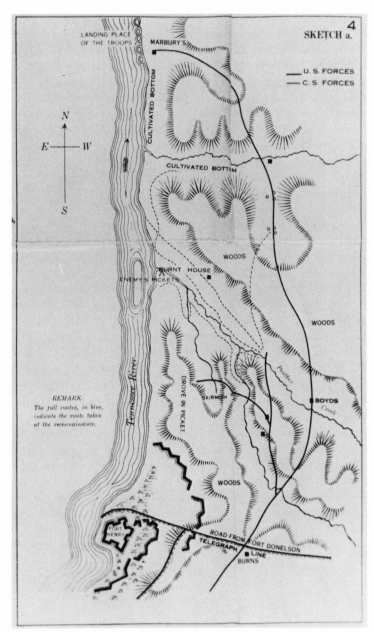

MAP 3. Environs of Fort Henry, 1862. U.S. Army Infantry School.
Military History Methods of Research Compilation of Sources (Fort Benning, 1937).

tery. C.F. Smith's column would move on the opposite side of the river from Pine Bluff Landing to take Fort Heiman. Then, leaving an occupation force, he would retrace his march, be ferried across the Tennessee, and reinforce McClernand. Both divisions would carry two days' rations, and a company of the 23d Indiana would be detailed to act as sharpshooters aboard the gunboats. Grant informed Foote of the scheme, but the alert naval officer realized that the muddy roads would slow the land movement. Why not stagger the time of the joint advance so as to permit the soldiers to get into final position before the naval assault? Grant obstinately refused, failing either to study the poor road conditions or to consider some stiff resistance from the Rebel pickets at McClernand's probing advance about noon on the fifth. Grant's stubbornness promised coordination difficulties.[33]

That evening, Grant and Foote enjoyed a moment of sardonic humor at their own expense. Foote had been off that afternoon delivering one of his typical pre-battle sermons to his crews about trusting in Divine Providence. He also warned them about wasting Uncle Sam's ammunition since "every charge you fire from one of these guns cost the government about eight dollars." By dusk, he was back aboard the *Cincinnati* where he, Grant, C.F. Smith, and McClernand all stood watching as Phelps and the *Conestoga* deposited one of the Confederate torpedoes on the flagship's fantail. Curious about the device (which Commander Henry A. Walke of the *Carondelet* styled "polar bears" because of their shape in the water), the four senior Federal leaders all walked over for a closer look. As a naval armorer unscrewed a powder cap at one end, the weapon emitted a loud sizzling noise. McClernand and Smith immediately threw themselves to the deck, but Foote and Grant sprang for the ladder leading back to the gundeck. Sheepishly—for all of the observing Jack Tars were now laughing at the spectacle—Foote asked Grant, "General why this haste?" The usually unruffled Grant replied, "that the navy may not get ahead of us." Everybody understood the barb, for it had been Foote who had loudly proclaimed to his land comrades earlier, "I shall take [Fort Henry] before you will get there with your forces." The morrow would decide just who would win this Confederate prize.[34]

CHAPTER 7

The Gunboats Win a Victory

TORRENTIAL RAINS POURED ON FRIEND AND FOE alike overnight, but February 6 dawned "mild and cheering" with a light
breeze. This would help blow away the smoke of battle, thought Commander Walke. Sleepy soldiers were more interested in coffee, however,
and the Confederate leaders worried about the still rising river. The waters stood almost waist-deep in places, and Haynes could not get into Fort
Henry when he arrived from Fort Donelson. Early in the morning, he
simply rowed into the fort, concluding immediately that the fort was untenable and ought to be forthwith abandoned. A council of war agreed,
but a thoroughly frustrated Lloyd Tilghman received assurances from
artillerist Taylor that he could hold out. Selecting fifty men from Company B, 1st Tennessee Heavy Artillery to service the guns with Taylor,
Tilghman decided that his only chance was to delay the enemy every
moment possible and retire the command toward Fort Donelson, "resolv-
ing to suffer as little loss as possible."[1]

Tilghman reasoned that a defense of Forts Henry and Heiman would
aid Fort Donelson either in its own successful defense or to buy time
for reinforcements to arrive from Bowling Green or Columbus. With
admirable hindsight, he recalled later, "the fate of our right wing at Bowling Green depended upon a concentration of my entire division on Fort
Donelson and the holding of that place as long as possible," since reinforcements could then get in the rear of any besieging force at Dover.
Scouting reports placed increasing numbers of Federal soldiers ashore
below Fort Henry. So Tilghman moved all but his "forlorn hope" artillerymen out to the shallow rifle-pits, which formed a semicircle some
three-quarters of a mile to the rear of the main work. Here his infantry
would escape the naval gunfire. Then Tilghman rejoined Taylor to await
the approach of the gunboats. They did not have to wait long.[2]

Foote hoisted his signal pennant to prepare for battle about 10:20 A.M.
Unknown to the navy, Grant's soldiers were still in camp, and confusion
slowed their departure to join the attack. Thirty minutes later, Foote
moved upriver, his gun crews standing silently at the ready beside their

Foote's Flotilla Attack on Fort Henry, February 6, 1862. Sketch by S.O. Hawley, Massachusetts Order of Loyal Legion Collection, U.S. Army Military History Institute.

cannon. Each gunboat passed through the Panther Island chute without mishap and re-formed into divisional lines. The ironclads were forward, with their wooden companions located to the right rear. Fort Henry lay almost before them at eye-level due to the floodwaters. This was fortunate, for the naval cannon had elevation limitations and would mean that Foote could employ point-blank fire against the fort. Still, Fort Henry's eight-foot high parapets were formidable, and the fourteen-feet of earth could absorb much beating from enemy guns. Twelve of Tilghman's heaviest guns would bear upon the flotilla, including the 10-inch Columbiad hurling a 128-pound shot, a rebored 24-pounder firing a 62-pound ball, and two 42- and eight 32-pounders also capable of doing great damage. The naval gunners could see the black muzzles of these cannon peeking through embrasures formed from the sand-filled cotton sacks.[3]

Foote's watch showed 12:30 P.M. He had no idea where Grant's men were; nor did he care. He would take the fort alone. Turning to flagship commander Roger N. Stembel, he gave the order to fire. Well within range of the naval guns, the opening shots were fired at 1,700 yards and fell short. Second Master James Laning of the *Essex* recalled Foote's earlier rejoinder to be sparing with the ammunition, remarking caustically, "so there was twenty-four dollars worth of ammunition expended." Finally one of his own gunboat's shells found its mark atop Fort Henry's parapet. Undaunted by such marginal gunnery, Foote later told his wife: "we were in sight of the fort for 2 miles. I opened the fire with rifle guns and soon they were returned by the fort. I ran up rapidly to the distance of 700 yards. It was a fearful struggle." And so it was, as the gunboats closed rapidly, firing only their bow guns. The Confederates replied, firing first with the Columbiad, then the rebored rifle, and finally the other guns as the range narrowed. Taylor directed each of his gun captains to concentrate upon one particular vessel and "to pay it especial compliments." Flagship *Cincinnati* took numerous hits, and Foote explained subsequently: "We were struck with rifle and heavy shot and shell 30 times, I had the breath, for several seconds, knocked out of me, as a shot struck opposite my chest, in the iron clad pilot house on deck."[4]

The accuracy of both sides improved as the gunboats moved closer to the fort. The cannon shells ripped the cotton sacks "as readily as a Navy Colt would pierce a pine board," exclaimed Captain Jesse Taylor. The action was "hot, rapid, and accurate as one could wish" for the first hour, with the advantage inclining toward the Confederates. In fact Porter's single stack *Essex* received a stunning hit from the Columbiad, causing the Rebels to think they had struck a mortal blow to enemy hopes

Confederates Defend Fort Henry, February 6, 1862. *Frank Leslie's Illustrated Newspaper,* March 1, 1862.

for quick victory. Porter's young aide, Acting Master's Mate Samuel B. Brittan, Jr., had died only a short time before as a cannon ball took off his head, thus earning a place among Union heroes as the "Boy Brittan" of Forcyethe Wilson's poem. Then came the Columbiad shot that exploded a boiler, scalding Porter and many of his crew. James Coffey was on his knees passing a shell from an ammunition chest to a loader when the steam caught him squarely in the face, and he died in that position. Master Laning declared subsequently that the carnage below deck was "almost indescribable." The gunboat drifted downriver and out of the fight, having fired seventy-two shots but carrying with it 10 dead, 23 wounded, and 5 missing from the one Columbiad shot alone. According to Taylor, with the *Essex* out of the battle line, the Yankee flotilla hesitated, halted, and seemed about to retire when a succession of catastrophes happened in the fort that restored the confidence and advance of the flotilla."[5]

The accurate Rebel fire broke and shattered the ironclad plating "as if it had been putty, and often passed completely through the [wooden] casemates." Foote held grimly to his task, feeling "it must be victory or death." Just then the 24-pounder rifle in Fort Henry burst, killing or disabling the whole crew. Shortly thereafter, the Columbiad was inadvertently spiked when a priming wire jammed and bent during loading. Several of the 32-pounders were knocked out, and Confederate hopes plummeted. Everyone wondered if the remaining cannon could withstand the shock of full charges of inferior powder. When the blacksmith failed to free the broken vent of the big gun and point-blank naval fire raked the parapets and spread death and destruction, Tilghman's garrison melted from their stations in fear. By 1:30 P.M., the Kentuckian faced a moment of truth. Dismembered bodies lay beside shattered guns, fires had kindled combustibles in the fort, and demoralized officers and men milled about. Tilghman hesistated to strike his colors; he threw off his coat and jumped to serve one of the remaining cannon himself, exclaiming that he would not give up the fort.[6]

Haynes also opposed surrender, although only four cannon were still in working order. Gilmer and Heiman thought it useless to fight on, yet the German emigré declined to intervene, since Tilghman "must be his own judge in regard to this affair." Tilghman ordered Heiman to send fifty new gunners from his regiment, but now he too began to waver in his determination. The end came about 1:50 P.M. Hoping to allow his main force to escape, Tilghman sought to parley with the Federals. Unsure of the position of Grant's land force, he reluctantly affixed a small white cloth to a stick and mounted the parapet. The dense battle smoke

S.B. "Boy" Brittan, Aide to
Commander Porter, killed at Fort
Henry, February 6. *Frank Leslie's
Illustrated Newspaper,* March 1, 1862.

hid this flag, however, and the conflict continued for another five minutes. Tilghman then ordered Taylor to strike the Confederate colors
from the main flagstaff. Orderly Sergeant John Jones braved the Federal's fire, ran to the flagstaff, clambered up to the yardarm, and lowered
the Stars and Bars. When reports of this reached Haynes, he sought to
raise the flag again and yelled at Tilghman: "I will not surrender, and
you have no right to include me in the capitulation as an officer of this
garrison, I being here only for consultation with you." He then rushed
off to join the escape column headed for Fort Donelson.[7]

Heiman also saw the Confederate flag flutter to the ground as he tried
to collect fifty volunteers for Tilghman. He hurried back to his commander, only to be told that he too should escape. Even Gilmer, who had
done so much to prod Tilghman to surrender, managed to go free, ostensibly because, like Haynes, he was only a consultant and not a member
of the garrison. Oddly enough, W.W. Mackall later wrote Gilmer's wife
that it was a question of whether he should have left the post after the
flag came down and whether he might have to be turned over to the
Federals. Such fine points in the southern code of honor displayed more
attention to form than determination to defend the forts to the death.
At any rate none of the trio went back to surrender, thus establishing
important precedents for escape in the face of capitulation.[8]

Foote thought the white flag a ruse at first. Finally ordering the gunboats to cease fire, he awaited developments. Once the Confederate flag
had been lowered, pandemonium broke out in the flotilla. Even the old
sailor lost control of the men aboard his flagship as "a cheer ran up from
this ship, a yell in fact & I had to run among the men & knock them
on the head to restore order." Surgeon John Lidlow especially "hollered
& bawled [and] I told him that he ought to be ashamed of himself,"
wrote Foote to his wife. Lidlow told his commander that it was like coming back to life, as he had expected to be killed, and thus could not help
roaring with all his might. Everywhere it was the same, as each gunboat
vied with another to take the actual surrender of the post. Contrary to
Foote's wishes, the *St. Louis* got there first, with *Cincinnati* and *Carondelet*
jockeying with one another until the latter ran aground, and Foote's sten-
torian voice boomed out for Walke to hold back. To Walke it was all
quite humorous, as the flotilla commander was yelling at the top of his
voice while his flagship drifted with the current, and the cheers, orders,
groans, and general confusion all accompanied the rush to gain Tilghman's sword. It was all quite amateurish really, but it was still the first
Union victory for men from Halleck's department. A white yawl came
out from the fort with Tilghman's adjutant and an engineer seeking permission for their leader to meet with Foote. The naval officer agreed,
meanwhile instructing Stembel and Phelps to take actual possession of
the fort. With infinite relish, the pair enjoyed rowing back through the
sallyport to raise the Stars and Stripes to replace the Stars and Bars. Returning with Tilghman to the *Cincinnati,* they watched as the proud Kentuckian reputedly greeted Foote, "I am glad to surrender to so gallant
an officer." The victory-stirred New Englander snapped back, "You do
perfectly right, sir, in surrendering, but you should have blown my boat
out of the water before I would have surrendered to you."[9]

Other witnesses pictured Foote as more solicitous to his prisoner, although the terms of surrender were no less than "unconditional." Tilghman did extract the promise that his officers could retain their sidearms. Foote told one friend that Tilghman had appeared aboard his
flagship shell-shocked, "wringing his hands and exclaiming, "I am in despair, my reputation is gone forever." Foote then reassured the man of
his gallantry—"more than two thirds of your battery is disabled, while
I have lost less than one third of mine," he said. Foote promised to forever attest to Tilghman's valor, and the naval officer not only wrote to
his own superiors to that effect, but encouraged his prisoner to do likewise to Richmond authorities. Foote then turned, saying, "come, gen-

eral, you have lost your dinner, and the steward has just told me that mine is ready." Arm-in-arm, the victor and vanquished disappeared into Foote's cabin. Whatever the truth of this story, Tilghman certainly escaped the indignity imposed upon his subordinates as they were rounded up by the sailors.[10]

Fort Henry was clearly a Union naval victory. While Grant's men marched off "as merry as a wedding party," at 11:00 A.M., feet and vehicles became mired in mud. Private Thomas F. Miller of the 29th Illinois said in his homespun manner that he and his comrades ran through water waist deep, but it was all to no avail: before they got to the fort, the enemy had left, and "we did not get to fire a gun but we had a good time." It was the same across the river with Smith's column, and neither force found itself even close to its objective when the opening sounds of Foote's naval fight reached them. "Now the ball is opened," one 7th Illinois soldier told his mates, as they plunged into cold, flooded sloughs "cheering and yelling like tigers." Still it was a fruitless effort to push through what a *Cincinnati Gazette* reporter likened to soft porridge of almost immeasurable depth. No one in Grant's army gained the environs of Forts Henry and Heiman until mid-afternoon.[11]

Colonel Isham G. Haynie of the 48th Illinois declared that the Rebels were "beaten, whipped, shelled out, and fled." Several of their steamboats had gone upriver without stopping to pick up survivors of the battle. Even Tilghman's land contingents departed quickly upon a roundabout twenty-two-mile march, crossing creeks ten times, with "indifferent" artillery horses pulling the light artillery, while the young and inexperienced infantrymen shed baggage and overcoats — even firearms — to lighten their loads. Panic-stricken cavalrymen of Lieutenant Colonel George Gantt's battalion rushed pell-mell through the infantry column defying orders to form a rear guard. Federal pursuers finally caught the tail of the Confederate retreat in a sharp skirmish that left two officers of the 15th Arkansas and 3d Alabama battalion dead and thirty-eight men prisoner, with the loss of only one Yankee trooper. Worse, several of the cannon had to be spiked and abandoned. The more resolute Confederates finally beat off the attackers and reached the Cumberland safely, the 10th Tennessee claiming not to have broken ranks during the retreat and actually having retrieved many of the firearms and equipment jettisoned by others. In truth, for the next two days most of the Fort Henry force simply straggled into the Fort Donelson-Dover environs. Gone was any semblance of an organized military force. A survivor such as Randal McGavock was quite angry that the Federals were back in his old camp, rifling his trunk, drinking his whiskey, and "I suppose publish my journal, and sell it to help pay the expense of the war." McGavock's journal was in the trunk![12]

While detachments of cavalry chased the fleeing Confederates, most of Grant's army rushed to be the first to reach the enemy camps near Fort Henry. Wet and tired Federals spent the evening of February 6 streaming into the dry areas near the Tennessee River forts. Lew Wallace drew a dram from C.F. Smith's flask and wondered aloud about "a stiff fight" if the Confederates had chosen to stay and defend Fort Heiman. Nobody quite understood why the enemy had left such immense quantities of food, clothing, and equipment without more struggle. A few men like Logan's 31st Illinois made good use of the gray uniforms, wearing them until their own dried out over still smouldering Rebel campfires. Other men settled in to consume the abandoned corn pone, ham, and biscuits in Rebel cooking pots and to bed down in the Confederate tents and huts. Soon they were writing letters home on captured stationery, puffing on captured meerschaum pipes, and chuckling about the evident war weariness of their enemy. The men rifled through abandoned valises and knapsacks, and read the Confederate recantations of secession and their desires to go home. Many of the young Federals became convinced the war was about over; others complained about the naval victory denying them a chance to do battle. Wilbur Crummer of the 45th Illinois observed years later about how foolish they had all been at the time. "We had enough of fighting ere the war was o'er," he decided, "and after the first battle we never begrudged other forces the honor of gaining victory without our help." That night, as temperatures dropped and many regretted leaving their overcoats and blankets back at Bailey's Ferry, the soldiers were kept warm by recalling that they had helped gain control of what Lieutenant Colonel Levi Merchant (28th Illinois) termed "this outlandish portion of seceshdom."[13]

Grant and his staff finally rode up to Fort Henry about 3:00 P.M. and immediately went to congratulate Foote. The general was obviously irritated that his partner had made good his boast of victory, and Foote wrote his wife that night, "we go ahead of the Army all to pieces . . . the army is rather chop fallen." Yet neither man could dwell on the matter. The Rebel force had escaped to fight again (a fact downplayed in official dispatches), while Tilghman, 12 other officers, and 64 men at the fort, as well as 16 convalescents from the hospital boat *Patton,* plus large quantities of captured supplies, all needed attention. Foote brooded over his scalded sailors aboard the *Essex* and vowed "never again will I go into a fight half-prepared." He noted petulantly that the injured Porter made

THE GUNBOATS WIN A VICTORY III

too much of his "little skirmishes" while the flagship *Cincinnati* had borne the brunt of the battle, in Foote's view. He promised to get Stembel's son into West Point for that officer's valuable service as Foote's aide during the battle. The bottom line for the staunch Calvinist, however, was that "we have made the narrowest escape possible with our Boats and our lives." As he told his wife, "A good day's work and I mean always to thank God for it."[14]

The tension and anxiety of the action also took its toll of Grant. He wrote Julia that night that the fort had been taken, that he was unhurt, and that she must not expect lenghty letters, for he was tired. If the words sounded testy, Grant quickly sealed the note with his customary, "kiss the children for me," before sending it off. His mind lay on the morrow—and Fort Donelson. Penning an equally terse note to Halleck, the expeditionary commander stated, "I shall take and destroy Fort Donaldson [*sic*] on the 8th and return to Fort Henry." There would be no hesitancy, no turning back, no time to fret about who won the victory at Fort Henry. The war had to go on.[15]

News of the fall of Fort Henry flashed across the divided nation by telegraph. The event so cheered people north of the Ohio that they had little time for anything but "three cheers, and another, and yet another, and one cheer more," as the *Cincinnati Gazette* put it. No one at home worried that the fleet had captured the fort, although both the *Boston Journal* and *St. Louis Democrat* carped about Grant's lackluster performance in allowing Tilghman's army to escape. Overall, the capture of Forts Henry and Heiman, when announced simultaneously with another Union victory at Roanoke Island, North Carolina, brought welcome relief after months of false hopes and promises. On the other side, Confederate citizens were distraught; Tilghman was immediately vilified; the garrison's artillerymen, gallantly serving their guns so that the infantry could escape, were overlooked. Powhatan Ellis, a young Virginia officer recently sent west with Floyd, wrote home on the eleventh that slanderous reports were being circulated about the treason, treachery, and avoidance of duty at the fort. He cited Tennesseans' bad feeling toward Tilghman for harsh discipline of their kinsmen and surrender of a Tennessee fort. The colonels of the Tennessee regiments refused to support the Kentuckian, said Ellis, and helped crucify him for the disaster. "Such is the reward of a man's doing his duty," he sighed; "when he meets with a reverse, which he had forseen," he remains at his post despite the absence of any measure of help from superiors.[16]

Even the first southern newspaper accounts displayed general ignorance of the conditions on the twin rivers. Finally, as the truth surfaced, the *Richmond Dispatch* stated: "Our Tennessee exchanges give us gloomy prospects for the future in that part of the Confederacy." The *Memphis Avalanche* suggested that "the people apprehend an immediate advance of the Northmen." From Johnston's headquarters, W.W. Mackall, his chief of staff, confided to Loulee Gilmer in Savannah that while her husband had escaped disaster, the situation looked bad, and he hoped that the southern people would meet it coolly and calmly and not prove as "recreant as they have been boastful." Very few homefront Confederates seemed as prescient as Dr. Lunsford Yandell, Sr., the Louisville physician working in a Memphis hospital. He confided in his diary that the Fort Henry defeat "brings the enemy into counties where we have many enemies who will gladly welcome them." He was alarmed at Confederate prospects and feared for the future. After all, it was only two weeks since the Mills Springs defeat, he noted; "God be on our side and help us."[17]

Reaction from the Confederate high command in the West seemed strangely mixed, however. Johnston quickly wired Richmond that while he had no reliable particulars about the loss, the garrison had escaped and an attack on Fort Donelson seemed imminent. Instead of outlining what he planned to do about that situation, he prattled about the defeat opening Tennessee River navigation to the enemy all the way to Florence, Alabama, and how Fort Henry "indicates that the best open earth works are not reliable to meet successfully a vigorous attack of iron clad gun boats." Suddenly he injected the notion of retirement from central Kentucky. "The movements of the enemy on my right flank would have made a retrograde in that direction to confront the enemy indispensible in a short time," he concluded in reference to the presence of George H. Thomas on the upper Cumberland at Burkesville. Apparently he could see no recourse but to get all of his scattered forces back behind the river at Nashville and re-group rather than trying to rush to counter two serious threats from Thomas, and then from Grant and Foote. Still, Davis and his advisers must have wondered precisely what was transpiring in Tennessee. Confident of his friend's capabilities, the president deferred to Sidney Johnston's judgment on the scene.[18]

As for the situation upriver from the breathrough point at Fort Henry, Johnston sent a volley of telegrams to local authorities telling them to burn "every stick of steamboat wood on the Tennessee River," to dispatch local defense units to protect the Decatur railroad bridge, and to get any remaining steamboats beyond the danger from Foote's gunboats, since "we may want them for transportation." This thought must have provided scant comfort to those citizens in the path of the Federal invasion, and J.G. Norman of Tuscumbia, Alabama, for one, wasted little time in writing Secretary of War Benjamin about abandonment to the enemy. It was now too late to worry about Bushrod Johnson's alleged error in siting Fort Henry on the Tennessee River flood plain, or that Tilghman, Heiman, and Gilmer had been negligent or tardy with torpedo defense or the placing of heavy cannon in the inadequate Fort Heiman. General neglect of the threatened twin rivers sector ran from authorities at Columbus and Bowling Green all the way to the top in the Davis government, in a sense; yet none of this was apparent to citizens such as Norman or Yandell. Johnston himself may have been unaware of any local culpability for conditions at Fort Henry, because he had never bothered to visit the site. All officials recognized that this loss of key positions on the Tennessee River had dealt a severe blow to the Confederacy in the West. This was made quite plain within the week by a raid upriver to Muscle Shoals by Phelps's three timberclad gunboats.[19]

Foote quickly dispatched Phelps with his gunboat division to capture the vital M.C.&L. railroad bridge near Danville, Tennessee. He discovered that the Confederate guards had fled in haste, first jamming the draw span of the 1,200-foot-long trestle and then abandoning camps and stores. The intrepid Phelps landed a party to repair the span, which it did in about an hour. Then additional orders caused him to burn some of the trestle, and destroy track so as to render the whole bridge temporarily inoperable. Eventually the advancing Federal armies would want to re-utilize the bridge, but for now it was to be denied to the Rebels. Phelps also scattered some other river craft nearby and captured more supplies ashore which had been destined for Fort Henry. Phelps reported that the "fiendish rebels" had fired all of the remaining boats on the river in the area, and one boat filled with gunpowder had exploded directly in front of a local Unionist's house, demolishing both. Phelps continued to the landing in Hardin County known as Cerro Gordo, where the Confederates were finishing the gunboat *Eastport*. The boat crew tried to scuttle the craft before fleeing, but once more Phelps's sailors rushed ashore and saved the vessel, along with hundreds of feet of ship lumber. Leaving the *Tyler* to guard this prize, Phelps took the other two gunboats upstream, spreading havoc and destruction in his wake.[20]

Alabama citizens sent deputations to meet Phelps and to plead with the hated Yankees to spare wives and daughters from molestation. The Union naval officers—whom the locals styled "Lincolnites"—must have smiled as they assured town fathers that they were neither "ruffians nor savages, and that we were there to protect them from violence and to enforce the law." Phelps agreed to spare the local railroad bridge linking Florence and Tuscumbia, more as a sign of good faith to the citizenry than anything else. In subsequent weeks, the Federals would regret such a favor which enabled Johnston's army to escape completely from Middle Tennessee. Yet for the moment none of this was apparent to an understanding Phelps, anxious to win the hearts and minds of the enemy to reunion. While all this was going on, local home guards fluttered about trying to organize resistance to the gunboats, and the local Memphis and Charleston railroad superintendent, A.J. Hopper, managed to move his rolling stock and locomotives out of the raiders' reach. On February 9, President Davis boldly sent word that "The number of men who can have been transported by four gunboats [*sic*] should never be allowed to tread upon our soil and return." The words were empty; the home guards accomplished nothing. Phelps retraced his steps in due course, dispersing a Rebel training camp near Savannah before tying up at Fort Henry on the tenth, amidst cheers from Grant's soldiers.[21]

Phelps devoted much of his after-action report to a graphic description of the warm Unionist response among the people upriver. These were the "enemies" mentioned by Yandell in his diary, and Phelps recorded that crowds by the hundreds gathered on the river banks and "shouted their welcome and hailed their national flag with an enthusiasm there was no mistaking." He recounted tears streaming down the cheeks of old Mexican War veterans, and he reported hearing that "many people had the stars and stripes laid under their carpets and other places and gladly showed them now that they dared." At least twenty-five ardent young Unionists went aboard the gunboats to enlist. News of all this latent Tennessee unionism naturally received due notice northern newspapers once Phelps and his crews were interviewed. Most of the loyalists returned underground when the navy departed and Confederate troops restored their own law and intimidation to the region. Some of the Unionists fled northward. Mississippian Daniel K. Boswell had a price on his head for supplying Federal authorities with invaluable intelligence data, including Fort Henry's situation, the previous autumn. After the war large numbers of these closet Unionists swelled local Republican ranks during Reconstruction, thus proving that such wartime loyalty did exist. More than anything, however, Phelps's reports spawned false hopes that more widespread loyalism could be found "on the shores of Tennessee." Soldiers such as John S. Wilcox stationed in Smithland, Kentucky, wrote home, after talking with sailors returning from the expedition, that surely daylight was breaking. The next push at Fort Donelson and Bowling Green would cause the Rebels to further retreat, "gradually lessening in numbers and the rebellion will die."[22]

The reality was that Phelps's success proved short-lived as Confederate infantry re-occupied Paris Landing and the railroad crossing at Danville where the sailors had damaged the M.C.&L. bridge. In fact, the Rebels returned the very night Phelps passed upriver, and for the next several days these troops skirmished with small contingents sent by Grant to occupy the bridge site and guard the ruin. Finally Halleck directed Grant to dismantle the structure entirely, which men from the 32d Illinois accomplished with a flourish on the eighth. Actually, Grant had been unable to move immediately on Fort Donelson due to the high waters, and Foote needed time to swing around to the Cumberland and make necessary repairs to damaged gunboats en route. Meanwhile the naval officer basked in the limelight of his victory. Secretary of the Navy Welles sent appreciation for his services in forming and fighting the flotilla "which has already earned such renown [as] can never be overestimated." He also exchanged notes with Tilghman (temporarily incarcerated at Louisville) concerning Foote's erroneous reference to the use of mortar boats at Fort Henry. Foote told his vanquished foe that he would always appreciate his high courage but not his political views concerning Union and secession.[23]

Only the gunboat *Carondelet* remained available to protect Grant's army huddled in crowded camps awaiting dry roads. The unruly volunteers continued to loot and destroy property, their officers hugging warmer quarters aboard transports off-shore. The so-called "Jesse Scouts" caused Grant such trouble that he finally ordered McClernand to ship them back to Cairo. The generals spent time writing dispatches and reports and directing scouting expeditions. Actually Grant was in a tight spot — only he would not admit it. With the gunboats gone on one mission or another and his land force with its back against the swiftly flowing flood waters, there was surely reason for concern. A determined counteroffensive by Johnston could have proved disastrous. Still, Grant wrote his sister, Mary, that the scare and fright of the enemy seemed beyond conception and that he had absolutely no qualms about ultimate success. He told one departing newsman that he might wait a day or so, for the army was going over to capture Fort Donelson. When the reporter asked if he knew anything about the Rebels' strength, Grant replied that he did not but thought he could take the fort; in any event he would try. Ever restless, the general boarded a transport and ran up to inspect the railroad bridge at Danville on the eighth, and he wrote Secretary of the Treasury Salmon P. Chase about reopening "trade to the Southern states, as far as the Army goes." He knew of two staunch Paducah Unionists who might be given trading privileges as rewards for providing information useful to the campaign. A military professional,

Grant remained a midwesterner in focus, and he was sensitive to the political and economic factors of the expedition he directed into the Southern Heartland.[24]

There were other problems during this interlude on the twin rivers. McClernand's political agenda had begun to surface. His operational report brimmed with his own division's accomplishments at the expense of others in the army. Since Grant may have been wary of tangling with this powerful political general at this stage, he tried to overlook the fraternal squabbles in his army family. It hardly helped, however, to have McClernand brazenly entitle his base camp, "Camp Halleck," or re-style Fort Henry as "Fort Foote." More vexatious, perhaps, McClernand had taken to instructing Grant on how to conduct the campaign, including sending memoranda on the very eve of the Fort Henry battle advocating a night assault and four days later submitting an elaborate assault plan for Fort Donelson, with his division naturally leading the attack. Certainly it remained within McClernand's duties to provide his superior officer with advice, and he was the principal man on the ground at Fort Henry. His division conducted most of the reconnaissance for the roads and enemy works at Fort Donelson. It may only have been McClernand's previous proclivity for intrigue, and his personality which caused subsequent commentators to date the Grant-McClernand estrangement from this period.[25]

Each day Union cavalry patrols probed closer to Fort Donelson, and Grant accompanied one such patrol on February 9 to ascertain the condition of the Telegraph and Ridge roads leading overland to Dover. Grant was thinking offensively, which greatly disturbed Henry Halleck in St. Louis. The departmental commander telegraphed: "Hold on to Fort Henry at all hazards. Picks and shovels are sent, and large re-enforcements will be sent immediately." The two men were distinctly different. While Halleck talked about spades and entrenchment, said newsman Arthur Richardson, Grant seriously contemplated moving upon a "strong fort which he knew next to nothing about, with infantry and cavalry, and without a single field piece." Richardson stretched a point some, but when Grant called a meeting aboard his headquarters boat for the afternoon of the tenth, the flood waters had abated, and the ground had dried. He anticipated short, affirmative answers to his basic question: should the army move on Fort Donelson or await more men from Halleck? C.F. Smith obligingly answered for movement. McClernand agreed but pulled forth a lengthy memorandum placing his new division in the van. Undaunted by the fact that he had already passed the paper to Grant, McClernand proceeded to read it verbatim while

Grant fidgeted visibly during the performance. Newly promoted brigadier general, Lew Wallace thought later that it would have been better
for McClernand if he had kept the discussion short.[26]

Wallace was much less given to intrigue than McClernand. Still, he
was also a political general and had promotion and acclaim as his goal.
As junior member of the circle of generals, Wallace labored under the
cloud of prewar Democratic affiliation and militia service. He had actively schemed against C.F. Smith at Paducah before the campaign.
Wallace was an inspiring leader of men, however, and he too had connections in Washington. Grant certainly seemed pleased when Wallace
barked at the end of McClernand's lecture to the war council at Fort
Henry, "lets go, by all means; the sooner the better." This suited both
the expedition leader and his army. The men had grown tired of looting
camps, writing home about huge southern Bowie knives, and poking fun
at the "skeddadling rebels" who had left behind half-dressed sides of
beef, burning cook fires, and laundry drying before abondoned huts.
The Federals had become condescending in attitude, for like Ira Merchant of the 28th Illinois, they had seen enough of the dead Rebels from
the fight, and the abandoned Confederate camps. "Ye Gads is this a sample of Southern Chivalry," asked Merchant rhetorically, vowing that he
wanted no more to do with them after viewing such dead men. Obviously everyone had grown restive in the camps and were ready for a new
adventure.[27]

The troops seemed as thick as black birds in the autumn, declared
George Durfee of the 8th Illinois, with more arriving all the time. Eight
new infantry regiments, a cavalry battalion, and another artillery battery all disembarked from steamers at Fort Henry on the evening of February 8 alone. Illinois, Iowa, Missouri, Indiana—all were represented
by the newcomers, and a few, such as "Birge's Western Sharpshooters,"
came colorfully garbed and uniquely armed. This was a sharpshooter
regiment that was equipped with Dimmock plains rifles and target rifles,
and in every way, except for their uniforms, they fitted Army specifications. They had been John C. Fremont's pet unit in Missouri, and by
the time of the twin rivers campaign their gray coats and gray sugarloaf-
shaped hat with three black squirrel tails still connoted something special about them. Their reputations had preceded them, as Halleck himself would warn Grant: "Look out for Birge's sharpshooters, they have
been committing numerous robberies. I have the Col. locked up in the
Military prison." Still these were the kind of hard-bitten troops that Grant
needed for his volunteer force.[28]

As Grant struggled to get out of the Fort Henry mud, Halleck worked far to the rear at St. Louis to ensure the continuing success of his expedition as it crossed to besiege Fort Donelson. Neither Grant nor his subordinates had time to worry about rear area activities designed to provide re-supply and reinforcement to their mission. This could come only from a logistical lifeline which reflected Halleck's sense of priorities. Such activities as part of the higher art of war had not really jelled at this stage of the Civil War. As Grant struck hard and fast at the enemy defense line in the West, an overly cautious, poorly coordinated, and separately motivated command system behind him proved unresponsive to the rapid decisions required in modern conflict. As Halleck's biographer Stephen Ambrose noted, "Old Brains" was handicapped by a command system that wasted valuable time in fruitless debate. Of course the desk-bound Halleck contributed to this problem. He viewed Grant's move as merely an advanced base for something larger, and he wrote Buell on February 1: "at present it is only proposed to take and occupy Fort Henry and Dover, and, if possible, cut the railroad from Columbus to Bowling Green." This was vintage Halleck, the perennial textbook general who viewed operations in set stages and avoidance of a major siege or bloody set-piece battle. Grant would hold to his advance base, fan his forces out from this point to destroy Confederate lines of communication, and disrupt the countermoves anticipated of Johnston, Beauregard, and Polk, thereby maneuvering them out of their fortresses without major struggle. Then Grant's cautiously reinforced spearhead would build to the point where a new expeditionary commander such as Hitchcock could be sent in to execute the next well-planned and methodically executed maneuver. In Halleck's mind, "it will take some time to get troops ready to advance far south of Fort Henry."[29]

The Ohio departmental commander remained perplexed by the precipitous nature of Grant's expedition. Buell never doubted the veracity of the twin rivers approach, telling McClellan that the two forts were Johnston's "most vulnerable point, as it is also the most decisive." Yet, if he believed this, why had Buell persisted in devoting his main effort to the slow overland approach to Bowling Green rather than committing greater resources to a waterborne strike up the Cumberland? Halleck was in favor of his doing so. Halleck cornered the available transport force for his own purposes. Besides, Buell's people had advanced too far from their base to rapidly turn around and retrace their steps to use the Ohio-Cumberland axis of approach. Such would have uncovered the land route to Louisville for Johnston. So both Buell and Johnston became victims of their own overland strategy in central Kentucky. "My moves must be real ones," not diversions, Buell told both McClellan and Halleck, and such moves had to be on land, require all of his forces, and "the object must be accomplished by hard knocks." Fortunately the presence of two major Union armies in the field permitted an opportunity to end the stalemate.[30]

At first it took dozens of telegrams and letters to pry even a single brigade (Cruft) and six, raw and unbrigaded Ohio and Indiana regiments from Buell's department to send to help Grant. Then, as the Ohioan relented, he found it possible to dispatch an over-strength division to the Cumberland line of operations, just as Grant's command took to the roads leading to Fort Donelson. He wrote soothingly to Halleck: "There is not in the whole field of operations a point at which every man you can raise can be employed with more effect or with the prospect of as important results."[31]

Halleck still worried that he had unleashed something beyond his control on the twin rivers. Despite Grant's promise that the anticipated capture of Fort Donelson would be "more in the light of an advance guard than as a permanent post," Halleck did not trust the man; he wanted to insure his foothold in Tennessee. While trying to get cooperation from Buell, he alerted Brigadier General William T. Sherman at nearby Benton Barracks in St. Louis to "make your preparations to take a column or division on the Tennessee or Cumberland." He felt sure that the War Department would send him Hitchcock to supplant Grant as commander. Then, suddenly on February 10, the aged Hitchcock declined to take the field. This dislocated Halleck's scheme, and Sherman got no farther than an administrative slot at Paducah where he happily began to expedite the dispatch of men and matériel to his junior friend Grant. Despite Halleck's Machiavellian plan to replace Grant on the twin rivers, the expeditionary commander went about his business, completely unaware of the plot concerning his position.[32]

Halleck would not give up his scheme, and he urged McClellan to "create a geographical division to be called Western Division, or any other suitable name." It could comprise three departments: Buell's present Ohio setup, a revamped Missouri department covering only the area west of the Mississippi, and a new Mississippi department encompassing the area gouged out of the western Confederacy by Grant's victory. "I have no desire for any larger command than I have now," proclaimed Halleck, but he instructed McClellan that placing everything "under one head" would "avoid any clashing of interests or difference of plans and policy" as then existed in the West. Assistant Secretary of War Scott was convinced, but McClellan chose to temporarily ignore the whole idea. None of this prevented Halleck from dutifully working to help

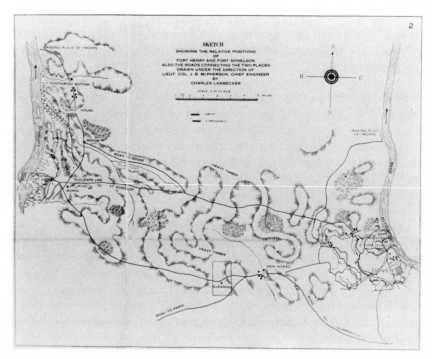

MAP 4. Country between Forts Henry and Donelson, 1862. U.S. Army Infantry School. *Military History Methods of Research Compilation of Sources* (Fort Benning, 1937).

ensure Grant's continuing survival. He rushed his own chief of staff, George Cullum, to Cairo "to facilitate your very important operations" (as Cullum told Grant), hammered Foote on the necessity of speeding up gunboat repairs, and tried to ensure that everyone going to the battlefront had proper arms and equipment.[33]

"Time now is everything to us," he brusquely told Cullum, "don't delay one instant." Foote and Cullum both wasted too much time worrying about a Confederate counter-stroke at Cairo from Columbus, and the army officer fretted about the large number of uniformed malingerers hovering around base as well as the "array of curiosity-mongers wanting to go to Fort Henry" on the government boats at public expense. Gradually more men and equipment moved down the logistical pipeline to Cairo. Governor Yates and his adjutant general rushed green recruits of the 43d, 57th, and 58th Illinois to the staging area by train, while other midwestern governors also pushed partially trained and equipped units forward. Brigadier General John Pope at Jefferson City, Missouri, strained to send cavalry from that area to help Halleck and Grant. When Colonel E.D. Baldwin's 57th Illinois refused to budge from a rest stop at Springfield until it received its five-months' back pay, Halleck snapped: "If the men refuse to obey, disarm them and confine them as mutineers. Also arrest every officer who does not assist in enforcing orders." He promised to have money available at Cairo for the unit, but "it is wanted and *must go*." Using a different tone to the dilatory Foote, he telegraphed simply on February 11. "Make your name famous in history by the capture of Fort Donelson and Clarksville. Act quickly even though only half ready." By 8:30 that evening, Foote wired back: "I am ready with three gunboats to proceed up the Cumberland river, and shall leave here for that purpose in two hours."[34]

Grant sent a similar note to Halleck the next morning. He had given orders the day before to begin the march on Wednesday, February 12, "at as early an hour as practicable." Then, with clearing skies and balmy weather, Grant changed his mind just before noon on the eleventh, directing McClernand to clear the crowded Fort Henry perimeter by dusk. The Illinois political general took his division several miles out on the Dover road and encamped for the night. Everyone would travel light, said Grant, with no more than forty rounds and two days rations per man. More would follow in the wagons, but little artillery would accompany the strike force. Lew Wallace would remain behind with three regiments to occupy Forts Henry and Heiman against surprise attack by Polk from Columbus. The ambitious Hoosier was "sick with rage" at this development, and he blamed C.F. Smith for it. Walke and the *Carondelet* would precede both Foote's main flotilla and Grant's land force to the Cumberland and be in place before Fort Donelson to commence the attack. A light, rapid stroke was Grant's plan, and he expected to make short work of the Rebels at Dover. He may have been unduly optimistic that the easy success of Fort Henry could be repeated.[35]

CHAPTER 8

The First Day at Donelson

THE YOUNG BLUECOATS WERE IN FINE SPIRITS as they marched away from Fort Henry on the morning of February 12. A truly southern winter, they thought as they quickly rid themselves of overcoats and blankets because nobody would need them in Dixie. Soon the roadside lay littered with such extras. Drums and fifes began to play, and a holiday mood gripped the marching columns. Even Grant, their leader, caught the spirit as he bantered with his staff, riding along the Telegraph road. When Surgeon John H. Brinton's steed pressed ahead of the rest, Grant observed drily: "Doctor, I believe I command this army, and I think I'll go first." Everyone laughed.[1]

Of course not everyone in the neighborhood was amused by the sight. The dreaded Yankees frightened Flora Sykes, who hid behind a chest of drawers as they passed her house. McClernand's men took the lead, with C.F. Smith's division following on the two roads leading to Dover. Grant had originally intended that his old teacher push one of his brigades first "into Dover, to cut off all retreat by the river, if found practicable to do so." All of this was premature, for the moment, and the men simply marched along, observing the heavy forests, isolated dog-trot cabins, and local ironworks, which stood eerily silent and deserted.[2]

Grant also expected to link up quickly with Foote's flotilla on the Cumberland. In fact Walke reported later that he had appeared off Fort Donelson by 11:20 that morning and had fired the requested salvo to alert Grant to his presence. Foote had found that refurbishment of his main flotilla took longer than expected and that some twenty-eight sailors had jumped ship after the unfortunate encounter with shattered boiler, scalding steam, and bloody gundecks of the Fort Henry battle. Foote spent the next week haranguing Washington officials for more recruits. He still lacked sufficient strength when Halleck prevailed upon him to leave for the Cumberland. Grant may have actually thought that he could win a victory without the gunboats. Confident and even jubilant at the prospect, he wrote his sister Mary on the ninth that he hoped to give Gideon Pillow (reputedly in charge at Dover) a "tug" before she actually received his letter. So, as his soldiers worked their way to within a mile or two of the Confederate outer works, everyone in blue seemed relaxed and optimistic. Neither army nor navy saw one another, yet each knew the other was present. Soon both services discovered numerous gray-clad Confederates, and they proved to be anything but passive before the advancing Federal host.[3]

Fort Donelson's garrison was just as cocky and expectant of victory as Grant's army. Young Powhatan Ellis, the Virginia staff officer, wrote his mother on February 11 that while the enemy was reported to have large numbers on the Tennessee River, "I think the danger has passed," as they would have attacked immediately after the fall of Fort Henry, in his view. Equally positive, Colonel Nathan Bedford Forrest's cavalry sought to block Grant's advance on the very doorstep of the Fort Donelson defense perimeter. They skirmished hotly that day, which should have alerted the Union commander to the fact that he would not move unopposed to invest this second fort. Then the next day some 1,300 troops fought for three hours several miles from the outer works and temporarily stymied Grant's land advance.[4]

Over the years since the campaign, one question has bothered veterans, descendants, and historians. Did the Confederacy intend to fight the crucial battle for Middle Tennessee and the Southern Heartland here at Fort Donelson? Lost in the rhetoric about Johnston's "command shock," mental paralysis, or "loss of command of himself and of the Army," as well as the series of controversial decisions and actions by subordinates on the scene, are the actual facts of Confederate intentions and actions. Agreement did exist apparently at the time that somehow Grant needed to be contained, if not actually destroyed on the Cumberland. A high level conference at the Covington House in Bowling Green on Friday evening, February 7, supposedly provided the direction. Present at the gathering were Johnston, Hardee, Mackall, and Beauregard (the latter apparently suffering from an old throat ailment so that his laryngitis that evening mingled with the gloomy forebodings of the others).[5]

A distinct air of defeatism hung over the meeting. This hampered the group from reaching a consensus as to the best course of action. Beauregard had been in the theater less than a month and had labored under the impression given him before leaving Virginia by Confederate military spokesman Colonel Roger A. Pryor, and others, that he could assume a deputy command under Johnston and take his personal staff to Kentucky, that a core of experienced officers would be elevated to key positions, and that, most important of all, the army in the West would be heavily reinforced, thereby making an offensive possible. The reali-

View of Dover, Tennessee. Sketch by H. Lovie, *Frank Leslie's Illustrated Newspaper*, March 15, 1862.

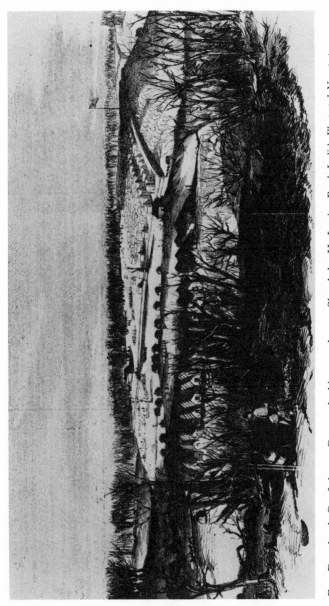

Fort Donelson's Confederate Camps, looking northwest. Sketch by H. Lovie, *Frank Leslie's Illustrated Newspaper*, March 15, 1862.

ties of Johnston's situation dashed such promises, and possibly embit-
tered Beauregard. He regarded the defensive posture of the army as
wasteful, while (as he contended after the war) the real positions war-
ranting attention were the twin river forts. Beauregard claimed to have
passed such views through his own chief of staff, Colonel Thomas Jordan, before leaving the Old Dominion. In any case he took those ideas
with him to the Covington House conference.[6]

Hardee supposedly visited the ailing Beauregard just before the meeting and discovered that he advocated a concentration of all available
force on the Cumberland to smash Grant. When the other officers joined
Beauregard later, they found him quick to advance this scheme (although
perhaps not with the "pertinacity" that he recalled after the war, claimed
historian T. Harry Williams). Surely Johnston's own seniority and aversion to sacrificing the huge depots at Bowling Green and Clarksville
would have offset Beauregard's ardor. Certainly what emerged from the
Covington House conclave was anything but Beauregard's bold move,
and presumably he acquiesced in the group's decision since the memorandum of the proceedings went forth over his signature.[7]

A picture of muddled indecision pervaded Johnston's headquarters.
his forces were spread all over the map, linked solely by telegraph, and
dispersed largely by the Union moves of January, Buell's ponderous advance, and the Confederate proclivity to guard everything and every
place with inadequate forces. In addition to Hardee's 14,000 at Bowling
Green and Polk's 17,000 at Columbus, bits and pieces of maneuver forces
were strung out—8,000 with Buckner and Floyd at Russellville, 2,000
with Clark at Hopkinsville, 2,000 with Pillow at Clarksville, and something approaching 5,000 on the twin rivers facing Grant. Van Dorn in
Arkansas, Crittenden in East Tennessee, and approximately 5,000 reinforcements coming from the Gulf Coast (as promised by Richmond
authorities) were too far away to be a factor. Secretary of War Benjamin
directed Johnston to break up East Tennessee forces and add them to
his own Bowling Green army, but there was no time for that. Priorities
set by Johnston seemed to be those of saving the Bowling Green supplies and blunting Buell—Beauregard's memorandum on the Covington House conference said as much.[8]

The generals at Covington House solemnly declared that Fort Donelson "not being long tenable," the army should evacuate Bowling Green
and retire to Nashville—perhaps even to Stevenson, Alabama, if necessary. "A strong point some miles below [Nashville] being fortified, forthwith, to defend the river from the passage of gunboats and transports"
would make this redeployment feasible. Obviously, if they thought Fort

Donelson untenable, then this strong point was to be Clarksville. Gideon Pillow (back in uniform after a month's convalescence from ill health, and apparently his earlier disatisfaction with the Columbus situation resolved) had telegraphed the previous day that Clarksville's fortifications were incomplete. Rising waters of the Cumberland also threatened the Clarksville position, and the lack of cannon and ammunition as well as cannoneers convinced Pillow that "if Donelson should be overcome, we can make no successful stand without larger force." Johnston, Beauregard, and others should have known that no reliance could be placed upon any defense at Clarksville. Gilmer had not finished his task. Fort Donelson alone provided the salvation for Confederate fortunes in Middle Tennessee.[9]

Pillow had rejoined the army by taking command of what was primarily a supply base at Clarksville. His political and organizational skills and renewed enthusiasm for the cause soon transformed that post into a well-functioning distribution point, especially for forwarding men and supplies downriver to Forts Henry and Donelson. Ever the loyal Tennessean, Pillow, more than Johnston, remained aware of the twin rivers as the gateway to his native state. Perhaps he also sought glory for himself (the thought was never far from the minds of his detractors), but on February 7 all that he received from headquarters in reply to his candid report about Clarksville were instructions to cross his 2,000 men to the south side of the river, leaving "sufficient force" to protect the factories and warehouses, "in the saving of which the Confederate Government is interested." Nobody told him how to divide his men to cope with both directives or what he was supposed to do once he reached the south side. Pillow replied dutifully: "General Johnston may rely upon my doing all that is possible." Actually, Bowling Green headquarters temporarily lost sight of Pillow's activities as it worried about withdrawing Polk back to the Memphis area and defending Mississippi River strong points like Island Number 10 and Fort Pillow to the last extremity. The Confederate high command assumed that various subordinates knew how to make "bold stands" and fight to the last, yet extricate their men when the propitious moment arrived so as to avoid future disasters like Fort Henry.[10]

Johnston's dispatches during this week showed a desire to make only token fights at key places in order to buy time but not to engage in major battle. Running throughout were thoughts about the fluidity of the situation, contradictory reports from the front, and frenzied activity. Johnston wanted information with which to form a clearer picture of Federal activity, and he directed Pillow to provide such data via telegraph, boat, or courier. He wired Richmond pessimistically: "I think the gunboats of the enemy will probably take Fort Donelson without the necessity of employing their land force in cooperation, as seems to have been done at Fort Henry." Still, if Sidney Johnston truly felt intimidated by the Union fleet, why did he bother to reinforce the Cumberland position at all?[11]

The man knew little about the fort and its occupants, and he relied entirely upon subordinates such as Pillow for guidance. Johnston's mind was set upon withdrawing everyone behind the river at Nashville, where he assumed state officials were busy gathering supplies and finishing emergency defenses. Everything was done hastily. Crisis hung heavily in the air, and the key to Johnston's thinking could be found in four telegrams which he sent to Pillow and Floyd on the seventh. Floyd was to concentrate his force across the river from Clarksville, "to support Donelson," but so as to leave his route open to Nashville. Pillow "will move his force to Donelson" and assume command there, reuniting with Floyd "if the fort has fallen." Just why Pillow needed to go there remains unanswered because Bushrod Johnson had just gone downriver from Nashville under Johnston's instruction to assumed command of the Fort Henry survivors. Sidney Johnston may have had more confidence in Pillow, or—as seemed to happen repeatedly—everyone simply forgot about Bushrod Johnson. At any rate the departmental commander's third telegram of the day told Floyd that when he had crossed at Clarksville, he would "determine his future movements with regard to the enemy as he may find judicious." Here was all that was necessary to plunge the Confederate cause into confusion. Yet, from Johnston's perspective, he had little choice but to allow subordinates some discretion. Therefore, at 10:00 P.M., he wired Pillow: "reports are so contradictory, that you must do the best you can, under orders you have recd. until Floyd arrives when he will execute them." He added: "If your service or Buckner's or both are most important at Donelson, go there." With that, Albert Sidney Johnston implicitly passed the marshal's baton to eager, local commanders. They, not he, dictated strategy on the twin rivers for the next week.[12]

The fog of war began to lift for Johnston when Floyd reached Clarksville on the eighth and reported by telegraph. He told his superior that a large portion of the force intended for Fort Donelson had gone forward and that he would try to determine Grant's plan, but he warned against expecting much on that point except "what can be gathered from general deduction." He too had doubts about defending against the dreaded gunboats, as "they are nearly invulnerable, and therefore they can probably

General John Bell Floyd.
National Archives.

go wherever sufficient fuel and depth of water can be found, unless met by opposing gunboats." He predicted that the Federals would use their naval capabilities to destroy towns on the river and every bridge across the stream. He felt that they could be confined to the waterways, but only at heavy cost and inconvenience "with the obstructed transportation we will have." He reaffirmed Clarksville's weakness, blaming the engineers, but suggested "this place is capable of being made very strong indeed." The fact was that Clarksville was not strong at that moment, and that made the difference. Then Floyd concluded with the most helpful comment of any that week: "I wish, if possible you would come down here, if it were only for a single day. I think in that time you might determine the policy and lines of defense." But Johnston was not listening. His telegrams of afternoon and evening on February 8 reiterated that Floyd could deploy his force at his discretion. "I cannot give you specific instructions," he wrote the Virginian, "you will therefore ascertain the probable movements of the enemy and distribute your forces as you think proper."[13]

Conflicting intelligence information reached Bowling Green in a steady stream. That same day Buckner wired from Russellville that his Louisville contacts indicated that Buell viewed Halleck's operation as "chiefly a diversion." Still, reported Buckner, his spy had noted five gunboats and sixteen transports convoying some 12,000 men for that diversion. On the ninth, Buckner relayed information from his Clarksville aide, Major

Alexander Casseday, recounting still more spy reports of a 900-wagon supply train leaving Lexington, Kentucky, for Thomas' force in southeast Kentucky. Johnston's intelligence network was feeding more information than could be absorbed at headquarters. Yet the situation on the Cumberland clarified slightly when on that day Pillow took direct command at Fort Donelson. His arrival solidified Confederate determination to stand and fight at the post. Before dark, Pillow had ridden around the fort and camps, talked with officers and men, and conferred with Bushrod Johnson (whose tenure as commander of the garrison had lasted all of forty-eight hours). Johnson had done little more than stockpile matériel sent from Clarksville, send the fort's sick by return boat, and study the situation. The two generals undoubtedly discussed the incompleted defenses, unmounted Columbiad and 32-pounder cannon, and the lack of tools, lumber, and artillery necessary for a proper defense.[14]

Pillow took special note of the deep gloom which hung over the troops as a result of Fort Henry. He watched the soldiers hard at work on Gilmer's outer defense line of earthworks, clearing fields of fire for artillery and preparing abatis for the works. But he sensed their apprehension. He learned that not only were remnants of the Henry garrison now at Fort Donelson — as well as the original four infantry regiments, six cavalry companies, and a small number of artillerists of the Cumberland post — but additional line regiments which had come in since the seventh included the 51st and 56th Virginia from Floyd's brigade, the 2d Kentucky, 3d and 18th Tennessee from Buckner's division, and the four-regiment brigade accompanying Pillow himself. Given these facts but principally persuaded by a desire to defend Tennessee soil, both Pillow and Johnson agreed that the decisive battle should — and could — be fought at Fort Donelson. This fact decided upon, Pillow acceded to his aide and local Dover resident, Major J.E. Rice, that the general use his residence as headquarters. Settling into the command post, Pillow took pen and paper in hand to inform Floyd, Johnston, and Governor Harris of the situation.[15]

Pillow's message to all three men was essentially that while the fort was not in the best state of readiness, "the place *will not be surrendered*," and his younger aide, Lieutenant John C. Burch, added privately to the letter sent to Harris, "he *don't think* it will be taken." Pillow told Floyd that the Federals remained encamped at Fort Henry, although scouts and local Secessionists reported two gunboats down the Cumberland about eight to ten miles below Dover. His men needed tents, said Pillow, and he wanted Buckner sent to Fort Donelson, but he promised to keep the

Virginian informed by telegraph and courier so that he might relay the data to Johnston. Then the political general turned to improving morale and organization in his new assignment. His special order of February 9 was vintage Pillow.[16]

Pillow told the garrison that he relied upon their courage to maintain their position. That was fair enough, but then he enjoined them to "drive back the ruthless invader from our soil and again raise the Confederate flag over Fort Henry." He "expects every man to do his duty," added Pillow, invoking both God's help and a Nelsonian touch. "Our battle cry, 'Liberty or death,'" must have occasioned more than a few laughs in the ranks, but Pillow persisted. The next day he used the occasion of a visit to the water batteries, where Captain Saint Claire Morgan's company of the 10th Tennessee was drilling, to add another oration. Recalling that he had Irish soldiers with him in Mexico and at Belmont, Pillow declared: "You are Irishmen and I know you will prove true to your adopted South. I come here to drive the Hessians [sic] from this neck of land between the rivers, and I will never Surrender!" The word was not in his vocabulary, he shouted, suggesting that many of the Sons of Erin knew him personally or by reputation; then he ordered them to work. Randal McGavock, second in command of the 10th, knew Pillow too well and noted in his private journal that he regretted Pillow's appearance at the fort, for he held no confidence in him as an officer. He feared that the days ahead would require all the skill and talent that could be brought to the field by the Confederates.[17]

Pillow and Johnson brigaded the various units and formed them into two divisions, one to be commanded by Johnson and the other by Buckner when he arrived. Gilmer and the local engineer, Joseph Dixon, continued to work on the trench lines, and Gilmer wrote that all this activity gave him renewed confidence that the position could be held. A water attack would be more difficult to stop, but he now concluded that it might have been "want of skill in the men who served the guns" rather than gunboat invincibility that lost Fort Henry. Pillow abandoned the idea of constructing a boom across the flooded river but told headquarters that he, given ten extra days, hoped to make bombproof quarters for the heavy artillery. The Confederates would not receive such a gift. In fact Pillow worried that Grant might strike southward through the rugged and broken country behind Fort Donelson and Dover, reaching the river upstream and cutting his line of communications with Clarksville. He eventually dismissed this notion since the terrain and absence of food and fodder dictated against its success. He told Floyd that he was accordingly "pushing the work on my river batteries day and night;

also on my field works and defensive line in the rear." He asked Floyd to send Clarksville's heavy guns down to strengthen Fort Donelson, then told the other brigadier general that he would do so himself in a couple of days. "Upon one thing you may rest assured," he telegraphed Governor Harris, "I will never surrender the position, and with God's help I mean to maintain it."[18]

Pillow's tone was upbeat as long as he commanded at the fort. Suddenly a new danger surfaced, and it came from within rather than outside the Confederate command structure. It developed largely at Pillow's own instigation. The arrival of Simon Bolivar Buckner on February 11 injected a sour note as prewar animosity welled to the surface once more. Whether the residue of bitterness from the earlier 1857 political imbroglio concerning the U.S. Senate race caused the ensuing command troubles at Fort Donelson cannot be established positively. For his part Pillow attempted to solidify the Donelson team by naming Buckner not only a division commander, but also leader of the army's right wing. Still the proud Kentuckian was placed subordinate to Pillow, whom he considered a fool. Other perceptive officers sensed trouble; McGavock, wondering how the two would work together in crisis, noted that Pillow was a vindictive man and not likely to forget earlier problems. At the very least it hardly helped the situation that Buckner carried direct orders from Floyd that he should be allowed to withdraw his division from Dover by water should he think that course advisable.[19]

Floyd and Buckner had discussed an operations plan just before Buckner left Clarksville for the fort. Floyd had been told again by Johnston that he had full authority to make all dispositions of his troops for the defense of Fort Donelson, Clarksville, and the Cumberland. Thus Floyd and Buckner formulated a plan whereby their forces would concentrate at Cumberland City, where the railroad left the river and headed overland toward the Tennessee River crossing, "with a view of operating from some point on the railway west of that position in the direction of Fort Donelson or Fort Henry, thus maintaining communications with Nashville by way of Charlotte." The plan offered good strategic mobility for inferior forces and would ensure that such forces would neither be cut off by the gunboats nor outflanked in the hilly scrub country by Grant's land column. The Confederates could operate against Grant's logistical line back to Fort Henry. As far as Floyd and Buckner were concerned, just enough force would be left at Fort Donelson "to make all possible resistance to any attack which may be made *upon the fort*, but no more." Colonel J.S. Scott's Louisiana cavalry would range up and down the opposite side of the Cumberland to prevent Federals from land-

ing there. The plan sounded good — depending upon how Sidney Johnston's orders to Floyd were interpreted.[20]

Pillow chose to interpret such plans as a repetition of Lloyd Tilghman's sacrifice at Fort Henry, and he wanted no part of that role. He
doubted that the scheme truly reflected Johnston's intentions, and he refused to entertain Buckner's departure with his division until he had
spoken directly to Floyd. So shortly after daybreak on February 12, Pillow boarded a steamboat and went upriver to Cumberland City to find
Floyd. He left Buckner temporarily in command at Dover with strict
orders that a planned reconnaissance toward Fort Henry by Forrest's
cavalry should not bring on a general battle. He saw no evidence yet of
any advance of the enemy. When he reached Cumberland City, Pillow
learned that Floyd had gone to Clarksville to untangle logistical and
transportation difficulties. He did not know that Floyd had communicated his plans to Johnston that very morning. Two telegrams from headquarters the previous day indicated Johnston's displeasure with Floyd's
apparent vacillation. "Twice today I have telegraphed you to command
all the troops and use your judgment," said Johnston. Therefore, Floyd
had taken great pains to reassure his chief that he did indeed have a plan
and that Buckner, at least, agreed with it. "I have been in the greatest
dread ever since I reached this place at [the forces] scattered condition,"
he wrote, noting that his troops were inadequate to defend any line forty
miles long which could be attacked from three different directions. "We
can only be formidable by concentration," Floyd declared, and he added
that he intended to construct rafts which might be jammed against the
railroad bridge abutments and piers at Clarksville as a sort of bulwark
against the gunboats should they pass Fort Donelson.[21]

Pillow certainly wanted to argue his case in person, and may have
done so, but the record remains unclear. At some point a steamboat
brought the disturbing news that the Federals were advancing by land
and river against Fort Donelson. It was far too late now to make any
change in dispositions, so the Tennessean sent telegrams from Cumberland City to Floyd, Harris, and Johnston, stating that he was returning
in haste to Dover, adding, "shall suspend order for Buckner to fall back
at present." Then, when he reached the now endangered fort, he sent
what one historian has termed a grossly misleading telegram to Johnston. Pillow stated:

If I can retain my present force, I can hold my position. Let me retain Buckner for the present. If now withdrawn, will invite an attack. Enemy cannot pass this place without exposing himself to flank-attack. If I am strong

enough to take field, he cannot ever reach here; nor is it possible for him to subsist in the country to pass over, nor can he possibly bring his subsistence with him. With Buckner's force, I can hold my position. Without it, cannot long.[22]

Here was a plan fully as plausible in theory as the Floyd-Buckner scheme, but it was delivered to higher authority at the very moment of Federal attack. Cumberland City telegrapher R.C. Wintersmith wired Harris, for example, that the gunboats had actually opened fire on Fort Donelson and between 10,000 and 12,000 Federals "have landed in force." By the time that Floyd returned to his headquarters in that town, Johnston had fired off his 3:00 P.M. telegram to Floyd, in effect endorsing Pillow's plan. His terse comment to Floyd stated simply: "I do not know the wants of General Pillow, nor yours, nor the position of General Buckner. You do. You have the dispatch, Decide. Answer." Floyd had little time to waver, and he knew it.[23]

By evening, everyone had copies of Pillow's statement as to that day's cavalry skirmishes, a gunboat bombardment, and the arrival of Grant's land forces before the fort. Pillow telegraphed frantically: "We shall have a battle in the morning, I think certainly, and an attack by gun-boats." The enemy surrounded his position within ten minutes marching time, he claimed, and yet he added, "I have done all that it was possible to do, and think I will drive back the enemy." The pivotal moment for withdrawal from Fort Donelson had vanished. The Floyd-Buckner plan for concentration at Cumberland City passed into a footnote to history. Given Confederate steamboat shortages on the river, it is quite doubtful that the scheme could have been implemented at all. All things being equal, Johnston's 10:30 P.M. telegram to Floyd saying that he should take the remainder of his men to Donelson that night was about the only option left. Faced with news of Grant's appearance, as well as the actions of subordinates on the scene, Johnston had been forced to play his hand. As he told President Davis a month later: "I determined to fight for Nashville at Donelson, and gave the best part of my army to do it." Still, if he had reached this decision before February 12, he had not communicated it clearly and forcefully to the four subordinates who were sent to implement the plan.[24]

Pillow may have overstated the case of low morale and defeatism when he first arrived at Dover, but he found the command less apprehensive than previously when he returned from Cumberland City. Soldiers such as W.H. Farmer of the 30th Tennessee and his friend J. Wesley Murphey assured loved ones optimistically that they expected success if attacked.

Murphey told his sweetheart: "I'll stand by my cannon, I'll let balls and grape shot fly; I'll trust in god and Davis, but keep my powder dry." T. Joseph Brigham of Company B, 50th Tennessee wrote his mother that blistered feet, mud over shoe-tops, weighty knapsacks, and a headache plagued him more than fears of the Yankees. Many of these men had been at Fort Donelson since autumn, and by mid-winter the boredom, camp fevers, homesickness, and incessant drills were eagerly replaced by the anticipation of combat. Sleepy Dover had long since passed in interest. Little more than a layover for riverboat traffic and a connecting point for overland stages between Clarksville and Paris, this county seat had become overshadowed by the military activity within the town environs. The innocuous public square, the court house, the few stores, and offices of doctors and lawyers — even the two local inns of any repute were all taken over for army purposes. F.P. Gray's large Dover hotel, for example, located at the upper steamboat landing afforded the best lodgings in town, and it was destined to figure prominently in the events about to unfold on the Cumberland. Across the street stood the town jail, and up the unimproved lane could be found additional structures pressed into service by quartermaster, ordnance, and hospital personnel. Several roads fanned out from the town leading overland toward the Tennessee River crossings, and upriver toward Cumberland City and Clarksville, as well as inland to various ironworks and forges. Private Thomas H. Riddell of the Goochland (Va.) artillery later remembered "this little village . . . situated on a hill interspersed with small trees and overlooking the river," but more hardbitten Rebels held less kindly thoughts about the sleepy hamlet.[25]

The presence of Pillow and Bushrod Johnson somewhat quieted the fears of the garrison about the Union gunboats, as communicated by the Fort Henry survivors. George Wiley Adams wrote his wife that the nearly 13,000 soldiers now gathered about Dover would hopefully bring better luck. Yet everyone talked about Tilghman's treachery in surrendering Forts Henry and Heiman, and there was grumbling about loss of confidence in the officers and the Southern Cause. Captain Reuben R. Ross (whose Maury County artillery battery had traded its light field artillery pieces for the heavier fortress guns upon its arrival on February 12) recorded in his journal that had he been drilling and preparing his defense for some days before, he would not have felt alarmed, but the short preparation time and want of his men's familiarity with their new weapons brought "a feeling of deep solicitude as to result over me." Nevertheless, these Tennesseans decided that there was no time for despondency.[26]

The Federal naval victory at Fort Henry caused the Donelson defenders to look mainly to conditions in their own water batteries. Fatigue details strengthened the earthen parapets to a thickness of ten to sixteen feet from top to base. Observers noted that the lower battery stretched obliquely down the slope from the main hilltop fort for a distance of 150 yards. Its exterior crest ran in a straight line at right angles to the river, while its interior crest formed a *crémaillère* since the left was more elevated than the right, with gun positions occupying different elevations. The smaller, upper battery (again actually located slightly lower on the slope of ground but upstream from the lower battery, hence the two terms) formed a semicircular work and lacked the embrasures and bombproofness of its partner, but it possessed the same coffee and cotton sack sandbags and rawhide-lined embrasures, and it too had a powder magazine of its own. The two positions by this stage obviously incorporated rudimentary "lessons learned" from the Fort Henry battle.[27]

Milton Haynes increased the arduous training for the cannoneers by February 11. Some twelve pieces of artillery poked their muzzles from these batteries. Eight 32-pounder smoothbore seacoast cannon and one 10-inch Columbiad (all mounted *en barbette*) formed the complement of the lower battery, while two 32-pounder carronades (naval guns) and a 64-pounder (also styled in reports as "6.5 inch rifle," "68-pounder," or "128-pounder rifle gun") formed the armament of the upper battery. Haynes tested the Columbiad at the extreme left of the lower battery on the sixth, only to have the twenty-pound powder charge dislodge the piece from its platform and damage the carriage. He set his men to work repairing the damage and ordered replacement parts from the Cumberland Iron Works, and restored the cannon to service prior to the Federals' appearance. Still, most of the Confederates lacked confidence in the repaired cannon, and Captain Bell G. Bidwell at the upper battery added to their pessimism by declaring his carronades to be utterly worthless. With distinct ordnance problems, no one thought that the water batteries could stop the Union gunboats after the dismal Fort Henry performance.[28]

The water battery preparations formed only part of the weeklong activities in the Confederate positions on the Cumberland. With the arrival of the Fort Henry survivors and Colonel Gabriel C. Wharton's 51st Virginia of Floyd's brigade on the seventh, a steady influx of new units probably reminded some of the young Rebels of their grandfather's stories of the great gatherings at the Watauga settlements or Boonesboro in the Indian wars. Each night the steamboats *General Anderson* and *May*

Duke shuttled more Confederates from the railhead at Cumberland City into the Dover perimeter. These newcomers stepped off the steamboats onto the frozen mud of the landings, and many of them lacked cooking utensils, tents, and other camp gear. Nearly all of them seemed disgruntled to discover that their first major activity was only the fatiguing work of adding to the earthworks or other chores.[29]

Josephus C. Moore of the 18th Tennessee remembered that they slept on the cold ground and worked on the rifle pits both day and night. His unit finally got some of its baggage on the eleventh, but they had to haul it nearly two miles to their positions and even then did not have time to pitch their tents. Captain Calvin J. Clack, commanding A company of the 3d Tennessee, also groused in his memoirs that his regiment had been hiking all over wintry Kentucky for most of the previous month, and thus their eating habits had become poor at best. "Green beef boiled on coals, and frequently without salt, and often bread without grease or salt, cooked upon sticks held over the fire," he complained. They luckily found comfort from comrades in the 53d Tennessee who shared camp facilities, tents, and rations, and "contributed in every way they could to our comfort," said Clack.[30]

Pillow's arrival brought Colonel John M. Simonton's 1st Mississippi, Colonel Thomas J. Davidson's 3d (23d) Mississippi, Colonel Harlan B. Lyon's 8th Kentucky, and Colonel John M. Gregg's 7th Texas also to Dover. The bombastic Pillow soon posted Roger Hanson's over-strength 2d Kentucky on the extreme right of the line next to Hickman's Creek to guard the road from Eddyville. Then, in sequence down the line, he sited the brigades of John C. Brown, Gabriel Wharton, Adolphus Heiman, Joseph Drake, and Thomas J. Davidson. Grant marched virtually unopposed to Fort Donelson largely because Pillow was too busy bolstering his defenses and posting his commands to lash out and strike the Federals on the march. Even the reputedly aggressive Buckner missed his opportunity for such glory when in command during Pillow's absence on February 12. Of course his orders forbade precipitous action, although it seems strange that the Kentuckian would have bowed so easily to strictures of his erstwhile nemesis. In any event, everyone from general to private on the Confederate side thought in terms of defense, not offense, as the Federals closed in on them.[31]

Even Commander Walke and the *Carondelet* failed to draw Confederate fire when the gunboat arrived below the fort. By dusk on February 12, McClernand's side-slipping his units via the Ridge and Pinery roads brought his division opposite the works held by Heiman and Drake.

Elsewhere, Colonels John Cook and Jacob Lauman filed their brigades off to the left past a humble farmhouse belonging to the Widow Crisp, where Grant would soon make his headquarters. Breathing heavily, the men crested a ridge opposite Hanson's command and drew fire. Immediately withdrawn behind the summit, they bivouacked for the night. Meanwhile at Mrs. Crisp's place, the double feather bed and large open fireplace beckoned to a fatigued Grant and his staff. Nobody cared much what the Rebels were doing that night. For sure, Pillow's army would not mount a night attack.[32]

Even without further fighting, neither side anticipated a restful night. Scouts such as Adam Rankin Johnson ranged far out from Pillow's works, searching for information about the enemy. Union counterparts conducted similar missions of their own. Then suddenly a savage north wind turned the weather bitterly cold. The Federals shivered and cursed the fact that they had left blankets and overcoats far to the rear where supply personnel would have to bring them forward later on. The Confederates were just as uncomfortable, although encamped in the hollows and ravines behind their entrenchments. George Washington Dillon and messmates of the 18th Tennessee remembered cooking some thirty scones of flour and five or six nice hams, but they were the exception. Most of the southerners suffered from lack of sleep, irregular meals, and overwork. As Chaplain Thomas H. Deavenport of the 3d Tennessee recalled, they had been working night and day for nearly a week. Roger Hanson told his wife that while he had seen some pretty stiff times during the Mexican War, nothing compared with the siege at Fort Donelson. Sleep proved impossible, work unending, and when the Kentuckian tried to rest, he awakened with frostbitten ears. Neither side would be very anxious to begin the battle when dawn broke on February 13.[33]

Floyd arrived at the upper landing about daybreak and immediately took command of the army. He brought the remainder of his brigade with him. Like Pillow, Floyd was more the flamboyant politician than the great battle captain. He had bickered with superiors during the western Virginia campaign. He enjoyed the dubious distinction of having served as President James Buchanan's secretary of war just before the war, and Floyd earned the North's enmity for ostensibly stockpiling southern arsenals with war matériel. Some people claimed he was flexible to a fault and prone to falling under the influence of the last person to talk with him. Still Johnston may have thought his compromising skill would provide some tempering influence on Pillow and Buckner. Floyd undoubtedly stepped off the boat firm in the belief that he enjoyed his superior's confidence that he could make decisions. To this day, however, it remains a mystery just why Johnston sent this particular man to command the major portion of his western army, at the crucial battle, and at a place which even Floyd considered "illy chosen, out of position, and entirely indefensible by any re-enforcements which could be brought there to its support." What was equally strange was the fact that Floyd proceeded to stand and fight for that position for three long days![34]

Johnston's reasons apparently lay with his subsequent comment to Davis: "When the force was detached, I was in hopes that such dispositions would have been made as would have enabled the forces to defend the fort or withdraw without sacrificing the army." Floyd understood this premise. But timing was crucial. He needed to hold until he received the news that Johnston had safely evacuated Bowling Green and had the Central Army of Kentucky back at Nashville. Only then could Fort Donelson be evacuated. Meanwhile Grant had to be contained. After setting up his command post, Floyd rode with Pillow to survey the garrison. He found a vast array of winter huts, a sea of white tents, and numerous supply and munitions dumps, but he also came away convinced that the outer trench line had been injudiciously constructed because it exposed the Confederates to heavy sharpshooter fire as they went to and from the works. Yet none of the generals saw any alternative now but to fight it out. Furthermore, no sooner had Floyd completed his inspection tour than the battle opened, making questions of strengths and weaknesses of the position moot.[35]

The Confederate command at Fort Donelson may not have been as divided and confused as later commentators contended. If anything, it was Grant and his captains who were in a quandary at this point. Sitting over breakfast in the Crisp kitchen, the Federal commander pondered prisoner interrogations and scouting reports which suggested that possibly 25,000 enemy troops were behind the strong earthworks in front of him. Grant had only 15,000 men with him at this juncture, and he knew nothing of the whereabouts of Foote and the main flotilla. In actuality the naval force was steaming very slowing toward Dover, battling the heavy flood current of the Cumberland all the way. Grant sent messages to Lew Wallace to bring over the rear echelon from Fort Henry, and to Walke to advance his lone gunboat at 10:00 A.M. as a diversion, while McClernand and C.F. Smith tightened their cordon around the Confederates. Grant also wired Halleck to speed all reinforcements to Fort Henry, where they could march across the neck of land to Fort Donelson, if necessary. Meanwhile, like Pillow, he told his subordinates to avoid battle. Patrols might go forward, a reconnaissance made, and the investment completed, but no one was to make any impetuous rush on the main Rebel lines.[36]

Thus, in the soldier jargon of the era, "the ball opened." Few of the soldiers huddled against the cold had thoughts of garden cotillions that morning. The day itself dawned "as clear and serene" as previous ones, and everyone rolled from their fitful slumbers to the warming rays of the sun, which "seemed to smile upon the efforts of the National troops," proclaimed the *New York Times* correspondent. Birge's sharpshooters were already active between the lines in the predawn darkness. Clad in their subdued uniforms, these marksmen had an air of authority about them. Each one carried a whistle, which they used in signaling movement to right or left, forward or back. A reporter thought that they moved through the forest like Indians and "wanted no better fun than to creep through the underbrush and pick off the Rebels." Indeed they would take their toll of Confederates that day—until southern counterparts joined the deadly game. Even Nathan Bedford Forrest took a turn with a May-nard rifle, felling one of Birge's men from his treetop perch. Still, Birge's boys were up early on the thirteenth, ensuring that their place would be recorded in the history books.[37]

Three bloody and significant battles unfolded that day, despite Grant's orders. All of them began in the morning, extended into the afternoon, and gave both sides their first taste of real fighting on land. The actions provided their share of human drama and tested both tactics and mettle of the soldiery. All three of the battles convinced Grant that Fort Donel-son would be harder to reduce than Fort Henry. The first fighting began on C.F. Smith's front as his division tried to move closer to Buckner's position in the Eddyville road sector. Nobody had accurate maps of the area, and to goad the Confederates into disclosing battery positions, Smith directed Battery D, 1st Missouri Light Artillery to employ its four 10-pounder Parrot rifles at long range. The noise of artillery as well as small arms fire began to echo across the countryside behind Fort Donel-son. After a hearty breakfast, Smith called for a simultaneous advance of two of his brigades with Lauman on the left and Cook on the right, John McArthur in reserve. By 10:00 A.M. these men from Indiana, Illinois, and Iowa had formed around the Crisp farm, moved up through heavy undergrowth on the steep slope, and reached the crest of the ridge facing Buckner's lines—1,400 yards away. Colonel James G. Veatch of the 25th Indiana claimed later that the timber was so thick that they could see only portions of the Confederate line, and could gain no idea of its range or extent. Unslinging knapsacks and other gear, Lauman's men fixed

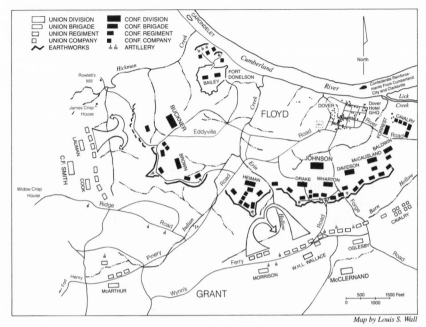

MAP 5. Action, February 13, 1862.

bayonets, dressed their lines, and descended the slope so that they might accomplish Smith's directive to close within cannon range of the enemy. Why anyone thought this would not violate Grant's orders about a general battle was unclear.[38]

Cook's brigade proceeded in the same fashion to the right of Lauman. The brush and Rebel abatis clogged the ravine and stymied the Federals. Probing fire from a Union supporting battery drew a response from Porter's Tennessee gunners in the apex of Buckner's line, and soon Hanson and Joseph Palmer added their musketry to the din. The closely packed Yankees discovered too late that a simple reconaissance had become an all-out assault on the enemy position. By afternoon, Lauman and Cook managed to extricate their commands and consolidate them on the ridge above the Crisp farm. The sector quieted down with only sporadic artillery outbursts and sharpshooter activity continuing in the wintry air. Volunteers on both sides had seen comrades cut down in battle — nearly one hundred of them from the 25th Indiana, 7th and 14th Iowa, and the 13th Missouri. As one Iowan realized, the men experienced the first shock of hearing the discharge of artillery, knowing that the guns were aimed "this way," and seeing wounded and dying men for the first time. Buckner's people experienced similar feelings. As William Lewis Mc-Kay of the 18th Tennessee recounted, all of the men were taken off-guard by the first rounds; they fell to their knees on the second; and at the third shot they fell flat to the ground.[39]

Meanwhile downriver, Walke got up steam aboard the *Carondelet* about 9:05 A.M. and headed toward Fort Donelson, firing the 8-inch Dahlgren and 42-pounder guns with fuses cut to explode at 10- and 15-second intervals. Water battery commanders were drilling their gun crews when the boat nosed around the bend, and it seemed that Walke's move "was diabolically inspired and knew the most opportune time to annoy us," said one. When the gunboat had appeared the previous day, Captain Reuben Ross's subordinate, Lieutenant Hugh S. Bedford of Mississippi, had tapped him on the shoulder and whispered that the enemy was coming. "I observed the pallor and seriousness produced by some extraordinary question," recalled Ross. At the time, he had shrugged off the feeling and continued with the gun drills to give his men time to regain composure as he communicated the news of the Yankees' arrival "in an indifferent tone." The next morning, however, it was different. "We began early," stated Ross confidently, "omitting all the ordinary morning duties such as combing, washing, & c."[40] Ross rebuked his men for so much disorder the previous day and ordered no talking above a whisper so as to inspire coolness and deliberation in serving the guns. Ross worked his 10-inch Columbiad and the 6.5-inch rifle—the only pieces capable of responding to Walke's long-range fire. The duel continued for nearly two hours, during which Confederate shots ostensibly struck the iron-plating of the gunboat with loud noise. Ross fired several of his 32-pounders too but with no effect. One 128-pound projectile did cut through a bulwark on the *Carondelet* spreading havoc by bouncing about "like a wild beast pursuing its prey," wounding several seamen with wood splinters and bursting a steam-heater before passing once more through the ship's side and into the river. In turn, the Confederates collected fourteen naval shells fired into their positions. Walke's most telling shot was the one which passed through an embrasure of Captain B.G. Bidwell's Number 2, 32-pounder, shattering the gun carriage and tearing loose a screw-tap which struck Dixon in the head, killing him instantly.[41]

Walke drew off temporarily to ascertain damages and transfer his wounded to the steamer *Alps*. He then resumed a long-range cat-and-mouse shelling from just around a bend in the river. Ross and Dixon's successor, Captain J.E. Culbertson, enjoyed the game all afternoon, but neither side drew further blood. The *Missouri Democrat* reporter claimed later that one Confederate commander told him the *Carondelet* fire that day did more damage than the bigger fight between Foote's whole flotilla and the water batteries the next afternoon. Walke's gunners fired 139 shots on the thirteenth, killing one besides Dixon and wounding five additional Rebels, including Captain J.P. Shuster, late of the U.S. Navy. More serious was the damage done to the Columbiad's front traverse wheels, which could not be easily repaired in the field. Yet, when Pillow and Floyd visited the batteries at nightfall, they found the men working hard to fix the damage, and no one indicated the slightest fear of the Union navy. If anything, the Confederates were now convinced that they had severely damaged or even sunk the *Carondelet*. About all that Walke accomplished was to exhaust the ammunition for his bow guns.[42]

Artillery fire also sounded that morning along McClernand's section of the battle line. The Illinois general had ordered subordinates to continue shifting past the besieged Confederates via the Wynn's Ferry road and to strike the river above Dover, thus completing the encirclement. The 2d and 4th Illinois cavalry soon reported from Dudley's Hill, which overlooked the flooded backwaters of Lick Creek where it emptied into the Cumberland. They could see a few enemy troops opposite them, beyond a ravine known as Barn Hollow. So McClernand ordered Colonels Richard Oglesby, W.H.L. Wallace, and William R. Morrison to push their brigades on quickly to close with the cavalry. Disputing their movement, Captain Frank Maney's Humphrey County artillerists opened a hot fire from the salient in Heiman's sector of the outer trenches. Maney's gunners laid down periodic barrages on the roadway every time they saw the marching Federals through gaps in the intervening trees. Farther down the line, D.L. French's six-gun, Cumberland Kentucky battery joined in the fray. When the Federals returned the fire, the Confederate guns fell silent, only to resume when the Union gunners pulled out. Finally, McClernand's patience snapped. Defying Grant's orders, he decided shortly after noon to rush Maney's battery and silence it.[43]

At some point McClernand also received a message from Grant that the gunboats and steamboats bearing reinforcements had left Smithland but that C.F. Smith had been repulsed in his morning action. McClernand now feared that his own command might be exposed to a Confederate sortie. Both he and Smith had been spoiling for a fight ever since the navy got to Fort Henry first. This fact, combined with Maney's shelling (galling to all in the ranks, claimed young Wilbur F. Crummer of the 45th Illinois), and a general desire to punish the Rebels led to McClernand's attack. At any rate, Morrison's brigade stood close at hand, and McClernand ordered the brigade commander to take his 17th and

General John A. McClernand. National Archives.

49th Illinois, as well as the 48th Illinois from W.H.L. Wallace's neighboring brigade, and storm the enemy battery position. By about 1:00 P.M.,
the force had been assembled and stood poised to attack.[44]

Just then, Colonel Isham G. Haynie of the 48th Illinois rode up to
coordinate with Morrison. Haynie, a prewar lawyer and sometime member of the legislature as well as judge of the Common Pleas Court at
Cairo and presidential elector for Stephen A. Douglas in 1860, simply
pulled rank on fellow lawyer and legislator Morrison in order to command this select mission. Morrison bowed to the inevitable, and the pair
agreed to take the objective together. (Years later McClernand told Haynie's son that he had ordered his father to lead the charge and that he
placed him over men his senior "because I considered him an abler soldier.") Haynie's and Morrison's commands swept down the slope from
the Wynn's Ferry road and into Erin Hollow where parade ground alignment disintegrated in the heavy undergrowth and uneven terrain.[45]

As with C.F. Smith's attack that morning, abatis, accurate and heavy
enemy fire, undisciplined volunteers, and the terrain broke apart the
Haynie-Morrison assault. It was all over in fifteen minutes, although
McClernand's men got to within forty or fifty yards of the nettlesome
battery. "They fired down hill at us and shot over all the time," claimed
Luther H. Cowan of the 45th Illinois, who witnessed the action. The
Federals never fired more than ten rounds but took solace in having
driven every Confederate behind the breastworks—and "not a devil of
them dared to show his head." Still, some 147 Federals fell in this costly
and abortive assault. Moreover, one of those melodramatic but memorable moments in the "war between brothers" came near the end of the
fight. The dry leaves in front of Maney's lines caught fire from exploding
shells, threatening a horrible death to scores of Yankee wounded lying
in "no man's land." Graves' battery beyond Indian Creek, and other Confederate units kept the main body of Federals at bay, thus preventing
rescue of their fallen. Some of Colonel William A. Quarles 42d Tennessee (who had just arrived from the *General Anderson* in time to join the
battle) rushed to aid Heiman's men in a daring rescue of the very enemy
they had been shooting down moments before. Such heroics aside, Mc-
Clernand, like Smith and Walke, accomplished little beyond bloodying
raw troops, expending ammunition, and bolstering the morale of the
Rebels.[46]

The unsuccessful aspects of the day escaped several of McClernand's
young men, however. Two Illinois walking-wounded encountered Grant
on their way to the rear area dressing station. The army commander
noted: "You look disfigured—been hunting bear?" Almost gleefully they

replied that they had the animal "treed" and would bring him down the next day, to which Grant chuckled and rejoined, "you didn't hurt anyone, did you?" One of the pair answered: "Why General, I dunno—I reckon I just scared 'em and they fainted." Grant motioned them on to a field hospital nearby. He was not pleased by his generals' actions. As the day wore on, reports came in that Oglesby's men had moved to within several hundred yards of Confederate lines in the Forge road area, and the sharpshooters continued to maintain their deadly work. Confederate artillery lieutenant John Morton's black hat sported a large feather which provided a particularly inviting target for them. One of Morton's men uncharitably muttered, "pretty bird, I'll catch him a worm in the morning," but hat and owner both escaped the aim of Birge's marksmen. Everyone waited for a general assault that never came. Grant remained unsure of the whereabouts of Foote's flotilla, but he had learned that he faced a plucky foe. Nevertheless, as one commentator declared, the Rebels made no effort to thwart the Federal investment—a mistake almost equal to unopposing the march from Fort Henry.[47]

CHAPTER 9

Gunboat Defeat
on the Second Day

ALL THAT DOUGLAS HAPERMAN OF THE 11TH Illinois remembered about the fighting on February 13 was that "we were kept
moving back and forth along the line all day." But nobody on either side
ever forgot "the most disagreeable and tedious" night that followed. Arrival of darkness brought with it a cold rain, then sleet, and finally, three
inches of snow, accompanied by bitter north winds. The temperature
plummeted to around twelve degrees Fahrenheit. W.H.L. Wallace reported that the night promised to be "one of great suffering and hardship
to the whole command." Some soldiers such as Daniel Harmon Brush
of the 18th Illinois tried to scoop leaves around them and catch some
sleep, only to be constantly called out on alert. It was impossible to keep
warm with the scant covering at hand, Brush remembered, adding that
to stay comfortable at all required officers and men alike to run around
in circles in the snow. He also recalled hearing two Irishmen lament-
ing to one another: "Oh, Pat, if we had now but one of the drams we
used to take when we didn't need 'em, wouldn't it go fine?" "Faith and
it would," replied Pat, but, as Brush allowed, no drams would come for
wishing it.[1]

It was the same over in the Confederate positions. It did not hamper
scout Adam Rankin Johnson from Forrest's band in his scouting of C.F.
Smith's lines. Nor did it bother his fellow Kentuckians in Roger Hanson's regiment, some of whom came equipped with a sort of butternut-
gray, hooded parka. Most of the southerners kept warm by digging earthworks, as William McKay of the 18th Tennessee noted how they literally
scratched logs from the snow and ice and carried them up very steep
hillsides to make the base for breastworks. It was so cold, said G.W. Dillon, "that we could hardly stand still during the hours of midnight."
Other Confederates could not wait to go off-duty and return to tents and
campfires far to the rear. All this ended with the next alarm, leading artillerist John Watson Morton to decide that no one knew the "terrible suf-

fering and horrible discomfort" of that fearful night so well as the hungry and exhausted soldiers of both armies.[2]

Down at the water batteries, Colonel James E. Bailey kept his 49th Tennessee busy bolstering the parapets and revetments, while Captain Ross at the upper battery lobbed an occasional shell upriver simply to keep the gunboat sailors awake beyond the bend. He half expected the Federals to try to steam past him during the storm. Returning at one point from some business in Dover, Ross thought he heard the sound of whistles, and he "was racked with fear." All he aroused with his impromptu cannonade, however, were the irate generals at Confederate headquarters, and Gideon Pillow sent an aide to the battery with the order to cease firing. The aide also handed Ross a flask of peach brandy to steady his nerves. Ross did not sleep much that night and was up before dawn—again uneasy that the gunboats might try to slip past just before daybreak, since he had read somewhere that military writers claimed this was the time when guards "are their least apt to be watchful." The return of Birge's pesky sharpshooters and the resumption of artillery duels broke the silence of the night at first light.[3]

February 14—St. Valentine's Day—was the kind of morning when everyone would have preferred to stay inside. Lieutenant Charles G. Nott, a former resident of New York City, declared that urban life was poor preparation for the field on a day like that. Icy ground covering and continued high winds brought land operations to a halt. Confederate surgeons readied another boatload of sick and wounded for shipment to Clarksville and Nashville hospitals. Skirmishers peppered away, and boys from the 50th Illinois took particular pride in finally felling one Confederate marksman they had dubbed "Old Red Shirt." They especially prized his "Mississippi Yager" rifle. Grant wired Halleck that the investment was at a standstill pending arrival of land and naval reinforcements. He still felt confident, he said, and the feeling was shared by his men. By 11:00 A.M. Lew Wallace's contingents from Fort Henry marched past the Crisp house, and Grant sent them to fill the gap between McClernand and C.F. Smith in the upper Indian Creek valley. He also designated them his "Third Division." Additional men poured off steamboats at a landing several miles downstream and marched to join the main force. Three regiments from Ohio—the 58th, 68th, and 76th—formed a brigade along with Colonel John M. Thayer's 1st Nebraska, and they went to reinforce Lew Wallace's command. The 2d Iowa went to strengthen C.F. Smith's force.[4]

Grant's principal concern was the navy. It was time for Foote's flotilla to join the fight. The onset of winter weather in enemy country, the unpredictability of volunteers under such stressful conditions, the logistical nightmare of an exposed line of communications, plus the abiding question of Sidney Johnston's intentions, all worried Grant, far more than his memoirs and later apologists have suggested. Certainly, he wrote Cullum back at Cairo that very day, the enemy was strong, well fortified, and having "not less than 30,000 troops," with all statements suggesting even a higher figure. Grant never lent much credence to spy and prisoner reports, and definitive figures have never been established for the Confederate command at Fort Donelson. The mere suggestion of 15,000 to 21,000, although imprecise, seems plausible and has been generally accepted through the years. Whatever the true figure at the time, Grant definitely looked to Foote's Western Flotilla to equalize the fight and possibly win a quick decision as it had at Fort Henry.[5]

About the time that Birge's sharpshooters had been purged as an annoyance to the Confederates that day, Ross noted through his telescope that many smokestacks could be seen just around the river bend. He immediately sent a runner to headquarters requesting permission to fire upon what he judged were transports disembarking enemy reinforcements. Floyd and Pillow, however, decided that a council of war was needed, so time elapsed while Buckner was summoned to the Rice house for consultation. Scouting reports suggested 15,000 to 20,000 new Federals had arrived. Furthermore they conveyed the equally dismal news that both the Wynn's Ferry and Forge roads to the south of Dover had been closed by McClernand's men. The Virginia brigadier general sent off a hasty telegram to Johnston: "The enemy have reached the ground near the fort with eight or ten gunboats I am uncertain which, and fifteen transports reported to have on board near 20,000 men. They are now landing. This makes their force nearly 40,000 strong." He added expectantly, "I will fight them this evening."[6]

Forgetting Ross's request completely, the war council decided to break free from Grant's encirclement and to march southeastward to Charlotte and then to Nashville to join Johnston. Pillow would lead the assault, with Buckner serving as a rear guard. Couriers alerted the various commands, and, as G.W. Dillon of the 18th Tennessee recorded, every man capable of bearing arms "arose from his dismal place of pretended repose," gathered gear and equipment, and marched to determined posts where they stacked arms, built good fires to keep warm, and rested "unmolested until late in the evening." Historians have termed this a half-hearted attempt to escape and have blamed an irresolute Pillow for the miscue. Apparently the shocking cold slowed the troop movements, and when the Confederates eventually started off into an attack in the Dud-

Water Batteries at Fort Donelson, looking downriver. Sketch by H. Lovie, *Frank Leslie's Illustrated Newspaper*, March 15, 1862.

ley's Hill area, conflicting orders soon brought them back to their camp-fires. One of Floyd's staff, Major Peter Otey, contended, twenty-two years after the battle, that he was at Pillow's side during the sortie and that a stray sharpshooter's bullet caused Pillow to exclaim, "Captain, our movement is discovered. It will not do to move out of our trenches un-der the circumstances." Otey protested, but Pillow sent the staff captain to tell Floyd that the attack should be deferred until morning. Floyd's reaction, according to Otey, was: "A concentrated thunderstorm in a room twelve feet square with 'blue damnation' for a non-conductor would hardly have expressed my idea of his views as expressed to me." Recover-ing his composure, Floyd told Otey to inform Pillow that "he has lost the opportunity not by being discovered, but by the delay in sending the message and the consequent delay in getting a message back to him at this late hour." It would be quite impossible to commence an attack at that time, so Pillow should indeed return the troops to the trenches. "Here was in my humble opinion," thought Otey later, "the fatal mistake at Fort Donelson."[7]

Few of the Confederate after-action reports even mentioned this sor-tie of the fourteenth. Forrest's scout, Adam Johnson, alluded to a brisk skirmish by his commander's units on that day. But most subsequent commentators, such as Johnston's biographer-son, attributed the aborted affair to a moral and psychological ascendancy of Pillow over his weak and irresolute superior, Floyd. The weather and its impact on flintlock muskets, and the fatigue of the men may also have weighed heavily on the situation. Perhaps it was truly too late in the day to have stolen a march on the Federals. True, Grant later told Buckner that reinforce-ments had not yet filled the gaps in his besieging line, but only three or four hours of sunlight remained on that snowy February afternoon, and, given the usual sluggish nature of battles during the Civil War, Pil-low and Floyd may have had a point. Buckner only shrugged stoically at Grant's idea, claiming that he had not been in command of the army at that point. The stillborn assault allowed McClernand time to slip Col-onel John MacArthur's brigade behind those of W.H.L. Wallace and Oglesby so as to strengthen his extreme right wing as it dipped down toward the river from Dudley's Hill. By mid-afternoon it was all aca-demic. Suddenly, Foote's flotilla hove into view intent upon engaging the water batteries. All thought of Confederate land action evaporated for both armies.[8]

Andrew Hull Foote had never been confident that his flotilla was ready to attack Fort Donelson. Tilghman's rough handling of the gun-boats at Fort Henry undermined Foote's optimism, despite the singular victory. The *Cincinnati* and *Essex* had been put out of action for at least two weeks. Repairs to equipment took time, but those to men's spirits took even longer. Foote needed men — at least 600 by his estimate — and nobody wanted to fight aboard his iron coffins. So, when Cullum arrived at Cairo on February 6, with orders from Halleck to push forward everything in support of Grant's isolated column, Foote had told him flatly that it could not be done, at least not just then for the navy.[9]

It took pressure from Cullum, Halleck, Grant, and the War department troubleshooter, Assistant Secretary Scott, to get the old sailor moving again. Foote finally took the hint, and grumbling by letter to Navy Secretary Welles that he would do all in his power to render the gunboats effective for a fight (however improperly manned) because "General Halleck wishes it," he ordered his boat captains to rendezvous at Paducah. Foote could not take the incompleted mortar boats, and the *Essex* and *Cincinnati* remained behind for more repairs. At 7:45 P.M. on February II, Foote cast off from the Cairo levee once more with the three Eads "City Series" ironclads, *St. Louis, Louisville,* and *Pittsburg,* while the three timberclads escorted heavily-laden troopships, *White Cloud, Fairchild, Baltic, Adams,* and *Tutt* upriver. Unfortunately, the *Lexington,* leaking badly, had to be left behind at Paducah.[10]

Finally, late in the afternoon on the twelfth, Foote's armada left Paducah for the Cumberland. The trip proved exciting for the new recruits aboard both gunboats and steamboats. Abandoned farms of unharvested corn and tobacco, deserted houses, and ransacked properties attested to the winds of war. At Eddyville, Kentucky, "fair women and brave men" turned out to wave handkerchiefs and small Union flags and even mobbed one Rebel sympathizer who dared display the Stars and Bars in defiance. Cheer after cheer went up from the fleet as the pro-Union crowd tore the hated banner from its staff. Fifteen miles upriver, the famous Hillman Brothers rolling mill represented further manifestation of Secessionism, yet, as reporters with the expedition noted, only more loyal women greeted the passage of the boats.[11]

The steamer *Alps* met the flotilla near Canton, for Grant had sent the boat to help tow the gunboats against the raging floodwaters of the river. Foote learned from her captain that the battle had already opened on land, and this irritated the naval officer. He ordered "full speed ahead" and, above Line Port (eleven miles from Fort Donelson), he signaled both gunboats and transports to close up and prepare for action. Guns were run in, loaded, and placed in battery; ammunition brought up from the holds and placed in magazines; sights adjusted on the cannon; and the decks cleared for action. But, darkness descended on the river and the onset of that bitter night of snow and sleet prevented the start of a naval attack. It was nearly midnight when the convoy came in sight of the *Carondelet's* mooring four miles below the fort.[12]

Grant and his staff rode up to the landing at 9:00 A.M. on February 14. The general immediately ordered the troops out of their comfortable berths aboard the transports. Then he went aboard Foote's flagship *St. Louis,* where he found the naval commander adamant about the flotilla's unpreparedness for combat. We know little of the ensuing discussion except that Grant convinced Foote that not only could the gunboats suppress the water batteries, but several could probably run by them and reach the Confederate rear at Dover. Thus the combined pressure from army and fleet would cause the Rebels to surrender; it was only a question of time. So persuaded, against his better judgment, Foote acquiesced to Grant's demands, and the general left the meeting in obviously high spirits—"confident of an easy victory," was the way one newsman saw it. Grant told bystanders, as he mounted his horse, that aided by the gunboats, he could capture every man in the fort.[13]

After Grant's departure, Foote signaled his boat captains to come aboard the flagship for instructions. Reviewing the situation, Foote reiterated his hesitancy to engage in battle. Firepower was less than he had possessed at Fort Henry, although the gunboats now before Fort Donelson mounted some fifty-seven heavy cannon against twelve Confederate guns. Each of the gunboats had a variety of smoothbores and rifled cannon, but Foote wanted to await arrival of his mortar boats for their high angle, long-range fire that could save him from the pounding inflicted at Fort Henry. Foote sulked for want of those mortars (sidetracked by railroad officials somewhere in Illinois, he was told before leaving Cairo) and his subordinates who knew of the slaughter aboard the boats at Fort Henry sympathized with his dilemma.[14]

The duty-bound Foote finally told them that orders must be followed, even from the army, so the attack would go forward. He wanted his captains to replenish coal bunkers, protect their steam boilers and unarmored decks from enemy fire, and, when everybody was ready, navy signal Number 958 would be hoisted and orders given to cast off. Commanders Walke *(Carondelet)* and Benjamin Dove *(Louisville),* as well as Lieutenants Hiram Paulding *(St. Louis),* Egbert Thompson *(Pittsburg),* Phelps *(Conestoga),* and William I. Gwinn *(Tyler),* then returned to their boats and directed their crews to pile chains, lumber, bags of coal, and crew hammocks against exposed areas. Tarpaulins were drawn over those white hammocks to hide them from Rebel gunners. Promptly at 1:45 P.M., the six gunboats steamed slowly out into the floodwaters of the

USS St. Louis, "City Series" Ironclad. National Archives.

Cumberland. A quarter mile above their moorage, Foote signaled to deploy for battle with *St. Louis, Louisville,* *Pittsburg,* and *Carondelet* taking the van from right to left. The timberclads, which the ironclad Tars derisively styled "la bandboxes," followed a quarter mile to the rear. At a speed of about three miles per hour (nearly a mile per hour under capacity speed in such waters), Foote's flotilla rounded the bend into full view of the fort about 2:35 P.M.[15]

Meanwhile, Confederate headquarters personnel finally remembered Ross's request to fire on the Yankee transports. By this time, however, most of the Federals had gone ashore. Despite Culbertson's reluctance to join Ross in such fire, for fear that it might bring on a counter-bombardment, the Confederate gunners fired several well-placed rounds. They apparently clipped the bows of several transports and caused much consternation among the boat captains. Then, just as Ross really applied himself to such work, Foote's squadron appeared. Several of the gunboats lagged behind, claimed the Confederates afterward, and Foote's flagship seemed to lose control in the swift current and almost rammed the river bank. Gradually, however, the gunboats regained control and steamed slowly forward in battle array toward the guns of the fort.[16]

The opening shots of the engagement occurred about 2:38 P.M., with firing becoming general for both sides within the half-hour. Neither antagonist drew blood at first, for the wild firing merely sought the range. The water batteries confined their fire to the Columbiad and 6.5-inch rifle. In fact, Pillow's strict orders caused Culbertson to hold back with his 32-pounders until the gunboats reached a barrier of intertwined logs and tree limbs in the river, about nine hundred yards from the batteries. High water had negated the obstacles' effectiveness, but the Confederate gunners knew the range at this point. As the gunboats came closer, the Confederates clearly picked out the poorly camouflaged white hammocks piled high against the *St. Louis's* pilot house. The wind had blown away the tarpaulins, and cannon from both shore batteries opened with a fury on the boats. As Ross suggested in his private journal, the air above and around was full of shot, solid case and shell, while the river below was almost continuous spray.[17]

The gunboats first opened a slow, deliberate return fire from their bow guns, while advancing steadily against the swift current. Foote signaled Walke at one point to ration his fire until they came within point-blank range — the tactic which had worked so well against Fort Henry. The timberclads remained so far behind as to be quite ineffective, although they initially drew off some of the Confederate gunners' attention from the ironclads. Very soon into the fight, a priming wire became lodged in the vent of the 6.5-inch rifle at the upper battery, causing its crew to think an enemy shell had knocked the piece out of action. Soon they were able to work it once more, only to have it jam again. Just as the situation looked hopeless to Ross, ten or twelve of his men under Sergeant Patrick Cook, who died later in captivity at Chicago, sprang to the rear of the position, grabbed a large log, and then mounted the parapet in front of the cannon to drive home the cannon ball which was causing the problem. At another point in the fight, one of Ross's nervous young cannoneers lost his rammer over the parapet during the loading process. Ross told him to retrieve it, as "we must have the rammer." The youth coolly mounted the earthwork and secured the tool despite the fact that "a shot from the enemy could easily have killed six or eight of the men had it come in the neighborhood," noted Ross. Such acts of heroism took place all over the water batteries that afternoon.[18]

The tempo of battle quickened as both sides increased their rate of fire with the clock approaching 3:15 P.M. As the gunboats closed to point-blank range, their fire increasingly overshot the water batteries, arching ineffectively over the hill and into the Rebel camps beyond. A newsman aboard the flagship thought that the Confederate fire was far more accurate, and Ross himself decided that "a singular paralysis" took possession of the flotilla while the southerner's fire "was better sustained." Nonetheless, Foote's boats pressed to within four hundred yards of the lower battery by 3:30 P.M. Both sides now felt the full fury of the short-range battle. The naval Tars thought for sure that their shots had caused many Rebels to abandon their works in terror. Confederate spokesmen later denied such allegations of cowardice. Ross claimed, "our work grew very warm yet the men became cooler, in proportion." By this time, many Confederate onlookers had gathered from the outer defense perimeter to see the spectacle, among them, Nathan Bedford Forrest and his staff. Caught up in the pandemonium, the profane cavalryman turned to his preacher aide, Major D.C. Kelly, and yelled, "Parson, for God's sake, pray; nothing but God Almighty can save that fort."[19]

The Confederate generals may have had the same thought. Only moments before, Floyd had wired Johnston (ostensibly now at Edgefield opposite Nashville) that the gunboats were advancing, with fighting becoming general along the whole line. "I will make the best defense in my power," Floyd assured his superior. As the river battle reached its crescendo, Floyd telegraphed again excitedly, "the fort cannot hold out twenty minutes. Our river batteries working admirably." Obviously, Johnston would not understand what was really happening. Pillow sent a similarly vague message to Governor Harris, and down at the water batteries many of the gunners were not sure whether victory or defeat lay within their grasp. Men dropped dead, wounded, or just exhausted around the guns, and the Union naval shells tore up the earthworks and sandbag revetments as well as knocking down the flagpole.[20]

Yet, Foote had miscalculated, and the carnage proved worse aboard the gunboats. One 32-pounder shot struck the *St. Louis* pilothouse, passing through an inch and one-half of iron plate and more than fifteen inches of oak timber. Shell fragments ricocheted around in the pilothouse, mortally wounding one pilot, F.A. Riley of Cincinnati, and catching Foote himself in the ankle. The grizzled but game old salt seized the wheel from the dying Riley and steered the craft despite yet another wound in the arm. By now other shots riddled the *St. Louis,* making her unmaneuverable. Deck planking and armor plating were both battered and crushed, boat hoists blown away, the "chimneys" or smokestacks perforated with their guy-wires snapped — the boat was a shambles. Boat captain Paulding told Foote that the steering mechanism had been badly damaged by the shot which killed Riley. The gunboat slowly drifted out of the fight.[21]

Elsewhere, the *Louisville* took one 128-pound projectile at an angle formed by the upper deck and pilothouse; a 32-pounder swept the craft from bow to stern; another Columbiad shot shattered the gun carriage of an 8-inch Dahlgren gun, spattering Commander Dove with blood and brains from three decapitated crewmen serving the piece. Still a fourth shot (which some claimed actually came from the *Tyler* by mistake) put this gunboat completely out of action by severing her tiller cables. Only the *Pittsburg* and *Carondelet* remained in the fight. The *Pittsburg's* captain soon retired because his craft was in danger of sinking, and his crew could not serve guns and pumps at the same time.[22]

The Confederates rejoiced at their success. The close range — some claimed 350 yards or less — produced a thirty to thirty-five degree depressed, right angle fire against the boats. The gunners could see their shots going home aboard the gunboats. Private John G. Frequa on one of the 32-pounder gun crews in the water batteries shouted to his mates: "Now boys, see me take a chimney!" True to his word, his next shot carried away both the smokestack and flagstaff of the *St.Louis.* "Come on, you cowardly scoundrels, you are not at Fort Henry," he screamed, tossing his cap in the air. He sent his next shot through one of the vessel's gunports for good measure. The shriek of the heavy shells over them was enough to strain the nerves of the strongest man, recalled Adam

Rankin Johnson, who watched the fight nearby. But fright turned to elation as the sight of a wavering enemy cheered the powder-blackened defenders of the fort.[23]

The Union navy had not expected such punishment from the Confederate batteries, despite Foote's hesitancy to attack. Only the *Carondelet* continued to brave the Rebel fusillade—by its standing so close to the batteries, Ross worried that the gunboat would send landing parties to capture the works. Everybody had determined to sell their lives dearly, claimed Ross, using staves, handspikes, and sponger staffs in the place of customary but non-existent cutlasses. Ross need not have worried. Within minutes, this lone gunboat was also reduced to a floating hulk, with smashed decks, shattered stauncheons, and anchors, as well as red-tipped smokestacks and flagstaff shot away. Adding insult to injury, one of her gun crews improperly loaded a 42-pounder in the heat of battle, with a resulting explosion which prematurely wounded everyone at the station. Then, the retiring *Pittsburg* rammed *Carondelet's* stern, damaging its starboard rudder and forcing Walke's boat to ease even closer under the Confederate guns, to avoid a rocky shoal on the opposite side of the river. The defenders used this as a pretext to try to sink the boat as it backed and hawed to get downstream. As a final gesture, the water battery gun captains focused upon the boat's less-protected parts by skipping their cannon balls across the surface of the water. Another shot went through one of *Carondelet's* bow portals, decapitating more Tars, who had defied their leader's orders to duck when a shot could be seen coming their way. "We had then no mercy on them," was the way an exhilarated Ross summed it up.[24]

Foote subsequently tried to rationalize his bitter defeat. The gunboat assault "would in fifteen minutes more, could the action have continued, have resulted in the capture of the fort bearing upon us, as the enemy was running from his batteries," he contended officially. A week later, he told his wife, "we came within an ace of getting it as 200 yards further would have placed us so that their guns could not bear upon us and then we would have mowed them down." He slighted the Confederate victory as "the hotly contested, but unequal fight," since "the accident rendering two of our gunboats suddenly helpless in the narrow and swift current," as well as the fact that "the enemy must have brought over twenty guns to bear upon our boats from the upper battery and the main fort on the hill," while "we could only return the fire with twelve bow guns from the four boats." Foote overlooked some salient points. The Cumberland River, even at flood stage, was much narrower than the Tennessee River at Fort Henry. His four gunboats could not advance quickly due to the current, and they could not maneuver to apply broadside fire to the fort. Confederate marksmanship with plunging fire ensured that Foote would not run past the batteries and get into their rear.[25]

The Confederates also had some answers to Foote's contentions. If his boats had fired with the deliberation and accuracy of the *Carondelet* on the previous day, decided Lieutenant Bedford, he could have dismounted the Columbiad and 6.5-inch rifle, demolished the 32-pounders at his leisure, and shelled the fort "to his heart's content." Certainly Foote's decision to close rapidly with the Confederate guns remained questionable, if explicable from his Fort Henry success. His longer-ranged ordnance could have hammered the Confederates at ranges up to 1,600 yards. The consistent overshooting of the shore batteries during the fight proved this fact. Writing to Admiral David D. Porter the next November, Rear Admiral John Rodgers, who but for politics might have commanded on the twin rivers instead of Foote, observed that ironclad vessels were made to fight wooden vessels and forts at distances which would leave the ironclads impenetrable to enemy gunfire. The enthusiastic but misguided Foote had violated that tenet, Rodgers claimed. Foote was from the old school of sea-fighting sailors—rapid fire at close range to batter the opponent into submission. As Bedford observed, "flushed with his victory at Fort Henry, his success there paved the way for his defeat at Donelson."[26]

The water batteries' fighting ended about 4:30 P.M., with three of the four ironclads drifting helplessly downstream with the flood. Cheer after cheer echoed all over the Confederate positions, until the hills and hollows surrounding Dover reverberated with shouts of victory. Lieutenant Colonel Alfred Robb of the 49th Tennessee passed a flask of spirits among the tired gunners in the water batteries, helping celebrate victory and revive body and spirit. Floyd and Pillow rode down to the river to congratulate the defenders. Singling out Lieutenant Bedford, the generals promised him that if the batteries would continue to keep back the enemy gunboats, the infantry would hold the Federal land forces at bay. In light of what was about to transpire, Bedford remembered ruefully some twenty-nine years later that his earlier observation of the thousands of Yankee reinforcements pouring ashore from transports on the morning of February 14 caused him to wonder "if these officers were able to fulfill the promise, or if they were merely indulging in an idle habit of braggadocio."[27]

The Confederate celebration continued long after dark. Floyd sent a cryptic telegram to Johnston about 5:15 P.M.: "The gunboats have been driven back, two it is said seriously injured. I think the fight is over today." But he made no mention of any plans for a counterattack. Pillow, signing himself "Commander," penned a more verbose and enthusiastic communique to Polk at Columbus (still his nominal superior, one supposes, for why else would he suddenly remember to send him a telegram?), and the euphoria of victory had overcome the realities of the situation. There was cause for rejoicing—no loss of guns, a few wounded, and only one subaltern killed inside the main fort by a stray shot. All this despite nearly three hundred shells lobbed into Confederate lines by Foote's gunboats. Statistically, the Rebel gunners had retaliated with about the same number of shots, but they at least hit 50 percent of their shots. What a fillip for cold, tired, and besieged defenders.[28]

Downstream it was different. Dusk and gloom settled over the defeated Union flotilla. All four ironclads were out of action; the *Pittsburg* was leaking so badly that it could not even make the berthing at the landing; the captain simply tied fast to a tree along the riverbank about two miles below the water batteries, prompting Confederate rumors that the ironclad had been sunk completely. Foote made ready to take the whole flotilla back to Cairo for repairs. He had lost eleven seamen killed or mortally wounded, and over forty otherwise incapacitated. His men's morale was crushed, and his own health seriously impaired by injuries. That evening he fumed in his cabin. "To see brave officers and men, who may say they will go where I lead them, fall by my side," he wrote a friend; "it makes me sad to lead them to almost certain death." He would never admit miscalculation, but he told a newsman after the fight that he had been in six other engagements with forts and ships, "but never was under so severe a fire before." Even the correspondent decided that he had seen enough of war afloat. "My curiosity is satisfied," he declared, henceforth he would prefer a land view.[29]

Grant had watched the naval debacle, and it sickened him also. Saying nothing officially about the battle, he would let the navy make its own excuses for defeat. He had done nothing to supplement the gunboat attack with any land diversion—joint army-navy cooperation had not progressed that far at this stage of the war. He confided in his memoirs many years later that the sun set that evening, leaving the army confronting Fort Donelson anything but comforted over its prospects for victory. He wrote his wife, Julia, that night that the taking of the fort "bids fair to be a long job." Due to the heavily fortified and re-inspired enemy, he did not know just when it would end, and he bluntly urged her to pack up and go to her sister's family for the duration. He did not know when he might return to see her. The navy had definitely jolted Grant's timetable and morale.[30]

Halleck knew nothing of the critical turn of events on the Cumberland that evening. Bothered more by numerous small irritations that plagued his efforts to reinforce Grant and Foote, the general seemed irritable to all around him. He fretted about extension of the telegraph line across the Ohio River and on to Fort Henry. Until it was finished, he could get news of the twin rivers expedition only by steamboat. Various ill-disciplined reserve units at Cairo and Quincy, Illinois bothered him. He wanted lame ducks weeded out of his department, and he told Cullum to put one unit to work on constructing earthworks so that they could make some sort of contribution to the war effort. When Senator Milton S. Latham wired from Washington about rumors of C.F. Smith's alleged intemperance and disloyalty, Halleck shot back: "Don't permit C.F. Smith's nomination [for higher rank] to be rejected. He is the best officer in my command." Indeed, Halleck had his troubles, but Grant's safety remained uppermost in his mind.[31]

Would Polk attack Grant's line of communications at Cairo? Halleck ordered Cullum to reconnoiter in that direction. Until Halleck received Foote's somewhat evasive report about the gunboat defeat at Fort Donelson, he had little to worry about concerning Grant's communications with Paducah. Matters seemed so well in hand that Halleck named Grant to command a newly formed District of West Tennessee and gave Grant's old Cairo district to William T. Sherman. Sherman and Cullum were working hard to both speed reinforcements and guard Grant's rear. Lurking behind every move in the West, however, was fear of what Albert Sidney Johnston would do about Grant's force.[32]

For a time, the Federal high command believed the Johnston would surely concentrate his army on the Cumberland. Grant's dispatches hinted at reinforcement of the Fort Donelson garrison, and McClellan in Washington wrote Buell on February 13: "Watch Fort Donelson closely. I am not too certain as to the result there." Buell was unsure also, and he continually queried Halleck to make sure "Old Brains" knew what he was doing. Buell's own ponderous movement effectively fixed Johnston, and the Ohioan dismissed any threat to Grant, telling McClellan at 6:00 P.M. on the fourteenth: "The only apprehension I have now is for his gunboats."[33]

Buell's fears for Foote came from erroneous intelligence about low water in the river, not the water batteries defeat. The Ohio departmental commander reported dutifully to Washington that he sent reinforcements to Halleck but that his own line of communications was stretched thin and open to Rebel raiders. In some ways Buell stayed in touch more with Washington than Halleck. All told, the top Union generals played

war on the map and via telegraph. Only Foote and Grant prosecuted
the conflict in earnest before Fort Donelson. Regrettably, at this very moment, some of the worst headquarters machinations took place concerning replacement of Grant himself.[34]

Following Halleck's failure to secure Ethan Allen Hitchcock for command on the twin rivers, he turned to Buell, offering to transfer Grant
and Sherman to operations solely on the Tennessee axis, if the Ohioan
would go down and take over the campaign on the Cumberland. Nothing happened, and on February 14, McClellan deflated Halleck's latest
scheme for theater unification under his personal charge by suggesting
that David Hunter in Kansas would actually outrank Halleck (who had
Hunter in mind for one of his own subdivisions in the unified command). Moreover, wired McClellan, what disposition did Halleck intend to make of Hitchcock? "If you do not go in person to the Tennessee
and Cumberland," said McClellan to his St. Louis subordinate, "I shall
probably write Buell to take the line of the Tennessee, [sic] so far as Nashville is concerned." Halleck wired back that for the moment he had no
definite plan beyond the capture of Fort Donelson and Clarksville. Anything other than that would depend upon the Confederates. Blissfully
unaware of such concerns, Grant recorded in his memoirs that he had
entertained absolutely no idea that there would be any other engagement on land "unless I brought it on myself." The generals at St. Louis,
Louisville, and Washington thought otherwise.[35]

Union fears of a Confederate concentration against Grant proved
groundless. Johnston and Beauregard apparently accepted the notion
that the pivotal battle would occur at Dover, and the Creole wrote his
friend, Rodger Pryor on the fourteenth, that the loss of Fort Donelson
would be followed by "consequences too lamentable to be alluded to." All
Beauregard had to offer were words. "General Johnston is doing his best
but what can he do against such tremendous odds?" he lamented. The
Confederacy had to give up some minor points and concentrate to save
the most important ones, or "we will lose all of them in succession," Beauregard told Pryor. Therein lay the rub, however. Just what was "minor"
versus "important?" At some point on St. Valentine's Day, Johnston read
the frantic dispatches from Floyd and Pillow, and they caused him to
urge Hardee to speed the retreat from Bowling Green. To the generals
at Fort Donelson, however, Johnston could send only his cryptic and forever enigmatic wire: "If you lose the fort, bring your troops to Nashville
if possible." For over a century, people have tried to fathom precisely
what Sidney Johnston meant with those words.[36]

Method, not goal, became the problem. That night, in a war council

held at one of the general's headquarters in Dover, the Confederate command attempted to comply with Johnston's orders. Floyd claimed later
that two days of battle had convinced him of Grant's aversion to attacking again but that he had "no doubt whatever that their whole available
force on the Western waters could and would be concentrated here if
it was deemed necessary to reduce our position." The Confederates did
not know how many men Grant now had arrayed against them, but they
estimated nearly 40,000. They saw that their own recourse lay in dislodging Grant's forces "on our left, and thus to pass our people into the
open country lying southward towards Nashville." That had been the battle plan interrupted by Foote's intrusion. There was no reason why it
should be changed for action on February 15.[37]

Then, Pillow took the floor. His scouts provided a clear picture of the
enemy situation in the attack sector. McClernand's division covered
both the Forge and Wynn's Ferry roads south of town. Moreover, the
water-borne reinforcements reaching Grant had partly bolstered the
Union right flank, claimed Pillow, erroneously, for they had really gone
to Wallace and C.F. Smith. Pillow also assumed incorrectly that the Federals had massed siege artillery covering each debouchment or access
road through Confederate lines. Finally, the political general viewed the
Federals as concentrated in three distinct "encampments" rather than a
continuous line, and that the thick undergrowth of brush and black-jack
between such concentrations made "it impossible to advance or maneuver any considerable body of troops." So, he proposed an attack plan of
his own. He wanted to launch the assault on the left using Bushrod Johnson's division and the elite 2d Kentucky from Buckner's division. Once
this attack had sent McClernand's men fleeing along the Wynn's Ferry
road, and compressed upon the Union center, then Buckner could attack with the rest of his command and catch the panic-stricken enemy
in flank and rear. Grant would be pinned against the river at his downstream landings — or so Pillow thought.[38]

When Pillow finished, Buckner injected his own views. He immediately vetoed the Tennessean's use of Roger Hanson's crack Kentuckians.
Pillow backed off, claiming only that he wanted a more substantial unit
to bolster the assault waves since "a very large portion of the force I had
to fight [with] were fresh troops and badly armed." Buckner then advanced a modification of Pillow's plan. He would intervene more directly in the battle by cleaning out Federal artillery positions along the
Wynn's Ferry road at the same time that Pillow was rolling up McClernand's extreme right flank closer to the river. Buckner felt that this would
"lessen the labors" for Pillow, and "strike the enemy in a more vital point."

Pillow agreed, and the two decided to leave Heiman's brigade at his important post in the Confederate center, using this unit as a hinge around which the attacks would pivot, as well as shield for Buckner's right flank during the attack. Floyd gave his blessing to the plan that called for the attack to begin at dawn.[39]

The trio then sent for Bushrod Johnson (who had not been privy to the council despite his rank), and the brigade commanders. It was past midnight when these men walked into the council room, knocking snow from boots and overcoats. At least one brigade commander, Colonel John W. Head who was in charge of the main fort, did not attend or send a deputy. This proved unfortunate since one of his regiments—the 30th Tennessee—would cover Buckner's whole evacuated sector of the outer trenches on the far right. At any event, once Floyd had called the briefing to order, Pillow took charge, outlining scope and purpose of the attack and designating each unit's place in the assault. Only Heiman raised the issue of inadequate manning for the evacuated outer earthworks. What if the Yankees counterattacked, he asked? Floyd brushed him aside saying that he could fall back into the fort "or act as circumstances would dictate." To Bushrod Johnson, "all the plans were skillfully and minutely adjusted" even to the point that in the event of failure, "a rallying point, far beyond the enemy's lines was designated," for survivors. Chief Engineer Gilmer was not as sure. He recalled later that details for carrying out the plan remained unclear when it came to rations to be carried, whether blankets and knapsacks were to be taken or left behind, what would be the marching order for the actual escape after the battle, as well as who would take the advance, and who would command the rear of that escape column. Even Bushrod Johnson admitted, several months later, some procedural weaknesses with the planned attack, noting: "How and when the retreat should commence was not determined in conference, and these were clearly things to be determined at a subsequent period." There was no proposition made to retreat from the battlefield, he added, "and no determination made to do so." If such had been the case, then the details of provisions, clothing, and additional ammunition would have been discussed, "and such preparations made previously to the battle would have greatly loaded down and encumbered the men in the fight," claimed Johnson in retrospect.[40]

The council of war broke up about 1:00 A.M., having established a planned jump-off for the assault of 5:00 A.M.—well before daylight in February. Meanwhile, the brigade commanders were to move their units into position by 4:30 A.M. Every participant left the meeting with a different notion as to what would happen after the successful attack. Pillow held that his troops would return to the defenses and that victory would be so complete that time would permit retrieval of equipment, rations, and the units guarding the trenches and main fort during the assault. Then everyone could commence the retreat. Buckner and his subordinates thought that nobody would return to the trenches after the battle. Thus Colonel John C. Brown's brigade packed three days' rations in their haversacks and appeared in "heavy marching order" to commence the attack. In Buckner's view, Head, Heiman, and the rest of the garrison would have to be sacrificed — a notion which incensed Tennesseans such as Randal MacGavock when they learned about it.[41]

No doubt the plans were poorly conceived, hastily made, and improperly implemented on the crucial issue of what would happen after the attack itself. Such a product of divided command and divisive personalities became apparent only after the fact. For the moment, everyone was determined and enthusiastic about success. Pillow vowed to stand and fight for Tennessee soil and to destroy the invader. Buckner was equivocal, even at this point, having been forced out of his beloved Kentucky and not at all sure when he and his fellow Kentuckians might return to reclaim the state for the Confederacy. Bushrod Johnson — ever the cipher — seemed to one onlooker "as gloomy and wore as anxious a look when it was known that the boats had been driven off as when the fight was hottest." Nobody could say what the adopted Tennesseans felt about the plan. That left Floyd, who knew Sidney Johnston's orders were to save the army. He alone, as senior commander, should have ensured that battle plans were made clear to all participants — perhaps he thought they were, at the time. His subsequent actions implied agreement with Pillow's understanding of the scheme. In any event, this was the situation when the Rebels started to break Grant's stranglehold on Fort Donelson in what Gideon Pillow would style, "the battle of Dover."[42]

CHAPTER 10

Confederate Blunders on the Third Day

St. valentine's day did not bring the decisive result expected by Grant and feared by his opponents. The vaunted gunboats had not reduced Fort Donelson. Now, shortly before dawn on February 15, the high-pitched Rebel yell surged up from Barn Hollow—a screeching sound symbolizing men's frustrations with cold, snow, and Yankee bullets; a searching cry for freedom and warm food. All during the predawn hours, Bushrod Johnson's division had shuffled through mud and snow, against a biting wind to take positions far to the left and 200 yards outside the Confederate defense perimeter in anticipation of mounting the attack. His massed regiments sat astride a little-known road—noted variously on maps as the East Road, or simply a river road leading to the Cumberland Iron Works and eventually upriver to Cumberland City and Clarksville. Buckner's division slid from its earthworks and camps closer to the main fort and occupied the trenches evacuated by Johnson's men. Slick roads and tired soldiers delayed both movements, and the attackers straggled into place later than planned by the generals. Still, Sergeant Spot F. Terrell of Stewart County's own 49th Tennessee noted that Saturday, the fifteenth, came on cold but with snow already melting by the time the sun "was shooting forth her butiful [sic] rays upon the tree tops.[1]

At the water batteries, the gunners had repaired battle damage from the previous day, and awaited reappearance of the gunboats. Captain Ross surmised that the reason the enemy never attacked in the morning was because of the sun's rising upriver in the direction which would affect the naval gunners' aim. Nonetheless he wanted to be ready. Torches provided heat and light for overnight preparations, which included fashioning makeshift gunsights—"disparts" he called them—to compensate for the disparity between thickness of muzzle and breech in aiming the heavy cannon. These triangular contraptions, when lashed to the top of the barrels, would ostensibly enable Ross's gunners to "aim exactly" at the enemy using Foote's run-in-close tactics displayed the day before and at Fort Henry. Ross also had his ordnance sergeant fill shells with molten lead to increase their striking power against the ironclads. All the preparations proved unnecessary, for the night passed peacefully on the river, and sunrise would see the battle elsewhere.[2]

The staging operation out on the defense perimeter produced some anxious moments for the Confederates. Because of his ill health, Colonel Thomas Davidson's brigade left late for the attack rendezvous. Brown's brigade also lingered in its trenches near the Eddyville road, waiting for the garrison troops from the main fort to replace them. Brown finally left, marching off disgustedly in defiance of Buckner's specific order to hold fast. He left only a token force behind him. When Head's people finally appeared, they found that they had to cover three-quarters of a mile of earthworks, facing C.F. Smith's entire Federal division massed on the ridge across the ravine to the west. Even Buckner had to drop off some of his men in other undefended areas of the outer trench line, nominally held by Johnson's people, in order to support the artillery which would not leave the lines in the assault. Fortunately, Federal pickets detected none of this commotion during the dark, stormy night.[3]

Meanwhile, Pillow massed Bushrod Johnson's division in column-by-brigade formation for the attack. Forrest's cavalry took the lead, and sometime around 6:00 A.M. (Pillow claimed 5:15 A.M., subordinate Federal commanders noted an earlier arousal, but McClernand emphatically stated "6 o'clock A.M.", and Randal MacGavock insisted the attack was made at least one hour after sunrise) the whole mass of men started off into the murky half-light. A cross-section of young southern manhood embarked on their first real crusade in battle. Some 8,000 to 10,000 strong, they aimed at the Federal flank anchored atop Dudley's Hill. Moving to within a third of a mile of this landmark, they began to draw skirmish fire from sleepy Union pickets. Skirmishers of the 26th Mississippi and Captain J.F. Overton's company of cavalry clashed with outposts of Colonel Isaac Pugh's 41st Illinois, as the attackers struggled up a country lane into a field of 400 or 500 acres atop the hill.[4]

The snow and underbrush plus inexperience nearly confounded the Confederate attack at this point. The Mississippians tried three times to form, yet the intricate drill maneuvers of the era left them fifty yards to the rear and right of the exact place where their battle line should have been. Such comic gyrations of unit drill seemed deadly serious at the time to brigade commander Baldwin, and even Forrest decided that the natural obstacles of this battlefield would make it difficult for his cavalry to "act with celerity and cohesion." Pugh's brisk and well-sustained musketry further added to the confusion, enabling McClernand's main units to fall into formation. Nevertheless, Pillow and Johnson made contact with the enemy long before Buckner's units even reached the earthworks astride the Wynn's Ferry road egress. The third day at Fort Donelson already promised to be a long, bitter if somewhat poorly coordinated struggle between the young soldiers.[5]

The Rebel attack caught McClernand's division passing another cold and restless night. Sharpshooter activity led Lieutenant Colonel Thomas G. Ransom to turn out his 11th Illinois and place them in line of battle for two hours at one point. The division generally stayed in makeshift bivouacs, Daniel Brush recalling that nobody anticipated the onset of general battle since the troops had become quite accustomed to continual picket firing. When the widespread firing indicated something more serious at dawn, the Federals took their places in line with deliberation but no particular sense of urgency. Still, even noncombatants such as the 44th Indiana's sutler, James R. Devor, grabbed a musket. The Federals soon discovered that they had too much ground to cover—McClernand's cavalry had found that out the day before. The East or river road crossed flooded Lick Creek at Dr. Smith's ford beyond Dudley's Hill, and no one could be sure that route was adequately blocked to an enemy sortie. McClernand had sent McArthur's brigade to do the job late on Friday afternoon, but the time of day, the gunboat battle, and general troop fatigue had left the task incomplete. McClernand planned more attention to his right on the fifteenth, although Grant had assured him that the Confederates would not bring on a battle. Suddenly it was dawn, and the army commander was proven wrong. The "Long Roll" sounded on the drums indicating trouble, and neither McClernand nor McArthur had time to worry about the river road.[6]

Somewhere off to the Federal right near the river, Colonels Silas Noble and T. Lyle Dickey had their Illinois and U.S. regular cavalrymen patrolling the area, but even that had been left to luck in the cold winter night. A portion of Dickey's command had actually ridden two miles out on the Forge road and remained bivouacked at Randolph's Forge that morning, completely out of contact with the threatened division. Only infantry pickets warned that "the enemy were advancing in strong force," leaving McClernand's officers and men no time even for a customary cup of coffee. Throughout the commands, men went hungry and were even pitifully short of ammunition since their supply wagons had not kept pace with army movements. By 7:00 A.M. a formally arrayed Confederate line of battle, covered by artillery fire from inside the trench line, swept onto McClernand's position. The tenor of the fighting became well established over the next two hours: there were sharp fire-fights between individual regiments and brigades, slashing thrusts by Confederate infantry and cavalry in combined assaults, and stubborn resistance from determined Federals. Localized Confederate gains came only because their opponents ran out of ammunition and suffered deci-mating casualties which forced withdrawal through scrub oak and thick-ets, across gullies, intermittent fields and woods, and over a battlefield obscured for the most part by black powder smoke from muskets and cannon. Both sides came poorly equipped for the battle, with many southerners handling single-shot squirrel guns and shotguns, even old "Buck and Ball" muskets, while the northern soldiery fared no better with their many Austrian muskets. It proceeded to be a slugfest at close range, with one Virginia battery commander noting the battlefield so covered with woods that he had to follow the progress of the fight more with the ear than with the eye, and several times his unit ceased firing because of difficulty distinguishing friend from foe. The overall picture of the morning's work was one of a progressive bending back of the Union line until it stood nearly at a right angle to the main axis of Mc-Clernand's position along the Wynn's Ferry road.[7]

McClernand was in trouble by 8:00 A.M. Confederate infantry and cavalry had passed around the eastern and southern slopes of Dudley's Hill and into the upper valley of Lick Creek, where they cleaned out cavalry resistance and rapidly outflanked McArthur's position. While the compacted Federal line thus provided more concentrated firepower for stopping the main thrusts of Simonton, McCausland, Baldwin, and Wharton against the bluecoats at the Forge road, this overlapping of the Federal right flank by superior numbers of Confederates and an exhaus-tion of ammunition forced regiment after regiment to pull back. Then, regimental and company officers such as Colonel Michael Lawler of the 18th Illinois went down with wounds, contributing to local demoraliza-tion. McArthur's men soon bolted and ran.[8]

McClernand called for help. Instructing his brigade commanders to hold as long as possible, he sent two staff lieutenants, Erastus S. Jones and Julian Carter, off to inform Grant and Lew Wallace of the impend-ing disaster. Wallace had already heard the muffled sounds of battle, alerted his own regiments, and awaited developments. The Hoosier gen-eral wondered about what was transpiring off to his right; he thought McClernand might be up to his old tricks of commencing a fight despite Grant's orders. Wallace realized his mistake only when Major Mason Brayman, McClernand's adjutant, rode up breathlessly to explain the situation. Great danger portended, shouted the gray-haired Brayman,

adding that no one could predict the result if McClernand did not receive immediate help. Wallace tried to calm him, but there was little that
he could do because his orders were to "prevent the enemy from escap-
ing." Without more information, said Wallace, he could only send his
own courier, Lieutenant Addison Ware, to get more instructions from
headquarters.[9]

Several messengers therefore descended upon Mrs. Crisp's farmhouse
about 8:30 A.M., looking for Grant and bearing news of action on the
right wing. They received no guidance, however. During the night, the
injured Foote had summoned his friend Grant to consult aboard the flagship. The naval officer explained that he was too incapacitated to mount
a horse and ride through the sleet and snow to visit the army commander. Grant, feeling that the Rebels would do nothing in his absence,
obligingly rode off to the steamboat, landing at first light. He wanted
to see the damaged gunboats anyway. He left orders that neither McClernand nor Wallace were to bring on an engagement until further orders,
but C.F. Smith apparently received no similar directive, nor did he know
of Grant's absence.[10]

The threatening news caused Captain William S. Hillyer, one of
Grant's aides, to saddle his horse and dash for the steamboat landing.
He reached the river just as his superior emerged from Foote's gunboat. Apparently, the intervening woods and river bends had muffled
the sounds of battle, and Grant was visibly upset from his discussion
with Foote about the return of the gunboats to Cairo for repairs. Foote
was obviously shaken from his defeat and from the task of burying hor-
ribly mutilated corpses of his seamen on the riverbank. All he could
think of was getting the mortar boats and the more powerful gunboat,
Benton, before returning to the battle. He promised Grant that he would
leave two relatively undamaged gunboats, but the general saw scant comfort in that. Carnage lay in evidence all over the gundecks, and Grant
realized his army had no alternative to a lengthy siege. Thus he was in
no mood for Hillyer's ill-tidings. Hillyer seemed livid with fear, recalled
Grant later, so the pair lost no time in galloping over mud-frozen and
slick roads to headquarters.[11]

Meanwhile, the aides had returned to McClernand and Wallace with
the news of Grant's absence. Wallace had already decided to send reinforcements to his colleague. By 8:45 A.M. Colonel Charles Cruft's brigade
(25th Kentucky, 44th Indiana) had marched to the sounds of the battle,
leaving only Thayer's men and random skirmishers to cover the upper
Indian Creek valley. Cruft found McClernand completely engaged, but
the Illinois general still placed these reinforcements in reserve, a fact

which raised Lew Wallace's ire when he learned of it later. He could not understand McClernand's request for help if he had no immediate need for the men. Apparently the Confederates were not alone with person-ality problems among their senior commanders.[12]

Buckner finally committed his division in a desultory attack across no-man's land in the Wynn's Ferry road area held by W.H.L. Wallace's brigade, and near McClernand's command post at the Ambus Ross house. Unfortunately for the Kentuckian and his men, Rebel artillery support stampeded some of the grayclads by dropping short rounds among them, and McClernand was permitted the luxury of time to shift units to counter the new Confederate surge in this sector. The relent-less pounding by 6- and 12-pounders from the guns in the Confederate trenches and the steady, mounting pressure of southern infantrymen along the whole line simply wore down Union resistance. Even when Cruft's men were finally thrown into the battle, the effort ended disas-trously. Colonel James Shackelford's 25th Kentucky mistook Oglesby's 8th and 29th Illinois for Confederates as it dashed forward. Uniforms had become virtually indistinguishable by this time in the swirl of black powder smoke which hung over the battlefield. Some Federals still wore militia gray at Fort Donelson, while a sprinkling of blue cloth remained in evidence among the Confederate ranks. As Oglesby noted later, "the enemy skulked behind every hiding place, and sought refuge in the oak leaves, between which and their uniforms there was so strong a resem-blance." Shackelford's mistake was explicable, if fatal. Holding cartridge boxes aloft to indicate the cause for withdrawl, Oglesby's men melted to the rear. They joined countless others in Bufford Hollow near a hospi-tal at the Rollins house, where even medics of the 25th Kentucky soon came under hostile fire.[13]

Thus by late morning, Pillow and Bushrod Johnson had carried Con-federate fortunes to the threshold of victory. "Our success against the right wing was complete," declared Gilmer. The attack had opened both river and Forge roads and had driven two of McClernand's brigades off the field in disorder. The way to Nashville and freedom lay open to the southern army. Avowedly, Federal defeat resulted mostly from fatigue, supply shortages, and several inept tactical moves. Curiously, however, the Rebels could not administer a *coup de main* and end the fighting. Much of this resulted from tactical doctrine of the day. From what his people could see through the intervening brush, recorded Captain S.B. Marks (who succeeded Lawler in command of the 18th Illinois), the Con-federates advanced in columns six or eight files deep. This formation was well suited to street fighting: a surge forward, delivery of fire, and brief retirement to reload while the next rank repeated the maneuver — the whole mass presenting a steamroller effect. So rapid was the firing, said Marks, that he could distinguish no interval, and this unrelenting pressure consistently pushed the Federals back.[14]

These were battlefield lessons from the Mexican War, supplemented by peacetime tactical manual authors such as Jomini, Mahan, Scott, and Halleck. These lessons had been imparted that previous summer and autumn in training camps by citizen-soldier leaders. Effective musketry demanded close-order formations — a line, or when a decisive impact on a defender might be desired, by column. Small columns applied to a salient point worked well, but large ones proved unwieldy, pronounced the sages of the era, although it remains difficult to know which one truly distinguished the fighting on the Cumberland. Columns certainly deprived a formation of much of its firepower, and apparently the Confederates were given to using the unwieldy large column at Fort Donelson. Perhaps the tactic of firing and falling back in rapid repetition offset the firepower problem, and it may be that Pillow and Bushrod Johnson actually followed the Jominian precept that a skillful mixture of deployed lines and columns, acting alternately according to circumstances, would ultimately produce success. The usual command and control problems on nineteenth-century battlefields were also a factor, and the noise and confusion of this battle hampered perfect coordination of action by commanders. Bushrod Johnson's fetish for maintaining "a regular, well-connected line" certainly clashed with snowy and rough terrain, and the evident fatigue which showed on Rebel faces by mid-day reflected the toll of the relentless pressure on attacks as well. The Confederate generals had all of their units on-line, whether in column or otherwise, and reserve depth was lacking at crucial moments for any *coup de main*.[15]

Federal fire did not decimate the attackers. Mississippian John Simonton remembered that "the enemy kept up a continuous volley of musketry," but with little effect, since most of the bullets passed over his men. "The spirit and determination that insured success" ultimately worked for southern soldiers in a fight where progress could be measured in yards from hillock to hillock. In fact, after-action reports on both sides were sprinkled with phrases such as "the enemy pressing us very hard," the ground being "hotly contested," and the holding of positions "under galling fire." Sometime between 11:00 and 12:00, the Confederates concentrated upon reducing the Union salient at the triangle formed by Wynn's Ferry Road and the narrow feeder lanes to the Forge road and Bufford Hollow. "Commands were scattered and mixed in fragments,"

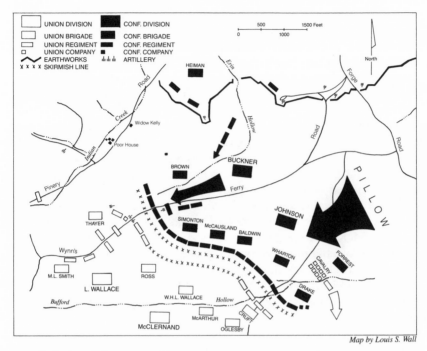

MAP 6. Action, February 15, 1862 — 12:15 to 1:00 P.M.

claimed Nathan Bedford Forrest. Here the intensity of the action was reflected in one Confederate's comment later that Fort Donelson was about the only battle in the West where he witnessed the bayonet being used so extensively. Another participant recalled seeing a young Mississippi lad, calling for his regiment to re-form and charge the Yankees, while tears rolled down his face from the excitement. "I think he would have gone alone if an officer had not taken him to the rear," declared the observer.[16]

By this time the rear areas in Dover began to see the human wreckage from the battlefield. Exploding Federal shells had already wrought havoc among the few remaining townsfolk, and commissary or teamster personnel located there. Quite a few stragglers from the attack had simply gone back into town "and were around the fires and up and down the river bank," noted Forrest. Some had purportedly gone back for more ammunition, others simply to get warm, still others to help wounded comrades to hospitals. Not a few were merely skulkers. Private V.K. Farris, a hospital steward with the 41st Tennessee remembered that by 11:30

A.M. hospital boats had arrived and that he was helping doctors in one of the vacant hotels. About that time, Federal artillery fire began to pepper the area, he noted (the same kind of misdirected Confederate fire plagued Federal surgeons behind McClernand's lines at the Rollins and Cherry houses), and it took about one and a half hours for the Confederates to get the enemy fire shifted by raising hospital flags high enough to be seen.[17]

Each of the Confederate generals seemed to be fighting his own isolated battle, only marginally coordinated with the others. We cannot be sure of Floyd's whereabouts — one hospital steward claimed to have seen him with the brigade surgeon about 11:00 A.M. behind the trenches formerly occupied by Colonel Robert Farquharson's 41st Tennessee at the Wynn's Ferry road egress. Buckner ostensibly stood nearby, for Lieutenant Selden Spencer of Graves's battery noted his presence there, and William McKay of the 18th Tennessee sighted the Kentuckian walking to the crest of a hill fifteen or twenty paces from the trench line. Buckner was pacing back and forth oblivious to solid shot and bullets nicking the dirt before and behind him. McKay could not recall how long Buckner remained under fire, but anticipated seeing him fall at any moment. He guessed that the general did this to inspire the men, but such risks failed to prod a sluggish and poorly developing assault. Perhaps the Federal fire kept Buckner's troops pinned down; perhaps he only waited for the battle to pass across his front to his designated attack sector. At any rate Floyd did nothing to accelerate the pace; as senior leader, he merely let the action run its course rather than directing a decisive, slashing advance by Buckner's division across a flat quarter-mile space which lay between the trenches and McClernand's reeling Federals.[18]

Pillow and Bushrod Johnson were more active, by comparison. Johnson could be found personally "pressing the left wing, keeping a regular, well-directed line, and in guarding the left flank." Actually he might have better exploited his left flank superiority rather than just "guarding" it. Pillow was the most energetic of the lot, ranging over the field, berating laggardly field officers to move up, and urging the weary foot-soldiers to greater effort. Of course this was the Tennessean's battle, his moment of glory. In many ways he assumed the guise of army commander and senior leader — a role which soon caused problems for everyone. About mid-morning, he rode to Heiman's command post atop the hill guarded by Maney's battery. This position afforded the best view of the wooded ravines and ridge-studded terrain, even though it lay over a quarter-mile west from where Buckner and Floyd watched the action. Elated by what he could see of the Confederate success, Pillow dashed off a telegram to Albert Sidney Johnston. "On the honor of a soldier, the day is ours," he said. And so it seemed for the moment, but precious time slipped away, and still the battle reached no definitive conclusion.[19]

The fog of battle continued to befuddle both sides. Lieutenant Spencer noted that sometimes the musketry would be steady and even continuous, telling of another stubborn Federal stand, and then scattered discharges told of their retirement. None of the Confederate batteries advanced onto the field with the infantry but offered only indirect fire over the heads of the attackers. Captain John H. Guy's Virginia battery had the satisfaction of seeing "fully and without obstruction" only the combined arms attack by Hanson's 2d Kentucky infantry and Forrest's cavalry which overcame one stubborn pocket of Yankee resistance. Such were moments which later on became legend for the Lost Cause. Actually, Forrest's horsemen had been riding around the field for most of the morning looking for trouble spots. Finally they came upon McCausland and Simonton as they struggled with the Federals at the Forge road salient. Seeing great possibilities for a team operation, Forrest persuaded Hanson to cooperate in an assault which caught Ransom's 11th Illinois in the left flank and rear. Vicious hand-to-hand fighting ensued. Union regimental and national colors changed hands several times. Ultimately the bluecoats broke for the rear. Ransom's command folded, its young colonel fell wounded, and Colonel John Logan's 31st Illinois (next in line) gave out despite the wild-eyed, fiery enjoinder from its commander to "suffer death men, but disgrace never, stand firm."[20]

Forrest's troopers gathered over one hundred prisoners from this single attack. The shattered Federals scampered back into Buford Hollow to the shelter of the hospital area, although a few apparently kept on running. One wag in a Hoosier regiment claimed that a very scared lieutenant from his unit continued running all the way to Fort Henry, found a boat just starting downriver, got aboard, and reached his home in southern Indiana before he learned that Fort Donelson had surrendered. Apocryphal, perhaps, but the situation for McClernand's division was tight by noon on the fifteenth. At this point, it became W.H.L. Wallace's turn to feel the full fury of the Confederate juggernaut. His unit rallied around a small earthen redan occupied by 24-pounder howitzers of Captain Edward McAllister's Battery E, 1st Illinois Artillery. Momentum lay with the victorious Rebels, as once again Forrest and Hanson teamed up to repeat their earlier success at dislodging tenacious Yankees. Buckner also sent Brown's Tennesseeans to move frontally from Erin Hollow against this position. Maney, Green, and Graves would play artillery fire from positions directly across from McAllister. It was high noon when the Confederates moved "at quick time" to break this final stand of Mc-Clernand's division.[21]

Buckner's command marched out under a distinctive battle flag. The Kentucky general's wife had sewn such banners while her husband's men were encamped at Bowling Green. Buckner had heard Sidney Johnston expressly wish for a "battle flag so distinctive in character that it could not be mistaken for the flags of either nation." Buckner proposed "a flag which has no artistic taste about it, but which is perfectly distinctive"—a white oval on a dark blue field. The new banner differed little from traditional United States Army regimental flags or even some state flags on both sides, but such subtleties mattered little at Fort Donelson, where it was first unfurled in combat. Hanson's 2d Kentucky was already attired in the distinctive hooded parkas, so the battle flag was but one more unique touch to the snowy combat. Whether beneath the strange banner or distinctive winter garb, all of the Confederates swept forward across a two-hundred-yard open space, formerly an encampment, and pitched into W.H.L. Wallace's resolute Federals.[22]

"It was not, strictly speaking, a 'charge bayonets,'" declared Hanson later, "but it would have been one if the enemy had not fled." Forrest claimed that his horsemen did most of the dirty work, braving tangled undergrowth and Wallace's well-directed musketry. His men actually got in among McAllister's gunners and did fearful damage. As the peripatetic Captain Guy discovered later while riding over the area, the dead "lay as thick as men generally lie in a tent." When it ended, Wallace's brigade was also in full retreat up Wynn's Ferry road, leaving cannon, prisoners, ambulances, and hospital tents in the hands of Forrest's troopers. Hanson and Brown mopped up survivors, and Brown then turned his men into the roadway in pursuit of the fast disappearing troops of W.H.L. Wallace. The Illinois brigade commander wrote his wife that the Rebels seemed a "strange and snotty crowd," but that they shot "terribly sharply."[23]

The Confederate battle line now arched for fully a mile from Brown's contingents moving westward astride Wynn's Ferry road, to Drake's brigade dipping down into Bufford Hollow to the southeast. Opposing the Confederates at this moment were only packets of disjointed and dispirited Federals, each one fighting for its own survival. Buckner sensed that the time was ripe for moving his reserves from the trenches, and he also ordered Graves to limber his guns and join Brown's pursuit. By 1:00 P.M., the way out of the Fort Donelson trap lay wide open. McClernand's division virtually ceased to exist as an organized fighting force. The Confederates stood within a hair of smashing Grant's army. Only that was not to be.[24]

Unknown to Brown's advancing column, a new body of Federals had moved into a blocking position astride the critical Wynn's Ferry road. Thanks once again to the intrepid, if insubordinate, reaction of Lew Wallace (who had dispatched a second reinforced brigade to aid McClernand without permission from Grant), this new group would turn the tide of battle. The background for the move was colorful. Shortly after news of McClernand's predicament reached army headquarters, Grant's adjutant, Captain John A. Rawlins, rode over to check on matters himself for his absent chief. He encountered Lew Wallace, and as the pair chatted astride their horses, they noticed a horde of stragglers and "a compound of shots and yells, mixed with the rattle of wheels and the rataplan and throbing rumble of hoofs in undertone," as the flotsam of McClernand's destroyed command began passing on that ill-defined section of Wynn's Ferry road where it crossed the upper valley of Indian Creek. Soon a very distraught and bareheaded officer dashed by, shouting "we're cut to pieces," which prompted Wallace to recall that he had never seen a case of panic so perfectly defined. Rawlins reached for his pistol to shoot the wretch on the spot, but Wallace restrained him. Soon an orderly rode up to report the road jammed with wagons, as well as mounted and dismounted troops —"on the plains we would call it a stampede," he proclaimed. Then and there, Lew Wallace decided to deploy his third brigade to the critical point on the field. Moving his own men aside to let the fugitives pass, he told Rawlins of his intentions, and the adjutant then rode off toward headquarters but at a slow gait so as not to panic C.F. Smith's division en route.[25]

By 10:00 A.M. Lew Wallace had Thayer's brigade, reinforced by Lieutenant Peter Wood's six-gun Battery A, 1st Illinois Light Artillery (the Chicago Board of Trade battery), plus the 46th, 57th, and 58th Illinois regiments moving to help McClernand. He sent a courier to inform C.F. Smith that Wallace was commiting his last brigade. Then he remembered to retrieve Cruft's skirmishers from the Indian Creek valley, thereby leaving a gap in the Federal line. Fortunately, Wallace noticed the absence of friendly troops there as he rode off, so he detached the 68th Ohio to block that escape route for the Rebels. as the Union infantry and artillery marched along, they encountered increasing numbers of demoralized stragglers, moving to the rear in whole squads and companies, but still carrying arms and regimental colors. The panic had subsided, and these men were simply jaded and out of ammunition. They repeatedly cried out to Wallace, "cartridges, cartridges, we're looking for ammunition. Got any?"[26]

Lew Wallace saw a ranking officer coming toward him, one leg casually thrown over the pommel of the saddle like a farmer homeward bound at the end of a work day. This was W.H.L. Wallace, with some four or five hundred men of his broken brigade strung out behind him. Lew Wallace spurred his horse forward, inquired after the other officer's name, and discovered that both men not only bore the same surname, but had commanded the 11th regiment of their respective state volunteers (which must have caused great profanity in the army post office, mused the Hoosier). The two then compared notes as to the course of the battle. W.H.L. Wallace reiterated his lack of ammunition and asked if his new acquaintance commanded the rapidly closing reinforcements on the road. Lew Wallace replied that he did, asking in turn whether the enemy was close. W.H.L. Wallace responded, "Well, you will have time to form line of battle right here." The Hoosier expressed his thanks, the pair shook hands, and each man turned to his perceived task. Nonchalantly, W.H.L. Wallace turned in the saddle and, with his survivors, pushed on toward the ammunition wagons which Lew Wallace said were back in his old sector.[27]

General Lew Wallace realized that indeed Thayer's people had to be deployed right where they were—a spot where Wynn's Ferry Road slipped off the ridge toward the oncoming Confederates. To his left the ridge dropped off more precipitously into the upper reaches of Erin Hollow, while to the right it stretched through the woods toward Bufford Hollow. The position was ideal for defense. Undergrowth and blackjack sealed the flanks and channeled an attacker onto the roadway. Wallace decided to place his artillery in the road, beside two guns of Captain Ezra Taylor's Illinois battery, left by the retiring W.H.L. Wallace. Flanking the artillery would be Thayer's infantry. Lew Wallace sent a rider galloping back through Thayer's column to locate Wood's battery and "to stop at nothing" in rushing it forward. The loquacious Hoosier recorded in his memoirs the thrilling sight of Wood's unit rushing into line. Horses running low, riders standing in their stirrups plying their whips, guns and caissons bouncing over root and rut like playthings, the men clinging to their seats like monkeys, he said. There was no shouting, only Wood in front waving his sword. "I fancied the trees trembled as the wheels rolled by them," wrote Wallace; "I know the ground shook earthquake like." It was stuff worthy of an Old World painting.[28]

Taylor would be piqued later that Wallace's after-action report accorded Wood's people all of the fame. For now the battle was at hand,

and everyone stood to their work. The line proved to be a strong one, indicating that citizen-soldier Wallace knew what was required at that moment. From left to right he arrayed the 58th Ohio, with Company A of the 32d Illinois flanking the artillery north of the road. The 1st Nebraska (Thayer's own unit) and the 58th Illinois filed to the right of the guns, south of the roadway. A cloud of skirmishers stretched off into the woods and undergrowth farther south and fused with McClernand's survivors regrouping near the Rollins house and hospital. Colonel Charles R. Woods's 76th Ohio lay down behind Wallace's main position, providing a ready reserve. Farther back, the 46th and 57th Illinois massed in columns of companies on the road "ready and anxious for a fight." Eventually four additional guns from Taylor's battery returned from replenishing their ammunition supply and anchored the left rear of the 58th Ohio, covering the Erin Hollow approach. Bits and pieces of the shattered 11th and 31st Illinois trickled through the defenders, headed for the rear with their wounded in blood-stained blankets, and shepherded by a seriously injured "Blackjack" Logan — visible signs of pain etched upon his face.[29]

Wallace's move came none too soon. As solid shot from Maney's Rebel guns cut through the trees overhead, the Union troops could now see butternut-clad infantry of Brown's brigade "coming up the road and through the shrubs and trees" on either side of the road. Both sides had jettisoned packs and excess equipment and had come prepared to fight. Young David Bodenhamer of the 32d Tennessee had been waiting all morning for this moment, having stood in a reserve line shivering from the cold. A *Chicago Times* correspondent captured the moment "as the rebels supposing we were on the retreat, came yelling out of their works into the road," he wrote. He added that the Chicago boys of Wood's battery poured a hail of grape and canister into them, slaughtering them by the dozens. Then Wallace ordered Thayer to open fire, and stood entranced as muskets of the Cornhusker and Illini soldiers rose and fell "steadily as if on a parade ground."[30]

For a while, the Confederates tried to perfect their alignment with "the brush on the slope of the hill mowed away with bullets." The Federals stood fast as Wood's gunners fired fifty-five double-shotted rounds into the enemy. The battery historian later declared that they had been under fire for thirty minutes and were pretty scared but stood their ground, and none ran away as far as he knew. In fact Brown's Tennesseans concentrated upon Wood's battery and the Nebraskans. Three times the Tennesseans tried to shift from their marching column of "files of four" into a battle line. Each time, deadly Federal fire stopped them, threw them into confusion, so that the Confederates simply retired in frustration. Wallace had no need for reserves. The accurate Federal fire cut down Rebel unit leaders such as Lieutenant Colonels Thomas M. Gordon of the 3d, and William P. Moore of the 32d Tennessee further confusing their men. Even the redoubtable Forrest, reconnoitering in front of the infantry, had a horse shot from beneath him, and had to leave the action rather ignominiously on foot. The 18th and 32d Tennessee regiments had an especially difficult time priming their flintlocks in the snow. "When I take a retrospective view of that charge," observed George Washington Dillon of Logan County, Kentucky, who was serving with the 18th Tennessee, "I can but shudder at the awful condition we were placed in at that time."[31]

Major Nathaniel F. Cheairs tried to rally the 3d Tennessee after Gordon went down but to little avail. Everybody was disheartened, and the whole Confederate attack gradually faded back some 150 yards to re-form and dry musket locks. Supporting artillery fire from Guy's and Graves's guns in the trenches had little effect. Distance, indirect fire, and faulty ammunition were the cause. Even Heiman, who had readied the 27th Alabama and 48th Tennessee to move to help the attackers, now held them back. By 1:30 P.M. the punch had left the Confederate breakout attempt. Wallace mounted no counterattack, despite Thayer's rather lame, post-battle claim that "nothing but the thick underbrush prevented a charge with the bayonet." Truth was, Wallace and his Federals remained content with having simply stopped the determined Rebel drive.[32]

Brown's repulse marked the end of Confederate success that day. Fatigued soldiers on both sides simply stopped moving, as their officers tried to reorganize units broken and mixed or scattered over the field. The lull proved pivotal for both armies. While the precise timing of events will never be known, it seems likely that some time after 1:30 P.M. both Union and Confederate leaders made critical decisions. The entire character of the battle of Fort Donelson as well as the twin rivers campaign changed abruptly.

For one thing, Pillow assumed that the first phase of the battle plan had been completed. He immediately ordered implementation of the second phase, as he understood it. Presumptuously, he ordered both Johnson and Buckner back to the trenches in order to consolidate, pack gear, draw rations, retrieve the artillery, heavy artillerists in the fort and the supply wagons, and then leave the perimeter. The precise time of evacuation remained unstated, but other senior officers from Johnson to Gilmer and Forrest substantiated Pillow's understanding of this scheme. Then the full implications of faulty communications came to the fore.

When a courier bearing Pillow's order reached Buckner, the Kentuckian exploded with indignation and refused to obey at first. The long-simmering political feud now erupted anew over a military matter. The Tennessean had prevented Buckner's artillery and Farquharson's 41st Tennessee from joining Brown's flagging assault on Lew Wallace, and Buckner was angry. Now the fruits of victory were about to be lost because of Pillow's order. Buckner dallied but realized that he could not evade a second directive from Pillow; just then the senior general rode up.[33]

As Floyd told it later, he had been watching the earlier Hanson-Forrest victory over W.H.L. Wallace and had told Buckner "on the field" that "My intention was to hold with Brigadier General Buckner's command the Wynn's Ferry road, and thus prevent the enemy during the night from [re-] occupying the position on our left which he occupied in the morning." Then, leaving the Kentuckian, Floyd had started for the right wing of the Fort Donelson perimeter, "my intention being, if things could be held in the condition that they then were, to move the whole army, if possible, to the open country lying southward beyond the Randolph Forge." Again no specific time was mentioned; Floyd said that "during my absence, and from some misapprehension, I presume, of the previous order given," Pillow had preemptorily ordered Buckner back to the trenches.[34]

So a surprised Floyd was confronted by a irate Buckner. "At his request to know my opinion of the movement," snapped Buckner later, "I replied that nothing had occurred to change my views of the necessity of evacuation of the post, that the road was open, that the first part of our purpose was fully accomplished, and I thought we should at once avail ourselves of the existing opportunity to regain our communications." Floyd seemed to agree, Buckner thought. The senior general then rode off to find Pillow and set matters straight. When Floyd eventually found Pillow, he demanded: "In the name of God, General Pillow, what have we been fighting all day for? Certainly not to show our powers, but solely to secure the Wynn's Ferry Road, and now after securing it, you order it to be given up."[35]

A contrite Pillow used all of his political talents to convince the Virginian of the correctness of his action. Pillow cited worn-out troops, the need for food and ammunition replenishment, the character of the snow-covered terrain which hampered re-supply, the totality of battlefield victory, and the inhumanity of leaving the wounded on the field without medical treatment and in freezing temperatures. He also noted the knavery of any sacrifice of the main garrison. Besides, said Pillow, the withdrawal had been nearly completed by this point, so why not continue it, regroup, and move out later on? Again, nobody set a specific time for evacuation. By this stage, both generals had become immobilized somewhat by reports of some 20,000 fresh Union troops pouring into the battle area. This new element might destroy a combat-fatigued army such as the one they now commanded. The two generals turned field glasses toward Buckner's old trenches on the Eddyville Road and thought they caught sight of great activity in C.F. Smith's lines opposite. Partly with cause, partly from fear of Grant's massive reinforcements, and mostly from their own exhaustion and irresolution, Floyd and Pillow persuaded one another that the whole army, including Buckner, needed to return to the perimeter at this time.[36]

What really caused this turn of events will never be known for sure. Buckner may well have reinterpreted the decisions of the previous night's war council in light of the battlefield success, or even subsequent events of the next two days when he later wrote reports of the affair. Pillow too may have elapsed into selective memory by the time he penned a rationale for his actions, or he may have reverted to his determination to defend his native soil to the death, no matter what had been decided by the council of war. The tactical victory of the morning may have given him a convenient excuse to urge retirement, leading then, not to evacuation, but to continued fighting until either Grant departed the area in defeat, or Sidney Johnston arrived with a relief column. All of this must forever remain conjecture. We do know the reaction among the Rebel soldiers. Captain Guy thought: "The general opinion among the Colonels seemed to be that Genl. Pillow was so elated with the success of the attack, that he abandoned the idea of retreating." Mississippi Lieutenant Spencer of Graves's Kentucky battery concurred, claiming: "His head was turned with the victory just gained, and he was too short sighted [Spencer crossed out the words "a fool"], to see that it was entirely thrown away, unless we used it to escape." Pillow might telegraph Nashville that he had gained a great victory, continued the lieutenant, but "he was doomed to be made wiser by experience before he was twelve hours older."[37]

Even Lew Wallace later joined this derisive chorus by proclaiming: "General Pillow's vanity whistled itself into ludicrous exaltation." Imagining Grant's whole army in defeat and flight, noted the Hoosier, Pillow "deported himself accordingly." Yet Floyd's own after-action comments indicated that however naive the Confederates may have been in retrospect, the day's success did seem to guarantee that an evacuation was still possible at a time of the Confederates' own choosing. Here was the problem — the imprecision of the evacuation timetable; was it to be mid- or late afternoon, that night, or the next day, and from which place, the battlefield or the defense perimeter? None of this had been made clear, either from the council of war on February 14 or from consultations during the lull in battle the next day. Just why Floyd eventually deviated from his original plan of using Buckner's men as a screen also remains vague. Perhaps Floyd forgot about it, although the recorded excuse has come down in his own words. "As the enemy were pressing upon the trenches," he noted, "I deemed that the execution of this last order [Pillow to Buckner] was all that was left to be done." It seems, then, that in all the dithering of the southern generals during the lull in the fighting, they permitted the Federals to regain the initiative by default and to dictate just how the battle would end.[38]

It was probably close to 1:00 P.M. when Grant finally arrived back at headquarters where Rawlins and the rest of his staff briefed him on the seriousness of the crisis. Again the sequence of events is unclear. Grant apparently realized that he must commit everything at hand to the fighting. He told in his memoirs of seeing everything favorably along the line from left to center, but when coming to the right, "appearances were different." Somewhere along the way, he dropped a terse but revealing note to Foote, whom he assumed to still be at the riverboat landing. If all the gunboats capable of doing so would make an immediate appearance before the Confederate river positions, he penned, "it may secure us a Victory." Otherwise, the army stood on the verge of defeat. He admitted to some of his army to being surprised, and demoralized, but told the naval officer that he thought the enemy was even more so. He did not expect a full battle from the flotilla, he said, but just a diversion. "I must order a charge to save appearances" was the way Grant described what was necessary, and if the gunboats did not appear, this would reassure the enemy and further demoralize the army.[39]

Grant then rode to the sound of battle, passing C.F. Smith's command post and pausing to learn what he could from his old friend. He found Smith sitting calmly under a tree but quite willing to render aid once he received Grant's orders. Why he had not taken more initiative like Lew Wallace did remains a mystery too. In any event, in receipt of Grant's permission the division commander dispatched Colonel M.L. Smith's reserve brigade to the endangered right flank. By this time Grant and his staff were picking their way through the remnants of McClernand's division en route to the disaster area. All of this delayed the army commander's appearance at the critical spot on Wynn's Ferry road until after Thayer's repulse of Brown's assault.[40]

Meanwhile Wallace had decided to retrieve Cruft's brigade which he had sent earlier to help McClernand. He found the unit in Bufford Hollow and eager for another engagement. Wallace told Cruft to hold his ground at all cost, and, returning to Wynn's Ferry road, he encountered McClernand. The pair dodged stray bullets as they talked, and soon Grant and his staff thundered up on horseback. The gathering moved quickly to serious business. Grant noticed many of the soldiers were "standing in knots, talking in the most excited manner." No officers seemed capable of giving orders, he recalled, while the soldiers themselves lacked only ammunition to get back into the fight, and "there were tons of it close at hand." Furthermore, Grant heard some of the men say that the enemy had attacked with filled knapsacks and haversacks. This immediately alerted him to the fact that the Confederates were prepared to fight, so long as they had provisions, and that they were probably attempting to escape. At first he told Wallace and McClernand to entrench and await reinforcements. Then, realizing that more drastic action was necessary, yet exuding an air of calm which impressed onlookers, Grant changed his mind. Clutching a fistful of dispatches and chewing on a ubiquitous cigar, he unpretentiously told his subordinates: "Gentlemen, the position on the right must be retaken." Then he swung his horse around and took off at a gallop.[41]

Grant confided to one senior staff member, Colonel J.D. Webster, that some of the men seemed badly demoralized, but that the enemy was even more so, for he had attempted to force his way out and then had fallen back. The one who attacks first now will be victorious, declared the general, and the enemy "will have to be in a hurry if he gets ahead of me." He correctly surmised that Floyd had pulled everyone out of the trenches for the assault but pickets, and that C.F. Smith could easily storm the works in his front. Therefore he rode back to Smith's command post, telling Webster to slowly pass through the disorganized soldiers and pass the word to fill cartridge boxes and get back into line because the Confederates should not be permitted to escape. The result proved electrifying, said Grant in his memoirs, for the men only wanted a leader.[42]

Late afternoon shadows crept over the landscape before the Federal counterattacks got started in both sectors. Smith's division had been waiting impatiently since morning, standing under arms but at ease in line, listening to every sound of battle, and eagerly anticipating the call to action. Their commander had been shifting units around most of the day; Birge's sharpshooters had been active; and reserve contingents had filled gaps such as those left by M.L. Smith's men passing to the right wing. Still it was C.F. Smith's division which jumped off first that afternoon to redeem the morning's disaster. McClernand and Wallace vacillated in trying to decide who could best mount the type of assault needed to fulfill Grant's wishes in their area. It would be Smith's attack which caused a fatal rupture in Confederate defenses and dislocated Floyd's evacuation plan.[43]

C.F. Smith's response to Grant's proclamation — "General Smith, all has failed on our right, you must take Fort Donelson" — was simply, "I will do it." Grant's confidence that the older man faced nothing but token defenders prompted further response. The stern, yet popular C.F. Smith rode off to start work. His plan was concise: feint with Cook's smaller brigade while launching the main assault with Lauman's larger one. Riding over to his favorite 2d Iowa, he shouted; "You must take the fort; take your caps off your guns, fix bayonets, and I will lead you." About 2:15 P.M. his division moved off its ridge-top toward Buckner's old works. The order held — rely on the bayonet, no firing until inside the enemy's works. Regimental formations became ragged once the men reached the bottom of the ravine and crossed the small stream there. Complete confusion attended their ascendance of the opposite slope and entry into the Rebel abatis. They emerged from that obstacle onto slippery slopes, directly within the gunsights of the waiting Confederates.[44]

Turning in his saddle, the sixty-year-old Smith bellowed: "Damn you, gentlemen, I see skulkers." Suggesting that they had enlisted to die for their country, he now offered them that chance. Scared to death, one young volunteer confessed that Smith's tactic worked. He saw the old man's mustache over his right shoulder and kept on going. Still another soldier thought it incredible that they could go up the hill and keep any sort of order at all. He felt that a rabbit could scarcely get through the brush and logs. Everyone, however, got through behind the white-haired general on horseback, carrying his sword aloft with hat on the blade tip.[45] Again it was the stuff of heroic paintings, and the aghast Confederates held their fire until scarcely twenty yards separated them from the onrushing Yankees. Only three battalions of the 30th Tennessee under Major James Turner held these works, and their double-barrel shotguns proved no match for the northerners' cold steel. "Right gallantly was the duty performed," beamed Smith later. By 3:00 P.M. his men had cleaned Turner's people out of the trenches and watched as the Rebels scampered across the ravine behind the earthworks to an adjacent ridge spur, some five hundred yards to the rear. The Federals had cracked Fort Donelson's outer defense line, without firing a shot.[46]

Gallant deeds attended Smith's assault. Color Sergeant Henry J. Gran-

Grant on the Battle Line, February 15, 1862. Painting by Paul Philippoteaux, Library of Congress.

nis of the 12th Iowa spent the rest of his life claiming to have implanted the first flag "*inside* the enemies works," although he admitted that the 2d Iowa had the honor of "being the first *on* the works." This was terribly important to young, impressionable volunteers who had suffered the cold nights, as well as the heat of battle. Corporal Voltaire P. Twombley of Company F, 2d Iowa "took the colors after three of the color guard had fallen . . . and although almost instantly knocked down by a spent ball, immediately rose and bore the colors to the end of the engagement." On March 12, 1897, he would be awarded a Congressional Medal of Honor for that deed in 1862.[47]

Most of Buckner's division were just returning to their old trenches when C.F. Smith struck, and were not yet in position to blunt the attack. Many like G.W. Dillon in the 18th Tennessee had just stacked arms, eaten a little snack, and "in short almost worn out from so much exposure and loss of sleep." But they were up the line from the immediate breakthrough area, and with Hanson's Kentuckians and the 14th Mississippi, the Tennesseans were soon called upon to seal off the threat, as Lauman and Cook began scrambling up the steep sides of the ravine toward the ridge spur where Turner's people had taken refuge. Most of the Federals were in high spirits; victory did that. Robert J. Price of the 52d Indiana recounted that nobody minded the zip-zip of bullets hitting tree trunks as they removed their wounded because everything was quite exciting. Smith was urging them on and had moved up sections from Batteries H and K, 1st Missouri Light Artillery to provide close support for the next assault.[48]

The Federals' elation quickly subsided, for C.F. Smith's attack now bogged down when Buckner's main force joined Turner along the second ridge. The two sides blazed away at one another for the rest of the afternoon, and the Confederates tried desperately to throw the bluecoats out of their newly acquired earthworks. Somebody yelled "charge," remembered William McKay of the 18th Tennessee, and some of his colleagues, not thinking of "the absurdity of one little regiment charging three lines of battle of the enemy across a deep ravine," started down the hill in a run. They lost their drum major who had predicted his own death in their first fight. Probably the most famous episode of this see-saw fight came with the action of young First Lieutenant James W. Morton of Captain Thomas K. Porter's Tennessee battery. With his commander cut down, young Morton (who went on to command Forrest's horse artillery) took over (he was later memorialized in James R. Randall's poetry as "the lad in the flush of martial pride," who kept up his word not

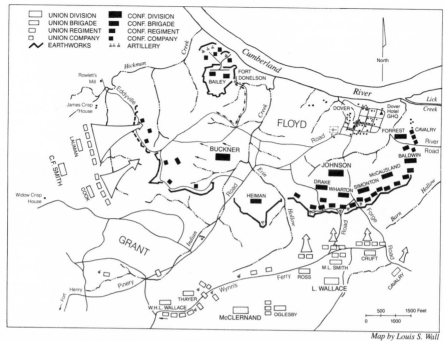

MAP 7. Action, February 15, 1862 — 2:00 to 5:00 p.m.

to give up Porter's guns). By nightfall, the fight had gone out of both sides.[49]

Buckner and other Confederate unit commanders thought their new position was even stronger than the old, and they sought to have their tired men erect new barricades. Most of the troops were too worn out, and, like Nathaniel Cheairs, drank a hot mug of coffee, tumbled on the ground, and slept as if dead. It was the same in Smith's new lines. His men built fires in the old Rebel trenches and tried to sleep, while their leader worried about the morrow. When queried about Sunday morning's plans, C.F. Smith replied, pointing across the ravine, "Take it, sir!" Some 357 of his men killed or wounded disturbed him, but what really mattered was victory. The Federals had broken the shell of Confederate defenses which protected the main fort.[50]

Meanwhile, on the far Union right, another Federal drive gained momentum on Saturday afternoon. When Grant ordered McClernand and Lew Wallace to retake the lost ground of the morning, McClernand told Wallace that his own command was too cut up and dispersed to do much, but he agreed that Grant was correct — the road "ought to be recovered." McClernand understood this to be Forge road which bisected his former position, and Wallace probably understood this from talking to him. Grant may have meant only Wynn's Ferry road, for that was the only road apparent at the time of the council. Wallace realized that his own division and whatever other units he might scrape together would comprise the counterattack. McClernand offered two regiments from Morrison's brigade which had been badly handled two days before during the Maney's battery attack. It seemed out of character for McClernand not to want the glory to offset the sting of morning defeat, but perhaps his ego had been badly bruised by the disaster. Wallace told him sharply: "It is getting late, and what is to be done must be done before night." Like Grant and C.F. Smith, Wallace turned to the task at hand.[51]

As McClernand rode off to re-form his command, Wallace surveyed the terrain with his aides. Desultory firing continued, endangering the general as well as nearby hospital personnel. Actually, surgeons such as Dr. Thomas W. Fry almost welcomed the enemy fire, for it discouraged McClernand's stragglers from lingering around the aid station. The fluidity of the situation permitted Wallace to move about, taking stock of the situation through gaps in the heavy timber, and to plan their best move. They spotted Bushrod Johnson's Rebels "walking about and blanketed" on a ridge about six hundred yards northeast of the Rollins place. This would be the Federal's objective. Lew Wallace shifted M.L. Smith's brigade into the hollow to cooperate with Leonard F. Ross (now commanding Morrison's old brigade) and Cruft. W.H.L. Wallace's men had replenished cartridge boxes and returned to the field, and they moved into the gap between Thayer on Wynn's Ferry road and McClernand's disorganized mass in the hollow. Left to right, Lew Wallace arrayed Ross and Smith, while Cruft would operate across the little spur road, screened on his right flank by Colonel Lyle T. Dickey's dismounted 4th Illinois cavalry. The force had no artillery, but neither did the Confederates. Once more, it promised to be an infantry slug-fest in the brush and snow among limestone ridges and ravines.[52]

Many of the Confederates had spent the time after Brown's repulse collecting arms and equipment and removing numerous wounded from the battlefield. Forrest's troopers alone reputedly gathered 5,000 small arms and sent them to the rear. The Confederates later claimed that most of their force had actually withdrawn by the time Lew Wallace's assault surged forward. Certainly this was not the way the Federals remembered it. No matter, Lew Wallace rode among his ranks much as C.F. Smith had done, chiding the men to inspire them. He inquired

General C.F. Smith. National Archives.

from his own Hoosier lads of the 11th Zouaves about which hotel they had passed the night, and received a cheerful answer that accommodations had been cold but cheap. He playfully assured them that he was now answering their long-standing complaint about never getting into a fight—"its here now," he noted, and asked what they had to say about that. "We're ready, let 'er rip," came back the answer. Wallace tried to tell as many as could hear him about the desperate character of the work at hand, but only cries of "forward, forward" were shouted back. Turning to let M.L. Smith light a cigar, Wallace called out, "Forward it is then!" Like C.F. Smith, he led the attack.[53]

Lew Wallace soon dropped off to establish his command post near the Rollins house. Since the Confederates were already beginning to pour a hot fire into the attackers from their ridge-top position, Wallace instructed Smith to practice his "zouave training." As such, the men would fight in loose order, creeping along the ground when the enemy's fire was hottest, rushing forward when it slackened, and, as Wallace observed, being nimble on their hands and knees far beyond the ordinary infantryman. They had been trained to load muskets on their backs, then roll over, and fire. They were "instantly observant of order in the midst of disorder," suggested their former teacher. The men thus clambered up the slippery slope with amazing speed, using rocky outcroppings and dense underbrush to good advantage. While Smith's unorthodox tactics were not copied by Ross and Cruft, the Federal assault made rapid progress.[54]

M.L. Smith's cigar soon fell victim to a Rebel bullet. Calling for a match, Smith waited indulgently until a young soldier dashed up to comply. Thanking the young man, the Missouri colonel added: "Take your place now. We are almost up." Then, puffing calmly on his new smoke, Smith urged his mount forward into the quickening Confederate fusillade. This fire seemed punctuated by lulls and furious outbursts, accompanied by taunts of the Rebels—"Hi, hi, there you damned Yankees. Why don't you come up? What are you waiting for?" To the chagrin of the taunting defenders, the Federals answered with a volley. Lew Wallace declared later that to get an impression of the assault, one had to think of nearly two thousand men simultaneously squirming or dashing up the steep, frost-covered slope; he likened them to "so many black gnomes burrowing in a cloud of flying leaves and dirty snow." Off to the right and across the lane, Cruft's infantry and Dickey's men, the latter armed with breech-loading Sharps carbines, tried to turn Bushrod Johnson's flank.[55]

Colonel Hugh Reed claimed after the war that his 44th Indiana really

Decisive Bayonet Charge by 2d Iowa, February 15, 1862. Sketch by H. Lovie.
Frank Leslie's Illustrated Newspaper, March 15, 1862.

General Lew Wallace.
National Archives.

broke the Confederate line at this point. This contention would be dis-
puted by other veterans in typical veterans' squabbles about who was
"first." No such controversy developed on the southern side. Johnson
had realized earlier that Drake's brigade could not handle any serious
counter-thrust in this sector. Therefore the general had returned to the
trenches seeking aid, only to be rebuffed by others, who now realized
that the threatened locale lay with Buckner's old trenches, not with the
Wynn's Ferry road area. Floyd especially vetoed Johnson's "hazzarded
suggestion" that the enemy in front of Drake should be pressed by a general advance from the entrenchments. Johnson was told to "display"
Drake's men as a cover for general withdrawal. Only Forrest's cavalry
rode back to help Johnson, and the horsemen, mainly under Major D.C.
Kelly, temporarily blunted Cruft's turning movement. Even Forrest recognized that Wallace's drive had too much momentum behind it. Together,
Drake and Forrest conducted a fighting withdrawal. For a moment, it
appeared that Lew Wallace's power might carry over the Confederate
works in the same fashion as C.F. Smith's. Then, last minute massing
of Confederate fire from behind the protective trenches checked Wallace's drive.[56]

Much of the late afternoon action took place on the ground of the
morning's fighting, "with the dead and wounded lying where they had
fallen," noted Wallace. At this time Commander Benjamin M. Dove,

from the gunboat flotilla, finally brought the *Louisville* and *St. Louis* up-river in answer to Grant's urgent request for help. These ironclads lobbed heavy shells in the general direction of the battlefield, many of them impacting in the very area of Wallace's advance. The Hoosier claimed later that Dove's support had "distracted the enemy's attention" and saved the gunboats' reputation in the minds of army men. Few Confederates, however, mentioned any naval fire on the fifteenth in their reports, although the water battery captains cited the appearance of one gunboat that "fired several shots, but did no damage." Perhaps by this stage of the fighting, none of the tired Confederates could distinguish between naval and field artillery gunfire.[57]

Many of Wallace's men stopped to tender care to the wounded from the earlier fighting. Lieutenant James O. Churchill had been one of those left to suffer when his 11th Illinois fell back. He lay among the fallen, watching Rebel scavengers rifle the pockets of the dead and wounded. He suffered rejection from Confederate surgeons who told him flatly that they had insufficient means to retrieve their own wounded, much less those of their enemy. So Churchill lay there reciting Thomas Campbell's poem about the cold December battle of Hohenlinden, and reviewing Napoleon's return from Moscow so as to maintain consciousness. Volunteers stopping to aid wounded friends of course slowed Wallace's advance. As one perceptive Confederate later contended, their own "buck and ball" cartridges could kill one and wound three Yankees, thereby causing one wounded man to take three out of action because "it takes two men to help him off the field." This was definitely the case with Lew Wallace's late afternoon attack, although men like Churchill gave that little thought as they struggled to avoid freezing to death.[58]

Caring for the wounded, the setting sun, and unfamiliarity with the terrain forced Wallace to resign himself to recovering the lost ground of the morning. Confusing instructions reached him from Grant that Wallace was to wait until morning to exploit the Union turnabout victory. Obviously the army commander had no idea that Wallace might drive all the way to the Confederate trench line, or that he might actually break through with one final determined burst. Therefore Grant's orders were to "fall back out of cannon range and throw up breastworks." Wallace protested to the messenger, Grant's chief-of-staff, Colonel Webster, asking, "the General does not know that we have the hill?" Webster stammered that he was only conveying orders, but he sensed that Wallace's rejoinder to tell Grant that "I have the order" would not prevent the Hoosier from trying to complete his success. Nonetheless it was not to be that evening, for as one of his own 11th Indiana zouaves sensed:

Lew Wallace's Federal Counterattack, February 15, 1862. Sketch by H. Lovie, *Frank Leslie's Illustrated Newspaper,* March 15, 1862.

"We were right under their guns; to have made a charge would have been madness." Wallace wisely made a reconnaissance of the enemy line, ordered M.L. Smith to establish pickets, and they placed the rest of his force in bivouac on the reverse slopes just south of the Wynn's Ferry road ridge.[59]

The battlefield gradually quieted as nightfall found the Confederates and Federals roughly where they had been that morning. McClernand's people trickled back into old campsites, while Oglesby and Ross took up a position north of Wynn's Ferry road opposite Maney's battery. Details from all commands combed the battlefield for wounded. While Colonels Noble and Dickey sent cavalry vedettes back to the vital Forge road area, contemporary evidence suggests that the Federals were not at all vigilant to the need to re-close that artery or the East or river road to Confederate escape. An important gap remained in the reestablished Federal cordon. It was not clear that either side realized this fact at the time. Pillow's "Battle of Dover" closed with some 3,000 fallen on both sides and relatively little accomplished, according to the original plan. While the Confederates had managed to gather sizable quantities of military supplies, including nine pieces of artillery, this was not what the breakout attempt had been all about.[60]

Participant memoirs suggest that all the soldiers were pleased when the battle ended. Some of them held a morbid fascination with death and destruction in their first battle. Union Major James A. Connolly of Charleston, Illinois, spoke of the vast number of dead horses, the frozen pools of blood on the field, noted that he had picked up over twenty hats with bullet holes in them together with pieces of skull, hair, and blood inside. Captain Guy stated that the duration of the conflict had not prepared him for such a slaughter, and he mentioned the dead lying about in every conceivable position, shot in every part of the body. He mentioned the ground strewn with blankets, canteens, haversacks, knapsacks, guns, and other equipment. The trees and saplings were all torn and many cut down by the firestorm of shot and shell, he said. Above all, the dead impressed him most as whenever a face was turned up to view, "its ghastly pallor was rendered more horrid by contrast with blood and gaping wounds."[61]

For others, such as George Washington Dillon, losing blankets and personal belongings because of Buckner's original orders to leave them behind in the attack festered more than anything else. When his unit returned to their old position, they found everything in disarray, and he complained bitterly about some men who had no respect whatever for a brother soldier's possessions. Grant's own servant, a broken-English immigrant named "French John," had been anxious to see the battle, but he returned that night to headquarters muttering: "I have no more curiosity; it is satisfied; it is all gone." Grant said little about the battle and sought refuge once more before Widow Crisp's fireplace, while his men endured another night of cold and snow. Like their enemies across the lines, they may have been more benumbed by memories of the day's action than the frigid night. The fate of battle and campaign now lay in other hands. Some three miles away, three Confederate generals met to decide their army's future in yet another council of war.[62]

CHAPTER 11

A Surrender Most Disgraceful

ONCE MORE A BITTER WIND WHIPPED SNOW and cold around the dead, the dying, and the cheerless living at Fort Donelson during the night of February 15. All evening, Rebel ambulance corpsmen went about gathering the wounded from local hospitals to put them aboard the steamboats with prisoners and the residue of garrison sick. About midnight, under orders from Floyd, the boats steamed upriver for Clarksville and Nashville. This proved to be but one of many blunders that night. Notwithstanding better medical care for the wounded at those cities, the departure of the boats denied the besieged army a means of escape. Meanwhile, out in the trenches, the tired but victory-flushed Confederate soldiers awaited their leaders' orders. The enemy campfires blazed brightly all around them and looked cheerful to men such as C.W. Tyler of the 50th Tennessee. He added that the men stamped their feet in the snow to keep warm and expected orders to cut their way to freedom once again. This too proved a false hope[1]

The actual sequence of events becomes imprecise once again. Apparently Floyd and Pillow returned to army headquarters once fighting died down in Buckner's old trench zone. Randal McGavock found them there discussing the day's events and preparing dispatches for Albert Sidney Johnston. Buckner soon joined them, but the fourth brigadier general, Bushrod Johnson, again remained out with the army, reorganizing the left wing. Nobody seemed to care; they had paid the man scant attention during the siege anyway. For the moment the trio warmed themselves before a raging fire with hot toddies in hand, argued about the day's success, but remained irresolute about the next move. Even Floyd's 11:00 P.M. telegram to Johnston was a curiously bland recital of the day's activities, with scant hint as to what would come next. McGavock left headquarters at some point with the impression that the battle would be renewed in the morning "with great vigor."[2]

About 1:00 A.M. Floyd summoned all regimental, brigade, and division commanders to a council of war. Ostensibly, it took place in Pillow's quarters at the Rice house, one block south of the square in

Dover. Time was short, and messengers arrived twice during the meeting to warn Buckner about enemy activity in front of his lines. Floyd added to the tension by mentioning the scouting reports of additional Union reinforcements landing downstream. He now estimated that Grant had over eighty regiments (the actual figure was half that, although a fourteen-steamboat convoy had disgorged five new regiments that night). Everyone was stunned and the war council focused on another escape attempt. Floyd ordered that quartermasters should burn their stores at daybreak and that all artillery should be spiked. Subordinates would collect their commands as they had the previous morning, precisely at 4:00 A.M. on the far left of the lines. The army would cut its way out again if necessary.[3]

At last someone among the Confederate generals had given a simple, direct order with a set time for escape. The three leaders sat back anxiously awaiting the hour of departure. Adjutants such as Colonel John Burch and Major Gustavus A. Henry, Jr. gathered headquarters records preparatory to evacuation. Then disturbing news began to come in from the pickets. They reported sighting rekindled Union campfires and hearing barking dogs opposite Pillow's sector. They assumed this meant that the enemy had reoccupied their previous positions. The generals began to waver on the army's ability to escape. Floyd sent for Major J.E. Rice, their host and Pillow's voluntary aide, to ask him about alternative escape routes. Rice told the officers that he understood the roads out of town were water covered, and chances of escape "decidedly unfavorable." Upon Rice's recommendation, Floyd sent another local resident — Dr. J.W. Smith, who owned the farm where the river road crossed flooded Lick Creek — to ascertain conditions. Smith rode out, found the backwater "just high enough to reach the saddle-skirts on a horse of medium size," and reported back optimistically that he thought the creek could be easily forded; furthermore he had seen no Federals at all in the vicinity.[4]

The generals remained unconvinced, and when Nathan Bedford Forrest joined the meeting, they questioned him about reinvestment. The cavalryman claimed to have ridden across the battlefield several times earlier in the evening and traveled two miles upriver "on the road to the forge" without seeing any enemy, but he agreed with Pillow that scouts should be sent to check all possible creek crossings. Two of these scouts accompanied Smith and returned with information that river road was impassable to infantry with the mud in Lick Creek valley about one-half leg deep, and the water indeed reaching saddle skirts of the horses. Other scouts such as Adam Johnson and S.H. Martin had passed out

Forge road and found no Federal activity, the wind and the wounded having rekindled the fires spotted by pickets. Precious time passed, and the army's medical director, Dr. W.D. Lyles, suggested that frostbite and pneumonia would claim most of the army if it tried to ford the one hundred yards of icy Lick Creek, and that most of the force was too broken down from fatigue, hunger, and low morale anyway to make the attempt. Pillow finally remarked that it was difficult to determine what was best to be done, but that he favored fighting their way out. Floyd turned to Buckner, possibly hoping to hear similar remarks from the loyal Kentuckian. Instead Buckner continued in the morose mood which had characterized his previous performance, according to some observers. His answer provided only a recital of hopelessness.[5]

Buckner apparently was the first to propose surrender. "I cannot hold my position half an hour after an attack," he exclaimed. Pillow retorted: "Why can't you?" and added, "I think you can hold your position; I think you can, sir." Buckner rejoined haughtily: "I know my position; I can only bring to bear against the enemy about 4,000 men, while he can oppose me with any given number." Buckner had obviously lost his grip as he ripped off a round of excuses—fatigue, shortages of food and ammunition, superior enemy numbers, and the health of his men, and even the return of Foote's gunboats—"sweeping with the fire at close range the positions of our troops." It would cost them three-quarters of the command, if the army tried to cut its way out again, and no general, claimed Buckner, "had the right to make such a sacrifice of human life." One can almost sense the shock of disbelief among council members, as Buckner dolefully concluded that it would be a virtual massacre and more disheartening in its effect than a surrender.[6]

In retrospect, Buckner's argument was weak. The army's stores were well stocked with food and medical supplies, and a steamboat bearing ammunition was due at daybreak. The generals knew how the water batteries had handled the gunboats, and, with the exception of Buckner's personal intercession to keep even his favorite "orphans" of the 2d Kentucky in battle array at day's end, there was little evidence to suggest that the rest of the force was too broken to renew the attack the next morning. Buckner had determined upon surrender, for he claimed that even if the army did escape, Union pursuit would cut the column to ribbons—a contention immediately rebutted by the feisty Forrest. Tempers began to flare, as it seemed only the Tennesseans wanted to fight their way out. Pillow especially felt they could hold out another day, so that the steamboats could return to ferry the army across the river. Whether the few boats available could have done so or whether the damaged rem-

General Simon B. Buckner.
National Archives.

nants of the Federal flotilla would have prevented such evacuation was not discussed. At least here was an option. Buckner was insensitive to any suggestion from Pillow, and reaffirmed his inability to contain C.F. Smith. Finally Floyd caved in, the opportunity for escape now passed.[7]

The scene rapidly approached bittersweet comedy. Floyd and Buckner rationalized that the army had fulfilled its mission to buy time for Johnston. Pillow finally bowed to the pressure, concluding, "there is only one alternative, that is capitulation." But he vowed not to be a party to it, saying that no two persons in the Confederacy were more sought by the United States government than he and Floyd, and the discussion degenerated after that into moral issues surrounding a general officer's action in this regard. Floyd was afraid of being tried and hung for alleged misdemeanors while serving as the prewar secretary of war. Pillow's reasons remained vague — perhaps his bombastic avowals of secession or his openly bantered image as a military buffoon concerned him. At any rate, having led the generals into this fix, Buckner now chose the martyr's role, as he declared it to be his considered duty to remain with his men and share their fate.[8]

The conversation continued as minutes passed. Floyd asked Buckner, "if I place you in command will you allow me to get out as much of my brigade as I can?" Buckner agreed, provided that Floyd left before the enemy received his surrender proposal. Events moved swiftly, as Floyd turned to Pillow, saying, "I turn the command over sir," and Pillow, for-getting now the future of his own troops, replied, "I pass it." Buckner resolutely affirmed, "I assume it," and asked for pen, ink, paper, and a bugler. Thus passed the torch of command at Fort Donelson, and with it the fate of over 15,000 Confederates. An enraged Forrest asked Pillow what he should do, and was told curtly to cut his way out. Uttering some explosive oath typical of this hardened warrior, Forrest told the generals that he thought there was more fight left in the army than they supposed. He turned on his heel and strode into the night, vowing to escape if he saved only one man.[9]

Floyd would later call Forrest back to prepare his command to escort Pillow and the Virginian to safety and the generals passed more time trying to set the record straight for official reports as to what each of them specifically felt about the surrender decision. Pillow particularly worried about his image and continued to declare his willingness to fight on. He told his colleagues that he understood their position and that it would mean the loss of 75 percent of the army to which, "I agree that it would be wrong to sacrifice them for the remaining fourth." Floyd and Buckner sighed wearily: "We understand you, general, and you under-stand us." Buckner then countermanded the orders to destroy excess com-missary stores, and the council ended—a war council possibly unparal-leled in American history.[10]

Forrest's confidence in the army's mettle proved perceptive. Almost to a man, they were shocked when told of their generals' plan to surrender. After the earlier council with senior unit commanders, these subordi-nates had returned to muster commands and begin the movement once more to the rendezvous on the army's left. By 3:00 A.M. Pillow's wing was in position. But some of the troops got no farther than Dover. They marched about one-half mile and halted, recalled Reverend Deavenport of the 3d Tennessee, and there remained in the cold for nearly two hours, when they saw a white flag passed "which caused us to think all was not well." Captain Guy had received conflicting orders about sending one of his cannon and six of his best horses to the steamboat landing, and he was puzzled because he thought that all of the artillery was to be spiked before the retreat. Deciding not to speculate, he simply rolled over in his blanket for another nap. Not so with Randal McGavock, who became impatient "and began to smell a rat." Queries up the chain of command only produced more confusion. Finally Bushrod Johnson, for one, decided to ride to headquarters to find out what was happening. By this time, noted McGavock, the forces within his view had become restive and began passing off up the riverbank singly and in pairs on their own.[11]

Johnson eventually appeared with news of the impending capitulation and with orders that everyone should return to quarters. McGavock marched his 10th Tennessee back "in sorrow, humiliation, and anger." The appearance of white flags on the trenches at dawn caught everyone off-guard. Captain R.L. McClung of the 15th Arkansas passed a battery behind his regiment and asked a gunner what the white rags were for. "We are all Surrendered G-d d-m you, that's what it means," replied the distraught artilleryman. McClung was upset too but more that the white flags were merely torn tents, not some large white silk flag more appropriate to a formal surrender. Others were mad as hornets, said Guy, with some raving and cursing, while another portion stood in shock. Astonishment soon gave way to "bitter regret and loud expression of discontent," he noted in his journal, and he claimed that no subordinate officer or soldier ever understood the necessity of capitulation or at all approved of it. Men from the 1st Mississippi wept hysterically and wrung their hands, while their officers broke their swords and tossed them away, recorded Lieutenant LeGrand Wilson of that unit. Lowly Private Spot F. Terrell of the 49th Tennessee thought it heartrending to surrender the place after so many glowing victories, but he added stoically, "we had to content ourselves as best we could under the circumstances."[12]

Not all of the Confederates acquiesced to the thought of captivity, however. Most notably, Nathan Bedford Forrest gathered his command together and offered to lead anyone who would ride out of the trap. Only Lieutenant Colonel George Gantt of the 9th Tennessee cavalry battalion and several companies of the 1st Kentucky cavalry attached to Forrest's command declined to make the attempt. Just after 4:00 A.M. Forrest led his men out of their ravine encampment and turned onto the road leading to the Lick Creek crossing. Five hundred shivering troopers stretched behind him, with an additional two hundred foot-soldiers holding to saddle skirts. Even some of Porter's gunners unhitched the battery horses and joined in. A three-man patrol soon conveyed the unwelcome news that Yankees now blocked the passage. Forrest called for volunteers to confirm the fact, but when he received no response, he determined to check personally. Turning over command temporarily to Kelly, Forrest and his younger brother Jeffrey moved out the road in advance of the main body, only to discover shadowy fence posts, which they suspected had "spooked" the scouts. Forrest even decided that this same

Colonel Nathan Bedford Forrest.
National Archives.

specter had frightened the scouts earlier that evening, leading to their reports which had weighed so heavily in the surrender decision.[13]

The Forrest brothers then rode onto Dudley's Hill, where they found small groups of wounded Federals huddling before makeshift fires. These men volunteered information that only scouts and scavengers roamed the battlefield that night. The Confederate officers thereupon wheeled their mounts around and headed back to the main column. Forrest felt he should pass this information to headquarters but hesistated until crossing the flooded creek. Lacking volunteers to test the depth of the Smith ford, he led the column himself across the icy waters and then hesitated again about alerting Buckner to the situation. Ostensibly at this point, he heard the first notes of the bugle call for "parley" and realized that it was now too late to alert Buckner. Riding on, he left a rearguard under Kelly at the junction with a road leading to the Cumberland Iron Works. Turning the main column into this road, Forrest threw out scouts and flankers, and set a deliberate marching pace. By nightfall on February 16, the command was twenty miles from Dover, having seen no Federals after crossing Lick Creek. This march proved as arduous as predicted, with much suffering among the men due to the icy crossing. Yet all survived, disproving the best medical counsel to the Donelson high command. By 10:00 A.M. on February 18, Forrest's column reached Nashville unscathed.[14]

Meanwhile, back in the defense perimeter, the early dawn hours found numerous Rebels making individual plans for escape. Colonel Head and Captain Bidwell at the main fort pleaded ill-health, so Buckner allowed them to escape by boat before the surrender. Pillow and Floyd also sought individual means of flight, with Pillow's resourceful aide, Major Rice, procuring a small flatboat or skiff with which to convey his chief across the river. The fortuitous arrival of the steamboats also permitted Pillow's staff to cross the river and ride overland with their leader to Clarksville. For a time it seemed that Pillow's manservant and his personal baggage had been lost, but Floyd brought both with him aboard the steamboats which he soon commandeered for the use of his Virginia brigade.[15]

The story of Floyd's departure added one more questionable act to the morning's proceedings. Arrival of the *General Anderson* and a second, smaller steamboat occasioned a made scramble for their use. The larger boat brought some four hundred raw Mississippi recruits, and both boats contained ammunition and subsistence for the army. Men and matériel were deposited unceremoniously on the muddy riverbank as Floyd immediately commandeered the craft. Ordering Major W.N. Brown to use his 20th Mississippi to form a guard around the landing, Floyd explained "that we would embark according to the rank of commanding officers." Thus caught on the bottom rung of the command ladder, Brown and his people acted like veterans while silently and steadily ("though sullenly") guarding the embarkation of other troops and the army commander. For a brief time the two steamboats ferried first McCausland and then Wharton and their men across the river. By this time, news of the impending surrender had spread like wildfire through the army, and a near panic ensued as many soldiers flocked to the upper steamboat landing seeking to escape.[16]

Private Thomas J. Riddell of Guy's battery waded at least one hundred yards through the freezing Cumberland to get aboard one of the boats. Whether justified, he had a horrid conception of being captured and subjected to the rigors of the prison pen, he claimed after the war. Riddell made it, although nearly over his shoulders in the frigid water. A barrel of whiskey aboard the boat was soon bayoneted open by the fleeing soldiery, providing a stimulant to the survivors. On deck, with drawn saber, Floyd shouted to his men: "Come on, my brave Virginia boys." About then the overly punctilious Buckner sent word that

Union gunboats were coming upriver and that the surrender was about to take effect. Both Confederate honor and his own honor dictated adherence to the terms of capitulation, he said. Perhaps Buckner had simply tired of the charade at the landing, for he bluntly informed one colonel that unless the boats left immediately, he would have "a bomb thrown into it." Floyd and the others saw the expediency of prompt departure, and the Virginian queried the boat captains about additional evacuees. The rivermen demurred, claiming they would swamp the craft, so Floyd ordered the lines cast off and movement out into the stream. Major Brown swore that the boats departed only half full of people.[17]

Left standing on the shore to witness this last act, Brown's Mississippians, most of Floyd's artillerymen, and countless other panicky rebels howled in protest, but to no avail. Brown later avowed that his men simply stacked arms in perfect order, "without the least intimidation but full of regret." Captain Guy noted that as soon as thoughts of escape vanished, the soldiery began breaking open barrels of army stores, which lay about in quantity, and appropriated the sugar, whiskey, crackers, molasses, and clothing. Yet he was most angered by finding the gun which he had sent earlier to the landing at Floyd's request, now left standing with its horses and limber in a nearby street. Interestingly, this gun's dispatch to the landing had permitted Riddell to escape but not his battery captain. Similarly, Pillow and Floyd — like Forrest — along with uncounted others over the next week made good their escape in defiance of the naysayers who said that flight was impossible. Left to taste the bitter gall of surrender was the chief architect of that event — Simon B. Buckner, the man who said escape could not be done.[18]

This proud Kentuckian prepared for the formal act of surrender. He directed that white flags appear on the outer works, although nobody had white cloth. Ordnance Sergeant R.L. Cobb of the 50th Tennessee secured a white sheet for the main flagstaff in the fort. Buckner specifically forbade any such display on the water batteries, where the Confederates had been notably victorious. The problem of white cloth persisted when Buckner sent his aide, Major George B. Cosby, out to Colonel John C. Brown's sector with directions to mount a parley party to find Grant. Finally a cut-up tent sufficed. Then Major Cheairs (who was to lead the party) questioned the proper bugle call for parley since no one had any previous experience with a surrender. A thoroughly irritated Brown turned to the regimental band bugler of the 3d Tennessee and told him to blow every bugle call he knew, "and if that wouldn't do — to blow his d-n brains out!" Tempers were short in Confederate lines that morning.[19]

The Cheairs party passed beyond the trench line with Buckner's stuffy and formal surrender note that read: "In consideration of all the circumstances governing the present situation of affairs at this station, I propose to the commanding officers of the Federal forces the appointment of commissioners to agree upon terms of capitulation of the forces and post under my command, and in that view suggest an armistice until 12 o'clock to-day." The party found even the Federal lines greatly agitated at daybreak. Cheairs naively took this to mean that they were preparing to retreat back to Fort Henry, "as they were facing in that direction." Actually C.F. Smith (whose lines he reached) was preparing to attack, not retreat. It took nearly an hour for the bugle calls and white flag to arouse interest among the Yankees, but finally Cheairs and his group were taken before Smith, who received them with a curt, "I'll make no terms with rebels with arms in their hands — my terms are unconditional and immediate surrender." The old soldier passed the major along to Grant. Reaching the Crisp house, Smith and Grant consulted while Cheairs waited, and Grant apparently embraced Smith's reiterated oath —"no terms to the damned Rebels"— and so stated in a note back to Buckner.[20]

Indeed Grant's words (but Smith's sentiments) later echoed down through the subsequent years of American history. It earned the younger man a sobriquet and a place in the pantheon of national heroes. Still the philosophy came from the teacher, not the pupil, as Grant formally wrote Buckner: "Yours of this date proposing Armistice and appointment of Commissioners to settle terms of Capitulation is just received. No terms except unconditional and immediate surrender can be accepted. I propose to move immediately upon your works."[21]

This was no empty threat on Grant's part; he had tired of the inconclusive three-day combat and wanted to end it quickly then and there. He had already wired Cullum at Cairo about his dwindling ammunition, unpredictable supply line back to Fort Henry, and the uncertainty of the conflict. That morning Grant told McClernand and Lew Wallace to coordinate their final assault on Rebel lines when they heard C.F. Smith's guns and to finish the thing. Buckner probably suspected the immediacy of this assault, and his attempt at an armistice was designed to forestall such an attack. Of course the Kentuckian also expected more favorable treatment from his old friend Grant. He had loaned the man money some years before when Grant ran out of funds in New York while returning from California. Furthermore, thinking he might at least secure a parole for his half-frozen army, Buckner had prevented destruction of stores and munitions. Now all that he received from Grant was a rebuff. Buckner therefore replied somewhat peevishly: "The distribution of the forces under my command incident to an unexpected change of commanders and the overwhelming force under your command, compel me, notwithstanding the brilliant success of the Confederate arms yesterday, to accept the ungenerous and unchivalrous terms which you propose." This was the final barb of frustration; yesterday no longer counted. At least Grant did not make good his threat to open fire, for it took Cosby and Brown three and one-half hours to complete the round trip from Buckner's headquarters.[22]

Buckner's pique transferred itself to Cheairs in a final exchange with Grant. When queried by the general as to the Confederate strength, Cheairs noted only seven or eight thousand. Grant cut him short: "I didn't ask you for a falsehood, sir." Cheairs flared at this aspersion to his honor and replied that while Grant might be the enemy commander, his father had taught him to take insult from no man. He started to remove his coat as if to fight. Grant smiled, thought better, and apologized, but the unrepentant Cheairs had the final word. Under the circumstances, he told his captor, he would have to accept the apology, but he told him to be more careful of "your language to me in the future." Then the major led Grant and his staff into Dover and to the fateful meeting with Buckner at the hotel near the upper steamboat landing. Before departing, Grant instructed Rawlins to send orders to Smith and McClernand so that they would move forward and occupy the Confederate entrenchments. All public property would be closely monitored, he directed, and collected with no pillage or theft permitted.[23]

At this very moment, however, another Federal general officer was also moving into Dover. Lew Wallace had placed his brigades in battle array early that morning on the Wynn's Ferry road. Supported by McClernand, the massive assault was to pick up where it had left off the night before, or "about breakfast time," according to Wallace. Yet he was baffled at the lack of enemy activity in opposition to his preparations. Then he saw two riders coming toward him under a flag of truce. Not wishing them to discern his activities, he sent an aide to intercept them. One rider, Major W.E. Rogers of Mississippi, told Wallace of the parley, that the Confederates were drawn up in quarters with arms stacked, and that surrender was imminent. Wallace directed his brigade commanders to move forward to secure persons and property but to keep their own men under close check because he wanted the business done "as delicately as possible," with not a taunt or cheer. Then, feeling "a quick thrill" at the opportunity, and an "irresistible impulse" to see his old friend Buckner, Wallace asked Rogers for the flag of truce so that he might ride ahead. The Mississippian remarked that he would hardly need it, adding, "our people are in a bad humor, but I will be glad to have you go with me."[24]

Rogers took Wallace to the upper landing and to the large double-chimneyed, two-story frame structure known locally as the Dover hotel. Typical of taverns of the antebellum South, it had been constructed in the early 1850s and had passed to F.P. Gray's ownership from a T.D. Mockabee in 1860. Until that Sunday morning, the hotel played only a minor role in the Fort Donelson proceedings. Buckner had his headquarters there; Floyd's was just up the street; but both generals spent most of their time out on the field. The inn may have provided intermittent food and shelter to the pair and their staffs. The serious war councils took place elsewhere, apparently—the record is vague. Still, it was the Dover hotel that would go down in history as the place where both Wallace and Grant found Buckner waiting to surrender.[25]

Escorted by Rogers, Lew Wallace walked into the building before Grant and down a narrow hallway, which opened into the dining room. There he found Buckner seated at a table with eight or ten staff officers. The Kentuckian rose, "grave, dignified, silent." The grip he gave, noted Wallace, "was an assurance of welcome quite as good as words." Buckner declined to introduce his staff—"you know them all," he told Wallace, as the Hoosier had indeed met most of them during the 1860 encampment of the Kentucky State Guard in Louisville. Nobody seemed talkative, and one young staff officer broke into tears about the events then unfolding. They offered Wallace a niggardly breakfast of cornbread and coffee and then proceeded to discuss the battle and the war in general. The Confederates were convinced that Grant had nearly 50,000 men, and Wallace chose not to contradict them. He did comment how surprising for the Confederate Congress to give "up the old flag" for a new one. That prompted Buckner to lash out: "The old flag! I followed it when most of your thousands out yonder were in swaddlng clothes—in Mexico—on the frontier—and I love it yet." Wallace avoided a retort.[26]

The conversation then turned to a graver note as the Rebels asked what Grant would do with them. This question was important: would the United States government treat them as prisoners of war or traitors? Wallace did not know, but he told them that he knew Grant and Lincoln and that neither man was vindictive by nature. This relieved the southerners. Just then a knock on the door was heard and in strode Commander Benjamin F. Dove of the U.S. Navy. The navy seemed to be abroad very early, Wallace told an aide later; they were looking for swords, perhaps. But Dove had come upriver with the *Louisville* and *St. Louis,* under orders from Henry Walke to see if the navy could once more beat the army to a surrender. Lew Wallace flattered himself that he had gotten ahead of the naval officer by nearly an hour. The two Federals passed some terse comments, and Dove precipitously left the room. Wallace later softened his story of the army-navy rivalry, but by then he was serving as Dove's character reference. The navy department had been so upset by Dove's failure to take Buckner's surrender that it suspended him.[27]

Nearly an hour after Dove's exit, Grant and his staff clattered up on their horses. Their ride from Smith's lines had been a mixture of cheering Federals and sullen glares from the vanquished Rebels. An accompanying cavalry escort had drawn revolvers because of the antagonism etched on Confederate faces. Finally, however, Grant reached Dover and had a "very friendly" meeting with Buckner. The pair joshed about the battle, with Buckner noting that if he had been in top command, Grant would never have laid siege to the place. Grant replied gallantly, that if Buckner had been in command: "I should not have tried in the same way that I did." The Federal commander remained unaware of Pillow's escape, whereby Buckner chided that he thought Grant was too anxious to capture him personally. Grant smiled and replied that if he had captured Pillow, he would have turned the Tennessean loose, for "I would rather have him in command of you fellows than as a prisoner." This banter stood in marked contrast to the talk between Buckner and C.F. Smith when the older officer arrived at the hotel. Smith had also taught the Kentuckian at West Point, yet he now refused to shake his hand. "General Smith, I believe I am right," said Buckner. The unforgiving teacher replied: "That is for God to decide, not me, for I know I am right."[28]

Grant and Buckner eventually discussed surrender terms. Grant asked about Buckner's strength, and Buckner replied that he was unsure, possibly 12,000 to 15,000. The Confederate general requested permission to send burial parties onto the battlefield, and Grant agreed, regretting later that the Federal guards became so familiar with the sight of Confederates passing freely that many of the captives got beyond the pickets and escaped. The two commanders also discussed the hungry Confederates, and Grant freely suggested that Union rations would be issued, while officers might retain sidearms and servants and the enlisted ranks their clothing and blankets. Other slave laborers (milling about in the streets of Dover) would be pressed into Union work gangs. With that, Buckner retired upstairs to his quarters, and Grant worked with aides to prepare supplemental orders affecting prisoner transfer and tabulation of captured stores. The hotel now became temporary headquarters to the victors, pending arrival of Grant's own steamer, *New Uncle Sam.*

Out on the trench line, despite Grant's orders, the elated Federal soldiery thundered volley after volley of cheers and victory salutes into the frosty air.[29]

Surgeon John Brinton asked Grant about the formal, traditional surrender ceremonies where Buckner would hand over his sword and the Rebel force would pass before the government troops. Grant quietly advised him that the surrender was fact. He had the fort, the men, and the guns, so why go through with vain forms to mortify and injure the spirits of brave men, "who, after all, are our countrymen and brothers?" Mississippean Selden Spencer penned an appropriate epitaph to the whole affair in his journal, writing: "So after four days hard fighting without rest & exposure to severe weather, having defeated the enemy in every engagement & signally on Saturday, with no hope of relief, exhausted, surrounded by four times our number, cut off from succor, we yielded to fate and were Prisoners of War."[30]

Grant's army now moved to secure the fruits of victory. Bands struck up "Yankee Doodle" and even "Dixie" as the brigades of Cruft, Oglesby, Ross, and W.H.L. Wallace marched into Dover. Tennessean John M. Porter and his friends thought bitterly, "never did music sound so much like the wails of the dying." C.F. Smith's men soon had the Stars and Stripes floating over Fort Donelson itself, and "Bohemians" of the news corps soon disembarked from steamboats to fan out like locusts through both Union and Confederate armies to seek stories. Indomitable reporters Charles C. "Carleton" Coffin, Franc B. Wilkie, Junius Henri Browne, and others put into words what sketch artist Henri Lovie and his friends captured with pencil and pad. "A motley, care-worn, haggard, anxious looking crowd" of Rebels was the way *Boston Journal* reporter Coffin described the human flotsam at the Dover landings. They proclaimed loudly their battlefield victory, he noted, and cursed the discord and disloyalty of their generals. Floyd always was "a damned thief and sneak," declared one dissatisfied prisoner, while others swore that they would shoot Floyd "as they would a dog, if they could get a chance."[31]

The dejected Confederates stood around glumly in groups, drinking heavily from liberated whiskey and brandy stores, and even their officers showed little concern about the rabble. A few downcast prisoners worried that the Federals would start shooting them, but the victors were too busy looting Confederate camps (despite Grant's orders) or seeking out friends and relatives among the vanquished to share the "influence of sweetened dram" to kill anyone. A brisk trade sprang up between the erstwhile antagonists — Rebel tobacco, bowie knives, and trinkets being exchanged for Yankee beef and biscuits. Such trading was of course forbidden, but few paid any attention to orders. The desolate shambles of Dover also proved too alluring, and the riff-raff on both sides soon broke open stores and rifled civilian houses and shops for brass candlesticks, mirrors, and civilian clothing. Grant caught one Federal merrymaker, cavorting in a woman's straw bonnet embellished with a flower, and a long strip of blue tarlatan was thrown over his shoulders. The army commander ordered the man strung up by his thumbs aboard the headquarters boat to set an example, but even the sober John Rawlins, as trustee of Grant's own abstinence, gave in to several victory toasts. A general relaxation affected both armies in the aftermath of the battle.[32]

Still, serious work lay ahead. At first, chaos made it difficult to determine priorities. At some point Grant sent a terse telegram announcing his victory to Halleck, and then followed with more detailed dispatches. The telegram said simply that Grant had taken 12,000 to 15,000 prisoners, including General Buckner and General Bushrod Johnson, 20,000 stand of arms, 48 pieces of artillery, 17 heavy guns, 2,000 to 4,000 horses, and large quantities of supplies. Grant's letter cited the near disaster of the fifteenth, his consultation with the wounded Foote, and the overriding news of the unconditional surrender of the post. At least this time Grant got the spelling of Fort Donelson correct.[33]

Reporting duties concluded, Grant and his staff tackled the problems of the dead, wounded, and prisoners. It had been a long time since American officers had taken the surrender of a whole army in the field. Grant wrote his wife that it was the largest capture ever made on the continent, in his opinion. Quite possibly, the Union officers simply did not know how to handle the task. At least three sets of specific orders prescribed procedures for the POWs, yet in Buckner's opinion there seemed to be no concerted action between different parts of Grant's force in managing the issue. Eventually, Buckner had to intervene, and by so doing he actually gained most of the concessions originally sought from his captors. Certainly the cooperation quickly allayed all fears about the hanging of Rebels![34]

After their initial meeting at the hotel, Buckner went aboard the *New Uncle Sam* to conclude formal arrangements with Grant. The meeting was stiff, but informative and satisfying to everyone. Buckner, clad in light-blue overcoat and checkered neckcloth, freely discussed his positions, forces, and intentions. Speaking quietly, while smoking a cigar like Grant, he again requested subsistence for his army. He also wanted small favors for his wounded officers, permission to communicate with Albert Sidney Johnston, and a chance for his subordinates to write loved ones at home. Buckner also thought that his men should be put aboard the transports quickly due to the cold weather. But Grant hesitated, claiming inadequate staff to treat such matters, whereupon Buckner volunteered his own to help. As Buckner and his companions rose to leave, Grant solicitously drew aside his old friend and offered him his purse. The proud son of the Bluegrass declined, however, although later commenting upon the Union general's remembrance of his own prewar gesture.[35]

If Grant seemed solicitous, many of his subordinates were not. The Reverend Deavenport complained about thieving Yankees stripping Confederates of their clothing and blankets, driving them through the cold mud en route to the steamboats. Even Buckner witnessed a young Federal captain marching two Confederate colonels to headquarters under arrest. He quickly wrote a bristling note to Grant in protest, suggesting that Federal guards honor Buckner's own passes, or that Grant appoint a provost marshal to sit with the Confederate general's staff to issue such passes. He also requested Grant to decide if privately owned horses of Confederate officers were their own to retain, or were to be passed over to U.S. property officers.[36]

When Grant issued an order incorporating Buckner's point about respecting Buckner's signature, he may have once more unwittingly contributed to the escape of additional Confederates. Still, security was lax with civilian-attired reporters such as Browne and Coffin freely roaming about the Dover neighborhood. Browne saw Coffin on the morning of the surrender, "doing the fortifications on the run with his head down like an animal which trails by scent," he noted. Who could distinguish him from the captives — many of whom were clothed in nondescript buffalo robes, tablecloths, carpets, patchwork quilts, and paisley piano covers over their uniforms. Even amply supplied Federal clothing helped cloak true identities. Thus many of the garrison easily escaped by walking out through the lines. James M. Cooper, adjutant of the 20th Mississippi, did so, taking his commanding officer's young son with him. Lieutenant LeGrand Wilson (a doctor serving as a line officer) simply hid out in a Dover loft until he could sneak through the lines. Bushrod Johnson, the highest ranking Confederate to escape, accompanied Captain J.H. Anderson of the 10th Tennessee out through Heiman's old sector, and he noted later that he had not heard of any soldier attempting to escape as having failed. Few Confederates excoriated his conduct as did his Ohio hometown newspaper. Those homefront Unionists probably were angered by the confusion of a reporter who thought Grant had bagged Sidney Johnston, not the more prosaic Johnson. At any rate this flurry of post-surrender flight proved the validity of escape as an option for the Donelson army, not as an organized force but rather as individual or small groups of fugitives.[37]

Grant took greater care with captured property; even this matter, however, soon got out of hand too. War trophies were everywhere, from personal effects of the captives to splendid guns, equipment, and regimental banners. Most Confederates tried to conceal their unit symbols, but the diligent Federal search in Dover uncovered caches of shotguns, food, ammunition, uniforms, and equipment — all of which had not been distributed to needy southerners during the battle. Much of this bounty disappeared as most of the Federals tried to send home booty from this signal victory in the West. Grant ordered McClernand and Lew Wallace to search all out-bound steamers, and he telegraphed Cullum to do likewise at Cairo. The relics went north in great numbers, however, with one rear echelon gunboat officer telling his sweetheart that he would send her a trophy from the battle as soon as he could trade for one. Lieutenant H.L. Brickett of the 25th Indiana would fall late in April at Shiloh, but he sent home a leather armlet from Fort Donelson, which some Rebel had fashioned into a percussion cap dispenser. Grant could do little to stop the pilferage.[38]

Days passed, and Federal officers still had no clear or accurate tabulation of the captured matériel. One Federal report enumerated 400,000 rations of rice, 300,000 rations of beef packed in boxes marked "Nashville," 150,000 rations of pork, as well as 400 barrels of new molasses and 20 hogsheads of sugar in Dover. Grant thought that he had enough supplies to feed his army for twenty days and enough rice for the duration of the war. The eighteen pieces of ordnance captured at Fort Henry were added to those at Fort Donelson, making at least seventy-five cannon scooped up by Federal forces in the twin rivers campaign. As to the wounded and prisoners, Christian Commission officials, who arrived quickly from Cairo after the battle, estimated that injured Confederates alone filled the twenty-three log-house hospitals at Fort Donelson and Dover. Best modern estimates suggest that possibly 20,000 to 21,000 Confederates had been available for the defense of the Cumberland, with fully 16,500 to 17,500 delivered over to Grant in the course of the surrender. Buckner could not have known precise numbers, and most certainly would have misrepresented them to his enemies. Confederate strength and casualty figures acquired a mythic quality from the very date of the infamous surrender.[39]

Arriving reinforcements from Brigadier General Stephen Hurlburt's division of Buell's army immediately went on guard duty, as well as policing the battlefield for overlooked wounded, dead, and discarded equipment. Federal injured were moved to makeshift hospitals all over the area. McClung of the 15th Arkansas watched much of this from a sick bed in a Confederate infirmary in Dover, and he reported how Yankee burial details unceremoniously collected frozen Confederate corpses on fence rails and dumped them, fifty to seventy-five bodies each, into mass graves. Given the frozen ground, the recently overturned earth of the rifle pits probably served as gravesites. Christian and Sanitary Commission delegations, as well as some participants' wives, arrived by boat to tend to the wounded with Mary "Mother" Bickerdyke and Mary Newcomb helping minister to wounded from both armies. Grant effected a prisoner exchange with Confederate authorities upriver (thus recovering some of his command taken on February 15 in trade for twenty-five Kentuckians). Later, other Kentuckians like John M. Porter, serving as a Confederate scout in the battle, would gain freedom by feigning civilian status. Grant also wrote on behalf of young Horace H. Lurton (who Buckner claimed was a discharged minor from Clarksville, present merely to witness the great battle), and Captain P.K. Stankiewicz, a Polish emigré battery commander of the siege artillery in the main fort. Grant knew Stankiewicz as a noncommissioned officer in the old army, and he could not believe that his erstwhile acquaintance had shed his loyalty to the Union.[40]

Soon Grant issued obligatory "victory" messages to his troops, suggesting that Fort Donelson would soon be marked in capital letters on maps across the country, and that veterans of the fight would live long in the memory of a grateful nation. He wrote his wife that he expected one more hard battle and then the rebellion would be suppressed, adding that Fort Donelson was one of the most desperate affairs of the war. Buckner echoed this thought in his final letter to his own wife, Mary, then at Columbus, and dispatched by Grant's courtesy. The note was heavy with pathos, as Buckner declared that he was left to bear the "blunder of my superiors" but that the lost campaign had produced something poignantly important. The surrender, said the Kentuckian, had unified a band of brothers in adversity—"noble fellows; we are linked together by ties which can never be loosened." With this thought, Buckner and his noble "Indians" (as he styled them) passed off to captivity.[41]

Unfortunately, the trauma for the Confederates did not end as they steamed away from the Dover landings. In fact the trip northward to prison continued both tragic and comic by turn. The cold weather continued, and absence of fire and proper body covering bothered everyone. The soldiers had been stripped of their ferocious-looking bowie knives, but they retained their dirty and pest-ridden clothing and bed-

Federals March into Fort Donelson, February 16, 1862. *Frank Leslie's Illustrated Newspaper*, March 15, 1862.

ding. They gathered in groups to keep warm aboard the boats and to maintain some semblance of cheer while eking out an existence until fate disclosed their future. J.T. Lowry of the 3d Tennessee pronounced that his boat should have been consigned to a junk pile years before and that he felt as much danger aboard it as when facing Yankee bullets. Cooking raw rations issued by Federal commissary personnel also proved a problem. An old-fashioned wood stove provided the solution, but its depressed top became a burning receptacle for meat drippings, as scores of men thrust raw meat on pointed sticks into the flames. They threatened to set fire to the whole boat. All in all, the disdainful Rebels came away heartily sickened with Federal treatment aboard the transports.[42]

The Confederates additionally faced local derision, as well as drafty and unsanitary craft such as the *Decatur, Tecumseh,* and *White Cloud,* when the boat captains stopped to procure wood at landings along the way. Grant's policy of keeping officers and their men together lessened the need for vast numbers of guards, but the few Union troops aboard the boats also voiced scorn of the prisoners. "A motley a crew as ever a mortal knew," suggested one Illinoisan, and he pointed to the lack of clothing uniformity and a distinct undertone of restiveness among the Rebel rank and file, for the "privates say they have been badly fooled." This guard found some Mississippi officers to be gentlemanly and reasonable aboard the *Decatur,* but the majority he felt were ignorant and low bred, and he concluded that if they were the flower of Magnolia State youth, "I can hardly conjecture what the leaves must be."[43]

Cullum took charge of the POW shipments when the boats reached Cairo. Just as Grant feared, the matter became a hassle. Halleck ordered separation of the prisoners into packets, with some 3,000 enlisted men going to Springfield, Illinois, and Indianapolis, Indiana, and the remainder to Chicago. Officers were sent to Columbus, Ohio. The same inexperience and unpreparedness attended these moves as had been present at Dover. Earlier prisoner exchanges in the West were in effect no longer; Henry-Donelson numbers were too great, and official Washington frowned on anything suggesting even tacit recognition of the Confederacy as a nation. So thousands of captured Confederates, thrust upon Federal authorities by Grant's victories, became not only a great embarrassment, but also a massive management problem.[44]

Certainly the small number captured at Fort Henry provided no precedent. They had been quietly shipped to Paducah under Grant's orders to get them out of the way of the campaign. At first Grant wanted them held incommunicado in confiscated Secessionist homes. Then he softened to the point of recommending parole and freedom of the town.

Halleck agreed, but when everybody realized that the city was Lloyd Tilghman's home and would pose problems to Sherman's control of the place, Grant suggested that the Fort Henry prisoners be sent to Cairo, where Halleck had them transferred to the Alton, Illinois, prison. Even then the officers were given their parole and could stroll about town. All of this ceased when Secretary of War Stanton and General McClellan learned of it. They telegraphed their opposition to paroles and exchange, despite Halleck's assurances. At one stroke, Washington hardliners swept away all felicitous local attempts to shape POW policy. The Rebels would be incarcerated as prisoners of war.[45]

Halleck continued to protest, citing the negative effect upon the reputed Unionism growing in Kentucky and Tennessee. We can afford to be generous, he claimed, and "if they violate [parole] I will hang them." Washington remained firm, however; the senior officers were to be sent to Fort Warren in Boston harbor. Halleck did manage to effect equal treatment for Confederate and Federal wounded, but if any prisoner tried to escape, "put them in irons," he instructed. He finally stripped sidearms from the prisoners, but as late as March 5 he received reports of Confederates roaming about the streets and into the saloons of Columbus. Finally his patience ended toward such liberties.[46]

The first indication of Halleck's change came with a telegram from the Illinois governor that it was unsafe to send prisoners to Springfield because of the large number of Secessionists there. In fact, sizable expressions of friendship for the southerners accompanied their journey to places such as St. Louis, Springfield, and Alton. Many friends, relatives, and sympathetic northerners tried to ameliorate the plight of the POWs. McGavock noted on February 20 that their arrival at St. Louis occasioned a most cordial reception from the locals, many of whom went to the boats with articles of clothing and other necessities. He also mentioned their pleasure at reunion with old Fort Henry friends on parole. Certainly Halleck, Cullum, and their seniors had reason to change all this familiarity with the enemy.[47]

Solutions could not be found overnight, however. Illinois Adjutant General Allen C. Fuller wrote Halleck that his state had a lease on Camp Douglas at Chicago for use as a training ground until May 1. It could accommodate 7,000 prisoners, but what about breaking the lease? What was to be done with the black manservants of some Rebel officers, queried Indiana governor Richard Morton. Small towns such as Lancaster, and New Lisbon, Ohio, volunteered warehouse space for the prisoners, but other communities recognized the potential incumbus of rebellion by doing so. Mayor J.S. Ramsay of Chicago complained about the lack of a fence around Camp Douglas, and while a Secessionist element in Lafayette, Indiana, might fete the vanquished from Donelson, he felt "our best citizens are in great alarm for fear that the prisoners will break through and burn the City." Halleck was unmoved and shot back testily, "raise a special police force if necessary. I have taken these Confederates in arms behind their entrenchments; it is a great pity if Chicago cannot guard them for a few days."[48]

Halleck's temper was not improved by news from Cullum that the wives of Buckner and Roger Hanson, among others, had come up from Columbus, Kentucky, under a flag of truce, seeking to be with their husbands. Precedent existed from previous arrangements between Grant and Polk, but that had since passed, and the Missouri department commander quickly slammed this door shut. When the prisoners had been properly disposed of, he suggested, there would be time to decide about family visitation. Besides, Buckner had already proven troublesome. The ever combative Kentuckian had used his departure from Dover to lecture one impertinent Union colonel, who asked if the band's playing "Yankee Doodle" did not rekindle fond memories of the old army for Buckner. Buckner answered by noting how one of his men was drummed out of the regiment for some offense just before the surrender, and the unit band had struck up the customary "Rogue's March." "Stop," cried the victim, "you have mistaken the tune. Play Yankee Doodle; a half million rogues march to that every day." No, Buckner did not leave the place quietly, nor would his passage to prison prove easy either. Reaction in northern Kentucky to Buckner, Hanson, and other Kentucky Rebels threatened to turn violent as they passed upriver toward captivity in Massachusetts. Civil authorities had issued a warrant for Buckner's arrest, "on the charge of treason against the State of Kentucky," Buell wired Halleck on the nineteenth. Assistant Secretary of War Scott, also present in Louisville, warned that "many threats are made of lynching him if he is brought into Kentucky." The matter exceeded local control, and newsmen in the North suggested that Union officers' lives could not be sacrificed merely to gratify the "natural longing of Kentucky" to hang one of its own traitors. Certainly Buckner could not be exchanged, and for several days following the surrender the United States government was unsure of what to do with him.[49]

The *Louisville Journal* also reported gleefully the capture of Roger Hanson. The editor promised a demi-john of whiskey to "comfort and gladden" his heart in prison. Just across the Ohio in New Albany, Indiana, the citizenry remembered courtesies extended by State Guard Kentuckians during prewar militia drills. In any event the Lincoln government wanted Buckner, Tilghman, Hanson, and other high-ranking officers captured on the twin rivers and taken out of the South as quickly and quietly as possible. On February 25 Halleck directed Colonel Richard Cutts to escort the Confederate officers by train to Boston and Fort Warren. Heavy snows and curious but antagonistic crowds in Buffalo, Rochester, and Albany in New York delayed their arrival until early March. Several times Cutts sought to avoid unpleasant incidents at stops along the way by offering his blue overcoat to hide Buckner's gray uniform. Each time the sensitive southerner declined, avowing that he was a Confederate soldier and that he did not propose to disguise himself "to prevent your people from disgracing themselves." At Rochester, Buckner actually quipped with hecklers that he and Tilghman were unused to public life, and he wondered why the crowd wanted to deprive them of popular ovations. Finally, on March 3, Buckner's group passed safely behind the cold prison walls of Fort Warren on windswept Georges Island in Boston harbor.[50]

By this date, Buckner's army had disappeared into similar prison pens such as Camp Douglas at Chicago, Camp Morton at Indianapolis, Camp Chase at Columbus, and Camp Butler at Springfield. Smaller contingents went to Alton, Terre Haute, and Lafayette sites, and some would cross to Johnsons Island in Lake Erie. Passage to those camps left Rebel heads unbowed. Despite the rigors of the journey which further damaged moral and health for many, the insults of Yankees, and the primitive prison conditions, most of the Confederates took their fate in stride. One irate prisoner remembered the wide-eyed Chicago onlookers, claiming, "to them it was far better than a menagerie. They seemed at a loss to determine what we were, whether men or animals, whether 'spirits or health or goblins damned.'" The *Chicago Tribune* declared, "a more woebegone appearing set of men" would be hard to imagine, and the *Indianapolis Journal* observed that here and there could be seen a man or two who had the appearance of being intelligent or educated, but these were noted exceptions. In spite of the constant northern carping about nondescript uniforms, multihued knapsacks, or ersatz outer coverings, the Henry-Donelson survivors appeared virtually unvanquished to most observers as they marched into confinement. Reverend Deavenport captured this irrepressible southern spirit quite nicely when he observed his unit's mascot:

> The orderly of my company had a favorite chicken, raised in camp called Jake, this he carried to prison. On getting off the cars he set him on his knapsack and as Jake thus rode through the city [Chicago] every few steps he

would crow. He seemed to possess something of the unconquerable spirit of the boys. At last we drew near the prison and over the street the "glorious old stars and stripes" were hanging for us to walk under, but the column parted, one half going on each side.[51]

"Jake Donelson"— as the unconquered Rebel rooster came to be called throughout the imprisoned army— provided the symbol of this captive but undaunted host. He provided an antidote to what Nathaniel Cheairs declared was "the most disgraceful, unnecessary and uncalled for surrender that occurred during the four years of War."[52]

CHAPTER 12

A Season of Lost Opportunities

WHEN SECRETARY STANTON LEARNED OF Grant's victory, he wired Halleck: "The brilliant results of the energetic action in the West fills the Nation with joy." Indeed northern cities and towns went wild with the news. Fireworks, patriotic bunting, enthusiastic handshakes reflected the enthusiasm. Senators at the U.S. Capitol forgot their own rule against applause, while cannon salutes thundered from the Army of the Potomac across the river. Halleck told a group gathered outside his St. Louis headquarters that he would suspect the loyalty of any male in the city who could be found sober enough to walk within the next half hour. He ordered a hamper of champagne for this assemblage. A local newspaper in Macomb, Illinois, declared reverently: "Light is breaking, God Speed the Right." But in Richmond, Jefferson Davis solemnly pronounced that "events have cast on our arms and hopes the gloomiest of shadows."[1]

Probably too many northerners thought the war was about over. Possibly, at first, too many of them attributed the victory to Halleck, McClellan, even Stanton and Lincoln, rather than to Grant. Suddenly everyone wanted to visit the victory site. Cincinnati's intrepid newsman, Whitelaw Reid, said that crowds of people gathered from all over the Midwest to make the pilgrimage. Fortunately for Grant and his army, the Cairo and Paducah choke points stifled steamboat travel to the twin rivers. Grant wrote Sherman that he wanted to see as few civilians as possible at Dover and that ladies, especially officers' wives, were quite troublesome. Nevertheless, scores of reporters, artists, speculators, and plain sightseers would join doctors and nurses in slipping through the army net and reaching Fort Donelson in the weeks following the battle.[2]

Writing in his memoirs in 1885, Grant contended that in February 1862 he had felt the way was open for conquest of the western South. Others had agreed, and all that had been needed, claimed Grant, was a single head to direct operations, in what might be called "unified command." Such an arrangement would have permitted rapid movement to Chattanooga, Corinth, Memphis, and even farther south, using vast numbers of new volunteers pouring down from the North. Writing as an aged warrior beset with throat cancer and with only indistinct memory in 1885 of the actual situation in 1862, Grant was clearly not at his best, but his suggestion nevertheless remains intriguing. Was this one of the truly missed opportunities of the war? Could three additional years of carnage and suffering (and the whole era of harsh reconstruction) have been averted by more perceptive and responsive Union leadership? Or were such things mere dreams of old men looking back, forgetting that the ingredients for a final blow at the rebellion were not yet in place at the time of Henry-Donelson.[3]

Grant said little about such opportunities immediately after the battle. He confided to his wife that affairs such as Forts Henry and Donelson were terrible and that he wanted to avoid them in the future via maneuver. He felt that Halleck agreed. In fact Halleck, not Grant, now claimed center stage in the drama on the western rivers. Three days after Buckner's capitulation, the department commander wrote Assistant Secretary of War Scott at Louisville, suggesting that with Buell's help, they could end the war in the West in less than a month. This goal, however, ran afoul of differing agenda among the generals, logistical difficulties with supply and movement, communication problems, and the uncertain intentions of the enemy.[4]

Men were also tired. Even Halleck's chief of staff, George Cullum, complained: "It is mighty hard to play everything from corporal to general and to perform the functions of several staff departments almost unaided as I have done for the past two weeks." Halleck should have sensed this. His own communiques to Washington contained rising fears born of fatigue. "The crisis of the war in the west" and "we are certainly in peril" echoed through missives to McClellan and the administration. Halleck worried that Beauregard was moving on Paducah or Fort Henry with Polk's command from Columbus. He fretted that Johnston would move downriver from Nashville and strike Grant before Buell could move to his assistance. In short, men in the West had expended their energy conquering Forts Henry and Donelson and now fell victim to their own worst fears.[5]

One problem was a veritable babble of voices and ideas. In addition to Washington, St. Louis, and Louisville officials, Grant, Foote, Cullum, and Sherman offered their own comments pertinent to the next stage of operations. Buell continued to push his overland approach to Nashville; Halleck alone saw the western rivers as the great line of opportunity, and said so in every message. He wanted a Napoleonic grand design, for Halleck remained the master of map maneuver. He told Washington that the principal effort should be up the Tennessee River and into the Heartland. All railroad communications between Nashville, Memphis, New Orleans, and other points connecting with the bastion at Columbus could be threatened, effectively dividing the Confederacy. Halleck wanted everything unified under his own control. "Make Buell, Grant, and Pope [another of his western generals], major generals of volunteers," he wired McClellan on February 17, "and give me command in the West." "I ask this in return for Forts Henry and Donelson," he added presumptuously.[6]

Actually Halleck's scheme was far more elaborate, for he wanted something styled "the Department of the West," "Division of the West," or "The Armies of the West." He cared not for the precise name, so long as he commanded it. Under his charge, Major General David Hunter would continue to direct the Department of Kansas (for Halleck credited him with sending reinforcements which saved Grant at Fort Donelson). Buell would similarly conduct affairs in Ohio and Kentucky. The venerable Ethan Allen Hitchcock (still envisioned as emerging from retirement for duty on the rivers (would lead forces in Missouri and Tennessee. Some 50,000 reinforcements from the eastern armies would enable Buell to finish his drive on Nashville and free Grant's men to return to the center piece of Halleck's plan — the Tennessee River thrust. Foote's naval force would threaten but not attack Columbus, and Grant could circumvent the citadel. Halleck would orchestrate it all, and even Scott waxed ecstatically ("with this organization, there can be no such thing as fail"), as he transmitted the idea secretly to Washington.[7]

The Lincoln administration rejected the idea. Lincoln, Stanton, and McClellan were themselves dabbling in western strategy, and the President was much too overcome with grief at the recent death of his beloved eleven-year-old son Willie to rationally comprehend Halleck's visionary idea. He called for Halleck's cooperation with Buell, as well as "vigilence, energy, and skill" to prevent the Rebels from surprising Grant and destroying his army. Lost in the telegraphic exchanges were simple concepts. McClellen understood one, however, when he wired Halleck on February 16: "Should Donelson fall, you will move on Nashville by either route which may at the time be quickest."[8]

The quickest route was by water, and the way was "perfectly clear," said one bystander at the state capital after the fall of Donelson. Everyone there had panicked, and while northern leaders dithered about grand strategy, their opponents provided opportunities for further success. Buell's scouts, as well as both Grant and Foote, reported the evacuation of Clarksville, and the retirement of the Rebels through Nashville. Astonished by Halleck's directive not to let his gunboats go beyond Clarksville, Foote pleaded: "The Cumberland is in a good stage of water, and Genl. Grant and I believe that we can take Nashville." His own subordinate, Phelps, who had done more ranging up and down western rivers than anyone else, argued that Nashville "will be surrendered without a fight if a force proceeds at once against it." Grant sent a similar suggestion, but Halleck hung back. Nashville lay in Buell's jurisdiction, and he awaited McClellan's pleasure.[9]

Flood waters, downed telegraph lines, and Rebel sympathizers among the telegraph operators plagued communications between the generals. So affairs stood on February 22, George Washington's birthday, and the date set by Lincoln for a general advance of all Union armies. Impractical as that order was, the western forces were already in the field. News of Sidney Johnston's apparent evacuation of Nashville should have quickened their movements. Suddenly Buell wanted Halleck's transports to convoy his divisions by water to Nashville. Chiding subordinates like Cullum for pulling Buell's chestnuts from the fire by providing such craft, as "it disconcerts my plans," Halleck now turned back to his idea of the move up the Tennessee. Buell could march unchecked to Nashville, and Grant could now leave Dover and move overland to the Danville crossing where he would again board the steamboats for a waterborne invasion. Middle Tennessee no longer interested Henry Halleck by February 24, and apparently he thought he had persuaded McClellan likewise.[10]

The message traffic that week showed contradictory thinking, reversals of plans and orders, and general confusion in the Union high command. McClellan mirrored the pitfalls of absentee strategy-making. "We must not forget Eastern Tennessee," said the general-in-chief; he wondered if a force could not be sent to cut the vital Virginia and Tennessee railroad near Abingdon in southwestern Virginia. He also wanted both subordinates to key upon Chattanooga and the Decatur-Stevenson section of north Alabama for those railroad junction targets would "very nearly isolate A.S. Johnston from Richmond." Buell could move overland and Halleck by water against those targets. Columbus, Kentucky, could be allowed to wither or be evacuated without a battle. Then McClellan rambled on about taking Corinth, not Decatur, in a telegram to Halleck, and he twice reminded Halleck to cooperate with Buell "until Nashville is securely ours." McClellan wanted strength figures from everyone before he could decide how to outflank Johnston, reputedly at

Murfreesboro, south of Nashville. Both McClellan and Buell worried well into March about a counterstroke from the southern chieftain, although intelligence estimates placed him safely behind the Tennessee River in north Alabama, and of no particular threat to Middle Tennessee. Halleck wrote caustically to his Ohio department counterpart on March 4: "If Johnston has destroyed the railroad and bridges in his rear he cannot attack you." He suggested, why not come to the Tennessee and operate with Halleck in cutting Johnston's line with Memphis and the Mississippi forts?[11]

While the three top Federal generals fought the war by map and telegram, their people in the field faced more practical issues. Bottomless muddy roads and footsore soldiers plagued Buell's force doggedly marching toward Nashville. Halleck's troops were stretched painfully thin with incompleted repairs on the gunboats, unfinished mortar boats, and the limited pool of transports hampering their leader's grand design. Suddenly the rivers began to fall; when told that ten days would be necessary to repair Foote's damaged flotilla, Halleck exploded to Sherman and Cullum that they had a weekend and should get mechanics from Chicago and Cincinnati if necessary. Foote proved particularly nettlesome since his wounds in both body and pride at Fort Donelson. Chafing because he had been prevented from seizing Nashville (he could have been in the city on February 22 had it not been for Halleck, he said), the sailor was also angry that army officers had received promotions for their role in the twin victories, while his own subordinates received no similar awards from the navy. He complained to everyone about the quality of 600 eastern sailors sent by McClellan to serve as flotillamen but who proved rebellious because they had not been paid. Foote blamed "jealousy on the part of McClellan and Halleck" for his problems, vowing to obey only orders from the secretary of the navy and the President and promising to raise a row if given a chance. "I can well afford to be independent," he declared.[12]

Little of this anger surfaced in official army-navy relations but could be found in private letters. Foote wrote his friend, Assistant Secretary of the Navy Gustavus Fox, that Halleck never stopped badgering him to take to the water again, despite his unreadiness. Although Foote had his naval builders add ten inches of solid oak to the front of pilot houses aboard the gunboats, he still could not get river pilots and "other newly made officers" to go aboard what they styled as "floating coffins." The vaunted *Mound City* broke down near the Tennessee Iron Works at Eddyville on the Cumberland as it steamed toward Nashville, and "all endeavors to get where there is some work to do are baffled," declared one irate ensign. Foote warmly praised Cullum for his help in correcting naval deficiencies, but Fox counseled caution, for Cullum was chief of staff to the general "that holds you back and ignores your existence." These army engineers were all alike, warned Fox; they were conceited, puffed up, imbued with contempt of the navy, and determined to prove impossible what Foote had achieved—successfully attacking forts with warships. Foote then lapsed into his familiar refrain in a note to Secretary Welles shortly after he and Cullum conducted a nebulous reconnaissance to Columbus on February 23: "The army will not move without gunboats, yet the gunboats are not in condition to act offensively at present."[13]

Only the timberclads preserved naval honor for the moment, as Lieutenant William Gwin in the *Tyler* repeated Phelps's earlier feat of steaming up the Tennessee to discover pockets of Unionist sentiment in the hinterland. Army transports finally deposited William Nelson's division of Buell's army at Nashville by February 25 and also discovered many persons who professed that they had always been Union men, although as brigade commander, Colonel J. Ammen observed, it was hard to believe it. At least the diehard ex-sailor William Driver of that city surfaced to coin the phrase "Old Glory," as he thrust his coveted U.S. flag (hidden from Secessionist neighbors for months) into the hands of a Federal officer with the wish: "I hope to see [it] hoisted on that flagstaff in place of that damned Confederate flag set there by that damned rebel governor, Isham G. Harris." Again Federal officials hoped that emerging Unionism would be one of the most positive results from Grant's success on opening the twin rivers.[14]

Still it would take a fortnight before army and navy forces in Halleck's department could effect a similarly bloodless capture of Columbus. Everyone knew from scouts and Memphis newspapers that Rebel evacuation was in the wind. Halleck planned for Foote's mortar boats to prod Polk's departure, but Foote's truculence and a general Federal aversion to pressing any attack on the citadel allowed the enemy to escape, with little effort necessary. Polk told his superiors that six months' supplies had been removed before Federal occupancy, but many Union soldiers thought otherwise, noting that even the disabled heavy cannon could be easily repaired. Cullum was moved to remark: "Columbus, the Gibraltar of the West is ours, and Kentucky is free, thanks to the brilliant strategy of the campaign, by which the enemy's center was pierced at Forts Henry and Donelson, his wings isolated from each other and turned, compelling thus the evacuation of his strongholds of Bowling Green first, and now Columbus."[15]

This was just what Halleck wanted, and he now proposed to extend the success by breaking Johnston's new defense line, "an oblique one, extending from Island No. 10 to Decatur or Chattanooga." We must again pierce his center at Savannah or Florence, he wrote Scott on March 7, warning that: "Buell should move immediately and not come in too late as he did at Donelson." But Buell seemed not to hear Halleck. Old Brains schemed in every way possible to secure Buell's troops — even sending commodity-laden steamboats to Nashville to disguise his real intent of using them to bring the Ohioan's men back to the Tennessee axis by water. All that ploy produced, however, was a loud outcry from Washington that cited a congressional prohibition against commercial intercourse with states in rebellion. Halleck wrote Stanton and Secretary of the Treasury Salmon P. Chase that his "opening of trade to Nashville was a military ruse." But he got no men from Buell.[16]

Halleck was on his own, and he acted accordingly. On March 1, he sent orders to Grant to move to the Tennessee with the object of destroying a railroad bridge over Bear Creek near Eastport, Mississippi, and severing connections at Corinth, Jackson, and Humboldt. He was to avoid any general engagement with the enemy, however. By the tenth, he had secured a promise from Buell to move overland and join forces at Savannah, although the Ohioan clung to the thought that "under no circumstances should [Middle Tennessee] be jeopardized," for both political and military reasons. That same evening, Halleck penned a strong note to McClellan. In it, he announced that the Tennessee River "is now the great strategic line of the Western Campaign." "Believe me, general," said Halleck in only the very thinnest veil to outright insubordination, "you make a serious mistake in having three independent commands in the West." Cooperation would always be lacking at the critical moment — "all history proves it," noted Halleck, growing bolder. "You will regret your decision against me on this point. Your friendship for individuals has influenced your judgment," Halleck concluded, referring to McClellan's long-standing esteem for Buell. Martyr-like, Halleck added: "I shall soon fight a great battle on the Tennessee unsupported, as it seems, but if successful it will settle the campaigns in the West."[17]

Actually Halleck's self-assurance rose measurably the next day when the telegraph brought Lincoln's announcement relieving McClellan of command of all the Union armies and giving Halleck his desired control in the West. Coupled with Major General Samuel Curtis' victory at Pea Ridge, Arkansas, Union fortunes shone more brightly than ever. "The new arrangement will not interfere with your command," Halleck told Buell on March 13. He made it clear, however, that he expected Nashville to be held by only a corporal's guard and the Ohioan to march rapidly overland to the rendezvous at Savannah on the Tennessee. "I know that I am right," he told Buell four days later, thus concluding the months-long struggle for control in the West. Unity of command had finally arrived. Would it have made any difference had it existed at the time of Henry-Donelson? Possibly not, given the limits of citizen armies, communication variables, and the foibles of conducting war in the winter. To many, the self-adulation of unaccustomed success may have also delayed pressing a beaten enemy. Halleck complained to his wife on March 5: "The fall of Columbus, the great 'Gibraltar of the West,' and the taking of New Madrid have followed as consequence of the victory of Fort Donelson, just as Bowling Green & Nashville were abandoned to Genl. Buell in consequence of the same strategic movements. The newspapers give the credit of these things to Stanton, McClellan & Buell, but fortunately I have recorded evidence that they even failed to approve them after I had planned them." Lost in the shuffle was the man Grant and his army. Lost also was a singular fact: the war was not over, Johnston not captured or destroyed. Divided Union command in the West had most certainly thwarted total exploitation of Grant's signal victories on the twin rivers.[18]

The Confederates seemed equally incapable of exploiting opportunities. Floyd's telegram announcing Fort Donelson's fall caught Sidney Johnston offguard. True, he and Beauregard had written off that position during the Bowling Green war council on February 7. Retreat to Nashville seemed the only viable option, but Johnston surely had hoped that Floyd and the other generals could save thousands of men caught up at Fort Donelson. News from them during the succeeding battle had fluctuated between confidence and despair, leaving their leader in a quandary. Johnston concentrated upon the footrace with Buell and upon getting Hardee's Central Army of Kentucky behind the line of the Cumberland safely. That in itself proved a major accomplishment, according to Johnston's admirers. In the process, however, they overlooked the fact that Johnston missed a great opportunity to join the fighting around Dover and destroy Grant's dagger thrust into the bosom of the upper Confederate Heartland.[19]

The evacuation of Bowling Green, like Columbus, proved costly and demoralizing to the Confederates. The Reverend Robert Franklin Bunting wrote home to Texas about burning 50,000 bushels of corn at the fairgrounds and some 250,000 pounds of pork at the slaughter house, and that many local gentry torched their own homes rather than surrender them to Yankees. Onlookers painted a scene of panic at the evacuation, with women and children fleeing into the snowy fields, and civilian conveyances joining the army trains in a stream of frightened humanity rolling southward toward Dixie. This was something new to southern soldiery, and while Johnston and Hardee conducted an orderly retreat of the main army, the experience affected the morale of this proud fighting force.[20]

Behind the army lay a wake of destruction, with the youthful Louisville and Nashville railroad wrecked from the Green River trestle all the way to Nashville, a burnt-out town at Bowling Green, and scenes of pillage on farms back to the Tennessee line. Rain and sleet soaked roads, bivouacs, and Confederate soldiery, who were bitter about uncooperative Unionist Kentucky farmers who took no pity on the bedraggled southerners. Louisiana cavalry and even Kentuckian John C. Breckenridge's brigade pillaged freely and required constant reprimand. It hardly seemed like an army which marched into Edgefield, across from Nashville, by the morning of February 15; rather it was a skeleton rabble requiring rest, succor, and renewal of spirits. Instead it soon received the bad tidings of Buckner's surrender. The telegrams from Pillow and Floyd about "one of the fiercest fights on record," "driving the enemy back with cold steel," and the "awful thrashing" of the gunboats created false hopes at Edgefield. Even Floyd's initial post-battle wire of 11:00 P.M. talked only of a sanguinary contest and failed to mention the purpose or result of the bloody breakout attempt. Even a more ominous, truncated message which followed at 3:45 A.M. the next day noted that large numbers of enemy reinforcements had arrived, that complete investment was taking place by "an army many times our own numbers," and that the "unanimous opinion" of all at Donelson was that "we cannot maintain ourselves against these forces." An anxious, yet expectant Johnston awaited further word.[21]

Could Johnston have done anything about the situation at this point? Reinforcement of the downriver garrison was out of the question. He commanded 10,000 pathetic and broken soldiers, even then clogging highways and streets in and out of the Nashville area. The men were in no shape for a flying march to save Fort Donelson. Lack of river transport eclipsed any significant relief for Floyd and his army. It was tragic, but everything was at this point, and Johnston was simply too busy salvaging the Bowling Green force, its supplies, and the Edgefield-Nashville crossing to strike back on the Cumberland. Johnston's vaunted interior lines had collapsed in crisis due to months of neglect and the general inadequacy of the Confederacy to conduct modern war based on logistics and transport — more important, perhaps, than fighting men.

It all fell in on Johnston during those fateful February days. With wintry weather, hundreds of refugees, 1,200 broken rails, plus repeated wash-outs of roadbed on the railroads south of the state capital, Sidney John-ston had little time to think about destroying Grant, even if he had really wanted to do so, and evidence of that desire remains remarkably missing in the records.[22]

The chance to correct affairs on the twin rivers slipped by Johnston like a moonbeam. At 11:00 A.M. on February 16, he received Floyd's final shocking telegram about the surrender. The Western Department com-mander had done too little, too late. Leonidus Polk's behavior during this period was equally inexplicable. Telegraph operations in West Ten-nessee and a local cavalry commander at Paris, Tennessee — Lieutenant-Colonel J.H. Miller — kept Polk even better informed than Johnston about the situation at Dover. Yet the fortress commander uttered only belated murmurs about a counter-offensive from his quarter — that thrust so feared by the Federal high command. Neither did Polk say anything about reinforcing the twin rivers or even attacking Grant's supply base at Fort Henry. Governor Harris' repeated enjoinders that Polk "make a demonstration" on Cairo or Paducah to hamper Grant's reinforce-ment met no response. Miller even delayed burning bridges so that sup-plies and survivors of the Union invasion might escape. The situation remained so unclear to everyone. Even Floyd's final telegram told noth-ing about how many men had been actually surrendered, except to boast of saving most of his own brigade, and then to whine: "I have attempted to do my duty in this trying and difficult position and only regret that my exertions have not been more successful." Johnston could only shake his head in disbelief and turn away. It was far too early to pinpoint cul-pability. Sadly, he sent a short, bitter note to Polk and Beauregard: "we are gone at Donelson we have surrendered."[23]

Johnston now learned that his own engineer, Jeremy Gilmer, had failed to woo "the Nashville Gods" or patrician elite into sending their slaves to prepare the city's defenses. Plans abounded — a twelve-gun bat-tery on a bluff below the city, a mine battery and chain barricade for the river, and a hyperactive Harris organizing independent companies in the eleventh hour. The state adjutant general even told one militia colonel to impress upon his soldiers that the revolution of 1776 had been won by the Tennessee rifle and that "we fight in defense of our homes and all that we hold dear." Most Nashvillians were not listening; they had relied on Fort Donelson, seventy miles downriver, for their defense.[24]

At 5:35 A.M. on the sixteenth, Johnston ordered his commanders to press the retreat since "news from our flank makes this advisable." This only further jammed the roads, occasioned periodic halts in the line of march, and further disrupted morale. The weather was fine that sabbath morning when Johnston crossed to Nashville to confer with Harris. The citizens were in church or at home, celebrating earlier news from Fort Donelson about victory over the gunboats. People from outlying districts had gathered in town, and posturings of southern heroics could be heard at every street corner. Johnston met quietly with Harris and his advisers at the capitol, and told them that since Donelson had fallen, the city could not be held. His army would retire to Murfreesboro, some thirty miles south. Word immediately spread to the streets, and the euphoria of victory evaporated in the thin, cold air. Rumors of the imminent arrival of the dreaded Yankee gunboats, wanton bombardment of a defenseless city, and the merciless bestiality of northern soldiers all surfaced quickly. Tension mounted when Hardee's desolate soldiery and the first survivors from Fort Donelson appeared with lurid tales of blood and gore. Deserters left the ranks in droves and headed home, and when ministers dismissed their congregations, "people were seen hurrying to & fro like crazy people," claimed newsman John Miller McKee later. Neither Harris nor Johnston displayed any leadership in this crisis. The governor reportedly suggested by mid-afternoon that women and children leave town to escape the enemy hordes. As the *Nashville Times* editor suggested subsequently, "while there may have been a military necessity for such a course of silence, the people cannot appreciate such reticence when a few words would have gone far to quiet their fears."[25]

Fears were not allayed, nor words of comfort forthcoming, and one Nashvillian recorded in her diary that by Sunday afternoon, everybody was on the move, houses were left empty to the ravages of the invader, and carriages were impossible to procure. Harris adjourned the legislature to meet the following Thursday in Memphis, producing more derision among the citizens. "Oh! Isham, gallant, chivalrous, courageous and swift on the run Isham—we are 'yours in haste,'" caustically wrote Virginia French in her private journal. Others simply spoke with their feet, joining the governor and Nashville bankers, who carried off their depositors' specie and other valuables in their flight. Local quartermaster officials such as Colonel V.K. Stevenson (also president of the Nashville and Chattanooga railroad) left with such haste and so little instructions for subordinates that questions were raised about desertion. Stevenson, however, telegraphed Harris from Chattanooga on February 19, explaining that he had gone there to supervise dispatch of more locomotives and cars to the capital, for he alone could unsnarl the line. Still, to men in Hardees's passing legions, the disintegration of the city was something new. Many, such as Bunting of the Texas Rangers, had seen public and private panic, but never "such a scene as the evacuation of Nashville." He hoped never to see it reenacted. But reenacted it would be, for Nashville was the first of many Confederate evacuations that included Memphis, New Orleans, Chattanooga, Atlanta, Savannah, and ultimately, even Richmond.[26]

Few, if any, Federals reached the outskirts of the city before February 23, yet panic and confusion prevailed for the duration of the Confederate occupancy. Floyd and Pillow arrived by steamboat from Clarksville at 7:00 A.M. on Monday, and Johnston, asking no questions of either man, placed Floyd in charge of a disintegrating city. Howling mobs of war-spawned proletaria threatened public order. Both generals joined Mayor R.B. Cheatham in explaining how superior Union numbers had overwhelmed the "10,000" cold, weary defenders at Fort Donelson. Pillow promised that the enemy would be with Nashvillians but briefly, adding bombastically: "I pledge you my honor that this war will not end until they are driven across the Ohio river." Surely the crowds had tired of Pillow's continual references to his honor. Anyway the Tennessean soon took a train for his home near Columbia, to sulk and prepare his official report on the Donelson affair. Floyd, Cheatham, the Edgefield civic leader General Washington Barrow, and some ordnance underlings such as Captain Nathan R. Chambliss and Captain Moses H. Wright took charge of affairs in the city. Assisted by the well-disciplined 1st Missouri infantry under Colonel John Bowen, as well as Colonel John Hunt Morgan's cavalry, they policed the streets. Chambliss, in fact, took command of the city's token fortification — the three-gun river battery known as Fort Zollicoffer, five miles downstream.[27]

Floyd found quite arduous the task of helping evacuate the city and yet maintain order there. He maintained communication with Clarksville authorities, and they pestered him about preserving the railroad bridge and what to do with the Donelson wounded. Nurse Blanche L. Lewis noted years after the war that the first boatload of wounded from the battle had reached Clarksville about 3:00 A.M. Sunday morning, and she remembered that for twenty-four hours a continuous line of ambulances and wagons from the river to the hospital brought the injured, many of them dying on the way. Two of Floyd's own Virginia surgeons, M.C. Burnett and J.A. Forbes, eventually helped transfer the wounded to already crowded Nashville hospitals. Added to this burden, Floyd's headquarters was deluged with queries about further evacuation of lunatic asylum inmates, rumors of Yankee incendiaries sent to burn the city's foundries and factories, and quantities of supplies floating off into the river from neglected levees. Floyd and his people tried to help secure war matériel for Johnston, but he and his Virginians "were nigh totally exhausted from the exertions and fatigues" of the battle. Even when the goods were loaded and sent off by rail, Floyd soon learned that trains sat idle down the line because of washouts.[28]

Floyd resorted to impressing all of the able-bodied men in the city for work gangs. Additionally galling to proud residents was the term "military necessity" when applied to destruction of two unfinished gunboats on Monday night and the railroad and prized suspension bridge across the Cumberland the next evening. Each day spawned new crises. When government warehouses were opened to citizens, the resulting riots forced authorities to employ firehoses as well as cavalry sabers of Morgan's and Forrest's men (the latter having now appeared after their legendary escape from Dover). By mid-week, most Nashvillians grew weary of their own leaders and the antics of the "Great Panic." Louisa Brown Pearl, wife of the city's prewar school superintendent who had fled to Michigan with their four daughters at the outset of the war, represented those homeowners who remained behind to protect their property, but who became disgusted with Confederate leadership in this crisis. She noted that the populace was without paper currency, a marketplace, bread, coal, or milk carts, and only drunken Confederate stragglers and a ceaseless downpour of rain to anticipate each day. She felt that she might even welcome the Federals, if only because they would frighten off the riff-raff.[29]

Floyd and the authorities abruptly closed the warehouses to the populace, for they had decided that more materiel could be saved for army use. A precious rifling machine and other ordnance equipment went off by rail to Atlanta. Forrest declared later that far too much was lost during the week-long binge. "With proper diligence" on the part of quartermaster and commissary officials, he claimed, all the public stores might have been carried to safety. He alone was later credited with saving 600 boxes of clothing, 250,000 pounds of bacon, and four wagonloads of ammunition. Perhaps Forrest remained angry about Floyd's actions at Fort Donelson, and once more he remained subordinate to him at Nashville. While Forrest might fault supply personnel, Floyd claimed, after watching the final loading of rail cars at 4:00 P.M. on February 20: "Much more could have been saved had there been more a system and regularity in the disposition of the transportation by rail." "Things which we can illy spare," wrote Bunting, as "there will yet be many a hungry man before many weeks roll by." One of Hardee's aides, Colonel St. John Liddell, unofficially speculated that negligence, poor transportation planning, the weather, and panic had cost the army fully half of its supplies. Even one Unionist in Nashville estimated $5 million worth of property was lost to the Confederacy.[30]

Whoever was at fault, the transport of sick and wounded southward from Nashville proved even more scandalous. Despite tireless efforts by ministering angels such as Mrs. Ella King Newsom, "the Florence Nightingale of the South," evacuation proved tragic. This Mississippi widow had helped administer Johnston's hospitals at Bowling Green, had moved to Nashville in time to care for victims of the battles at twin rivers, and accompanied the hospital trains to Winchester, Tennessee, afterward. Some snow-covered hospital trains went all the way to Chattanooga with injured and sick men in box and cattle cars without heat or attention for eighteen hours. Remarkably, only a few died. The removal of these soldiers was a military necessity, claimed Major Charles W. Anderson, the local transport officer at Chattanooga, "but why they were sent, unaccompanied or preceded by a proper corps of surgeons, medical supplies, and hospital attendants, I never knew." Given the haste of Nashville's evacuation, the wounded and sick received the same insensitive handling as army supplies.[31]

Sunshine finally broke through overcast skies on Sunday, February 23. Jefferson Davis had been installed as regular Confederate president the previous day on a most somber note, given the disasters of the month. The first Federal scouts appeared at Edgefield, causing a stampede of remaining Rebel malingerers in Nashville. Mayor Cheatham and another official lost little time in rowing across the river to surrender the city to a mere cavalry captain from Ohio. By this time southern citizens and soldiers alike were beginning to assess the previous week in realistic terms. Most deplored the loss of the forts, one Tennessee soldier attributing it all to "whiskey-headed" generals. Colonel W.N. "Sandie" Pendleton, reading of the western disasters from a comfortable bivouac in the Shenandoah Valley of Virginia, felt the men were thinking too much of "a whole skin, and too little of their country and the future." The severest stroke, said Reverend Bunting, was the evacuation of Nashville — "may God overrule it for our good and the good of our glorious cause." T.G. Pollock with the 51st Virginia in South Carolina simply thanked fate for an earlier order which had removed his regiment from shipment west to join Johnston and Floyd prior to Donelson.[32]

Johnston's harried army meanwhile defied mud, transportation breakdowns, and low spirits to pull back to Murfreesboro. Our retreat has been "most disastrous," was Bunting's assessment. The pike south of the capital was "one moving mass for miles," he noted, while other commentators recorded the whole episode as one sorry example of lax discipline and petty thievery. Many disconsolate soldiers plundered forest and farm for firewood and food, despite strict orders against such conduct. Whiskey cachés found great favor among the suffering army. When officers tried to limit consumption, they fell victim to derisive cries of "pour it out, pour it out," from hard-drinking rankers. Only the cavalry had work to do, it seemed, scouting back toward the advancing enemy and rounding up stragglers. Terry's Texas Rangers roamed through Nashville and downriver as far as Charlotte, collecting flotsam from Donelson, including men, horses, and mules. Benjamin Franklin Batchelor wrote his wife that women in the state capital waved handkerchiefs and cheered his men from balconies, and gray-haired matrons wept while urging: "go on brave Texans and may God preserve your lives; but never surrender." While the present appeared gloomy, he assured her, she should never lose faith in the goodness of God and the ultimate success of "our cause."[33]

The Cause was anything but successful that last week in February. Johnston retreated from Middle Tennessee, and on the twenty-seventh, reorganized the Central Army of Kentucky into three divisions of scarcely 17,000 men. He furloughed many to go home, recuperate, and recruit new volunteers. He planned to retire to Stevenson, Alabama, and regroup there, covering the important railroad and logistical bases in the area. Again, his mesmerization remained with the land access routes to the hinterland. Slowly and subtly, however, the persuasive arguments of a West Tennessee clique forced a change. The inert Polk was not so much a factor as the refugee governor at Memphis, a chorus of local officials and politicians in north Alabama, and that ever-aspiring, second-in-command of the theater, P.G.T. Beauregard. The Creole may have been an invalid for several weeks at Jackson, but his throat ailment hardly diminished his enthusiasm for retrieving Confederate fortunes. One observer, a northern traveler caught by the fluid wartime situation during a visit to his brother in New Orleans, heard Beauregard tell a Decatur, Alabama, crowd shortly thereafter: "We must win for never again will I live under a Yankee government."[34]

Beauregard was a man with a mission; some claimed it was Johnston's command, others looked to his patriotism, appetite for action, or even Gallic spirit. Whatever the cause, he certainly applied pressure to a reeling theater commander after Henry-Donelson. The very day that Grant appeared before Dover, Beauregard wrote Johnston outlining some blunt truths. He suggested that the fall of Fort Henry had opened the way for Federal outflanking of Columbus, Nashville, and even Memphis, and would most certainly destroy the east-west rail link of the Confederacy.

Departing from their February 7 agreement at the Covington House, the Creole now advocated abandonment of Columbus, defense of the Mississippi at Island No. 10 and Fort Pillow above Memphis, and concentration of Polk's forces at Jackson where they could contain any thrust by Grant up the Tennessee. This scheme reached Johnston just as he was conducting the Bowling Green evacuation. He made no immediate reply.[35]

Long after the war, when the two chieftains' followers argued once more, Beauregard and his biographer recalled another meeting, ostensibly at Nashville, as the deputy commander passed through en route to West Tennessee. It might have taken place—Johnston's aides never confirmed it, so we have only the word of Beauregard's faction that it did. He claimed that Johnston reconfirmed his intention to retire behind the Tennessee River at Stevenson. He agreed to evacuate Columbus, although requiring Beauregard to secure Richmond's permission first. Then the theater commander supposedly acceded to Beauregard's independent command in West Tennessee until the two wings of the army could be reunited. As before, Johnston's directives proved vague as to who commanded whom, but for a man of Beauregard's temperament, any hint of his taking over in Polk's area was interpreted as complete.[36]

Other voices urged the Richmond government to sacrifice all but the most important strategic points and to concentrate all of the dwindling Confederate forces in the West. Major General Braxton Bragg on the Gulf Coast and the ex-Confederate Secretary of War (now in a general's uniform at Tuscumbia, Alabama), Leroy Pope Walker, stressed the need to defend the line from Memphis to Virginia "at all hazards," and to concentrate at Corinth and Knoxville and retake the offensive. Suddenly Johnston saw where the primary threat lay, and he wired Davis on February 24: "This army will move on the 26th by Decatur for the Valley of Mississippi. It is in good condition and increasing in numbers." Johnston now relinquished Tennessee and Kentucky and chose to concentrate upon defense of the Mississippi Valley. Perhaps it was Beauregard's influence. The Creole hinted as much to his congressional friend, Roger Pryor, saying that he was seizing the helm of a sinking ship, with few men to man her, yet "we must defeat the enemy somewhere to give confidence to our friends." Indeed Beauregard did rally the southerners of the deeper Heartland to renewed effort.[37]

Pushing aside the inept Polk, Beauregard readied offensive plans. Using what remained of West Tennessee railroads, he planned a strike on Grant's vulnerable supply base. He would march on Paducah, seize the mouths of the twin rivers, and bottle Grant's army up at Dover. He would then turn and capture Cairo, even moving to threaten St. Louis. The ambitious plan would take 40,000 men, and Governor Harris as well as members of Beauregard's own entourage (Lieutenants S.W. Ferguson, A.R. Chisolm, A.N.T. Beauregard, Major B.B. Waddell, and Dr. Samuel Choppin) departed to convince Mississippi Valley leaders and other Confederate generals to send reinforcements for the scheme. Harris issued a proclamation to Tennesseans on February 19, calling upon all able-bodied white males to enlist regardless of age, and the next day he berated the rump session of the legislature at Memphis for not doing more to help retrieve the state's fortunes. Evoking the spirit of Revolutionary America, Harris' words could be read in every newspaper in the valley. People were inspired across the South, as one Montgomery, Alabama, editor suggested: "Those faint-hearted paltroons are a curse to the country, and if they are too chicken hearted to possess any confidence in themselves they should at least be made to hold their tongues in the presence of sensible men & women."[38]

Beauregard exceeded his mandate from Johnston. The Confederate War Department looked askance as his extraordinary attempts to recruit at the state level. His fiery appeal for plantation and church bells throughout the Mississippi Valley produced more verbal patriotism than bronze for cannon making. If he effectively organized supply depots from Union City in West Tennessee to Iuka in Mississippi, he simply lacked the time to reestablish such ordnance works needed immediately for rebuilding the army. Bragg brought 10,000 men from the Gulf, and new levies from north Alabama swelled the ranks. Then, just as this fever neared a crescendo, the Federal armies struck again, capturing New Madrid on the Mississippi below Columbus and remassing at Fort Henry for the Tennessee River strike. A chastened Beauregard shrank back from his move. The opportunity to destroy Grant's line of communications had passed. Beauregard retired to a miniature reproduction of Johnston's earlier cordon defense, and by late March both he and Johnston had decided upon Corinth, Mississippi, as a rendezvous point preparatory to adopting a new strategy.[39]

At last, even Johnston awakened from what historian T. Harry Williams once called his "command shock." Floyd had reached Chattanooga and telegraphed on March 11 that he had taken charge of defense of that place, with his Virginia brigade in excellent spirits after a march of 250 miles. Hardee's people had reached north Alabama and received an uplift of waving handkerchiefs, cheers, words of encouragement, and welcome from the local populace. Huntsville women gave the 6th Kentucky a new silk flag, and many of the soldiers quickly found the local grog parlors most felicitous. For Johnston, all this was a time of testing, and he admitted to his friend Davis: "The fall of Donelson disheartened some of the Tennessee troops and caused many desertions from some of the new regiments [but] I now consider the tone of the troops restored, and that they are in good order." By April Fool's Day, Johnston and Beauregard had unified the wings of the broken army and were ready for the serious task of rebuilding a fighting force.[40]

Johnston rejected the notion of raising guerrilla bands, for the "organization of the army will be preserved," and all troops in the service had to be subject to the articles of war as well as "discipline and such organization as may be necessary to render ours an efficient army." He recognized that success was the test of merit, telling an aide at one point, "critically it is not correct, but, as the world goes, it is true." As he tried to rekindle the fighting spirit in western Confederates, the proud soldier became increasingly stung by swirling criticism that now began to surface in the wake of the February defeats. This stigma had dogged him every footstep southward from Bowling Green. The Richmond government cited the pressure of those defeats both at home and abroad. As one of Floyd's aides at Donelson (and a Kentucky congressman besides), Henry C. Burnett, wrote his erstwhile general from Richmond on March 1: "Genl. Johnston's failure to send reinforcements to the Army at Donaldson has been generally criticized in severe terms here." In Europe, Confederate diplomats such as John Slidell in Paris, J.M. Mason in London, and P.A. Rost in Madrid noted their concern, Slidell saying it best perhaps: "I need not say how unfavorable an influence these defeats, following in such quick succession, have produced on public sentiment." If not soon counterbalanced by some decisive success, he warned, "we may not only bid adieu to all hopes of seasonable recognition, but may expect that the declaration of the efficiency of the blockade, . . . will be indefinitely postponed." Johnston was about to feel the ripple effect of earlier actions in his department.[41]

Southerners, especially Tennesseans, began to search for scapegoats. They had clung to every bulletin which had mingled hope, joy, and then despair as the full news of defeat crossed Dixie. Diarist Mary Chestnut suggested that the news of Fort Donelson as a "drawn battle" really meant "that we have lost it," while as late as March 7, radical Secessionist Edmund Ruffin complained bitterly at Richmond that nothing could be learned "near the main facts & all important tests of the result," by which he meant numbers and losses of those engaged. Such "skillful news mobilization," suggested a later military historian, A.L. Conger, was employed by the Davis government to soften the shock. Yet it did little good as the news trickled through the censors. Young "Lunny" Yandell at Columbus warned his sister of the day of the fort's surrender: "We are now at the beginning of the 'wild hour coming on.'" Mississippi planter Benjamin F. Bedford, whose son Hugh had been captured while serving the heavy water battery guns at Donelson, told a friend despondently: "I have given it up since Henry and Donelson were captured."[42]

Southern newspaper editors eventually joined the outcry, some counseling against eternal expectation only of victories, others seeking sterner answers. Moderates suggested "the secesh will have to suffer for their misdoings," as Kentuckian Albert C. Jewell remarked from his regiment's camp near Corinth. The public particularly chastised Johnston and Harris for inefficiency and cowardice in retreating before the foe. Panicky westerners wrote Davis, as early as February 21, that only the president's presence could restore patriotism and the will to resist. The Tennessee delegation in Congress declared on March 8, "right or wrong, confidence is no longer felt in the military skill of Gen. A.S. Johnston." Davis parried the barbs of his political foes such as Tennessee congressman Henry S. Foote or W.M. Brooks, president of the Alabama secession convention, as they called for Johnston's ouster. "If Sidney Johnston is not a general, the confederacy has none to give you," declared the chief executive. But privately, Davis wrote the general that, despite their years of friendship, he had expected a full report of events "precedent and consequent to the fall of Fort Donelson," since the people wholly misunderstood the "purpose of your army at Bowling Green" and the absence of an effective force at Nashville; they were holding the general responsible for the fall of the forts and the capture of Nashville. He further noted the public outcry about lack of effort to save supplies at the state capital, "and that the panic of the people was caused by the army." Davis respected Johnston's silence, he told his friend, but since the matter was really public, not private in nature, "such representations, with the sad foreboding naturally belonging to them, has been painful to me and injurious to us both." Davis promised help, a personal visit, but hinted: "A full development of the truth is necessary for future success."[43]

Johnston was stunned. Preoccupied with rebuilding his army, he was not accustomed to public scrutiny of military matters. He had already penned two reports, from Nashville on February 18 (concerning the Bowling Green evacuation) and from Murfreesboro a week later (concerning the Nashville evacuation). He had forwarded Floyd's and Pillow's reports on Fort Donelson to Richmond. Yet he was aware of public pressure, for Davis had told him on March 11 to suspend the generals and to secure answers and fix blame concerning the "unfortunate affair" on the

Cumberland. Johnston's replies mainly encapsulated the correspondence about the army's plight since the previous September, but in a rather telling indictment of his own judgment, Johnston confessed that he had been hasty in forwarding the generals' reports "without examining or analyzing the facts, and scarcely with time to read them." He simply wanted to avoid lengthy and unpleasant attempts at vindication of what had now passed.[44]

Finally on March 18, Johnston sent Davis a lengthy commentary on recent events. He admitted to overestimating Kentucky friendship, which had precipitated the Bowling Green advance. He claimed that he had determined to fight for Nashville at Fort Donelson, sending the best part of his army to do so, while retaining only 14,000 men to cover the railroad approach to the Tennessee capital. "Giving 16,000 to defend Donelson" was the way he phrased it. More condemning than statistical differences was Johnston's admission to a cardinal error of generalship: division of an army in the presence of any enemy. He said nothing about letting subordinates fight the major battle in the West, claiming merely that their "troops were among the best of my forces, and the generals — Floyd, Pillow, and Buckner — were high in the opinion of officers and men for skill and courage, among the best officers of my command." They were popular with the volunteers and had seen much service. They had requested no reinforcements, and Johnston pointed out that he had telegraphed Floyd on the fourteenth to save the army even if he lost the fort. Ever the gentleman-soldier, Johnston told the president: "it is possible this might have been done, but justice requires to look at the events as they appeared at the time, and not alone by the light of subsequent information." If the command had been "irregularly transferred," he commented, and subsequently devolved on the junior general, it was not "apparently to avoid any just responsibility or from any want of personal or moral intrepidity."[45]

Johnston was too soft on his ill-performing subordinates. He failed to properly chastise Polk for not moving to better aid the twin rivers forts — was it a question of a nearly forty-year friendship with the clergyman-soldier? Johnston also retained misplaced faith in Floyd and Pillow, reassigning them to duty while they appealed to Richmond, for, said Johnston to Davis, "I still felt confidence in their gallantry, their energy, and their devotion to the Confederacy." He explained away the discouragement among populace and soldiery, the inclement weather, excess flooding, and insufficient manpower as causing the further disintegration of his department in the evacuation of Nashville. Yet, he suggested, "most of the stores and provisions were saved and conveyed to new depots." Noting inaccurately that "in conformity with my original design," he had then marched southward "so as to cooperate or unite with" Beauregard for "the defense of the valley of the Mississippi." As for his long official silence after Henry-Donelson and the loss of Nashville, Johnston answered self-effacingly that it seemed the best way to serve cause and country. Lacking the true facts, "discontent prevailed and criticism or condemnation were more likely to augment than to cure the evil." He had refrained, "well knowing that heavy censures would fall upon me but convinced that it was better to endure them for the present, and defer to a more propitious time any investigation of the conduct of the generals," for in the interim their services and influence would be useful.

Mindful of the president's intercession, Johnston bowed "to a deep sense of the friendship and confidence you have always shown me," and disclaimed knowledge of political implications of his acts. Should the chief executive visit his army, however, "your presence would encourage my troops, inspire the people, and augment the army." If Davis actually went west and assumed command, Johnston felt "it would afford me the most unfeigned pleasure" to help his commander-in-chief gain victory and the country her independence. Even then Johnston seemed to be seeking someone else to make decisions and provide leadership, thus continuing the trail of such avoidance since Grant's first appearance on the twin rivers. "The test of merit in my profession with the people is success," he concluded, "it is a hard rule, but I think it right." Early in March, after brief investigation, the Confederate Congress vindicated Johnston's patriotism by a vote of 52 to 33. Three weeks later, Davis' friend and western commander lay dead of a Yankee bullet upon the field of Shiloh—the battle he knew that he needed most to win to recapture the people's vindication. Another defeat (some said Johnston's death was the cause) at Shiloh denied him that redemption for Forts Henry and Donelson and the loss of Middle Tennessee, but it provided him with martyrdom instead.[46]

CHAPTER 13

The Aftermath of Donelson

THE EXPEDITION THAT BROKE OPEN THE WAR in the West now languished in late February. Grant wrote Cullum on February 25: "I am growing anxious to know what the next move is going to be." For the moment, nothing happened as Halleck and Buell jockeyed for power, and the Federal government missed the Confederacy's jugular. Johnston and Beauregard failed to consolidate quickly enough to destroy the Federal incumbus in their midst. No Napoleonic "battle for the West" occurred, and the month following the twin rivers victories passed in deep frustration and mounting problems for Grant's army.[1]

Northern newspapers glowed with words about "Unconditional Surrender" Grant, as they now called him. They noted the type of cigars that he had smoked at the battle, and a flood of such smoking materials descended upon his headquarters. It may have been that Grant actually switched from pipe to cigar at this point in his life. He implied as much to his staff later, noting Flag Officer Foote's gift cigar on the morning of the decisive assault as the occasion for change. Thus his trusted naval comrade may have inadvertently contributed to Grant's future fatal bout with throat cancer. For the moment, however, cigars were the puff of victory. More serious were the facts that Grant's army was operationally inert, with mounting problems of physical exhaustion and illness from campaign exposure. Grant himself had contracted a cold at Cairo and nursed it through the campaign, and he was now recuperating while having to tackle consolidation of his exposed position on the Cumberland, occupation of southern territory within his jurisdiction, the reconditioning of his army for the next operation, and the unpredictable relations with Henry Halleck.[2]

Grant sent Foote with the gunboats *Cairo* and *Conestoga* to Clarksville on February 19, in an effort both to capture that hotbed of rebellion and to secure the railroad bridge from Confederate destruction. En route, Foote burned the Cumberland Iron Works, about six miles above Dover. He interrogated one of the proprietors, a Mr. Lewis, who claimed to be a Unionist. Why had this establishment worked for the Rebels when

Daniel Hillman's similar plant lower down on the river had not done so, queried Foote. Lewis replied quietly that while Hillman's establishment lay in neutral Kentucky, the Bell works stood above the Confederate fort at Dover. Since river trade was closed with the North, trade with the Confederacy was necessary for survival. Foote noted this man's Unionism, and the fact that he had kept his slaves at home in Clarksville rather than renting them for work on Fort Donelson. Still he took him aboard the gunboat as a prisoner, because of his war work, and destroyed Lewis's plant.[3]

Foote then steamed on to Clarksville. A local telegrapher saw the gunboats coming and wired Floyd at Nashville that he would ascertain how many troops were aboard. He also noted that the city garrison's officers had tried to burn the railroad bridge despite civilian protest and Johnston's orders not to do so, but the wet wood would not catch fire. The sailors arrived in time to quench the flames and take possession of several spiked cannon at Fort Defiance, the city's inadequate river defense post. Then they marched into town, where Mayor George Smith, the town's senior judge, and antebellum politician Cave Johnson (a friend of Foote's father) prevailed upon the naval officer to issue a proclamation calming the people. Foote claimed that this ran "contrary to my predetermination of never writing such a document," but he did so anyway, announcing "to all peaceably disposed persons that neither in their persons nor in their property shall they suffer molestation by me or the naval force under my command." Two-thirds of the residents had already fled town, he told the secretary of the navy, but the city was still in "wildest commotion from rumors that we would not respect the citizens either in their persons or their property." Telling the town fathers to surrender all military stores and to stop displaying "manifestations of Secession feeling," Foote felt rather good about the matter. As he wrote his wife, "the Clarksville affair will do me credit."[4]

Grant ordered C.F. Smith to garrison Clarksville that same day and accompanied the troops when they left from Dover on February 24. While the soldiers fanned out to occupy what W.H.L. Wallace termed a "beautiful village or town of 5 or 6,000 inhabitants," Grant took possession of an abandoned mansion on Second Cross Street and began the business of "reconstructing" a Rebel city. Only slaves and deserted streets welcomed the invaders. Wallace reported seeing but a single house with pleasant ladies at the door—and a British Union Jack hanging outside. Smith's division bivouacked at the local female seminary and in warehouses by the river. They rummaged about looking for Confederate stores, while medical personnel found some 130 wounded Confederates from the Fort Donelson battle and began sharing nursing duties with local women such as Blanche Lewis. The atmosphere between former enemies — both military and civilian — remained guarded at best.[5]

Four days later, Grant, McClernand, and an entourage of subordinates and newsmen made a day's excursion to Nashville. Everyone thought that city very lovely also (although Jacob Lauman deplored the coal-smoke smudged buildings), and reporter Franc Wilkie declared less favorably: "With its two beautiful bridges destroyed, with its landings marred by smoking wrecks of steamers, with its streets littered with the debris of a flying army, with its shops closed, and an air of gloom prevading the city, it was yet charming as a young widow in her weeds." McClernand and W.H.L. Wallace paid their respects to the widow of President James K. Polk, while Grant sought out Buell, who was now in the city. The lady received the Union officers, Wilkie observed, "polite, frigid, reserved." More happily, the invaders discovered some fifty-eight wounded Federals from Fort Donelson, forty of whom were from Wallace's 11th Illinois. Despite the Confederates' kind treatment, their commander noted that "scarce one of them but shed tears when I shook hands with them."[6]

The newsmen avidly sought out "secesh" for conversation both at Clarksville and Nashville. "Agate" reporter Whitelaw Reid commented about Clarksville: "Here is a piece just cut out of rebeldom, and still palpitating with its old life-blood." The people might eventually return to the Union, but "at that point, they took great pride in telling the Yankees that there were but six Union men in the town." The common assertion in Nashville, said Wilkie, was that only mechanics and the laboring classes harbored Unionist sentiment. What the reporters discovered was a bitter, unrepentent populace which blamed Donelson upon "the cowardice of Simon Bolivar Buckner" and the "excessive caution (with due emphasis on 'caution') of Floyd," thought Reid. To these Rebel zealots, the Federal forces were dangerous on the rivers, but "we can whip 'em anywhere, easy on land." Nonetheless, the newsmen saw the people eventually resigning themselves to Federal rule, for they had no immediate prospect of an alternative.[7]

Grant thought he saw increasing signs of southern Unionism among Nashville delegations who visited him at Clarksville, professing loyalty and obedience. Perhaps everyone was grasping at straws, yet Grant told his friend and patron, Congressman Washburne, as well as Halleck, that the effect of Fort Donelson's fall was quite marked upon the community and that the defeat was freely admitted. To the general, at least, "a powerful change is taking place in the minds of the people throughout this state," a thought confirmed by returning scouts of the 8th Missouri, who had penetrated all the way to Memphis. Actually, Confederate impressment attempts since the twin rivers disasters had sent many Tennesseans fleeing to Union lines, and such refugees "stand around our camps like lost sheep not knowing what to do," wrote one observer. Officers such as W.H.L. Wallace remained skeptical of sudden reversals in political ardor. He suggested to an old friend in Ottawa, Illinois, that he had seen little evidence of lingering memory or love for the old flag and government. Rather it would be only the "stern iron rule of the strongest" to provide anything like security, he concluded dismally, for it was bound to be a "union pinned together with bayonets."[8]

Grant worked with his soldiers to insure the safety of legitimate private property in Tennessee. It proved inevitable that many Dover residents, however, would appear at army headquarters demanding return of dry goods, buggies, mail coaches, and household and business property left within Rebel lines at the time of the battle and confiscated by the victors. The problem of fugitive slaves continued to fester, and Colonel Oglesby told his Illinois troops, "the spirit of the orders is not intended to make us slave catchers, and my command shall not be so used by any authority." He told his people to let the slave go out of camp, but "you will not deliver him to his master or to any men claiming to be his master." The *Chicago Tribune* proclaimed the sensitivity of this issue when it stated on March 4: "If [the soldiers] believe this war was against slavery, they would lay down their arms and go home."[9]

Grant thought that he had found a solution by ordering that slaves who had worked on the Dover and Clarksville fortifications would not be returned to their owners. They would go to quartermasters who needed army laborers. Thus Grant and his subordinates straddled a touchy issue since Halleck had decreed: "It does not belong to the military to decide upon the relation of master and slave. Such questions must be settled by the civil courts." Of course the fugitive slaves flocked to Grant's camps, serving as cooks and orderlies to the very receptive soldiery. One adjutant wrote home: "I am bound to have a half dozen if the war lasts much longer"; he vowed to get his wife a girl to help with the cooking when he returned from the war.[10]

Grant also chastised one zealous Missouri captain who pillaged and disrupted a slave community near the Bellwood iron furnace in the name of liberation. Federal authorities remained sensitive to the needs of all Tennesseans as the mounting specter of guerrilla warfare loomed following Fort Donelson's fall. Yet the full impact of such operations lay in the future, and nobody spent much time worrying about the full implications of such a contingency. In fact Grant sought to respond to reports of Confederate impressment of Unionists in West Tennessee, but Halleck told him that was not his business and to get on with planning the movement up the Tennessee River. For the moment, however, Grant was stymied by lack of supplies, a sick army, and then Halleck's open animosity. He confessed to his wife on March 1 that never had he been so crippled in resources.[11]

A chill settled over relations between the two generals as stinging criticism and accusations of improprieties in Grant's army reached St. Louis headquarters. While Grant told Julia how much he admired Halleck as his superior, the feelings were not mutual. As Grant said later in his memoirs, in less than two weeks after his twin victories both Halleck and McClellan were conspiring to get rid of him, and within three weeks he was virtually under arrest and without a command. Grant's problems were threefold. First, he had gone to Nashville (in Buell's jurisdiction), without Halleck's permission. Second, Grant had submitted neither reports nor strength returns, according to Halleck. Third, the unceasing tales of pilferage and general disorder in the expeditionary force led Halleck to conclude that Grant's army was more demoralized by victory than the Union army by defeat at Bull Run. Rumors of Grant's old drinking problem (perhaps the cough medicine for Grant's head cold) had surfaced once again. "It is hard to censure a successful general immediately after a victory," said his superior, but, satisfied with victory, "he sits down and enjoys it without any regard to the future." McClellan sent word to discipline such generals as Grant, and both men apparently thought a change of command on the twin rivers might be timely. Halleck especially considered only C.F. Smith as "equal to the emergency."[12]

Grant kept his temper and, aided by the slow communications, obediently explained how he had sent unit returns daily and why he had gone to Nashville to see Buell, and then he chattered about problems with high water, supplies, river transport, and the general condition of his force. The desk-bound Halleck was simply jealous and frustrated. He blasted Cullum about sending C.F. Smith's division to Nashville, querying: "What is the reason that no one down there can obey my orders?" What he failed to recognize was that delays in communication between field and headquarters were fouling the picture, and that the fog of war, an overly complex chain of command, short tempers, and growing impatience complicated relations at all levels between superiors and subordinates on the western rivers.[13]

Halleck's missives to Grant fairly dripped venom with statements such as: "The want of order and discipline and the numerous irregularities in your command since the capture of Fort Donelson are matters of general notoriety, and have attracted the serious attention of the authorities at Washington." By early March even Grant had tired of Halleck's insinuations. While wishing to avoid disrespect, disobedience, and relief from command, he said, the hero of Donelson suggested that perhaps Cullum had intervened in the communications line, for "it may be that many of [Grant's reports and telegrams] were not thought of sufficient importance to forward more than a telegraphic synopsis of." Halleck finally moderated his tone as the picture cleared and backed away from Grant's dismissal. He wrote Adjutant General Lorenzo Thomas on March 15: As he acted from a praiseworthy although mistaken zeal for the public service in going to Nashville and leaving his command, I respectfully recommend that no further notice to be taken of it." Frankly, Halleck could ill afford any public uproar that would attend Grant's cashiering. On March 13, he wired his subordinate, now at the end of a completed telegraph line at Fort Henry: "Instead of relieving you, I wish you as soon as your new army is in the field to assume the immediate command and lead it on to new victories." Halleck was a strange fellow, and he continued to chide Grant about enforcing discipline and punishing the disorderly since "the power is in your hands; use it, and you will be sustained by all above you." Grant never completely overcame either the problem or the damning publicity attending pilferage of property.[14]

The Grant-Halleck controversy simmered over various issues, and neither officer realized that communications lay at the root of their problem. High water and rough roads hampered extension of telegraph wires beyond Paducah to Fort Henry. All of this was dutifully reported to Halleck by Cullum, Sherman, and telegraph supervisors such as Major G.W. Smith and Colonel J.J.S. Wilson. The latter pair worked hard to correct the breakdowns. Even then, Grant remained skeptical of committing strength figures and other sensitive data on the wires where Rebel operators might intercept them. The army cipher and codes for transmitting long-distance traffic had not been passed to either Smith or Grant. The impatient Halleck never appreciated all of these facts or the impact of a stormy winter on this facet of field operations.[15]

While Grant tried to correct impressions at St. Louis headquarters, his subordinates and their men had irritations of their own. Ambitious junior and senior officers vied for recognition and power as a result of the Donelson victory. Lew Wallace incurred the animosity of one of Grant's aides by refusing to alter a report to reflect an inflated role of that officer in the affair. The ever ambitious McClernand courted further favor in Washington by sending Lincoln a copy of his battle report with the ink barely dry on the paper. Ten days later he followed with a rather pompous letter boasting "of all our land forces mine were the first to reach Camp Halleck, Fort Henry, Fort Donelson, and Clarksville." When Grant learned of this indiscretion, he told superiors that McClernand's report "is a little highly colored as to the conduct of the First Division" and stated that he had failed to hear the Illinois general's "suggestions spoken of about the propriety of attacking the enemy all around the lines on Saturday." Political generals such as McClernand and Wallace may have begun to weary regulars like Grant. At any rate, McClernand would be a man to watch closely in the future.[16]

This did not mean that Grant neglected those worthy of recognition. He recommended aides William S. Hillyer, Clark B. Lagow, Surgeon Brinton, Colonel Lyle Dickey's sons, as well as regimental commanders such as Morgan Smith and J.M. Thayer, and Commander Henry Walke of the navy. Of all the ambitious and eager army officers, only W.H.L. Wallace (soon to die at Shiloh) would tell his wife modestly that he did not feel like exulting at a proffered generalship. "I know the added responsibility of the position and pray for strength to fill it," he noted. Even Grant's head was turned by all the accolades until fellow officer William T. Sherman warned: "The moment you obtained a just celebrity at Donelson, by a stroke of war more rich in consequences than was the battle of Saratoga, envious rivals and malicious men set their pack of hounds at you, to pull you from the pinnacle which you had richly attained." By patience and silence, said Sherman, their noise can be quieted.[17]

Grant's army spent its final days along the twin rivers finishing overdue letters home, standing muster for pay, and nursing camp fevers, dysentery, and homesickness. The march back to Fort Henry and nearby landings for re-embarkation proved uneventful. By now most of the soldiers had tired of the rough woodland paths that traversed ridges and hollows. They wanted new adventures and warmer climes, and rejoiced at the "sublime spectacle" of steamboats massed at Fort Henry when they once more crossed flooded bottomland surrounding "this nasty hole" on the Tennessee. As late as March 28, Robert J. Price of the 52d Indiana noted the terrible stench of dead mules, horses, and cattle as well as discarded and spoiled meat from the troops. Herein lay part of the problem of Grant's sick army, or as Adjutant Joseph Drish put it: "Bad water, Salt Meat & hard Crackers are fast doing their work of destruction of a splendid body of men for the rebels[,] some thing they can't do themselves in a fight." Henry Dwight of the 20th Ohio echoed Drish, declaring "hardbread and fat pork is pretty poor diet for one who is sick with

the camp fever." Grant was ill; most of McClernand's brigade commanders were down with dysentery, colds, or lumbago. Dessicated vegetables
and potatoes did not help, and all that medic C.F. Tompkins could think
about was finding "the sunny South," walking into some orange grove,
and "helping myself to the best & call it 'Uncle Sams treat'"[18]

In time, the thrill of victory, the battlefield tours, and the homefront
accolades began to pall on the young army. "The boys are getting tired
of this kind of lazy idle life and want to be moving," thought Jacob Lauman. Eventually, they went aboard the transports and moved out into
the muddy stream opposite Fort Henry. "Behind us, down the river, the
sky was obscured by dense clouds of smoke, looking like angry storms,"
recalled James Dugan of the 45th Illinois. In every direction "the mighty
river monsters moved slowly onward, breathing fire & smoke, with dark-
mouthed cannon projecting from their sides, and with their cabins and
decks covered and literally jammed with armed men," in Union blue,
he continued. Others remembered it less poetically, with Sylvester C.
Bishop of the 11th Indiana Zouaves underscoring Grant's various irate
dispatches about inadequate river craft when he wrote his mother that
their trip upriver seemed more like "an open car loaded with hogs in
bad weather going to market." The lure of soldiering faded after Fort
Donelson.[19]

Soon after that battle the Reverend Mr. Robert Collyer of Chicago
had gone to Dover with a Christian commission delegation. Wandering
among Grant's army, he noticed that "the men do not swear and use profane words as they used to do." There was a touch of seriousness about
them, he felt. They were cheerful and hearty and might lapse into old
habits in a few days, "but they have been too near to the tremendous
verities of hell and heaven on that battlefield, to turn them into small
change for everyday use just yet," he decided. Within the month George
S. Durfee informed his family that the soldiery no longer spoiled for a
fight as before. They were ready to do their duty and make a good show,
he claimed, "but they have seen the fun they were so anxious to see, and
are satisfied." Will Tebbets of the 45th Illinois decided that despite all
the dangers, "it appears that the Lord has still more work for me to do."
Each man carried something quite personal away from his first battle
at Forts Henry and Donelson. As Durfee noted from Mineral Landing,
some four miles above Fort Henry on March 13: "There is a boat with
troops just passing, they are cheering. Our boys call them 'green hands'
as they don't hear so much noise from the old troops."[20]

Other survivors carried another legacy from the twin rivers. These
were the wounded and captives, and their legacy was one of pain and mis-

ery. Perhaps Clarksville's homefront saw it first with homes and churches quickly filled with Rebel sick and wounded from the Dover area. Ersatz nurses such as Blanche Lewis and her mother counted 110 deaths prior to the surrender with an additional 86 Confederates dying out of some 130 additional wounded who arrived in the city prior to evacuation. Many were buried on the local academy grounds and in the town cemetery with little concern for formality.[21]

Even Grant's medical advisor, Surgeon Brinton, felt that Union medical care was insufficient at Fort Donelson. He blamed Cairo quartermasters, but limited space aboard the transports proved the real culprit, for the army simply could not haul enough ambulances, tents, and medical chests to the fray. Although the two-wheel ambulances proved totally worthless, Brinton and his colleagues nonetheless performed as efficiently as possible. Regulations called for one medical officer per regiment in battle so as to provide emergency surgical attention under fire, while sending walking wounded to nearby dressing stations or field hospitals further to the rear. Union field hospitals were located quite close to the actual battle lines (thereby coming under fire), but an orderly evacuation of the wounded at least ensured a continuous line of conveyances plying back and forth between battlefield and hospitals. The Medical Department declared later that "the majority of the wounded on the battlefield were, in a few minutes, transported to points where every surgical attention could be rendered, and where their cases could be definitely acted upon."[22]

The gravest problem for the Federals (as compared to their opponents) hinged on finding adequate and suitable general hospital sites. At least Confederate surgeons could turn virtually every structure in Dover, plus many tents and winter huts, into makeshift hospitals, but, said Brinton, "hospital accommodations afforded by the two or three mean farm houses in the neighborhood were, at best, insignificant, and of hospital tents there were scarcely any." Grant's headquarters ultimately fell to medical use. Hay, straw, and canvas covers from quartermaster supplies were thrown on the snowy ground, while large fires were built to warm the wounded. Tea, coffee, and soup were prepared, "and thus the wounded were placed in a state of comparative comfort despite the inclemency of the weather," said the official version later. After Buckner's surrender, both Union and Confederate wounded swamped Dover facilities and eventually went aboard a transport for movement northward. Some 1,700 Federals and over 1,000 Confederates received rudimentary care in this manner, and "no case of death occurred under the knife, or following immediately any major operation," boasted Brinton.[23]

None of this prevented a legacy of suffering, however. "The benumbed condition of the men before being wounded, and their comparative exposure afterwards" contributed to the problem, said Grant's medical staff. The unavoidable exposure during the entire campaign "materially thinned the ranks of the army," they said. Plagued with camp disease after the battle, the only thing that Grant's army had not encountered was tetanus, although an outbreak of typhoid fever attended the crowding of men, animals, and equipment aboard the steamers going upriver to Savannah and Pittsburg Landing in March. All of this would lead to the first hospital fleet on western waters, but at Fort Donelson, claimed Brinton, "the want of a number of hospital steamers, properly fitted up and well officered, became painfully manifest." Indeed Grant, Cullum, Sherman, and Halleck as well as the midwestern governors and the War Department all discovered this sad truth about the nation's unpreparedness to cope with large numbers of sick and wounded.[24]

The army quickly accepted (although with bad grace), the help of civilians such as Governor Morton and the Indiana Sanitary Commission which rushed people to Dover, determined to aid the Hoosier wounded at least. Other states acted similarly, and some friction developed between private and government sectors over jurisdictional issues. Apparent need finally overcame legalisms, as even Halleck wrote one Iowan that "no distinction is made between states or between friends or foes. It is simply a question of humanity." Actually the civilians were shocked with what they found at Dover. Dr. J.S. Newberry of the Western Sanitary Commission from Cincinnati found "the individual condition of the wounded men deplorable," with lack of clean, fresh clothing, no extra blankets, inadequate bandages and dressings, and little food beyond cornmeal gruel, hard bread, and bacon. Even army surgeons requested medical supplies from this private group's chartered supply boat. After much argument the military permitted Newberry and company to take seventy-five to one hundred of the wounded aboard the *Allen Collier*, and back to Cincinnati. This mercy vessel provided food, clothing, and shelter beyond army capabilities. Some 400 or 500 wounded from Fort Donelson eventually went to that Ohio city for rehabilitation.[25]

River towns and cities from Paducah to St. Louis all received similar quotas of the injured. Nurses such as Mother Angela of the Sisters of the Holy Cross ministered to these men at Mound City, while the legendary Mary Bickerdyke, Mary Safford, and Mary Livermore (all midwestern women known to Grant for their humanitarian work in wartime) searched the battlefield for the fallen and provided subsequent care to the wounded. Ministers of the gospel tried to convert the heathen

in hospital wards, adding another dimension, but the legacy of the Donelson wounded soon became less the memories of the battlefield and
more the remembrance of the painful trip northward aboard vessels
such as *War Eagle, Fanny Bullitt,* and *Hazel Dell*—all whose decks literally
dripped blood and grime from the conflict. Then came the candle-lit
prayer vigils in stinking hospital wards with poor ventilation and the
moans of the wounded. Male nurse L.C. Stiles wrote home from Mound
City that he was sickened by sights of men with legs and arms shot off,
faces partially blown away, and many lying in their own blood. Lieutenant Churchill, who had remained unattended for so long on the battlefield, became something of a guinea pig for orthopedic quacks who
subjected his fractured thigh-bone to a contraption of hinged splints and
brass rivets that dug into the flesh. He survived bed sores, a throat infec-
tion, and the bullet wound—plus ignorant doctors at Mound City. Churchill reflected many of the Henry-Donelson wounded when one physician told him bluntly: "You are in a very precarious condition, and it
all depends upon your constitution, and your ability to bear up under
treatment." Precious few of the wounded came away with favorable impressions of the doctors. A few from the Sanitary Commission received
praise, but as George R. Lee said of his kindly old surgeon, he still had
a "hand like steel when the knife and saw had to be used."[26]

Still another kind of casualty was the result of the Henry-Donelson
experience—the Confederate prisoners of war. Writing about his imprisonment at Camp Douglas after Shiloh, Sir Henry Morton Stanley, the
world-famous newspaperman and African explorer, declared following
the war that it was an age of senseless brutality and heedless cruelty. It
was lavish and wasteful of life, he said, and had not the least idea of
what civilized warfare should be, except in strategy. Union and Confederate authorities proved this fact in their administration of prisoners of
war. The Federal government did not know how to handle the first size-
able prisoner haul from Forts Henry and Donelson. They turned former
northern training camps into POW compounds. Here the prisoners remained confined until summer and early fall when Union officials moderated their opposition to prisoner exchange. Meanwhile, Henry-Donelson
prisoners faced poorly fabricated facilities, camp areas alternately quag-
mires in spring and dustbowls in summer, with few opportunities for
escape. Cramped living conditions, a mixed assortment of bureaucrat-
ically oppressive camp guards and administrators, marginal food and
clothing, as well as the usual run of sickness, boredom, and low morale,
all sapped the stamina of a once proud army.[27]

Camp Douglas near Chicago was typical. Three miles of fourteen-foot fencing, sentry boxes at intervals along this fence, one-story wooden barracks housing 125 to 150 men each, and observation towers to guard against breakout provided a common profile at Douglas and elsewhere. A post hospital for prisoners was supplemented by one for the guards, a small "pest-house" for communicable disease patients, and a camp burials ground outside the fence. Wells and latrines were hardly segregated from one another, with predictable results. Such conditions soon siphoned prisoner interest away from the late battle. Survival, anguish about home-folks and spring planting, prisoner exchange, and the irritations about so little news from the outside all became matters of overriding importance to inmates at Douglas and the other compounds. Most prisoners feared Yankee censorship if they wrote home about Fort Donelson, and they seemed ready to leave the worry about that disaster to their officers; the latter having been quickly separated from their men by authorities so as to thwart camp rebellion, and also to induce the poorly educated rankers to renounce secession. Now the small farmers and other itinerant laborers who made up most of the Rebel enlisted force captured at Henry-Donelson had to fend for themselves. Gone was the comforting class structure whereby officer-gentry made decisions. These Confederates faced the new task of selecting camp spokesmen, who would then deal with Federal authorities, maintain camp discipline, esprit, and a modicum of unit cohesion during imprisonment. Northern newspapers and civilians derided the fall of vaunted "southern chivalry," with the *Sandusky* (Ohio) *Register* declaring upon arrival of Camp Chase transfers to Johnsons Island prison in April: "If there was anything about them superior to the 'greasy mechanics' of the North, which they affect to dispise, we could not see it." None of this bothered most prisoners. One cocky Kentuckian, when questioned about prewar occupation by a Camp Chase adjutant, replied disdainfully: "Lawyer, hell! I'm a gentleman. Put down my occupation 'Southern gentleman!'" Apparently the new leadership for the imprisoned army worked well at some camps, for as George Wiley Adams wrote his wife, back home in Tennessee, treatment was good, wholesome rations and warm quarters abounded, and he had nothing to do but eat, sleep, and enjoy himself. Few of his colleagues might have agreed, for prison camp was hardly enjoyable. The six months or so of imprisonment for the Henry-Donelson army, however, improved the soldier's capability to function independently of the civil and military social hierarchy of their native South, and to survive under duress.[28]

To some POWs it must have seemed like a repetition of winter encampment. Religious discussions and arguments flourished, and Lieutenant John Watson Morton of Porter's battery noted that the Johnsons

Prison Stockade, Camp Chase, Columbus, Ohio, 1862. William H. Knauss, *The Story of Camp Chase* (Nashville: Publishing House of Methodist Episcopal Church, South, 1906).

Island prisoners passed many hours in recreation, reminiscing about home and military life, and composing rhymes. Virginia battery captain John Henry Guy remembered his camp mates played marbles, baseball, cat, chimney, and town ball, as well as cards. "I see the games of which I was fondest when at school," he noted in his prison journal, but added that he refused to participate because "they do not tempt me from my books." A young lawyer in civilian life, Guy secured money and credit from friends on the outside to buy boxes of history, literature, and law books both for himself and his men imprisoned at Camp Douglas. Apparently he also plied his battery members with lengthy letters about making better use of their prison time than in gambling, play, and laziness. We know nothing of their response, since Guy penned his journal from Johnsons Island. Perhaps some took their leader's advice; probably others found it annoying at best.[29]

The prisoners quickly learned the power of the purse, and they went to great lengths to secure gold and credit from both home and the North. M.L. Vesey of the 14th Mississippi discovered that J.A. Mulligan's Irish Brigade guards at Camp Douglas could be quite friendly when properly bribed. "Instead of drawing the black molasses and wet brown sugar, we got good vegetables, cabbage, potatoes, etc. and fared fine from then on until we were exchanged," he recalled. Contemporary photographs of Fort Donelson prisoners at that camp show generally scruffy and sullen but adequately fed and clothed captives. No scarecrows of the infamous hell-holes at Andersonville or Elmira stared back from such pictures. True, some Rebels complained constantly about vermin, mud, and rats, while Captains J.H. George and R.L. M'Clung wrote postwar diatribes about the hellish conditions of deprivation, illness, extortion, and prisoner shootings at Johnsons Island. Stanley pointedly suggested after the war: "Were Colonel Mulligan living now, he would admit that a better system of latrines, a ration of soap, some travelling arrangements for lavatories, a commissioned superintendent over each barrack, a brass band, the loan of a few second-hand books, magazines, and the best-class newspapers (with all war news cut out), would have been the salvation of the two thirds of those who died at Camp Douglas." Obviously the prisoner's lot varied from camp to camp.[30]

Every unit captured at Forts Henry and Donelson left some of its members lying beneath Yankee sod at the prison camps. This was inevitable, and sparcity of accurate statistics notwithstanding, several hundred of the thousands taken on the twin rivers probably succumbed during confinement; others simply contracted health problems for later life. Postwar recriminations about Major W.S. Pierson at Johnsons Island or conditions at Camp Douglas weighed against postwar memorials to benevolent administrators like Colonel Richard Owen of Indiana's Camp Morton. What emerges is a mixed tale, from M'Clung's complaint about having to ride a half-mile in an open dump cart to a measles hospital and then sit on a muddy board across the top of his bed, to Adams' observation that he thought he was in better health at Camp Douglas than at any other time in his army service. One Indiana physician lamented: "The prevelant disease among them were typhoid fever and typhoid pneumonia, occuring in persons in whom the vital forces had been reduced to the lowest possible degree; many 'dropped dead' while walking about their quarters, without having manifested any disease, organic or functional, except great general debility." Yet no epidemics swept the prison compounds, and warmer weather greatly improved prisoner health. Generally speaking, the first large influx of prisoners of war in the winter of 1862 overwhelmed camp administrators and medical facilities everywhere. For enlisted prisoners from Henry-Donelson,

at least, it was less the prison camp conditions per se and more the prolonged rigors of the preceding campaign which enacted their toll.[31]

The senior officers of the captured army naturally fared better. True,
neither the families of Tilghman nor Buckner could join them in captivity (and both tried, while due to some fluke, Texas colonel John Gregg's
wife apparently stayed with him part way through captivity). Tilghman
and Buckner both suffered the indignities of solitary confinement (which
Buckner overcame by an ingenious use of newspapers as a means of com-
municating with his staff, without the knowledge of the Fort Warren
commandant). Certainly the wind and rain-lashed, stone-cold, and isolated bastion in Boston harbor offered few amenities away from its case-
mate barracks. Somehow the officers overcame such adversities. A spell-
binding view of the cradle of American liberty, including Bunker Hill,
Old North Church, and the Charlestown Navy Yard, could not be equaled
in midwestern enlisted camps. The camaraderie between upper-caste
Henry-Donelson officers and Maryland political captives provided in-
tellectual and social stimulation far beyond that suggested by Captain
Guy's literary program for Camp Douglas. Above all, the lavish dinner
parties, open consorting with prison officials, and an atmosphere more
reflective of a fine gentleman's private club marked confinement at Fort
Warren. Randal McGavock provided a glimpse of all this in his diary,
for on April 29 he noted a party with pickled oysters and bread from
Baltimore, ham and dried beef from Virginia, and Bourbon whiskey
from Kentucky. In addition to political and philosophical discussions,
some of the group entertained with singing. Later, this "mess" enjoyed
fresh salmon, roast and boiled mutton, macaroni, fresh cheese, green
peas, Irish potatoes, radishes, lettuce, and dessert, which Tennessean
McGavock passed off with a quip, "a splendid dinner for prison." Major
Cheairs explained that the prison commandant, Colonel Justin Dim-
mick, could furnish the best rations, cigars, liquors, and such for the
seventy-two inmates if they paid him $2.00 apiece per week.[32]

Getting good food and drink, hearing songs by staff and servants, flirt-
ing with any female visitor to the fort, securing the best mess stewards,
and worrying more about the hated Yankee oath of allegiance than the
plight of their men—these seemed to be the problems besetting Henry-
Donelson senior officers in captivity. McGavock captured the tone when
he observed that everyone was so kind that he fancied himself in the select society of congenial minds who had just happened "by some freak
of fortune in this inhospitable latitude." Buckner even found time to com-
pose poetry. Yet life at Fort Warren had unpleasant moments too. Col-

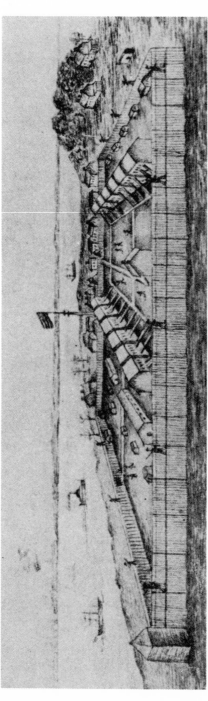

Johnsons Island Confederate Prison, Sandusky, Ohio. William H. Knauss, *The Story of Camp Chase* (Nashville: Publishing House of Methodist Episcopal Church, South, 1906).

onel Thomas Davidson of Mississippi proved to be the only senior officer from Henry-Donelson who died during confinement, although everyone else was ill at some point. Davidson, a widower, worried about his fifteen-year-old son, who had escaped capture at the surrender but who had not been heard from since. Cheairs mentioned that his own eyesight worsened during captivity, and, in late June, when Colonel John M. Lillard of the 30th Tennessee learned of his wife's death at home, he became very distraught. Cheairs was also troubled by the visit of W.G. "Parson" Brownlow of East Tennessee, who is *"gulling* these *Yankees* no little, & is making his trade . . . a very *profitable, paying business.*" Cheairs also fretted about Federal devastation of his beloved Rippo Villa near Spring Hill, Tennessee. McGavock, whose own family properties lay in the path of Yankee destruction at home, seemed to worry more that so few of his Boston friends cared to pay him a visit in prison. He did not realize that his friends worried about fraternization as indicating disloyalty to the Union. The incarcerated remained firmly committed to the justness of the Southern Cause and bemoaned loss of homefront confidence in leaders such as Sidney Johnston, the imposition of harsh Federal military rule by despised occupation leaders — military governor Andrew Johnson in Tennessee, for example — and the fluctuating war news. By summer most of these officers wanted to return to the war to avenge the disaster that had carried them to captivity.[33]

Of course some of the Henry-Donelson prisoners sought freedom from the start. Mississippian Edward Miller and Tennessean J.J. Montgomery and a few others managed to escape, but the vast majority simply awaited results of the rumored prisoner exchange that was always about to take place — but never did. A few petitioned some prominent northern officials (Johnson, Stanton, and Attorney General Edward Bates, for instance), while friends and relatives at home tried equally hard to have the Confederate government initiate a prisoner exchange. The pretexts always indicated health reasons, religious or moral scruples, or the fact that a particular soldier had been "impressed" into Confederate service. It became easier to win over the Henry-Donelson prisoners to the Union cause as their months of captivity increased. The ingenious Colonel Mulligan at Camp Douglas discovered that a number of Irish and other foreign-born captives could be induced to trade incarceration for enlistment in the U.S. Army, ostensibly for frontier duty. At least 328 such "galvanized Yankees" came from Mulligan's efforts with Henry Stanley, and a number of Heiman's 10th Tennessee captured at Fort Donelson. Others felt that Union service would be better than the horrors of prison and the fear of years of waiting until war's end.[34]

Exchange rumors became serious only in the summer. Major battles in the East and West left the warring governments with large numbers of captives. A series of negotiations took place which established the Dix-Hill Cartel and a system of exchange ranging from general officers to privates. Freedom for the Henry-Donelson captives resulted from this event, although the various prisoners departed their respective prison camps at staggered intervals. The Fort Warren captives went south at the end of July, as Buckner was traded for Union general George A. McCall, a Pennsylvanian captured near Richmond in June. The bulk of the junior officers and enlisted men did not leave their midwestern camps until August and September, although a trickle of individuals seems to have occurred all along. When the Fort Warren group stepped off the boat at the James River exchange landing in Virginia, every man seemed to draw a long breath, said McGavock. He added testily that the Confederate government failed to greet the returning prisoners, and everyone had to walk to Richmond. The experiences proved similar at western exchange points such as Vicksburg and Natchez. Passage down-river proved more tempestuous as several Tennesseans jumped ship in Memphis, seeking to get home sooner or simply to escape the antici-pated pressure to re-enlist that awaited their return to Confederate ter-ritory. Low water, sickness, and impatience bothered these restless POWs in the West, and Guy noted how the men cheered and shouted to every living creature they saw on the riverbanks during passage. Guy and his party landed at Vicksburg—"a great country village with scattered resi-dency & filled with yards and gardens and shade trees," he commented. Like McGavock in the East, Guy too lacked clean clothes and money, and "no provision has been made by our authorities for this." Appar-ently, Confederate officials provided only brief furloughs, followed by reorganization of the fighting units from the old Henry-Donelson army. By late September many of the Henry-Donelson captives were back in Confederate service despite their paroles. Spot F. Terrell, for example, re-joined a re-constituted 49th Tennessee under Colonel James E. Bailey near Clinton, Mississippi, in late September. Desperately short of man-power, the Confederacy simply violated the letter of prisoner exchange and parole in order to rebuild shattered ranks.[35]

Some Henry-Donelson survivors (John H. Guy for one) simply went home, and out of active service. Above all, the ordeal was over. Many parolees carried home small autograph books with names, addresses, and sentiments of fellow captives about shared experiences. Cheairs wrote that he had set February 15, 1864, as a date to gather and celebrate the battle of Fort Donelson at his home near Spring Hill, Tennessee, and that he had invited Buckner and all the Fort Warren prisoners to participate in what he termed "one big frolic." Less sanguine of ever meeting his mates again, Assistant Surgeon A.G. Alexander of the 15th Arkansas sent a farewell letter to stewards, druggists, commissary sergeants, and prisoner attendants of hospitals at Camp Butler where he had been incarcerated. Citing their noble sacrifice in the face of infectious disease, he wished them a long and happy life. Years later some of the Henry-Donelson prisoners would recall the six months after Donelson, a majority grimacing at the thought. A few such as Captain William B. Fonvielle of the 41st Tennessee doubtless smiled inwardly when remembering one moment of light in the darkness of Camp Chase. The Ohio governor had visited the place and promised to remedy the lack of "bedding and fire." "Parson" Brownlow was in charge, claimed Fonveille, and was universally hated "because of his arrogance and abuse of the prisoners." Everytime he spoke, the men would drown out his words with cat-calls. They knew that Brownlow had been cashiered for allowing his former regiment to be badly cut up and captured by Nathan Bedford Forrest. Returning one day to the prison camp with a new batch of captives, Brownlow was seen marching in front. One of the imprisoned Rebels with a "fog horn" voice had peered over the stockade wall in defiance of the guard. He shouted: "Old Parson Brownlow, did you see Forrest while you were gone?" Even the Union guards laughed at such hazing. The spirit of that cocky Rebel rooster, "Jake Donelson," never departed from the souls of those gallant combatants of Forts Henry and Donelson.[36]

CHAPTER 14

Henry-Donelson Remembered

P ASSAGE OF THE ARMIES FROM THE TWIN rivers ended neither
the bloodshed in the area nor the controversy surrounding the loss
of Forts Henry and Donelson. Three subsequent years of bitter guerrilla
warfare were punctuated by periodic, ill-fated Confederate attempts
to recapture the river positions and redeem the bitter defeat of 1862.
Long after the war, Buckner's surrender became part of the myth of the
South's Lost Cause; north of the Ohio, however, Union veterans chose
to remember larger and bloodier engagements of the war. The passage
of a century, and commemorative activities during the war's centennial,
brought about a modest resurgence of interest in the campaign.

Public clamor in the Confederacy rendered balanced judgment impossible for a time. The patience of the Davis administration toward Albert Sidney Johnston, his death at Shiloh, as well as the six-month captivity of the Henry-Donelson army, all hampered an official search for
truth about the disasters. Floyd, Pillow, Buckner, and Tilghman submitted after-action reports, as did lesser commanders in the fight. Pillow,
alone, would not remain silent in public. He quickly released his version
of events, claiming that the largest portion of the prisoners came from
his section of Tennessee and that their kinfolk demanded clarification.
His actions met the stern disapproval of superiors and the frank disbelief
of press and citizenry. Much was now made of the old Pillow-Buckner
feud, and eventually the Richmond government released the results of
its own rather supine investigation to Congress and the public.[1]

Other battles and other issues essentially stilled the controversy for
all but Gideon Pillow. He imagined enemies all about him, blaming
him for the defeat, and even fellow Tennesseans such as Senator G.A.
Henry goaded him with the fact that Davis "did not desire to do justice
to you or Floyd." Indeed the president suspected more culpability among
the generals than with his friend Johnston. Of course, blaming subordinates hid the unpleasant facts of the government's own niggardly support of Johnston in the West. Henry wanted Pillow to seek redress in
person at Richmond, but the petulant Tennessean hung back, using the

264

pen to embarrass the Davis regime. Officially he remained suspended from duty until August 22. Even then, Pillow had the remarkably poor grace to write the adjutant general: "Is the order of suspension simply removed, without anything being said relieving me from censure?" Richmond's response suggested several "errors in judgment" by the general that clouded the record. Relinquishing command to a subordinate rather than fighting it out or surrendering the command himself and the ill-timed order for retreat at the moment of victory on the fifteenth were the two grievous errors by Pillow. Everyone at the capital would have preferred that the Tennessean simply retire unobtrusively to his country home near Columbia and let the government prosecute the war.[2]

Pillow would not oblige them. His public bickering with former colleagues further embroiled men such as Lloyd Tilghman, who took Pillow to task over indiscreet words "directly reflecting upon me as a soldier and an officer connected with the defence of Fort Henry." Then, Pillow protested that Buckner had received command of the division which Johnston had long promised the Tennessean, when the Kentucky "hero" of Donelson returned from prison. Finally, personal problems intruded as Pillow wrote the secretary of war that Union troops had destroyed his properties and confiscated his slaves, and that he had personally burned his own cotton crop in response to wishes of the Confederate government. He faced a $5,000 property tax with no means of paying it, and "in this way I am reduced to poverty, with a large and dependent family of grown-up and unmarried daughters on my hands," he wailed. He told Richmond authorities that he had decided to retire from the service unless restitution could be done to his name and reputation. Such a retirement was precisely what Secretary of War James Seddon sought, and he immediately wrote back accepting Pillow's offer.[3]

Pillow now realized what he had done. On November 8, he wired back: "by no popular or legal interpretation can this language be construed into resignation nor was it so intended." Still, the general never formally received his perceived due, although a special order the following month revoked his "resignation," and several weeks later he led a brigade at the battle of Murfreesboro (Stones River) in gallant, if not exactly brilliant fashion. Soon, additional depositions reached the Davis government from Bushrod Johnson, Forrest, Gilmer, and various Stewart County residents, army scouts, and bystanders at Fort Donelson which reflected upon Pillow's case. How credible any of them were after the lapse of a year remains questionable. They permitted the Tennessean the luxury of continuing his assertion that surrender had been unnecessary as late as the morning of February 16, and that his version of the battle plan for regrouping back in the defense perimeter before evacuation was the correct one. He never retreated from that position, and persistence alone may have restored him to nominal command in Braxton Bragg's Army of Tennessee.

Still, Pillow remained an irritant even in that army, passing under the influence of the anti-Bragg faction of officers. He also bickered with his division commander, John C. Breckenridge, for supposedly not supporting him at Murfreesboro. Shunted off eventually to the task of gathering conscripts, volunteers, and stragglers by Bragg, the active Pillow sparked more controversy by his highly successful but unorthodox methods. Exceeding both his charter and his jurisdiction in Tennessee, Alabama, and Mississippi, Pillow also feuded with the central conscript bureau in Richmond. Finally, at the end of 1863, having drawn both praise and condemnation from governors, other conscript officers, and citizens, Pillow was relieved from this duty. As General Joseph Johnston noted: "General Pillow . . . not infrequently is compared to the press gang, sweeping through the country with little deference either to the law or the regulations designed to temper its unavoidable rigor." He passed to an innocuous cavalry command in north Alabama and botched one final field operation by marching his 2,000 cavalrymen nonstop forty-five miles to attack a 400-man Federal garrison at Lafayette, Georgia—yet failed to capture them. Finally, he ended the war as Confederate Commissary General of Prisoners, planning to trade cotton for foreign supplies to aid Federal POWs.[4]

Pillow probably fared better than Floyd, whose ignominious conduct followed him to his grave in 1863. After reaching Chattanooga and preparing the defense of that area, Floyd and his brigade were shifted northward to Knoxville in mid-March 1862. Here he received the government's demand for supplementary information about events on the Cumberland River the previous month, including evacuation of Nashville. Floyd responded that he had suggested to Johnston that only a token force be left at Fort Donelson and the main elements be concentrated at Cumberland City, and that he had consistently warned his superiors about the indefensibility of his position. He also recounted his fear that Grant would slip into Johnston's rear, but that all directives from army headquarters had been vague and indecisive. He asserted that his army had attempted to break the enemy's encirclement, but that arrival of enemy reinforcements had daunted the army and its leaders, leading to the transfer of command to Buckner and subsequent surrender. He concluded that as senior officer on the scene, it was his choice as to which troops might be evacuated, and that he had chosen his veteran Virginians, whom he considered more dependable for future needs of the Confederacy in the West than any of the untrained regiments from that section.[5]

Floyd, like Pillow, found himself stripped of command by presidential edict. Whatever the two generals' positions, they cast doubt upon President Davis' friend Johnston as a general. Influential Virginians urged Floyd to refute administration charges, but he too refused, claiming, like Pillow, that malicious men had the ear of the president. Floyd contended, "in my heart I feel that I have suffered the greatest injustice, but I have uttered no complaint." Indeed he kept silent, emerging only briefly the following August to write Buckner in an ill-concealed attempt to make amends for events leading to the Kentuckian's incarceration. But Floyd never returned to Confederate duty, passing instead to service with Governor John Letcher's Virginia state forces. His mission became that of guarding strategically important southwestern Virginia (actually, his home district), and a locale especially incensed by Davis' treatment of its native son. Floyd's attempts to recruit manpower ran afoul of the same conscript bureau people that confronted Pillow. But, contrary to the Tennessean's continuing lack of combat success, Floyd led troops to small victories against Union raids on the valuable Tennessee and Virginia railroad line and salt works in his area. Then, broken in health and reputation, Floyd sank beneath the burden and died on August 26, 1863, at his daughter's home in Abingdon, Virginia.[6]

Floyd and Pillow paid a high price for misjudgment on the twin rivers. Descendants of Virginia prisoners from Fort Donelson never forgave Floyd for "leaving all those people to surrender," while Captain Guy recorded in his prison journal that it was necessary to cashier and dismiss them from the service to show the world that southerners appreciate "their dastardly conduct and smart under the disgrace of the Surrender at Fort Donelson." Pillow's fellow Tennesseans imprisoned at Fort Warren were even more harsh. Major Cheairs declared that he understood Pillow had gone to his plantation "wishing himself dead, and if wishing would do any good, he could have any amount of help." Whatever their administrative skills, which had helped prepare their respective home state forces for the war in 1861, Gideon Pillow and John B. Floyd failed the test as battle captains, notwithstanding their combative spirit and zest for action. Tilghman, Bushrod Johnson, Buckner, and Sidney Johnston too were culpable for miscues and mistakes in the twin rivers campaigns. They, however, were ennobled by imprisonment and death, not censure.[7]

The Confederacy never retrieved the territory lost to Grant in February's campaign. The twin rivers area became a hotbed of partisan or guerrilla activities as well as a testing ground for Federal reconstrution efforts, a story largely overshadowed by more major campaigns of war. In August 1862 one band of partisans under Adam Rankin Johnson and T.G. Woodward recaptured Clarksville briefly before Union occupation forces thwarted their attempt to retake Fort Donelson and Dover. Recognizing the vitality of the rivers for Union logistical operations, Federal authorities regarrisoned Forts Henry and Heiman on the Tennessee River and constructed a new Fort Donelson, closer to the town of Dover and slightly upstream from the abandoned Rebel work. These positions, like Clarksville itself, became beacons to Confederate efforts to drive out the hated invader and to interdict Union control of the western waterways. Perhaps the most serious attempt to redeem the Henry-Donelson disaster took place in February 1863, when a combined cavalry force under Joseph Wheeler, Nathan Bedford Forrest, and John Wharton attacked the Dover garrison.[8]

Once again, command problems plagued Confederate efforts on the rivers. Both Forrest and Warton smarted under Wheeler's recent promotion in rank and command. Neither subordinate had confidence in midwinter campaign with broken-down horses, barely twenty rounds of ammunition per man, and possibly fifty artillery shells for six cannon. February weather again proved inclement, and Union authorities simply shut down river traffic in anticipation of the raid. Still, Wheeler wanted to prove himself, and the lure of bagging another Yankee garrison plus erasing the memory of the previous February urged the men onward. The Federal commander at Dover was an aging banker-in-uniform, Colonel Abner Harding of Illinois, whose abolitionist drive left him spoiling for a fight with the southerners. His 83d Illinois infantry, a four-gun battery, and a 32-pounder (retrieved from the abandoned Confederate water batteries and mounted in a makeshift arrangement in the town square) were outnumbered by Wheeler's force. Colonel William W. Lowe's 5th Iowa Cavalry (Curtis Horse) was too far away at Fort Henry to be of immediate aid, but dispatch riders went off to alert that force, and a steamboat rushed downriver with dependents to find roving naval patrols which might come to Harding's defense.[9]

The Confederate assault on February 3 found Harding strongly posted in the houses, cemetery, and town square of Dover. Uncoordinated Rebel attacks, massed Union musketry, and a determined Harding stopped the 4,500 seasoned Confederates. Again it proved a long, frustrating afternoon for the southern attackers. Enjoinders to surrender met Harding's rebuff, although Wheeler promised to treat the six hundred Federals as prisoners of war. Harding knew, however, that the Confederates had put a price on his head as a "felon," and while his troops tired and ran low on ammunition, he held out, awaiting dusk and the arrival of reinforcements. Finally, Wheeler saw the futility of further attacks— even Forrest's intrepid troopers had been roughly handled—and he ordered a retreat, just as a gunboat and Lowe's horsemen came into view. That night, during a nasty confrontation in the home of a local doctor at Yellow Creek Furnace, four miles from Dover, a thoroughly angry and beaten Forrest heatedly told Wheeler: "You know I mean no disrespect, you know the personal friendship I feel for you. But, you've got to put one thing in that report to Bragg; tell him I'll be in my coffin before I'll fight under your command."[10]

Wheeler accepted blame for the second disaster at Dover. His defeat marked the last serious attempt of Confederate forces to capture and hold a position on the twin rivers. Partisan activity and sporadic raids continued unabated, even into the summer of 1865 in this region. In 1864, between Forrest's temporary occupation of abandoned Fort Heiman during his famous Johnsonville caper and a passing attempt to hamper Federal resupply efforts in the Nashville campaign, Confederate regulars and irregulars caused Union officials much discomfort, but not catastrophic defeat. As in February 1862, the Tennessee and Cumberland Rivers became a synonym for defeat and humiliation in the battle for the Heartland. The Confederacy's failure to control these rivers reflected Sherman's appreciative comment from Georgia late in the war: "I am never easy with a railroad which takes a whole army to guard, each foot of rail being essential to the whole; whereas they can't stop the Tennessee, and each boat can make its own game." Such was the curse of Henry-Donelson's surrender upon the southern Confederacy.[11]

"We want to see discord superceded [sic] by peace; and demoralization corrected by honest industry," declared the *Clarksville Chronicle* editor in 1865. Slowly, a prostrated South arose from the ashes of defeat, although not before many returning veterans such as the Reverend J.H. M'Neilly found "a land of wasted fields, of ruined homes, of utter desolation" which he bitterly attributed to northern armies sent "with torch as well as sword and gun to burn, to pillage, and to destroy." Resumption of traffic on the twin rivers rekindled the golden prewar era of steamboating before an ascendant railroad industry slowly eroded such prosperity permanently. While Clarksville, Paducah, and other river towns recovered their vitality, and Stewart County, Tennessee, boasted 13,000 inhabitants by 1870, for example, some economic activity never recovered. The great iron industry slipped from its pinnacle of strength during the brief Confederate period, to a wartime nadir at the hands of destructive Federal raiders, and the return of peace witnessed greatly diminished commercial activity because the proprietary families now looked to Birmingham and Pittsburgh for healther production centers. Places such as the Dover hotel where Buckner had surrendered resumed service to river travelers until well after World War I, when steamboat traffic plummeted on the rivers. As a new South developed in the shadow of a powerful, unified nation, the unhappier memories surrounding events on the twin rivers in 1862 receded in time and memory.[12]

It proves impossible to trace the postwar lives of all witnesses to events at Forts Henry and Donelson. Some veterans surely returned to prewar lives as farmers, tradesmen, and laborers, and probably a few moved outside the law. Likewise, civilians from the area went home to reconstruct lives and fortunes. At least eighteen of the senior military figures did not survive the war, as was the case with hundreds of their men. Virtually all field grade officers and above in rank who fought on the twin rivers and remained with the colors for the duration moved on to greater honors and responsibilities. They parlayed such military glory into prominent political and commercial careers after the war, during an era which venerated veterans on both sides as no other period in American history has done. Tragic exceptions occurred, and two notable cases involved Adam Rankin Johnson and Gideon Pillow. Johnson was accidentally blinded in a guerrilla scrap late in the war just east of the twin rivers in Caldwell County, Kentucky. He relocated to central Texas after the war and, despite blindness, founded the town of Marble Falls and lived an additional sixty productive years. Pillow, by contrast, emerged from the war with huge debts stemming from personal sacrifices during his attempt to aid Tennessee mobilization in 1861, as well as subsequent destruction of property during Federal occupation. He joined a Memphis law partnership with his old friend Isham G. Harris, started a second family, and remarkably refrained from reopening old wounds about his controversial wartime exploits. Everywhere hung the onus of Fort Donelson for Pillow, and the comments of contemporaries such as Sherman that the Tennessean was "a mass of vanity, conceit, ignorance, ambition, and want of truth" never lifted. Little balance would ever accrue to Gideon Pillow's reputation.[13]

What did most survivors remember about Henry-Donelson? For southerners, the self-inflicted wound of the twin river forts never provided the material from which memories of the glorious cause could be molded easily. Within a year of the disaster, citizens such as Mississippi planter Benjamin F. Bedford, whose son had surrendered there, resigned himself to the defeat being the result of honest "differences of opinion" among the generals. Nearly everyone took Secretary of War Seddon's view that "Fort Henry and Donelson fell, with the loss at the latter of the gallant force who had victoriously repelled till exhaustion disabled them to meet overwhelming numbers." Only a few would echo Confederate ordnance chief Josiah Gorgas' realistic conclusion that "this was the great mistake of the war" and that a mere ten thousand additional troops would have converted catastrophic disaster into a great victory. Gorgas contended that had Grant been bested at Donelson, "as he might easily have been with proper disposition of troops," then the Union tide would have been swept back into Kentucky. Out of all this came the conventional southern view that Albert Sidney Johnston ranked with Lee and Jackson, Floyd and Pillow with the devil, and nobody even associated Bushrod Johnson, Polk, or even Beauregard with the affair. Buckner, of course, became a favorite martyr of the Bluegrass State, and even his celebrated visit to Grant's deathbed in 1885 resulted in no acknowledged discussion of their earlier and less pleasant meeting at Dover in 1862. The Henry and Donelson defeats were simply not talked about in postwar southern society, or among gentlemen officer-veterans who might have been expected to rehash the whole business.[14]

It was the same with the grayclad rank and file. Few Confederate enlisted men's reminiscences contain any other allusions to Henry-Donelson than as examples of the treachery of Floyd and Pillow. Even the great 1914–1919 survey of surviving Tennessee veterans by the state archivist uncovered relatively few responses of substance about service on the twin rivers. True, some 170 survivors of that campaign all suffered from eighty-year old memories by the time of World War I, and their record is more that of indecipherable handwriting and pardonable story lapses than insight. A few had unforgettable vignettes to recount — absence of a skirmish line in the Confederate attack on the fifteenth, the "fence-line spooking" of the scouts that night, and the overwhelming presence of shotguns as the main armament of the Rebel infantry. William McElwee of the 26th Tennessee claimed to have discovered the river road over flooded Lick Creek on the night of February 14, which permitted Forrest and his band to escape on the morning of the sixteenth. He also claimed to have heard Floyd sheepishly ask Pillow whether the pair might have used the two reinforcing steamboats that morning to convey the majority of the army upriver beyond frozen Lick Creek, and thus facilitate escape. Pillow's incoherent reply, said McElwee, was merely rambling about the issue having been decided by his prewar feud with Buckner. McElwee's comrade, Charles Fairfax Henley, could still ask rhetorically in 1915:

"why between seven and eight thousand unwhipped men flushed as they thought with victory, with both sides of the river open for their exit, should be thus ignominously surrendered is incomprehensible."[15]

One thread ran through all the reflections of the Henry-Donelson survivors. The cold and exposure, snow and sickness, and the broken physical condition of the southern fighting men had affected the results on the twin rivers. Reunions and reminiscences in the postwar South did not resound with war stories from this campaign. Perhaps most veterans agreed with what Virginian John Henry Guy had penned in his prison journal at the time: "I feel very little in a humour for indulging any lengthy comment on it here, where it will probably be never seen by any other Eyes than my own." A few such as John C. Stiles (commenting in the *Confederate Veteran* in 1917), may have sought refuge in such irrational observations as noting the large number of foreign names in Union battle reports (by this time published by the government and open to all readers): "We were surely fighting all Europe, in addition to the Yankees." Most typical, perhaps, was the opinion of one United Daughter of the Confederacy: "At Fort Donelson the Western South was not slain, it was only wounded." Clearly then, the New South dismissed the Henry-Donelson campaign as a mere prelude to the greater "what-ifs"—Shiloh or Gettysburg—averting their eyes from the unpleasant truths of failed southern leadership in a class-structured society but finding some solace in the value of southern fighting men.[16]

Relatively few northern veterans invoked Forts Henry and Donelson in disputes about their own wartime generalship. Memoirs from Grant, Lew Wallace, Henry Walke, and a few others kept the victories partially before public view, as did publication of government reports. The wartime deaths of C.F. Smith and Foote removed those figures before memoirs could appear and controversies begin. The reticence of Halleck, Buell, and McClernand all robbed posterity of any complete portrayal from the victor's perspective. The ubiquitous and wealthier unit associations of the Grand Army of the Republic clearly outperformed their southern brethren in recalling individual regimental glories of this campaign. Overall, even among ex-warriors of the Union, Forts Henry and Donelson paled beside the bloodbaths from Pittsburg Landing to Vicksburg, or Antietam to Cold Harbor. No marble shrines or cannon ball pyramids would mark the Forts Henry and Donelson battlefields as they did other sites. In fact these sacred shrines were mere steamboat stops upriver to more famous killing grounds for the Union veterans. Few in the North chuckled after the war as they had in 1862 with publication of sheet music lyrics about "Floyd's Retreat from Fort

Donelson," with its closing ditty: "He who fights and runs away, May live to run another day." Forgotten too were Herman Melville's sterner words about Fort Donelson and the horrors or futility of war. Perhaps the postwar generation in the North focused more upon the business of building the future.[17]

Through the years, eroding earthworks, resurgent fields and forests, and general neglect took over the battlefields of the twin rivers. Even the few people who went there saw little to quench their curiosity. What James Taylor Holmes of the 52d Ohio had styled "a most unpicturesque place to fight around" when he passed Fort Donelson in January 1863 reminded newsman Russel H. Conwell seven years later of Henry Wadsworth Longfellow's "forest primeval." Every trace of war was so effectively covered by foliage, he contended, that the visitor could not tell whether he had found "the artifical mound of wartime or primitive knolls of the forest." *Century Magazine* editors captured the same imagery in the 1880s with their various illustrations of the old battlefields. When they chanced upon the battle site, visitors from Holmes to Conwell could see little more than the Crisp farmhouse and clearing, original burial mounds of Union soldiers, or once-more sleepy Dover.[18]

Nevertheless, national authorities had been conscious as early as March 28, 1862, that a need existed for proper burial of Union dead. Adjutant General Lorenzo Thomas had conveyed Secretary of War Stanton's wishes in that regard to Halleck, but wartime exigencies prevented attention to the order until 1867. Finally, in that year, quartermaster officials began to supervise identification and reburial of some 670 Federal bodies (512 unknown) to a national cemetery on the site of the second, or Federal, Fort Donelson (which had itself been abandoned in the early summer of 1865). By 1882, the officer in charge of the new national cemetery suggested that these dead should be removed to a similar facility at Nashville as a cost-cutting measure. Quartermaster General Montgomery C. Meigs snapped, "let the men rest in peace," for the Fort Donelson National Cemetery "is a public historical monument to an important battle, a leading event in the history of the United States."[19]

Few people, besides Meigs, took notice. Local citizens, if they thought about the battle at all, did so from the perspective of the humble Christian Church in Dover, where a stained-glass window was installed in 1897 depicting Union and Confederate soldiers extending hands of friendship. Over in Clarksville, the original Confederate memorial was an orphanage for children of the dead soldiers of the area, but by the 1890s, money became available to erect a monument. Clarksville residents W.R. Bringhurst, Clay Stacker, and Charles H. Bailey served as figure

Modern Views of Fort Donelson National Military Park: Restored Gun
Position, Lower Water Battery and Trenches. Fort Donelson National Military
Park.

studies for the imposing infantry, cavalry, and artillery statuary adorning a Vermont granite shaft erected in picturesque Greenwood cemetery. Elsewhere in the city at the older Riverview Cemetery, some 125 unknown Confederates lay buried under a simpler monument, reputedly victims of measles, and other camp diseases while stationed on the twin rivers. The mystery of where the Confederate dead of Fort Donelson are buried persists, with legend continuing to hold that numbers of them still lie in the shallow battlefield graves and trenches around Dover. A movement to raise national consciousness regarding Fort Donelson sprang from the veneration of Americanism and heritage after World War I. But even then, proper commemoration and preservation of the fort remained a purely local and state project in Tennessee. Mrs. H.H. Leach, Clarksville resident and president of the Tennessee division of the United Daughters of the Confederacy finally succeeded in personally involving Congressman Joe Byrns of the Sixth District as leader of a movement to make Fort Donelson a national park like Shiloh, Vicksburg, Gettysburg, and others. On April 14, 1928, President Calvin Coolidge signed a bill into law accomplishing this goal — sixty-six years and two months after that snowy event on the Cumberland.[20]

Controversy and neglect did not end with establishment of a national park, however. The colorful story of Fort Donelson remained one of Confederate victory at the water batteries followed by degradation at the surrender table. Only one imposing monument — to the Confederate fighting man, atop Buckner's trenches — perpetuated the lingering theme which southerners wanted portrayed about the twin rivers. The words emblazoned on that monument said: "there is no holier spot than where defeated valor lies." Slowly, over time, the theme broadened at the park, even though boundaries never expanded to encompass either the Federal battle lines or the pivotal Confederate land victory of February 15. The onset of tourism and automobile travel after World War II opened the area to national and international visitors who wanted more than a panegyric to the Lost Cause. The Civil War Centennial, recreational development sponsored by U.S. government projects, and the permanent presence of the U.S. Army base at nearby Fort Campbell all stimulated economic progress in the area and wider vistas for other generations of Americans. While Fort Henry was swept away by Tennessee Valley Authority flooding for Kentucky Lake in the late 1930s, that agency's Land-Between-the-Lakes park (created in 1961) preserved not only outworks of the Civil War post, but the whole intriguing neighborhood of iron furnaces, dog-trot houses, and small farms, as well as programs to recapture the simpler life of people there long ago. At Fort Donelson,

Mission 66 plans have finally blossomed after a quarter century so that restored water batteries, Dover Hotel, visitor center, carefully marked troop positions, and interpretive automobile tours highlight the battle grounds. Dover and Stewart County have emerged as center pieces of a vast sports and recreational paradise, due largely to federal efforts. Certainly, this governmental activity now surpasses anything that aging veterans, self-annointed keepers of tradition, or grassroots politicians ever envisioned in original plans for memorializing this singular Civil War battlefield.[21]

Neither preserved battle sites nor marble monuments can provide anything beyond silent sentinels to the past, as we all know. For years, Henry-Donelson was brushed aside, overshadowed with dreams and myths reflected in a 1926 *Confederate Veteran* comment: "It is scarcely extravagant to say that had Albert Sidney Johnston lived the victory at Shiloh would have been complete, the whole character of the campaign in the West would have been changed, and with Lee in Virginia and Johnston in the West, the result of the war might have been far different." Forts Henry and Donelson remained dwarfed by the myth of Shiloh and Johnston. Only a few perceptive scholars captured the true significance. Such a respected southerner as Robert Selph Henry thought: "The fall of the river forts . . . was the critical event of the war," and historian James Ford Rhodes claimed in 1913 that the fall of Donelson was to the South what Bull Run had been to the North, "the first serious reverse and doubly bitter." Even then, these comments hardly express the full range of comprehension about the meaning of Henry-Donelson.[22]

Drunk with the intoxication of the 1861 triumphs, the Confederacy reeled from an event which started a domino effect on the whole setpiece pattern of the war. The Confederacy yielded too readily its economic and political base in the upper Heartland as a result of the defeat. Swept away were the South's principal powder mills on the Cumberland, the so-called "Great Western Iron Belt," verdant farms, as well as possibly the most important state capital of the region. Visible losses of tons of military supplies needed to prolong a war for independence also resulted from Henry-Donelson. Moreover the Confederacy yielded the moral ascendancy, an ascendancy so vital to a war of wills. Bell I. Wiley cited the campaign as one of the first cracks in the armor of southern resolve, thus elevating the campaign to decisive sociological importance in terms of national morale. Each section of the country—from New England to the Upper Midwest, and certainly the Deep South—saw the ability of the United States government and its soldiers to whip the vaunted flower of southern manhood in battle. They also saw the inability of the Richmond regime to succor an embattled state or region in major military crisis and Davis' credibility with Confederate westerners plummet. Into the vacuum of an abandoned region swept the power and control of centralized national government as Lincoln's military officials provided a stunning display of occupation government and political re-education to stamp out rebellion in the wake of Buckner's loss.[23]

Ultimate suppression of the Confederacy proved to be a slow, cumbersome process. Federal officials not only failed to exploit the opportunity provided by Grant and Foote, but they could not harness technological and organizational improvements in warfare for an immediate and permanent strike into the deeper Heartland. The fumbling efforts of Halleck, Buell, and Washington authorities after the fall of the forts appeared only slightly less bungling than the inability of Johnston, Beauregard, and the Richmond goverment to recapture the initiative in the West. Nonetheless, even with the month's lull following the battle, Federal military power rested squarely astride the arteries of advance and control for the region. The Union, thanks to efforts by Grant and Foote, had seized that crucial post-battle surge when psychological and matériel momentum becomes so vital to thrust and progress in warfare. Murmurs of Confederate resurgence were, perhaps, little more than ripples without substance, hopes with only fleeting promises of any permanent success. Reversing the tide or even blunting the Union surge would have required far more staying power than the Confederacy had available in the West after Henry-Donelson.[24]

A few historians such as A.L. Conger, Richard D. Goff, and Thomas L. Connelly have perceived the resonant economic and political effects of the loss of Middle Tennessee and western Kentucky to the Confederacy at Henry-Donelson. Others have focused more traditionally upon classic tenets of battle tactics, joint operations, leadership, and command — the predictable fabric of military history. Even the normally insightful Allan Nevins, whose cosmic view of the Civil War usually transcended mere combat narratives, focused principally upon Henry-Donelson as placing "the brightest laurels" upon the rank-and-file because the generalship had distinct flaws on both sides. Such a conclusion was stated more eloquently by John A. Wyeth, that older biographer of Nathan Bedford Forrest, who contended: "The annals of warfare will in vain be searched for an equal record of persistent courage, of heroic self-sacrifice, a valor that availed naught by reason of unfortunate leadership."[25]

The ultimate meaning of any singular military event will always be lost in time. Certainly Henry-Donelson can be used in various ways to study particular aspects of American history. Succeeding generations with their own agenda can learn much from the character of American leadership and decision-making in this campaign. They may also utilize the wartime drama to sense the meaning of rivers to America in peace and war. Moreover they may see Henry-Donelson as part of that interaction between national government and its citizenry in pursuit of the common political, economic, and social good. The campaign fits a continuum of governmental effort from antebellum concern about navigation and river commerce through the wartime bonding of man, technology, and organization. After the war, northernizing the South (as Richard Current terms it) can be seen really as "nationalizing" that section, and it commenced in wartime through national government intervention in an operation like Henry-Donelson. Eventually, rebirth of a region via the Tennessee Valley Authority, plus pivotal changes emerging from the Great Depression–Second World War era, extended this process to the grassroots level between the rivers. Today's Land Between the Lakes and national military parks which preserve portions of the Henry-Donelson sites are the final manifestations of this nationalizing process.[26]

In the end, of course, Henry-Donelson must always be studied from the military viewpoint. Here lay the gateway to a "glory road" for the North and a "trail of tears" for the South. The campaign lessons will continue to fascinate historians and buffs alike. The details of army-navy cooperation and the psychological effects of winter combat can only be truly appreciated by standing at the rivers on similarly snowy, February days to ask the eternal questions about these events — for the people and events of the past can only be properly judged in the context of time and place. Henry-Donelson was, after all, part of the story of nineteenth-century Heartland America. It was the story of western rivers, people, and their way of life. From that spun off the national meanings, suggested aptly by J. Milton Henry in his study of the land between the rivers when he noted that the area evolved from one best known for iron and timber resources, then subsequently for its importance in the Civil War, and finally to its modern role in the recreational fabric for all America. Francis Miles French suggested long ago in the poem, "The Blue and the Grey," that;

> No more shall the war-cry sever,
>   Or the winding rivers be red;

They banish our anger forever,
   When they laurel the graves of our dead!

Today, the graves and memories of those who fought at Forts Henry and Donelson have been laureled, and the anger of their era banished. Yet, how ironic that the ghosts of Blue and Gray will find their battleground turned into playground merely by the pen-stroke of a later generation.[27]

Organization of the Federal Forces

Army

GRANT (approximately 12,000, Feb. 6; approximately 25,000, Feb. 16.)
    37 infantry regiments + 1 company
    8 artillery batteries (field guns)
    2 cavalry regiments + 4 independent companies

First Division (McClernand)
1st Brigade (Oglesby)
    8th, 18th, 29th, 30th, 31st Illinois Infantry
    Battery D, 2d Illinois Light Artillery (Dresser)
    Battery E, 2d Illinois Light Artillery (Schwartz) (Gumbart)
    Companies A, B, 2d Illinois Cavalry (Noble)
    Company C, 2d US Cavalry (Powell)
    Company I, 4th US Cavalry (Powell)
    Carmichael's Illinois Cavalry
    Dollins' Illinois Cavalry
    O'Harnett's Illinois Cavalry
    Stewart's Illinois Cavalry (King)
2d Brigade (W.H.L. Wallace)
    11th, 20th, 45th, 48th Illinois Infantry
    Battery B, 1st Illinois Light Artillery (Taylor)
    Battery D, 1st Illinois Light Artillery (McAllister)
    4th Illinois Cavalry (Dickey)
3d Brigade (Morrison - wounded, Feb. 13, command passed to W.H.L.
    Wallace on Feb. 15, Ross senior officer present)
    17th, 49th Illinois Infantry

Second Division (C.F. Smith)
1st Brigade (McArthur)
    9th, 12th, 41st Illinois Infantry

Second Division (continued)
  3d Brigade (Cook)
    Battery D, 1st Missouri Light Artillery (Richardson)
    Battery H, 1st Missouri Light Artillery (Welker)
    Battery K, 1st Missouri Light Artillery (Stone)
    7th, 50th Illinois Infantry
    12th Iowa Infantry
    13th Missouri Infantry
  4th Brigade (Lauman)
    25th Indiana Infantry
    2d, 7th, 14th Iowa Infantry
    Birge's Western Sharpshooters
  5th Brigade (M.L. Smith)
    8th Missouri Infantry
    11th Indiana Infantry

Third Division (L. Wallace)
  1st Brigade (Cruft)
    31st, 44th Indiana Infantry
    17th, 25th Kentucky Infantry
  2d Brigade (attached to 3d Brigade)
    46th, 57th, 58th Illinois Infantry
  3d Brigade (Thayer)
    1st Nebraska Infantry
    58th, 68th, 76th Ohio Infantry
  Not Brigaded
    Company A, 32d Illinois Infantry
    Battery A, 1st Illinois (Chicago) Light Artillery (Wood)

Navy

FOOTE (6–8 iron- and timber-clad gunboats)

At Fort Henry
  Cincinnati (Stembel); *Essex* (Porter); *Carondelet* (Walke); *St. Louis* (Paulding); *Conestoga* (Phelps); *Tyler* (Gwinn); *Lexington* (Shirk)
At Fort Donelson
  St. Louis (Paulding); *Carondelet* (Walke); *Louisville* (Dove); *Pittsburg* (Thompson); *Tyler* (Gwinn); *Conestoga* (Phelps)

Organization of the Confederate Forces

TILGHMAN (approximately 2,700–3,300, Feb. 6, Fort Henry)
    6 infantry regiments + 1 battalion
    3 batteries of light and heavy artillery
    2 battalions + 1 company + miscellaneous cavalry

  1st Brigade (Heiman)
     10th, 48th Tennessee Infantry
     27th Alabama Infantry
     Culbertson's Light Artillery Battery
     Gantt's Battalion, Tennessee Cavalry
  2d Brigade (Drake)
     4th Mississippi Infantry
     15th Arkansas Infantry
     51st Tennessee Infantry
     26th Alabama (Garvin) Infantry (2 companies)
     Crain's Light Artillery Battery
     Alabama Cavalry Battalion (Hubbard, Houston)
     Milner's Cavalry Company
     Padgett's Spy Company
     Milton's Ranger Detachment
    Taylor's Company, Tennessee Artillery Corps

FLOYD (approximately 15,000–21,000, Feb. 13–16, Fort Donelson)
    27 infantry regiments + 1 battalion + 2 companies
    9 artillery batteries (field guns, siege, seacoast)
    2 cavalry regiments + 1 battalion

  Pillow's Division (B. Johnson)
  Heiman's Brigade
     10th, 30th, 42d, 48th, 53d Tennessee Infantry
     27th Alabama Infantry
     Maney's Tennessee Battery Light Artillery

Drake's Brigade
  4th Mississippi Infantry
  15th Arkansas Infantry
  26th Alabama (Garvin) Infantry (2 companies)
  1st Tennessee Battalion (Browder, Colms) Infantry
Simonton's (Davidson's) Brigade
  1st, 3d Mississippi Infantry
  7th Texas Infantry
  8th Kentucky Infantry
Baldwin's Brigade (-) (Buckner)
  26th Tennessee Infantry
  20th, 26th Mississippi Infantry
Wharton's Brigade (Floyd)
  51st, 56th Virginia Infantry
McCausland's Brigade (Floyd)
  36th, 50th Virginia Infantry
Artillery
  Guy's Battery, Goochland (Va.) Light Artillery (Floyd)
  Green's Tennessee Battery Light Artillery
  French's Virginia Battery Light Artillery (Floyd)

Buckner's Division
Brown's Brigade
  3d, 18th, 32d, Tennessee Infantry
  Porter's Tennessee Battery Light Artillery
  Graves' Cumberland Kentucky Battery Light Artillery
Baldwin's Brigade
  2d Kentucky Infantry
  14th Mississippi Infantry
  41st Tennessee Infantry
  Jackson's (Va.) Battery Light Artillery (Floyd)

Forrest's Cavalry Brigade
3d Tennessee Cavalry Regiment
Gantt's Tennessee Cavalry Battalion
1st Kentucky Cavalry Regiment

Fort Donelson Garrison (Head)
30th, 49th, 50th Tennessee Infantry
Maury Tennessee Battery Light Artillery (Ross)
Detachment Taylor's Company Tennessee Artillery Corps (Stankiewicz)
Water Battery Heavy Artillery (Culbertson)

Notes

ABBREVIATIONS

AC	Allegheny College
ADAH	Alabama Department of Archives and History
CHS	Chicago Historical Society
DUL	Duke University (Perkins Library)
FCL	Filson Club, Louisville
FDNMPL	Fort Donelson National Military Park Library
HL	Huntington Library
HSP	Historical Society of Pennsylvania
IHSL	Indiana Historical Society Library
ISH	Illinois State Historical Library
LC	Library of Congress
MC	Maury County
MDAH	Mississippi Department of Archives and History
MHS	Missouri Historical Society
MSUL	Murray State University Library
NARA	National Archives and Records Administration
SIU	Southern Illinois University Library
TSLA	Tennessee State Library and Archives
UIL	University of Illinois Library
UML	University of Michigan Library
UNCL	University of North Carolina Library
USAMHI	U.S. Army Military History Institute
UTA	University of Texas Library, Austin
UVA	University of Virginia Library
VHS	Virginia Historical Society

PREFACE

1. Connelly, *Army of the Heartland*, intro., and *Autumn of Glory;* Horn, *Army of Tennessee.*
2. Mockler, *Our Enemies the French*, ix; Fuller, *Second World War*, 36.
3. Undated newspaper clipping, author's files, FDNMPL.

4. *War of the Rebellion; A Compilation of the Official Records of the Union and Confederate Armies,* I, VII, 625, hereafter cited *ORA*.

CHAPTER I

1. Francis M. Finch, "The Blue and the Gray," 1867, in Browne, ed., *Bugle Echoes,* 327.
2. Coulter, "Effects of Secession Upon the Commerce of the Mississippi Valley," 275, 277–78; Francis H. Grierson quoted in Hubbart, *Older Middle West,* 83–84; Craven, *Growth of Southern Nationalism,* 21–27.
3. Douglas, *Steamboatin' on the Cumberland,* chs. 3, 4; Taylor, *Transportation Revolution,* 63; Kohlmeier, *Old Northwest,* chs. 1, 7, 8; Folmsbee, Corlew, and Mitchell, *Tennessee, A Short History,* ch. 15.
4. Kohlmeier, ibid., 106, 111–12, 168–71; Klein, *History of the Louisville and Nashville,* ch. 1; Sutton, "Illinois Central," 275–76; Black, *Railroads of the Confederacy,* ch. 1.
5. Coulter, "Effects of Secession," 276–78; Hubbart, *Older Middle West,* 146; Kohlmeier, ibid., ch. 8.
6. Hubbart, ibid., 223–26; Kohlmeier, ibid., 226; Coulter, ibid., 278–79; Earl J. Hess, "Mississippi River and Secession, 1861: The Northwestern Response," 187–88.
7. Sims, *Ohio Politics on the Eve of Conflict,* 21–22; *Nashville Banner,* Feb. 8, 1861; Kohlmeier, ibid., 231–36; Hess, ibid., 190–92; Coulter, ibid., 283–84.
8. Hess, ibid., 189–93; Coulter, ibid., 290–91; Hunt, "Fort Donelson Campaign," 63.
9. Coulter, ibid., 283–84; Weber, *Northern Railroads in the Civil War,* 95–96; Folmsbee, et al., *Tennessee,* 319–20.
10. *ORA,* 3, I, 67–68, 70, 81, 99.
11. Ibid., 3, I, 89–90, 113, 122, 158, 417–18; also I, LII, pt. 1, 137, 140–41, 144; Coulter, "Effects of Secession," 286–89, 291–93; Editor, *Confederate Veteran,* "Secession Spirit (1861) in Illinois," 5–6.
12. Kohlmeier, *Old Northwest,* 237–38; Coulter, "Commercial Intercourse with the Confederacy in the Mississippi Valley," 379; Hubbart, *Older Middle West,* 166–73.
13. *ORA,* I, IV, 176–77; Coulter, "Effects of Secession," 292–93.
14. *ORA,* I, LII, pt. 1, 159–60; Coulter, ibid., 299–300; Weber, *Northern Railroads,* 87.
15. Kreidberg and Henry, *History of Military Mobilization,* 90–93.
16. Randall quoted in Hesseltine and Wolf, "Cleveland Conference 1861," 258–65.
17. *ORA,* 3, I, 301; Hicken, *Illinois in the Civil War,* 2; Folmsbee, et al., *Tennessee,* 324; Livermore, *Numbers and Losses in the Civil War,* 42.

18. *ORA,* 3, I, inter alia contains correspondence on munitions procurement; also Horn, comp. and ed., *Tennessee's War,* 19–23; Coles, *Ohio Forms an Army,* 19–22; Jacobs, "Outfitting the Provisional Army of Tennessee," 257–71.

19. William Felts to Mary Fry, June 23, 1861, William H. Farmer collection, TSLA; Catton, *Grant Moves South,* 9,

20. Catton, ibid., ch. 1; Williams, *Lincoln Finds a General,* III, ch. 2.

21. In addition to standard biographies, see Warner, *Generals in Blue, Generals in Gray,* Faust, *Encylopedia of the Civil War,* or Boatner, *Civil War Dictionary.*

22. Nevins, *War for the Union,* I, 315; *ORA,* 1, IV, 155, 179–95.

CHAPTER 2

1. *ORA,* 1, III, 141–42; IV, 177–79.

2. Ibid., IV, 177–95; Connelly, *Army of the Heartland,* 52–55; Polk, *Leonidus Polk: Bishop and General,* II, 16–20.

3. Compare Connelly, *Army of the Heartland,* chs. 1, 2 with documentation in *ORA,* 1, LII, pt. 2, inter alia; IV, 180–89.

4. De Berry, diss., "Confederate Tennessee," 122–26, 128–29, 134–35; Horn, *Tennessee's War,* prologue, ch. 1, and *Army of Tennessee,* ch. 2.

5. *ORA,* 1, LII, pt. 2, 102–5, 112–14; Jacobs, "Outfitting the Provisional Army," 257–58, 267–68; Gideon Pillow to Adna Anderson, June 14, 1861, Dreer collection, HSP.

6. Connelly, *Army of the Heartland,* ch. 2; Horn, *Army of Tennessee,* 50–52; *ORA,* 1, LII, pt. 2, 112–13, 119–20, 122–23; IV, 475–76, 526–27; also Gideon Pillow to Isham Harris, June 19, Pillow to J.P. Walker, June 28, Harris to Pillow, June 30, F. Zollicoffer to Pillow, July 18, J. Thompson to B.F. Cheatham, Aug. 24, all 1861, all Dreer collection, HSP; also Harris to Pillow, June 20, 1861, Isham G. Harris papers, TSLA; and Charles Clark to Leonidus Polk, Aug. 10, 1861, Papers of Various Confederate Notables (Polk), RG 109, NARA.

7. E.B. Long, "Paducah Affairs," 253–76; Simon, ed., *Papers of Ulysses S. Grant,* II, 3, 10, 173–210 inter alia.

8. Long, ibid., 274–76.

9. Wilkie, *Pen and Powder,* 88–90, and Simon, *Grant Papers,* II, III inter alia, illustrates the learning process of war administration, while Grant family correspondence appears in II, 213–14, 237–38, 289–90, 299–300, 311–12, 327–8 e.g.

10. Ibid., II, 238; Henry B. Hibben to Emily Ross, Oct. 30, 1861, Ross-Kidwell papers, IHSL; Adolph Schwartz to Joseph Totten, Dec. 14, and "Anonymous" to Henry Halleck, Dec. 1, both 1861, both Box 1, Ltrs. Recd., Unnumbered 1861, Dept. of Missouri, RG 393, NARA.

11. Consolidated Report of Deficiencies, enclosure, John A. McClernand to Henry Halleck, Dec. 17, 1861, Box 1, Ltrs. Recd., Unnumbered 1861; Mi-

chael Lawler to Grant, Sept. 7, 1861, Registered and Unregistered Ltrs.-Repts. Recd., Cairo District, both Dept. of Missouri, ibid.; Simon, *Grant Papers*, II, 277, 309, 345, 351.

12. Simon, ibid., III, 114-56, inter alia, 202n, 204-5.

13. Ibid., II, 277; III, 4, 35-37, 45-47, 49n, 55, 56n, 177, 211-12, 220n-21n, 249-50, 251n, 272-73, 286-87, 329, 392-93; also Grant to C. Aster, Sept. 25; Grant to C.C. Marsh, Sept. 29; Grant to McClernand, Oct. 14, all 1861, all Ltrs. Sent, Cairo District, Dept. of Missouri, RG 393, NARA.

14. *Official Records of the Union and Confederate Navies*, 1, XXII, 280-86, hereafter cited *ORN;* Johnson, *Rear Admiral John Rodgers*, 155-68 inter alia; Milligan, *Gunboats Down the Mississippi*, 3-11.

15. Merrill, "Union Shipbuilding on Western Rivers During the Civil War," 17-18.

16. *ORN*, 1, XXII, 289-304.

17. Merrill, "Union Shipbuilding," 19-27; Boynton, *History of the Navy During the Rebellion*, I, 501-3; *ORN*, 1, XXII, 295-96, 299-303, 318-19.

18. Milligan, "From Theory to Application: The Emergence of the American Ironclad War Vessel," 126-28; *ORN*, 1, XXII, 297-99.

19. Merrill, "Union Shipbuilding," 23; Milligan, *Gunboats Down the Mississippi*, 15-17; *ORN*, 1, XXII, 305-8, 314-15; Johnson, *Rodgers*, 168.

20. *ORN*, 1, XXII, 318-22.

21. Ibid., 307, 321, 335.

22. Ibid., 354, 429, 444; Thompson and Wainwright, eds., *Confidential Correspondence of Gustavus Vasa Fox*, II, 5-6, 8-11; J.P. Sanford to Foote, Sept. 5, 10, 11, 21, 1861, Area File 5, Mississippi River 1861-65, Box 1, RG 45, Naval Records Collection, NARA.

23. Thompson and Wainwright, ibid., II, 11, 15, 23; *ORN*, 1, XXII, 448-52, 471; Milligan, *Gunboats Down the Mississippi*, 21-23; Montgomery C. Meigs to Foote (tel. and ltr.), Nov. 15, 21; George D. Wise to Foote, Dec. 18, 20, 22; James Eads to Foote, Dec. 30, all 1861, all Area File 5, Box 1, RG 45, NARA.

24. Stivers, *Privateers and Volunteers*, 235-57, details Foote's recruiting problems; Thompson and Wainwright, ibid., II, 12, 15; Fox to Foote, Oct. 28, Nov. 12, 17; Phelps to Foote, Nov. 15; R.N. Stembel to Foote, Nov. 22; Foote to wife, Dec. 17; Wise to Foote, Dec. 25, all 1861, all Area File 5, ibid.; also Henry A. Walke, "Gunboats at Belmont and Fort Henry," in Johnson and Buel, eds., *Battles and Leaders of the Civil War*, I, 359.

CHAPTER 3

1. Roland, *Albert Sidney Johnston*, 258-60; Connelly, *Army of the Heartland*, 59-61; Horn, *Army of Tennessee*, 52-53.

2. *ORA*, 1, IV, 173-95, 396, 402-5, 413-23; LXII, pt. 2, 146-47; *Memphis Appeal*, Sept. 12, 1861, quoted in Horn, ibid., 56.

3. ALC, "Fort Donelson," 61; Roland, *Johnston,* 259–62; Connelly, "The Johnston Mystique," 259–67: U.S. Cong., 37th sess., Sen. Ex. Doc. 1, *Message of the President, Vol. II, Rept. of Sec. of War, 1861,* 32–35, concerning Dept. of Pacific statistics.

4. Horn, *Army of Tennessee,* 55–62.

5. Connelly, *Army of the Heartland,* intro. ALC, "Fort Donelson," 55–62: Jacobs, "Outfitting the Provisional Army of Tennessee," 259–67.

6. *ORA,* 1, IV, 444, 452; LXII, pt. 2, 142–43; Black, *Railroads of the Confederacy,* 64; Reid, *Combined Operations in the Civil War,* 65; U.S. Bureau of Census, *Manufacturers of the United States in 1860,* 577–79, and *Agriculture of the United States in 1860,* 136.

7. Folmsbee, et al., *Tennessee,* ch. 17; Douglas, *Steamboatin' on the Cumberland,* ch. 4; J.B. Killebrew, *Introduction to the Resources of Tennessee,* II, 701–7, 760–67, 844–59, 922–36, 1108–17.

8. Horn, "Nashville During the Civil War," 8; Crabb, "The Twilight of the Nashville Gods," 291–95; Davenport, *Cultural Life in Nashville on the Eve of the Civil War,* ch. 9; Connelly, *Civil War Tennessee,* 14–15.

9. *ORA,* 4, I, 783; W.W. Mackall to M.J. Waldon, Sept. 20, 1861, ch. II, v. 217, Mil. Depts., A.S. Johnston's Command, Ltrs. and Tel. Sent, Sept. 1861–Apr. 1862, RG 109, NARA.

10. "W," "General Albert Sidney Johnston," 323; Black, *Railroads of the Confederacy,* chs. 2, 4; *ORA,* 1, IV, 414–15; Klein, *Louisville and Nashville,* 29; Spec. Orders 9, Sept. 24; Johnston to Harris, Dec. 2; Mackall to Stevenson, Dec. 31, all 1861, all ch. II, v. 217, ibid.; also Tels. n.d., President and Superintendent, Mobile and Ohio RR, to Johnston, Western Dept., Tel. Recd. Sept. 1861–Apr. 1862; and J.L. Williams to Polk, Nov. 28, 1861, Box 22, Ltrs. and Tel. Sent, 1861–64, Tel. Recd. 1861, Polk papers, all RG 109, NARA.

11. Douglas, *Steamboatin' on the Cumberland,* ch. 4, 103, 331–34.

12. *ORA,* 1, IV, 408, 421–23, 431–32, 449–50, 452–53, 468–70, 474–75, 502–3; LII, pt. 2, 150; Johnston, *Life of Gen. Albert Sidney Johnston,* 328, 340; Johnston to Davis, Sept. 14, 1861, Ltrs. and Tels. Sent, Sept. 1861–Apr. 1862, ch. II, v. 217, Johnston's command, RG 109, NARA; Roland, *Johnston,* 276–77.

13. Jacobs, "Outfitting the Provisional Army," 257–71; *ORA,* 1, IV, 401–2, 406, 410–11, 479, 512–13; LII, pt. 2, 158–63; also various tel. and ltrs. from ordnance officers, in Ltrs. and Tel. Sent, Oct. 1861–Apr. 1862, ch. II, v. 218, ibid., and Box 22, Ltrs. and Tel. Sent, 1861–64, Tel. Recd. 1861, Polk papers, both RG 109, NARA.

14. *ORA,* 1, IV, 475, 499, 525; VII, 766–67, 770, 795; LII, pt. 2, 218; Johnston, *Johnston,* 333; Steuart, "How Johnny Got His Gun," 166; James T. Mackey, "Camp Life in Tennessee, Kentucky, Mississippi, Louisiana, and Alabama," diary entries Dec. 12, 1861, Jan. 5, 9, 1862, Maury Co. Hist. Soc., Columbia, Tenn.; Mackall to Wright, Oct. 25, 1861, Ltrs. and Tel. Sent, Oct. 1861–Apr. 1862, ch. II, v. 218, ibid.

15. *ORA*, I, IV, 504–5, 553; LII, pt. 2, 189–90; Walker, "Building a Tennessee Army, 1861," 110–11.

16. Carter, *A Cavalryman's Reminiscences*, ch. 2; Stanley, ed., *Autobiography of Sir Henry Morton Stanley*, 168–69, 171–72, 177, 178–82.

17. Stanley, ibid.; Harrison, "A Confederate View of Southern Kentucky, 1861," 163, 175–76, 178; Rugeley, anno., *Batchelor-Turner Letters 1861–1864*, 1–4.

18. Claiborne, "Woman's Memoirs of the Sixties," 61–62; Robert Franklin Bunting to Editor, Nov. 9, 13, Dec. 19, all 1861, Robert Franklin Bunting collection; William Felts to mother, Nov. 24, 1861, William Farmer collection; Rev. Thomas Hopkins Deavenport diary, n.d., all TSLA; also Rugeley, *Batchelor-Turner Letters*, 5–6.

19. David W. Yandell to Lundsford Yandell, Dec. 22, 1861; Yandell papers, FCL; Johnson, ed., "The Early Civil War in Southern Kentucky as Experienced by Southern Sympathizers," 178–79; Davis, *The Orphan Brigade*, ch. 3.

20. Baird, *David Wendell Yandell; Physician of Old Louisville;* and "There is No Sunday in the Army," 317–22; "A Kentucky Physician Examines Memphis," 190–202, provides a full treatment of this family in war; also Harrison, "Confederate View," 170.

21. Stanley, *Autobiography*, 178–79; A.P. Merrill, "Health of Our Army," *Memphis Avalanche*, Jan. 30, 1862.

22. Connelly, *Army of the Heartland*, 65–77; *ORA*, I, IV, 194; VII, 813–14.

23. Johnston, *Johnston*, 327; Roland, *Johnston*, 268–70; Lundsford Yandell to father, Oct. 9, 1861, Yandell papers, FCL; Baird, "No Sunday in the Army," 322.

24. *ORA*, I, IV, 420; Polk, *Polk*, 36–37; Johnston *Johnston*, 322–23.

25. *ORA*, I, IV, 435, 437, 444.

26. Johnston, *Johnston*, 327; Stickles, *Simon Bolivar Buckner; Borderland Knight*, 106–9; Hughes, *General William J. Hardee; Old Reliable*, 82–83; Connelly, *Army of the Heartland*, ch. 3; *ORA*, I, IV, 455, 478, 528, 562–65; VII, 777, 781, 784, 797; J.F. Gilmer to wife, Oct. 17, Nov. 14, both 1861, Jeremy F. Gilmer papers, Southern Historical Collection, UNCL.

27. *ORA*, I, VII, 781–82, 792–95.

CHAPTER 4

1. *ORA*, I, LXII, pt. 2, 101–2; Connelly, *Army of the Heartland*, 39, 71–72.

2. Ash, "Community at War; Montgomery County, 1861–1865," 30–32; Davis, *Geography of the Jackson Purchase*, 6–8, 100–10; Killebrew, *Resources of Tennessee*, I, 406–7.

3. Henry, *Land Between the Rivers*, chs. 1, 4; Connelly, *Army of the Heartland*, intro.

4. Killebrew, *Resources of Tennessee*, 235–42; Lesley, *Iron Manufacturer's Guide*, 749, suggests "45 furnaces, and six or eight forges"; also W. L. Cook, "Furnaces and Forges," 190–91.

5. Tennessee Civil War Commission, *Tennesseans in the Civil War*, pt. I, 193–94, 285–86; Henry, *Land Between the Rivers*, 27–28.

6. William F. Foster, "Building of Forts Henry and Donelson," in Ridley, ed., *Battles and Sketches*, 64-66; Nichols, *Confederate Engineers*, 42-43; Horn, *Army of Tennessee*, 76-77; Bearss, "Fort Donelson Water Batteries," pt. 2, 3-5, FDNMPL.

7. Johnston, *Johnston*, 407; Henry, *Land Between the Rivers*, 99; Bushrod Johnson to Harris, June 11, 1861, Box 1, Harris papers, TSLA.

8. Kegley, "Bushrod Rust Johnson, Soldier and Teacher," 249-51; Cummings, *Yankee Quaker Confederate General*, chs. 1-4; Foster, "Building of Forts Henry and Donelson," 65.

9. *ORA*, 1, LXII, pt. 2, 122; List of Officers, Stations, Artillery Corps of Tennessee, Sept. 1861, encl., Governors Office to Polk, Sept. 1, 1861, Box 21; R. McGavock to Polk, Sept. 6, 1861, Box 22, both Polk papers, RG 109, NARA; also Frank, "Adolphus Heiman: Architect and Soldier," 35-57 inter alia; Patrick, "The Architecture of Adolphus Heiman," pt. I, 167-87, pt. II, 277-95.

10. *ORA*, 1, IV, 404-5, 427-28, 431-33; LXII, pt. 2, 166-67.

11. Ibid., IV, 440-41; LXII, pt. 2, 167-68.

12. *ORN*, 1, XXII, 371.

13. Ibid., 371-76; Phelps to Grant, Oct. 20, 1861, Box 1, Area File 5, RG 45, NARA; *ORA*, 1, IV, 446, 448; Read, "Reminiscences of the Confederate States Navy," 332-36; E. Wood to Polk, Oct. 4, S.R. Mallory to Polk, Oct. 21, Carter to Polk, Oct. 23, and Benjamin to Polk, Oct. 31, all 1861, all Box 22, Polk papers, RG 109, NARA.

14. H.L. Bedford, "Fight Between the Batteries and Gunboats at Fort Donelson," in U.S. War Dept., General Service Schools, *Source Book*, 656; Heiman to Harris, Oct. 14, 1861, Box 2, Harris papers; D.C. Cook to Nathan Brandon, Oct. 13, 1861, Brandon papers, both TSLA.

15. *ORA*, 1, IV, 453-59; *ORN*, 1, XXII, 379-84.

16. *ORA*, ibid., 460-62.

17. Ibid.

18. Ibid., 463, 488.

19. Ibid., 456, 463-69; LXII, pt. 2, 181; Mackall to A.J. Smith, Oct. 26, 1861, ch. II, v. 218, Johnston's command, RG 109, NARA; Jeremy F. Gilmer to wife, Sept. 25, Oct. 4, 13, 19; John Gilmer to Jeremy F. Gilmer, Oct. 13; John B. Peachy to Jeremy F. Gilmer, Oct. 13, all 1861, all Gilmer papers, UNCL; Nichols, *Confederate Engineers*, 433-34.

20. Gilmer to wife, Nov. 3, 1861, ibid.; *ORA*, 1, IV, 496-97, 506, 514.

21. Ibid., 514, 544-45; also Gilmer to Stevenson, Nov. 11, 1861, ch. III, v. 8, Engineer Dept., Ltrs. Sent, Chief Eng. Western Dept., 1861-62, RG 109, NARA; Gilmer to wife, Nov. 4, 6, 8, 13, 14, all 1861, Gilmer papers, UNCL.

22. *ORA*, 1, IV, 479, 480, 501, 526, 529; D.C. Kelly, "Forrest's (old) Regiment, Cavalry," Conger, comp., *Donelson Campaign Sources*, 148.

23. F. Hannum to Johnston, Oct. 17, Nov. 25; Johnston to Hannum, Oct. 17, both 1861, ch. II. v. 217, Johnston's command; also various dispatches, Clarksville Military Board to Polk, Oct. 15-18, 1861, Box 2, Polk papers, all RG 109, NARA; Johnston, *Johnston*, 416.

24. *ORA*, 1, IV, 481, 491–92, 495, 524–25.

25. Ibid., 511, 513–14, 519, 522, 539, 543.

26. On role of Belmont in Polk-Johnston coordination, see ibid., 532, 550–54, 557, 560; LXII, pt. 2, 225–26; Connelly, *Army of the Heartland*, 193–94; while a reevaluation of Grant appears in Simon, "Grant at Belmont," 161–66.

27. *ORA*, 1, IV, 523, 528, 560; Mackall to Polk, Oct. 21; I.B. Gray to G.W. Hillman, Oct. 31; W.B. Richmond to Hillman, Nov. 6, all 1861, all Box 21, Polk papers, RG 109, NARA; Editor, *Confederate Veteran*, "Gen. Lloyd Tilhgman," 318–19; General Service Schools, *Source Book*, 1427–29.

28. *ORA*, 1, VII, 685, 692–96, 698–700, 703–4, 709, 719, 723–24, 733–35; Connelly, *Army of the Heartland*, 104–5.

29. Polk to Mallory, Dec. 11, 17, 1861, Box 22, Polk papers; Mackall to Tilghman, Dec. 4; Mackall to Polk, Dec. 6; Mackall to Shaw and Lawson, Dec. 10; Johnston to Benjamin, Dec. 12; Cheatham to Johnston, Dec. 19; Johnston to Cheatham, Dec. 20, all 1861, all ch. II, v. 218, Johnston's command, RG 109, NARA.

30. *ORA*, 1, VII, 739–41, 745–46, 762–63, 769, 781–82; Johnston to Sam Weakley, Dec. 2, 1861, ibid.; Gilmer to Johnston, Nov. 26, 29; Gilmer to Harris, Dec. 3; Gilmer to Foster, Dec. 13; Gilmer to Sayers, Dec. 10, 13; Gilmer to Mackall, Dec. 10; all 1861, all ch. III, v. 8, Engineer Dept., all RG 109, NARA; also Gilmer to wife, Nov. 24, 26, 28, Dec. 1, 4, 8, 11, 14, 20, 22, 29, all 1861, all Gilmer papers, UNCL.

31. Johnston to Harris, Dec. 31, 1861, ch. II, v. 217, Johnston's command, RG 109, NARA; *ORA*, 1, VII, 752–53, 758, 779, 782–83, 793, 796–97.

32. Ibid., VII, 779, 813, 817–18; LXII, pt. 2, 239, 245–46.

33. M'Neilly, "Early Confederate Days," 208; Henry, *Land Between the Rivers*, 27, 29, 100–1, 118; Martin to cousin, Dec. 1861, William Felts collection, TSLA.

34. Brumbaugh, "A Letter to Fort Donelson," 33–34; McCord, "J.E. Bailey: Gentleman of Clarksville," 251; *ORA*, 1, VII, 143–44; Gower and Allen, eds., *Pen and Sword, The Life and Journals of Randal W. McGavock*, 85, 582.

CHAPTER 5

1. *ORA*, 1, VII, 533; Williams, *Lincoln Finds a General*, III, 159–64; Wilson, "Types and Traditions of the Old Army," 553–54.

2. *ORN*, 1, XXII, 431–81 inter alia; *ORA*, 1, VIII, 367–70; Simon, *Grant Papers*, III, 527.

3. Ibid., III, 235, 262, 350–58; Williams, *Lincoln Finds a General*, III, ch. 4; Brinton, *Personal Memoirs*, 97–98.

4. Catton, *Grant Moves South*, ch. 5; Jones, *"Black Jack": John A. Logan and Southern Illinois*, 116–18; Fletcher, *History of Company A, Second Illinois Cavalry*, 22–24; Avery, *Fourth Illinois Cavalry*, 47–48; Morsberger, *Lew Wallace; Militant Roman-*

tic, 66; *ORN,* i, XXII, 396, 436, 457, 461; Sylvester C. Bishop to mother, Dec. 25, 1861, Bishop papers, IHSL; Brinton, *Personal Memoirs,* 100-1.

5. Williams, *Lincoln Finds a General,* III, ch. 6; *ORA,* i, VII, 450-52, 457-58, 487-88, 520-21, 524; VIII, 402-3, 408-10, 419, 437-39.

6. Nevins, *War for the Union,* II, 15-17; Graf and Haskins, eds., *Papers of Andrew Johnson,* V, 57-60; Simon, *Grant Papers,* III, 204-7; IV, 34-35, 409.

7. *ORN,* i, XXII, 396-97, 426-27, 434-45, 454-58, 468, 473-74.

8. William T. Sherman, *Personal Memoirs,* I, 219-20; Reed, *Combined Operations,* 70-75.

9. *ORA,* i, VII, 524-36, 543, 547-48, 554, 928-29; VIII, 503-4; Williams, *Lincoln Finds a General,* III, ch. 7; Catton, *Grant Moves South,* ch. 6; Hattaway and Jones, *How the North Won,* 54-57, 61-64.

10. *ORA,* i, VII, 533, 537-38.

11. Ibid., 533-34; Ripley, "Prelude to Donelson; Grant's January 1862 March into Kentucky," 311-18, esp. 312; Entries Jan. 7-10, 1862, Indorsements to and from Grant, Military Ledger Books, McClernand papers; Civil War journal of Daniel Brush, Jan. 7-11, 1862, both in ISH; John B. Connelly diary, Jan. 8, 1862, IHSL; Brinton, *Personal Memoirs,* 101-2.

12. Thomas F. Miller to Benjamin Newton, Jan. 22, 1862, Miller papers, ISH; Ripley, "Prelude to Donelson," 314-15; Simon, *Grant Papers,* IV, 18-50 inter alia; Grant to C.F. Smith, Jan. 9, 1862, C.F. Smith papers, UML.

13. *New York Herald,* Feb. 2, 1862; Ulysses S. Grant, *Personal Memoirs,* I, 286; Brush journal, Jan. 15, 1862, ISH.

14. Douglas Haperman diary, entries Jan. 15-21, 1862, ISH; George S. Durfee to H.B. Durfee, Jan. 21, 1862, Illinois Historical Survey, UIL; J.M. Kidwell to mother, Jan 14, Ross-Kidwell papers, and Sylvester C. Bishop to mother, Jan. [29?], both 1862, both IHSL; *ORN,* i, XXII, 500-2, 507-10.

15. *ORA,* i, VII, 66-68, 72-75, 561.

16. *New York Times,* Jan. 24; *New York Tribune,* Jan. 18; *New York Herald,* Feb. 2, all 1862; Smart, ed., *Radical View; The "Agate" Dispatches of Whitelaw Reid,* I, 106; Whitesell, "Military and Naval Activity Between Cairo and Columbus," 120; Ripley, "Prelude to Donelson," 318; Williams, *Lincoln Finds a General,* III, 181-83.

17. Lyon, comp., *Reminiscences of the Civil War . . . Colonel William Lyon,* 14-16; Williams, ibid., ch. 7; Simon, *Grant Papers,* IV, 74-98.

18. Reed, *Combined Operations,* 78-80; *ORA,* i, VII, 561, 665-66.

19. John Lillyett to Henry Halleck, Jan. 18, 1862; Ltrs. Recd. 1861-67, Box 2, 1862, Dept. of Missouri, RG 393, NARA; Grant, *Personal Memoirs,* I, 287.

20. *ORA,* i, VII, 930; LII, pt. i, 198; *ORN,* i, XXII, 504-5, 515-16.

21. *ORN,* ibid., 502-3, 515-17, 523; Simon, *Grant Papers,* IV, 84-85; Avery, *Fourth Illinois Cavalry,* 51.

22. *ORN,* ibid., 517-19, 522-24; Milligan, ed., *From the Fresh-Water Navy,* 17-22; R.N. Stembel et al. to Halleck, Dec. 31, 1861; Stembel and A.W. Pennock

to G.W. Cullum, Jan. 24; Cullum to Halleck, Jan. 28, both 1862, all in George W. Cullum letterbook, AC; *ORA,* I, VIII, 535.

23. Connelly diary, Jan. 30, 1862, IHSL; McClernand to Logan, Jan. 5; Mary Logan to husband, Jan. 5; John White to Logan, Jan. 22; John Logan to wife, Jan. 29, all 1862, all Box 33, Logan papers, LC; Luther Cowan to wife, Jan. 25, 26, 1862, Cowan papers, TSLA; Huffstodt, "One Who Didn't Come Back: The Story of Colonel Gerret Nevius," 328-29; Wilkie, *Pen and Powder,* ch. 5.

24. Compare *ORN,* I, XXII, 524, 524n and *ORA,* I, VII, 120-21; also Brinton, *Personal Memoirs,* 10.

25. Halleck to McClellan, Jan. 24, 1862, Halleck papers, LC; Simon, *Grant Papers,* IV, 196-97n; *ORA,* I, V, 41; VII, 930-31; also Nevins, *War for the Union,* I, 407-8.

26. *ORA,* I, VII, 121, 571; *ORN,* I, XXII, 525-26.

27. *ORA,* ibid., 121-22.

28. *Missouri Democrat,* Jan. 30, 1862, quoted in General Service Schools, *Source Book,* 146-47; Bishop to mother, Jan. [?], 1862, Bishop papers, IHSL.

CHAPTER 6

1. *ORA,* I, VII, 828-29; John Adams to Major Williamson, Jan. 21, 1862, Tel. Recd., Circulars, 1862-64, Box 23, Polk papers, RG 109, NARA.

2. *ORA,* ibid., 823-25, 828-29, 832, 837, 845-47, 850-51; J.B. Wood to Polk, Jan. 20, 21, 1862, Polk papers, ibid.; Liddell, "Liddell's Record of the Civil War," 417-19, Hughes, ed. *Liddell's Record,* ch. 3.

3. *ORA,* I, IV, 1009, VII, 515, 807, 832; Short, "General John B. Floyd in the Civil War," ch. 1-3 esp.

4. Roland, *Johnston,* 274-81; Rugeley, *Batchelor-Turner Letters,* 16; Jeremy Gilmer to wife, Jan. 2, 1862, Gilmer papers, UNCL.

5. *ORA,* I, VII, 544, 563, 852-55; Rugeley, ibid., 10-12; Johnston to Pillow, Jan. 25; Johnston to Harris, Jan. 27; Mackall to Duncan, Jan. 29, all 1862, all ch. II, v. 218, Johnston's command, RG 109, NARA; J.R. Pope to "Ma," Jan. 26, 1862, Pope-Carter collection; Clark to Floyd, Jan. 20, 1862, Floyd papers, both DUL; Baird, *David Yandell,* 37-45.

6. *ORA,* ibid., 818; Johnston to Samuel Cooper, Jan. 8, 1862, ch. II, v. 218, Johnston's command, ibid.; Williams to Polk, Jan. 8, 13, 16, 1862, Box 23, Polk papers, both RG 109, NARA; also Tennessee Civil War Centennial Commission, *Tennesseans in the Civil War,* I, 172.

7. *ORA,* I, VIII, 728-29; Polk, *Leonidus Polk,* I, 72-73.

8. Johnston to Gorgas, Jan. 27, 1862, ch. II, v. 218, Johnston's command; various materials in Box 22, Polk papers; correspondence between Wright, Mackall, Tilghman, Gorgas, et al., ch. IV, v. 8, Ltrs. and Tel. Sent, Ordnance offices, Nashville and Atlanta, Dec. 1861-Apr. 1862, all RG 109, NARA.

9. Johnston to Tilghman, Jan. 8; Mackall to Tilghman, Jan. 14, 15, 18, 19, all 1862, Johnston's command, ibid.; Tilghman to Polk, Jan. 7, 9, 10, 13, 20, 24, all 1862, all Polk papers, ibid.; Wright to Mackall, Gorgas, Tilghman, as well as commanding officer and ordnance officer (Forts Henry and Donelson), all Jan.–early Feb. 1862, in Ordnance office files, ibid.; also *ORA*, I, VII, 74–75, 144–45, 834–35, 840; Jesse Taylor, "The Defense of Fort Henry," in Johnson and Buel, eds., *Battles and Leaders*, I, 368.

10. Mackall to Claiborne, Jan. 15; Mackall to Gilmer, Jan. 23, 29; Special Order 10, Jan. 18, and 19, Jan. 27, all 1862, all Johnston's command, ibid., Cummings, *Yankee Quaker*, 184–85; Gilmer to wife, Jan. 5, 7, 10, 14, 19, 20, 23, 31, all 1862, all Gilmer papers, UNCL.

11. *ORA*, I, VII, 132–33.

12. Ibid., 388, 409, 832–33; Cullum, *Biographical Register*, I, 707; Daniel, *Cannoneers in Gray*, 6.

13. Bedford, "Fight Between the Batteries and Gunboats," 136; *ORA*, I, VII, 388–89, 409–10, 870–71; various documents in ch. IV, v. 104, Record of Ord. and Ord. Stores Recd., Issued, Nashville, Atlanta, 1862–63, RG 109, NARA. Both contemporaries and historians called this cannon a "rifled colombiad," a "64-pounder rifled colombiad," a "128-pounder rifled gun," while Nashville ordnance officials claimed to have shipped a "6.4 inch," not a "6.5 inch" cannon.

14. Bailey to wife, Feb. 2, 6; David Clark to Maggie Bell, Jan. 18; George W. Adams to wife, Jan. 25, all 1862, all TSLA; Tennessee Civil War Centennial Commission, *Tennesseans in the Civil War*, I, 164, 283, 285, 293; McCord, "J.E. Bailey: A Gentleman of Clarksville," 253.

15. *ORN*, I, XXII, 528; Henry Walke, "The Gun-Boats at Belmont and Fort Henry," in Johnson and Buel, eds., *Battles and Leaders*, I, 364.

16. *Memphis Appeal*, Jan. 30, 1862; *ORA*, I, VII, 149, 153–54, 843, 855.

17. *ORA*, ibid., 121; Cullum to Smith, Feb. 1, Cullum letterbook, AC; Catton, *Grant Moves South*, 134; Simon, *Grant Papers*, IV, 131–32n.

18. *ORA*, ibid., 122–23; Paine to AAG, St. Louis, Feb. 4, 1862, Misc. Ltrs. and Repts. Recd. 1861–67, Box 5, Dept. of Missouri, RG 393 NARA; various materials, Richard Oglesby papers, VII, IX; Indorsements and Memoranda to and from Grant, McClernand papers, I, both ISH; Stonesifer, diss., "Forts Henry-Heiman and Donelson Campaign," 121–23.

19. Simon, *Grant Papers*, IV, 138–39; Welles to Foote, Jan. 31, Halleck to Foote, Feb. 3, both 1862; both Area File 5, Box 1, RG 45, NARA.

20. *ORN*, I, XXII, 522–34; *ORA*, I, XII, 809–10, 866, 874, 878, 881, 883–84, 887, 892; Sanford to Foote, Feb. 2; Foote to Phelps, Jan. 24, Phelps to Foote, Jan. 30, all 1862, all Area File 5, ibid.; Coffin, *My Days and Nights on the Battlefield*, 76–77.

21. Simon, *Grant Papers*, IV, 141–50; *ORN*, ibid., 528.

22. Wallace, *Life and Letters of General W.H.L. Wallace*, 153–54; Jones, "*Black Jack*," 119; Crummer, *With Grant at Fort Donelson, Shiloh, and Vicksburg*, 13; Fletcher,

Second Illinois Cavalry, 25–27; John Wilcox to wife, Jan. 27, 1862, Wilcox papers, ISH.

23. Colby quoted in Kaiser, "In Dusty Files a Coruscation," 298; Lyon, *Reminiscences of William E. Lyon,* 16; Milligan, *From the Fresh Water Navy,* 23–24.

24. Stonesifer, "Forts Henry-Heiman and Donelson," 125–26.

25. Simon, *Grant Papers,* IV, 145–49; *ORA,* I, VII, 126; Avery, *Fourth Illinois Cavalry,* 52; Grant, *Personal Memoirs,* I, 290.

26. *ORA,* ibid., 137.

27. Ibid., 148–50.

28. Ibid., 138, 153–54, 858–59.

29. Ibid., 138–39.

30. Ambrose, *History of the Seventh Regiment Illinois Volunteer Infantry,* 25–26; Luther H. Cowan to wife, Feb. 4, 1862, TSLA; Wallace, *Wallace,* 154; Gower and Allen, *Pen and Sword,* 583.

31. Taylor, "Defense of Fort Henry," 110; Bearss, "The Fall of Fort Henry, Tennessee," 11–12; *ORA,* I, VII, 580–87, 858–59.

32. Connelly, *Army of the Heartland,* 106–9; *ORA,* ibid., 136–39; Stonesifer, "Forts Henry-Heiman and Donelson," 146–50.

33. *ORA,* ibid., 125–26; Crummer, *With Grant,* 14–16.

34. *Boston Journal,* n.d. in Moore, col., *Rebellion Record,* IV, 374; Walke, *Naval Scenes,* 55.

CHAPTER 7

1. Ambrose, *Seventh Illinois,* 28; Walke, "Gunboats at Belmont and Fort Henry," 362–63; Taylor, "Defense of Fort Henry," 369–70; Stonesifer, "Forts Henry-Heiman and Donelson," ch. 8.

2. *ORA,* I, VII, 140, 151, 156.

3. Ibid., 132, 148, Atlas–Plate XI, figure 1; Walke, "Gunboats at Belmont and Fort Henry," *Battles and Leaders,* 362–63; Catton, *Grant Moves South,* 43; Milligan, *Gunboats Down the Mississippi,* 39; map accompanying ltr. James Drish to wife, Feb. 11, 1862, Drish collection, ISH.

4. Foote to wife, Feb. 6, 1862, Area File 5, Box 1, RG 45, NARA; Laning quoted in Walke, *Naval Scenes,* 61; Gower and Allen, *Pen and Sword,* 584; *ORA,* I, VII, 129, 134, 140, 146, 151.

5. Walke, "Gunboats at Belmont and Fort Henry," 364–65; *ORN,* I, XXII, 122–23; Sylvester C. Bishop to mother [Feb. 7, 1862], IHSL; Taylor, "Defense of Fort Henry," *Battles and Leaders,* 370; Walke, *Naval Scenes,* 56.

6. *ORA,* I, VII, 134, 141, 146, 151; Taylor, "Defense of Fort Henry," 371–72.

7. Stonesifer, "Forts Henry-Heiman and Donelson, 156–60; *ORA,* ibid., 141; Taylor, ibid., 371.

8. On Gilmer, see various tel. Mackall to Loulee Gilmer, Feb. 8, Loulee Gilmer to father, Feb. 10, all 1862, all Gilmer papers, UNCL.

9. Walke, *Naval Scenes,* 57, also "Gunboats at Belmont and Fort Henry," 366; *ORN,* I, XXII, 538; Foote to wife, Feb. 6, 1862, Area File 5, Box 1, RG 45, NARA.

10. Hoppin, *Life of Andrew Hull Foote,* 203-4.

11. Thomas F. Miller to Benjamin Newton, Feb. 10, Miller collection; Brush diary, Feb. 6; Ira Merchant to Yates, Feb. 26; all 1862, all ISH; Bishop to mother [Feb. 7, 1862], IHSL; Cowan diary, Feb. 6, 1862, TSLA; Crummer, *With Grant,* 19.

12. *ORA,* I, VII, 129, 142, 147, 152; Gower and Allen, *Pen and Sword,* 582-87; Isham G. Haynie diary, Feb. 6, 1862, v. II, ISH.

13. Lewis Wallace, *Autobiography,* I, 369-71; Avery, *Fourth Illinois Cavalry,* 52-55; Crummer, *With Grant,* 19-20; Cowan diary, Feb. 6, 1862, ibid.; Merchant to Yates, Feb. 26; Brush diary, Feb. 6; Haperman diary, Feb. 6, all 1862, all ibid.

14. *ORA,* I, VII, 124; Foote to wife, Feb. 6, 1862, Area File 5, Box 1, RG 45, NARA; Merrill, "Captain Andrew Hull Foote and the Civil War on Tennessee Waters," 86-87.

15. Simon, *Grant Papers,* IV, 155-60, 163.

16. *Cincinnati Gazette, St. Louis Democrat, Boston Journal,* all Feb. 7, 1862; Powhatan Ellis to mother, Feb. 11, 1862, Munford-Ellis papers, DUL.

17. Lunsford Yandell diary, Feb. 7, 1862, FCL; Mackall to Loulee Gilmer, Feb. 8, 1862, Gilmer papers, UNCL; Taylor to Polk, Feb. 6, 1862, Box 23; Pillow to Mackall, Pillow to Polk, both Feb. 6, all 1862, Box 20, all Polk papers, RG 109, NARA; *ORA,* I, VII, 157.

18. *ORA,* ibid., 130, 863; copy containing marginal comments attributable to either Beauregard or his biographer, Thomas L. Jordan, in Beauregard papers, DUL.

19. Tels. Mackall to Polk, Harris, Mayor of Tuscumbia, Shorter, et al., all Feb. 6-9, 1862, Ltrs. and Tel. Sent, Johnston's command, ch. II, v. 218, RG 109, NARA.

20. *ORA,* I, VII, 153-56; Moore, *Rebellion Record,* IV, 120-21; *New York Herald,* Feb. 10-13, 1862; *ORN,* I, XXII, 570-74.

21. *ORA,* ibid., 865-71.

22. Ibid., 155-56; John S. Wilcox to wife, Feb. 12, 1862, ISH; Henry, *"First with the Most" Forrest,* 477; *New York Independent,* Feb. 27, 1862; Graf and Haskins, *Johnson Papers,* VI, 310; Hoppin, *Life of Foote,* 218; Milligan, *From the Fresh-Water Navy,* 24-26; Cullum to Halleck, Feb. 7, 1862, Cullum papers, ISH; Coffin, *Days and Nights on the Battlefield,* 87-88.

23. Foote to Tilghman, Feb. 10; Halleck to Foote, Feb. 8, 11; Scott to Foote, Feb. 8 (3 tel.), and 11; A.H. Kilty to Foote, Feb. 9, all 1862, all Area File 5, Box 1, RG 45, NARA.

24. Welles to Foote, Feb. 13, 1862, ibid.; Hoppin, *Life of Foote,* 210; Simon, *Grant Papers,* IV, 164-75, 188; Wallace to wife, Feb. 8, 1862, Wallace-Dickey papers, Field Order 5, Feb. 9, 1862, Misc., McClernand papers, ISH.

25. Stonesifer, "Forts Henry-Heiman and Donelson Campaign," 183–84; Hicken, *Illinois in the Civil War*, 30n; McClernand to Grant, Feb. 5, 9, both McClernand papers, ibid.; *ORN*, 1, XXII, 544.

26. Richardson, *Personal History of Ulysses S. Grant*, 217; Simon, *Grant Papers*, IV, 171–72, 175–77, 182–83, 193–94n; Grant, *Personal Memoirs*, I, 294.

27. Simon, ibid., IV, 183–85, 188–91; Merchant to Yates, Feb. 11; James F. Drish to wife, Feb. 11; Brush diary, Feb. 7; Thomas F. Miller to Benjamin Newton, Feb. 10, all 1862, all ISH; Lewis Wallace to wife, Feb. 7, 8, 9, 11, all 1862, Wallace papers; John B. Connelly diary, Feb. 11, 1862, both IHSL; Ambrose, *Seventh Illinois*, 28–29; Brinton, *Personal Memoirs*, 113–14.

28. George S. Durfee to H.B. Durfee, Feb. 10, 1862, Illinois Historical Survey, UIL; Halleck to Grant, Feb. 13, 1862, Tel. Sent in Cipher by Halleck, Dept. of Missouri, RG 393, NARA; Eddy, *Patriotism of Illinois*, II, 65–69; Illinois Military and Naval Departments, *Illinois in the War for the Union*, 451–55; Edwards, *Civil War Guns*, 101–2, 142–43; Hanson, *The Plains Rifle*, 64–66; Lossing, *Pictorial History of the Civil War*, II, 210.

29. Ambrose, "The Union Command System and the Donelson Campaign," 78, 80–81; *ORA*, 1, VII, 576, 578, 601; *ORN*, 1, XXII, 583–84.

30. *ORA*, ibid., 583, 932.

31. Ibid., 936–37; U.S. Army Corps of Engineers. *Legends of the Operations of the Army of the Cumberland*, 5–7.

32. *ORA*, ibid., 592–95; Ambrose, "Union Command System," 83–5; Croffut, *Fifty Years in Camp and Field; Diary of Major General Ethan Allen Hitchcock*, 34.

33. *ORA*, ibid., 595; Kamm, *Civil War Career of Thomas A. Scott*, 109–10; also Halleck to Cullum, Feb. 7–12, 1862, Tel. Sent and Recd., RG 393, NARA; also Cullum to Halleck, Feb. 7, 9, 1862, ISH.

34. *ORA*, ibid., 603–4; *ORN*, 1, XXII, 582; Halleck to L.D. Baldwin, Feb. 6 (2); Pope to Halleck, Feb. 5, 10; Halleck to Yates, Yates to Halleck, Feb. 5, 11; Fuller to Halleck, Halleck to Fuller, Feb. 5, 6, 8, 9 (3), 11; Halleck to Todd, Feb. 7; Halleck to Saunders, Feb. 9, all 1862; and misc. corresp. concerning reinforcements, all Tel. Sent or Tel. Recd. Dept. of Missouri, RG 393, NARA.

35. *ORA*, ibid., 601, 612; Wallace to wife, Feb. 11, 1862, Wallace papers, ISH.

CHAPTER 8

1. Brinton, *Personal Memoirs*, 115; Ambrose, *Seventh Illinois*, 30.

2. *ORA*, 1, VII, 605; Brush journal, Feb. 12, 1862, ISH; Henry, *Land Between the Rivers*, 112.

3. *ORN*, 1, XXII, 550, 664; Simon, *Grant Papers*, IV, 180.

4. Powhatan Ellis to mother, Feb. 11, 1862, Mumford-Ellis papers, DUL; Jordan and Pryor, *Campaigns of Forrest*, 62–64; Wyeth, *Life of Forrest*, 37; Davis, ed., *Partisan Rangers*, 52–54.

5. Connelly, *Army of the Heartland*, 111–12; Walker, "Command Failure; The Fall

of Forts Henry and Donelson," 342–46; Roman, *Military Operations of General Beauregard,* I, ch. 15; Johnston, *Johnston,* 433–37; Roland, *Johnston,* 286–89.

6. Stonesifer, "Forts Henry-Heiman and Donelson," 169–73; Roland, *Johnston,* 289–90; Williams, *P.G.T. Beauregard,* 151–54; Roman, *Beauregard,* I, 221–23; P.G.T. Beauregard, "The Campaign of Shiloh," in Johnson and Buel, *Battles and Leaders,* I, 570; Jordan and Pryor, *Campaigns of Forrest,* 94–98.

7. *ORA,* I, VII, 861–62; Williams, ibid., 153.

8. Polk, *Leonidus Polk,* II, 74; various papers, Box 23, Polk papers, RG 109, NARA; *ORA,* I, VI, 823; VII, 862–63.

9. *ORA,* ibid., 861–62.

10. Tels. (2) Mackall to Pillow, Feb. 6, 1862, ch. II, v. 218, Ltrs. and Tel. Sent, Johnston's command, RG 109, NARA; Hamilton, *Battle of Fort Donelson,* 42–43.

11. *ORA,* I, VII, 863–64.

12. Tels. Mackall to Stevenson (4), Mackall to Pillow (3), Mackall to Floyd (4), all Feb. 6; Mackall to Pillow, Feb. 7; Mackall to Lindsay, Feb. 8, 9, 10, 12; Mackall to Wright, Feb. 6, 7, 9, 11; Mackall to Harris, Mackall to Gilmer, Mackall to Pickett, all Feb. 8; Mackall to Shiliha, Feb. 8, 10, 11; Johnston to Pillow, Johnston to Floyd, Johnston to Pillow or Floyd or commanding officer at Clarksville, Johnston to Pillow (10:00 P.M.), all Feb. 7, all 1862, all ch. II, v. 218, ibid.

13. *ORA,* I, VII, 865; Tels. Mackall to Floyd (1:45 and 7:00 P.M.), both Feb. 8, 1862, ibid.

14. *ORA,* ibid., 278, 864–65, 867; LII, pt. 2, 268; Cummings, *Yankee Quaker,* 190.

15. Pillow to Floyd [Feb. ? 1862], Floyd papers, DUL.

16. *ORA,* I, VII, 871; LII, pt. 2, 268; General Service Schools, *Source Book,* 630.

17. Gower and Allen, *Pen and Sword,* 589; *ORA,* I, VII, 867–68.

18. *ORA,* ibid., 868, 870–71; Lulee Gilmer to W.L. Alexander, Feb. 10; Gilmer to wife, Feb. 22, both 1862, both Gilmer papers, UNCL.

19. Johnston, *Johnston,* 435; General Service Schools, *Source Book,* 638; Stickles, *Buckner,* 40, 41; Gower and Allen, *Pen and Sword,* 190; Stonesifer, "Forts Henry-Heiman and Donelson Campaign," 202–3.

20. *ORA,* I, VII, 328–29; Johnston, ibid., 438–39; Connelly, *Army of the Heartland,* 115.

21. Hamilton, *Fort Donelson,* 83–84; Stonesifer, ibid., 203–5; Johnston, *Johnston,* 438; *ORA,* ibid., 272; LII, pt. 2, 269; J.S. Bransford to Floyd, and W.H. Armstrong to Floyd, both Feb. 12, 1862, Floyd papers, DUL.

22. Quoted in Johnston, ibid., 438; *ORA,* ibid., LII, pt. 2, 269, 271–72; General Service Schools, *Source Book,* 638–41, 645–46; Hamilton, ibid., 66–67; Stonesifer, ibid., 217–18.

23. *ORA,* ibid., 272; Johnston, *Johnston,* ibid.

24. *ORA,* ibid., 271; VII, 259; while the historical controversy can be followed best in Stonesifer, ibid., 217–20; Connelly, *Army of the Heartland,* 114–16; Hamilton, *Fort Donelson,* 40–43; Roland, *Johnston,* 293–97; Johnston, ibid., 437–39; and Walker, "Command Failure," 357–60.

25. Riddell, "Movements of the Goochland Light Artillery," 317; Henry, *Land Between the Rivers,* 112; Bearss, "The Dover Hotel," pt. 1, 9-11, FDNMPL; J.W. Stout, "Facts About Fort Donelson," *Stewart County Times,* Sep. 9, 1927; J. Wesley Murphey to Mary Grey, Feb. 6; W.H. Farmer to mother, Feb. 5, both in Farmer collection; Joseph Brigham to mother, Feb. 6, Brigham collection; James Hallums to M.E. Hallums, Feb. 2, all 1862, all Land Between the Lakes Project papers, TSLA.

26. Reuben Ross journal, III, Mar. 29, 1862, Ross family papers; George Wiley Adams to wife, Feb. 8, 1862, both TSLA; Gower and Allen, *Pen and Sword,* 587; *ORA,* 1, VII, 358.

27. Bearss, "Fort Donelson Water Batteries, Historic Structures Report," pt. 2, 42-49, FDNMPL; Ross journal, ibid., Mar. 29, 30, 1862, TSLA.

28. Bearss, ibid., 21-23.

29. *ORA,* 1, VII, 261, 276, 332, 349, 351; Davis, *Orphan Brigade,* 64-65; Davis, *Partisan Rangers,* 55-56.

30. Calvin C. Clack, "History of Company A, 3d Tennessee Regt. Infantry," undtd. typescript, TSLA.

31. Stonesifer, "Forts Henry-Heiman and Donelson Campaign," 204-5, 212-15; Grant, *Personal Memoirs,* I, 298, 313; Brinton, *Personal Memoirs,* 116-17.

32. *ORA,* 1, VII, 172, 184, 190, 193, 211-12, 215, 220.

33. Bailey, "Escape from Fort Donelson," 64; Wallace, "The Capture of Fort Donelson," in Johnson and Buel, *Battles and Leaders,* I, 410; Hanson to wife, Mar. 23, 1862, Hanson papers, LC; Thomas Deavenport diary, 7; G.W. Dillon diary, H, both TSLA; R.L. McClung diary, Barker Texas History Center, UTA.

34. *ORA,* 1, VII, 271; Stonesifer, "Forts Henry-Heiman and Donelson," 218-20.

35. *ORA,* ibid., 260, 267, 271, 330.

36. Ibid., 172, 184, 191, 279, 368; *ORN,* 1, XXII, 56; Stonesifer, "Forts Henry-Heiman and Donelson," 216-17.

37. Coffin, *My Days and Nights on the Battlefield,* 92-93.

38. Tactical action on the 13th can be followed in Hamilton, *Fort Donelson,* ch. 5; Stonesifer, "Forts Henry-Heiman and Donelson," 221-27; and Bearss, "The Fighting on February 13—The Assault on Maney's Battery," FDNMPL.

39. Reed, *Campaigns and Battles of the Twelfth Regiment Iowa Infantry,* 17, 32; W.L. McKay diary, 37, David S.M. Bodenhamer memoirs, 13-15, both TSLA; Selden Spencer diary, 1-7, MHS, and its published version, "Diary Account of Fort Donelson," 282-83.

40. Ross journal, III, 58-59, TSLA.

41. Water battery action on Feb. 13 can be followed in Walke, "The Western Flotilla at Fort Donelson, Island Number Ten, Fort Pillow, and Memphis," in Johnson and Buel, *Battles and Leaders,* I, 431-33, and in Walke, *Naval Scenes,* 75-76; Bearss, "The Ironclads at Fort Donelson; The Confederates Prepare for the Ironclads (Part II)," 80-84.

42. *ORA*, I, VII, 389-90; Ross journal, 68-69, TSLA; Bearss, "Fort Donelson Water Batteries," 26-28; Walke, *Naval Scenes*, 74-75.

43. Bearss, "Fighting on February 13," ch. 3; Stonesifer, "Forts Henry-Heiman and Donelson," 231-34; Browne, *Four Years in Secessia*, 74; Avery, *Fourth Illinois Cavalry*, 58-59; Morrison, *Ninth Illinois Volunteer Infantry*, 22.

44. General Service Schools, *Source Book*, 1398-99, 1407; *ORA*, I, VII, 172-73, 204, 212-13, 366-68; Gower and Allen, *Pen and Sword*, 590; Crummer, *With Grant*, 26-27.

45. Isham G. Haynie to "Pa" Mar. 22, 1862; Statement of Edwin C. Haynie, Aug. 1, 1895, III, Haynie papers, ISH.

46. Luther H. Cowan to wife, Feb. 19, 1862, TSLA; *ORA*, I, VII, 370; General Service Schools, *Source Book*, 677; Gower and Allen, *Pen and Sword*, 590.

47. Catton, *Grant Moves South*, 159; Bearss, "Fighting on February 13," 30-33; Brush journal, Feb. 13, 1862, ISH; Adam Badeau quoted in Johnston, *Johnston*, 448; Hubert, *History of the Fiftieth Regiment Illinois Volunteer Infantry*, 65; Morton, *Artillery of Forrest's Cavalry*, 29.

CHAPTER 9

1. Brush journal; Haperman diary, both Feb. 13, 1862, both ISH; *ORA*, I, VII, 194.

2. Dillon diary, Feb. 13, 1862; McKay diary, 137, both TSLA; Morton, *Artillery of Forrest's Cavalry*, 29-30; Davis, *Partisan Rangers*, 56. An example of the 2d Kentucky parka is in the Kentucky State Military Museum, Frankfort.

3. Ross journal, III, 63-66, TSLA; Bearss, "Ironclads at Fort Donelson, Part II," 84.

4. *ORA*, I, VII, 229, 243, 252, 612, 613; Wallace, *Autobiography*, I, 382-83; Hubert, *Fiftieth Illinois*, 67, 77-78; also General Orders II, Feb. 14, 1862, Indorsements, Memoranda to and from Grant, Military Copy Ledgers, McClernand papers, ISH.

5. Grant, *Personal Memoirs*, I, 302; Simon, *Grant Papers*, IV, 209, 209n for discussion of Confederate strength at Fort Donelson.

6. Floyd to Johnston, Feb. 14, 1862, Box 7, Floyd papers, Papers of Confederate Notables, RG 109, NARA; Ross journal, III, 72, TSLA.

7. *ORA*, I, VII, 330, 338, 379; Connelly, *Army of the Heartland*, 120; Walker, "Command Failure," 16; Hughes, "Why Fort Donelson Was Surrendered," 302.

8. Johnston, *Johnston*, 453-55; Stonesifer, "Forts Henry-Heiman and Donelson," 242-43; Davis, *Partisan Rangers*, 57-58; Casseday, "The Surrender of Fort Donelson," in Conger, *Donelson Campaign Sources*, 210.

9. Bearss, "The Ironclads at Fort Donelson: The Ironclads Sail for the Cumberland (Part I)," 1-9.

10. *ORA*, I, VII, 596-604, 937; *ORN*, I, XXII, 534, 583-84.

11. *New York Herald,* Feb. 21, 1862.

12. Ibid., also Walke, "Operations of the Western Flotilla," 433.

13. Grant, *Personal Memoirs,* I, 302; Simon, *Grant Papers,* IV, 209.

14. Stover, *History of the Illinois Central,* 98.

15. Pratt, *Civil War on Western Waters,* 213–33.

16. *ORN,* I, XXII, 592; Walke, "Western Flotilla," 433; General Service Schools, *Source Book,* 562, 660–61; Ross journal, III, 70–74, TSLA; Bedford, "Fight Between the Batteries and Gunboats," 660–62.

17. Ross journal, ibid., 73–74.

18. Ibid., 74–75.

19. Wyeth, *Life of Forrest,* 46–47; Catton, *Grant Moves South,* 161.

20. *ORN,* I, XXII, 611–12; Bedford, "Fight Between the Batteries and the Gunboats," 663–65.

21. Hoppin, *Life of Foote,* 228.

22. Bearss, "Fort Donelson Water Batteries, Part II," 28–33.

23. Davis, *Partisan Rangers,* 58; Bearss, "The Ironclads at Fort Donelson; The Gunboats Fail, Part III," 180–81.

24. Ross journal, III, 75, TSLA; *ORN,* I, XXII, 591–93; Walke, *Naval Scenes,* 78–79, 85–86, 89.

25. Foote to wife, Feb. 18, 1862, Box 1, Area File 5, RG 45, NARA; *ORN,* ibid., 584–85; Boynton, *History of the Navy During the Rebellion,* I, 528–31.

26. Bedford, "Fight Between the Batteries and Gunboats," 662–63; Johnson, *Rodgers,* 167–68.

27. Bedford, ibid., 665–66; *ORA,* I, VII, 159, 393.

28. *ORA,* ibid., 255, 880.

29. *New York Herald,* Feb. 21, 1862; *ORN,* I, XXII, 584–87; *ORA,* ibid., 391–96, 400; Coffin, *My Days and Nights on the Battlefield,* 109; Hoppin, *Life of Foote,* 224; Bearss, "The Ironclads at Fort Donelson, Part III," 181–82.

30. SIMON, *Grant Papers,* IV, 211; Grant, *Personal Memoirs,* I, 303.

31. *ORA,* I, VII, 612, 614; Tels. George H. Smith to Cullum, D.E. Williams to Halleck, Milton S. Latham to Halleck, all Feb. 12; Williams to Halleck, Feb. 14, 1862; all Tel. Recd. v. I; also Tels. Halleck to Williams, Halleck to Cullum, both Feb. 12; and Halleck to Latham, Feb. 13, all Tel. Sent, all Dept. of Missouri, RG 393, NARA.

32. Simon, *Grant Papers,* IV, 209, 230, 231n.

33. *ORA,* I, VII, 612.

34. Ibid., 608–14.

35. Grant, *Personal Memoirs,* I, 305.

36. *ORA,* I, VII, 800–1; Roland, *Johnston,* 291.

37. *ORA,* ibid., 263, 265, 268; *ORN,* I, XXII, 611.

38. *ORA,* ibid., 281–82.

39. Ibid., 282, 286; for a colorful if somewhat contrived dialogue between the generals, see Hamilton, *Fort Donelson,* 158–60, 358n.

40. *ORA,* I, VII, 365; also 267–68, 276–77, 318, 331, 347, 355, 360, 369.
41. Gower and Allen, *Pen and Sword,* 590.
42. Prison Journal of John H. Guy, Apr. 22, 1862, VHS; Bearss, "The Battle of Dover," 8–9, FDNMPL.

CHAPTER 10

1. "Map of the Battlefield, February 3, 1863," Joseph Latimer papers, USAMHI; Stewart County [1865], RG 77, NARA; *ORA,* I, VII, 276, 278, 286, 331–32, 338, 347, 350–52, 359–61, 380: Terrell, "A Confederate Private at Fort Donelson," 478.
2. Ross journal, III, 66, 75, TSLA.
3. *ORA,* I, VII, 337, 347, 358–59, 377.
4. Ibid., 175, 286, 339, 361, 371–72, 384–85; Gower and Allen, *Pen and Sword,* 583.
5. *ORA,* ibid., 339; Wyeth, *Life of Forrest,* 49.
6. Brush diary, Feb. 15, 1862, ISH; Avery, *Fourth Illinois Cavalry,* 59; *ORA,* ibid., 174–76, 199, 217–18, 339.
7. Ibid., 186, 216, 218; Avery, ibid., 60; Brush, ibid.; Guy, prison journal, Apr. 30, 1862, VHS; Hamilton, *Fort Donelson,* chs. 10, 11; Stonesifer, "Forts Henry-Heiman and Donelson," ch. 13; Bearss, "The Battle of Dover," ch. 2.
8. *ORA,* ibid., 176, 186, 190; *New York Herald,* Feb. 19, 1862.
9. Wallace, *Autobiography,* I, 389; *ORA,* ibid., 175, 327.
10. Grant, *Personal Memoirs,* I, 304; Alexander, *Grant as a Soldier,* 54–55.
11. Grant, ibid., 305; *ORN,* I, XXII, 585–86.
12. Wallace, *Autobiography,* I, 399–400; *ORA,* I, VII, 187–88, 243.
13. *ORA,* ibid., 185–87, 195, 201, 331; Brush diary, Feb. 15, 1862, ISH; Newsome, "A Kentucky Yankee's Story of Fort Donelson," 74.
14. *ORA,* I, VII, 190, 263.
15. McWhiney and Jamieson, *Attack and Die,* chs. 2, 3; *ORA,* ibid., 361.
16. M'Kay diary, 38, TSLA; Ben H. Bounds, "Civil War Memoirs," FDNMPL; *ORA,* ibid., 186, 371, 373, 787.
17. V.K. Farris to Mary, Oct. 31, 1862, Farris letterbook, TSLA; *ORA,* ibid., 387; Newsome, "Kentucky Yankee," 74.
18. Farris, ibid., M'Kay diary, 37–38; Spencer mss., MHS, and Spencer, "Diary Account" (published version), 284; Bearss, "Battle of Dover," 75; Stickles, *Buckner,* 142–43.
19. Walker, "Command Failure," 352n.
20. Spencer mss., and "Diary Account," 284; Guy prison journal, VHS; "A Soldier's Story, the Late J.H. Beadle at Fort Donelson," in Smith, *History of the Thirty-First Indiana,* 202; *ORA,* I, VII, 195–96, 199–200.
21. *ORA,* ibid., 208, 343, 485–86.

22. *Nashville Banner,* Dec. 11, 1909; Guy prison journal, VHS; *ORA,* ibid., 202–4, 352, 354.

23. W.H.L. Wallace to wife, Feb. 17, 1862, Wallace papers, ISH; *ORA,* ibid., 343–44, 385; Guy prison journal, ibid.; Davis, *Orphan Brigade,* 66–67.

24. *ORA,* ibid., 348.

25. Wallace, *Autobiography,* I, 401–2; *ORA,* ibid., 252, 257.

26. Wallace, ibid., 403–5; *ORA,* ibid, 237, 252–53.

27. Ibid.

28. Wallace, ibid., I, 406; also Wallace, "The Capture of Fort Donelson," in Johnson and Buel, *Battles and Leaders,* I, 420; *ORA,* ibid., 210, 237, 252–53; Ezra Taylor to G.J. Hulbard, Mar. 16, 1862, Taylor papers, CHS.

29. *ORA,* ibid., 238.

30. Bodenhamer memoirs, 6, TSLA; Cooling, "First Nebraska Infantry Regiment and the Battle of Fort Donelson," 141–43.

31. Kimble, *History of Battery A, 1st Illinois Artillery,* 38; G.W. Dillons book, L-M, TSLA; *ORA,* ibid., 238, 242, 253, 254, 369.

32. Colby and Kimball, "After Three Months Service," in Illinois, First Artillery, Battery A Association, *First Reunion,* 16–17; Cheairs account in John C. Brown autograph album; also M'Kay diary, 39, both TSLA.

33. *ORA,* I, VII, 265–66, 283, 318–19, 323, 332–33, 365.

34. Ibid., 269.

35. Ibid., 332–33; the possibly contrived dialogue can be found in M.B. Morton, "General Simon Bolivar Buckner Tells the Story of Fort Donelson," *Nashville Banner,* Dec. 11, 1909; and can be compared to Peter Otey's version in Hughes, "Why Fort Donelson was Surrendered," 303.

36. *ORA,* ibid., 318, 332.

37. Guy prison journal, VHS; Spencer diary, MHS.

38. Stickles, *Buckner,* 142–52; *ORA,* I, VII, 269; Morton, "Buckner Tells the Story," Wallace, "Capture of Fort Donelson," 419.

39. Simon, *Grant Papers,* IV, 214; Grant, *Personal Memoirs,* I, 306.

40. Greenawalt, "A Charge at Fort Donelson," 9–12.

41. *ORA,* I, VII, 169, 196, 238, 273; Grant, *Personal Memoirs,* I, 305–6; Wallace, *Autobiography,* I, 411–12, and "Capture of Fort Donelson," 421–22.

42. Grant, *Personal Memoirs,* I, 307–8.

43. Greenawalt, "Charge at Fort Donelson," Stonesifer, "Forts Henry-Heiman and Donelson," 319–20; Bearss, "Battle of Dover," 131–33.

44. Catton, *Grant Moves South,* 169; Editor, *Magazine of American History,* "Letters from Colonel Thomas J. Newsham," 40.

45. Catton, *America Goes to War,* 59–60; "Unfinished Report of Brigadier General C.F. Smith," General Services Schools, *Source Book,* 933–34.

46. *ORA,* I, LII, pt. 1, 7–9; Greenawalt, "Charge at Fort Donelson," 12–13.

47. Twombley, *Second Iowa Infantry at Fort Donelson,* 27; Bell, *Tramps and Triumphs of Second Iowa Infantry,* 10; Reed, *Campaigns and Battles of the Iowa Twelfth,* 19–20; Rich, "The Color Bearer of the Twelfth Volunteer Infantry," 98–99.

48. R.J. Price to father, Mar. 15, 1862, IHSL; Dillon's book, l-m, and Cheairs in Brown album, both TSLA; *ORA,* 1, VII, 225–26, 351.

49. Randall's poem in Morton, *Artillery of Forrest's Cavalry,* 35; M'Kay diary, 40, and Cheairs, ibid., both TSLA; Davis, *Orphan Brigade,* 67–68.

50. *ORA,* 1, VII, 222; Hubert, *Fiftieth Illinois,* 75; Ambrose, *Seventh Illinois,* 34–35; Greenawalt, "Charge at Fort Donelson," 13.

51. Wallace, "Capture of Fort Donelson," 422.

52. *ORA,* 1, VII, 196, 202–3, 207, 233–36, 238, 242, 245.

53. Ibid., 238, 361, 362, 365.

54. Ibid., 238–39; Wallace, "Capture of Fort Donelson," 423–24, and *Autobiography,* I, 417–18; McWhiney and Jamieson, *Attack and Die,* 102, 145.

55. Wallace, "Capture of Fort Donelson," 424; Rerick, *Forty-Fourth Indiana,* 273–74.

56. *ORA,* 1, VII, 361; Jordan and Pryor, *Campaigns of Forrest,* 84–85.

57. *ORA,* ibid., 361, 396, 401.

58. Conger, *Donelson Campaign Sources,* 165–67.

59. Wallace, *Autobiography,* I, 422–23; *ORN,* 1, XXII, 590; Bishop to mother, Feb. 19, 1862, IHSL; M'Kay diary, 40, TSLA.

60. *ORA,* 1, VII, 180, 187, 189, 190, 196, 207, 216, 239; Wyeth, *Life of Forrest,* 47.

61. Guy prison journal, VHS; Bodenhamer memoirs, 5, TSLA; Bearss, "The Battle of Dover," 147; Connolly, "Major James A. Connolly's Letters to His Wife," 232; *ORA,* ibid., 295.

62. Dillon's book, M-N, TSLA; Catton, *Grant Moves South,* 182–83.

CHAPTER II

1. *ORA,* 1, VII, 302, 386, 409; General Service Schools, *Source Book,* 1372; Stonesifer, "Forts Henry-Heiman and Donelson," 328n; Ferris letterbook, Oct. 31, 1862, TSLA.

2. Gower and Allen, *Pen and Sword,* 592; Bearss, "Unconditional Surrender: The Fall of Fort Donelson," 1–4; Hamilton, *Fort Donelson,* 362n.

3. *ORA,* 1, VII, 269, 283, 287, 296, 354, 357, 362, 370; Bearss and Jones, "Dover Hotel," NPS Study, 19–23.

4. Ibid., 287, 293, 295, 299, 367, 378; Wyeth, *Life of Forrest,* 65, 581.

5. Jordan and Pryor, *Campaigns of Forrest,* 88; Wyeth, ibid., 50; Stonesifer, "Forts Henry-Heiman and Donelson," 334; *ORA,* ibid., 273, 287–88, 295–97, 334, 385–86.

6. Ibid., 293–300, 333–35.

7. Wyeth, *Life of Forrest,* 52; Riddell, "Movements of the Goochland Light Artillery," 318; Stickles, *Buckner,* 152–57; *ORA,* 1, VII, 333.

8. *ORA,* 1, VII, 287–88, 293–97, 300; Bearss, "Unconditional Surrender," 10–13.

9. Stickles, *Buckner,* 157; *ORA,* 1, VII, 297–98.

10. Horn, *Army of Tennessee,* 93–96.

11. Gower and Allen, *Pen and Sword,* 593; Deavenport diary, 9, TSLA; Guy prison journal, VHS; Cooling, "A Virginian at Fort Donelson," 184.

12. For Confederate reaction, see Terrell, "Confederate Private," 480; Morton, *Artillery of Forrest's Cavalry,* 33–34; Spencer diary, MHS; Wilson, *Confederate Soldier,* 46–47; Gower and Allen, ibid., 593; McClung diary, 9, UTA; Cheairs, "Experience," II, 3, 4; M'Kay diary, 40–41; Dillon diary, O, Q, all TSLA.

13. *ORA,* I, VII, 295–96, 385–87; General Service Schools, *Source Book,* 1347–49; Wyeth, *Life of Forrest,* 55.

14. *ORA,* ibid., 386.

15. Ibid., 302.

16. Ibid., 274–75, 302, 381.

17. Riddell, "Movements of the Goochland Artillery," 316; *ORA,* ibid., 275, 305–6, 381.

18. *ORA,* ibid., 381; Cooling, "Virginian at Fort Donelson, 185–86.

19. Cheairs, "Experience," II, 4; McClung diary, 9, UTA; General Service Schools, *Source Book,* 1373.

20. *ORA,* I, VII, 160–61; Cheairs, ibid.; Brinton, *Personal Memoirs,* 129; *Source Book,* 935–36; Catton, *Grant Moves South,* 174–75; Davis, *Orphan Brigade,* 69–70, claims Private A.G. Montgomery, Company B, 2nd Kentucky, rather than Cheairs, carried Buckner's note to Grant, which is most unlikely because of his rank.

21. *ORA,* ibid., 161.

22. Simon, *Grant Papers,* IV, 212–19; Cheairs, ibid., II, 3, 4; "Original of General Grant's Famous 'Unconditional Surrender' Letter," *New York Herald,* Apr. 26, 1896, Dreer collection, HSP.

23. Cheairs, ibid.; Simon, ibid., IV, 219–20; *ORA,* I, VII, 625–26.

24. Wallace, *Autobiography,* I, 427–28; also "The Capture of Fort Donelson," 428.

25. Bearss and Jones, "Dover Hotel; Historic Structures Report," 10, 13, 23; Louise Runyon to C.L. Johnson, Mar. 14, 1934, both FDNMPL.

26. Wallace, *Autobiography,* I, 428–31.

27. Ibid.; *ORN,* I, XXII, 588–90.

28. Stickles, *Buckner,* 170–71.

29. Grant, *Personal Memoirs,* I, 313–14; Hamilton, *Fort Donelson,* 333–34; William H. Bigbee to friend, Feb. 23, 1862, Francis Brainerd papers, IHSL.

30. Spencer mss., 21, MHS, 282–83 (not in "Diary Account"); also Brinton, *Personal Memoirs,* 125–26, 133.

31. Coffin, *Four Years of Fighting,* 80–82; also *My Days and Nights on the Battlefield,* 140–41; Wilkie, *Pen and Powder,* 124; Porter memoirs, TSLA.

32. Sylvester C. Bishop to mother, Mar. 8, 1862, IHSL; Young, *What a Boy Saw in the Army,* 92; Smith, *Thirty-First Indiana,* 207; Brinton, *Personal Memoirs,* 131; Catton, *Grant Moves South,* 182; *ORA,* I, VII, 181, 187; Simplot, "General Grant and the Incident at Dover," 83–84; Deavenport diary, II, TSLA.

33. *ORA,* ibid., 159–60, 625; *ORN,* I, XXII, 595–96.

34. Cummings, *Yankee Quaker,* 207; Simon, *Grant Papers,* IV, 220-21, 229, suggests that "not since Saratoga and Yorktown had an entire army been captured on American soil," although he fails to mention that the capture of Vera Cruz during the Mexican War might have provided U.S. officers with a model.

35. Simon, ibid., 221-22, 233; Coffin, *Four Years of Fighting,* 83; Stickles, *Buckner,* 173.

36. Simon, ibid., 223; Deavenport diary, II, TSLA.

37. Simon, ibid., 221, 237-38; Coffin, *Four Years,* 81, 83; Smith, *Thirty-First Indiana,* 209; Cummings, *Yankee Quaker,* 207-13; Wilson, *Confederate Soldier,* chs. VI-XIV inter alia; Stiles, "In the Years 1861-1862," 163; Crozier, *Yankee Reporters,* 205.

38. Milligan, *From the Fresh Water Navy,* 30; Simon, *Grant Papers,* IV, 219-20, 233-34; Bearss, "Unconditional Surrender," 38; *ORA,* 4, I, 265-66, 1034-36; Deavenport diary, II, TSLA; *Nashville Times,* Mar. 10, 1862; Harding, "An Unusual Percussion Cap Accoutrement," 27.

39. Nearly all accounts differ as to strengths and losses, but Simon, *Grant Papers,* IV, 221, 226n, provides possibly the most comprehensive computation to date. For comparison, see Johnston, *Johnston,* 237-38, 241-42; and Smith, *Incidents Among Shot and Shell,* 63.

40. Simon, ibid., 232-33; McClung diary, 9, UTA; Newcomb, *Four Years of Personal Reminiscences,* 27-30; Porter memoirs, TSLA

41. Simon, ibid., 229-32, 240, 248; Stickles, *Buckner,* 175.

42. Lowry, "A Fort Donelson Prisoner of War," 334; Bodenhamer memoirs, TSLA.

43. John S. Wilcox to wife, Feb. 18, 1862, ISH; Gower and Allen, *Pen and Sword,* 595-96; Barnard, *Tattered Volunteers,* 12.

44. Lorenzo Thomas to Halleck, Jan. 20, 1862, Box 2, Ltrs. Recd., 1861-67; Halleck to Grant, Jan. 31, 1862; Ltrs. Sent, Nov. 1861-July 1862, both RG 383, NARA; *ORA,* 2, III, 238-39, 249.

45. *ORA,* ibid., 245, 247, 252-53, 267-68, 269, 275, 309-10.

46. Ibid., 271, 276, 277, 280, 287, 288, 290, 299; also J. Haines to John King, Feb. 20; King to Haines, Feb. 24; both Box 2, Ltrs. Recd. 1861; L. Noble to Halleck, Mar. 5, 1862, Tel. Recd. Nov. 61-Mar. 62, vol. 1, all RG 393, NARA.

47. Gower and Allen, *Pen and Sword,* 596; *ORA,* 2, III, 277.

48. Various aspects of the POW issue, including that of personal servants, can be followed in correspondence, RG 393, NARA.

49. *ORA,* 2, III, 279-80, 283, 314-15, 321, 340; Stickles, *Buckner,* 178-79.

50. Stickles, ibid., 180-81; Thompson, *Orphan Brigade,* 73-74.

51. Deavenport diary, II, 12, TSLA; McKinney, "A Rooster in Camp and in Prison," 419-20; Nye, "Jake Donelson, A 'Cocky' Rebel," 51; *Indianapolis Journal,* Feb. 24, 1862; *Chicago Tribune,* as quoted in *Harpers Weekly,* Apr. 5, 1862; Cooling,

"Virginian at Fort Donelson," 186; Lowry, "A Fort Donelson Prisoner of War," 334; Merrill, *Soldier of Indiana,* I, 317-18; Winslow and Moore, *Camp Morton,* 257-60.

52. Cheairs, "Experience," 6, TSLA.

CHAPTER 12

1. Davis quoted in Bill, *Beleaguered City,* 103; Catton, *Grant Moves South,* 179-81; Pratt, *Stanton: Lincoln's Secretary of War,* 168; Halleck quoted in Miles O'Reilly [Charles G. Halpine], *Baked Meats of the Funeral,* 166; Grant, *Personal Memoirs,* I, 316-17; *Chicago Daily Tribune, Indianapolis Daily State Journal,* both Feb. 18; *Macomb Journal,* Feb. 21, Mar. 28; *New York Daily Tribune,* Mar. 6, all 1862.

2. Smart, ed., *Radical View,* I, III-15; Simon, *Grant Papers,* IV, 260; Wallace, *W.H.L. Wallace,* 177-78; Wilkie, *Pen and Powder,* 136-37.

3. Grant, *Personal Memoirs,* I, 317; Reed, *Combined Operations,* ch. 3; Williams, *Lincoln Finds a General,* III, chs. XI-XIII; Hattaway and Jones, *How the North Won,* ch. 3.

4. Simon, *Grant Papers,* IV, 284, also 248, 257, 266, 278-79, 348-49; Hattaway and Jones, ibid., 76-77, 147-49; Ambrose, *Halleck,* ch. 3; *ORA,* I, VII, 637.

5. *ORA,* ibid., 620-45 inter alia, 942-43.

6. Ibid., 627-28.

7. Ibid., 595, 641-42; T.A. Scott to Stanton, Feb. 17, 1862, Stanton papers, LC; Catton, *Grant Moves South,* 187; Croffut, *Fifty Years in Camp and Field,* 434-36, 463, 473-74.

8. *ORA,* ibid., 624-25, 630-33, 642-45.

9. Ibid., 637-38, 645-49, 652; Cullum to Halleck, Feb. 19, 21; Scott to Halleck, Feb. 24 (2); E.C. Rush to Halleck, Feb. 15; H. Rumford to Halleck, and W. Hewitt to Halleck, both Feb. 18, all 1862, all Tel. Recd., Nov. 61-Mar. 62, Dept. of Missouri, RG 393; A.D. Wharton to Alfred Thayer Mahan, Feb. 7, 1883, Box 1, Area File 5, RG 45, all NARA.

10. *ORA,* ibid., 641, 645, 655-58; VIII, 591, 596, 602.

11. Ibid., VII, 660-68, 682; VIII, 591, 596, 602; Sherman to Halleck, Feb. 20, 1862, Tel. Recd. Nov. 61-Mar. 62, Dept. of Missouri, RG 393, NARA.

12. *ORA,* ibid., VIII, 657; *ORN,* I, XXII, 621-31; Milligan, *From the Fresh Water Navy,* 36; Thompson and Wainwright, *Fox Correspondence,* I, 39-55 inter alia.

13. Milligan, ibid., 32; *ORA,* ibid., VII, 665; *ORN,* ibid., 633-35.

14. Fisher, "Reminiscences of the Raising of the Original 'Old Glory,'" esp. 99-100; James Laning et al. to Jennie Glover et al., Mar. 15, 1862, CHS; Milligan, ibid., 28, 32-35; *ORN,* ibid., 633-35.

15. Frederic A. Starring to William Bailache, Mar. 12, 1862, CHS; *ORN,* ibid., 635-36, 565-69; Simon, *Grant Papers,* IV, 289-90; *ORA,* ibid., VII, 436-38.

16. *ORA,* ibid., I, X, pt. 2, 18-19.

17. Ibid., VII, 674; X, pt. 2, 24-25.

18. Ibid., VIII, 664, 668, 678; X, pt. 2, 33, 44; Williams, *Lincoln Finds a General,* III, 308; Halleck to wife, Mar. 5, 1862, quoted in Wilson, "Types and Traditions of the Old Army," 55.

19. Horn, *Army of Tennessee,* 99–104; Connelly, *Army of the Heartland,* 126–35; Davis, *Orphan Brigade,* 62–63; Johnston, *Johnston,* ch. XXIX; also Hughes, ed. *Liddell's Record,* ch. 4, 5.

20. Bunting to E.H. Cushing, Feb. 26, 1862, TSLA; Rugeley, *Batchelor-Turner Letters,* 19; Thompson, *Orphan Brigade,* 77.

21. *ORA,* I, VII, 418–19, 881–82; D.J. Noblitt, "Forty-Fourth Tennessee," in Lindsley, ed., *Military Annals of Tennessee,* 31; Klein, *Louisville and Nashville,* 30–31.

22. Black, *Railroads of the Confederacy,* 137–38.

23. *ORA,* I, VII, 864, 871, 887; Horn, *Army of Tennessee,* 100; Connelly, *Army of the Heartland,* 135; various tel. and dispatches in ch. II, v. 218, Ltrs. and Tel. Sent, Western Dept., Oct. 61–Apr. 62; also Harris to Polk, Feb. 15, (2); Johnston (telegrapher) to W.B. Richmond, Johnston to Polk, both Feb. 15; Miller to Polk, Taylor (operator, Humboldt) to Polk, as well as Johnston to Polk, Beauregard to Polk, all Feb. 16, all 1862, all Tel. Recd., 1862–64, Box 23, Polk papers, all RG 109, NARA.

24. Bunting to Cushing, Feb. 26, 1862, TSLA; McKee, "The Evacuation of Nashville," rpt. in Horn, *Tennessee's War,* 61; Hoobler, ed., "The Civil War Diary of Louisa Brown Pearl," 313; James Kemp Pope, "Recollections," 3, Pope-Carter papers, DUL; *Nashville Times,* Feb. 28, Mar. 1, 27, all 1862.

25. McKee, ibid., 61; *Nashville Times,* Mar. 1, 1862; Lytle, *Forrest and His Critter Company,* 81–82; Noblitt, ibid., 31–32.

26. Virginia French journal, Mar. 23, 1862, TSLA; V.K. Stevenson to Hardee, Pillow to Hardee, both Feb. 19, 1862, both Floyd papers, DUL; Morgan, "Experiences in the Enemy's Lines," 217–19; Bunting to Cushing, Feb. 26, 1862, TSLA; Sheppard, *Forrest,* 55–56.

27. Floyd to Mackall, Mar. 22, 1862, Box 1, Floyd papers; Special Order 29, Feb. 14, 1862, ch. II, v. 220, Western Dept., Orders and Special Orders, Oct. 61–Mar. 62, both RG 109, NARA; McKee, "Evacuation of Nashville," 63; Wyeth, *Life of Forrest,* 60; *Nashville Times,* Mar. 1, 1862; Boyce, "The Evacuation of Nashville," 60–62.

28. Blanche L. Lewis to Dr. C.W. Jones, Mar. 3, 1894, TSLA; Wickham to Floyd, Bransford to Floyd (2), both Feb. 18; Cheatham to Floyd, Rowland to Floyd, Leland (?) to Floyd, Winn to Floyd, all Feb. 19; Pickell to Floyd, Feb. 23; Floyd to Johnston, Feb. 24; H.C. Burnett to Floyd, Mar. 1; J.A. Forbes to Floyd, Mar. 8, all 1862, all Floyd papers, DUL; Coffin, *My Days and Nights on the Battlefield,* 149.

29. Floyd to Mackall, Mar. 22, 1862, ibid., McKee, "Evacuation of Nashville," 64; Hoobler, "Pearl diary," 316–17; Sheppard, *Forrest,* 56; Wyeth, *Life of Forrest,* 60; *Nashville Times,* Mar. 16, 1862; Graf and Haskins, *Johnson Papers,* V, 168, 169.

30. McKee, "Evacuation of Nashville," 67–69; Floyd to Mackall, Mar. 22, 1862, ibid.; Mackall to Hindman, Feb. 20, 1862, ch. II, v. 218, Ltrs. and Tel. Sent,

Western Dept., Oct. 61–Apr. 62, RG 109, NARA; Bunting to Cushing, Feb. 26, 1862, TSLA; *ORA,* 4, IV, 1035.

31. Anderson, "After the Fall of Fort Donelson," 289–90; Lewis, "The Florence Nightingale of the South," *Confederate Veteran,* 511.

32. James Kemp Pope-"Ma," Feb. 24, 1862, Pope-Carter papers; Hoobler, "Pearl diary," 318; *Nashville Times,* Mar. 3, 1862; Connelly, *Army of the Heartland,* 136; Graf and Haskins, *Johnson Papers,* V, 168; Bean, "The Valley Campaign of 1862 as Revealed in Letters of Sandie Pendleton," 326–65 inter alia; T.G. Pollock to Father, Feb. 19, 1862, Pollock papers, UVA.

33. Davis, *Orphan Brigade,* 72–73; Rugeley, *Batchelor-Turner Letters,* 21; various orders, Feb. 11–27, 1862, all ch. II, v. 218, Orders and Spec. Orders, Western Dept. Oct. 61–Mar. 62, RG 109, NARA; John T. Ellis to Charles Ellis, Mar. 27; R.T. Ellis to Powhatan Ellis, Apr. 8, all 1862, Munford-Ellis family papers, DUL.

34. Memoir of George Booth, 33–34, USAMHI; Connelly, *Army of the Heartland,* 138; Rugeley, ibid., 18; Mackall to Forrest, Feb. 24, Mackall to Quarles, Feb. 25; Mackall to Commanding General, Decatur, Feb. 27, all 1862, all ch. II, v. 218, Ltrs. and Tel. Sent, Western Dept. Oct. 61–Apr. 62, RG 109, NARA.

35. *ORA,* I, VII, 896–97.

36. Roman, *Beauregard,* I, 221–23, 232–33; Williams, *Napoleon in Gray,* 119–20; Roland, *Johnston,* 300–1; Johnston to Beauregard, Feb. 20, 1862, ch. II, v. 218, ibid.; *ORA,* ibid., 895–96.

37. *ORA,* ibid., 427; also LII, pt. 2, 887–89; Johnston to Davis, Feb. 24, 1862, ch. II, v. 218, ibid.; Roman, ibid., I, 275–76, II, 828; Seitz, *Braxton Bragg,* 82–84.

38. *ORA,* ibid., VII, 437–38, 899–901, 913–15; T.C. Hindman to Beauregard, Feb. 20, 1862, Tel. Recd., 1862–64, and Circulars, 1862–64, Box 23, Polk papers, RG 109, NARA; Governor's Message, Feb. 20, 1862, Box 2, Harris papers, TSLA; *Nashville Times,* Mar. 10, 11, 17, 1862, quoting *Memphis Appeal, West Tennessee Whig,* and *Montgomery Advertiser.*

39. Williams, *Napoleon in Gray,* 150–52.

40. *ORA,* I, X, pt. 1, 4; pt. 2, 370–72; Roland, *Johnston,* 303–4; Davis, *Orphan Brigade,* 73–76.

41. Johnston, *Johnston,* 725; Johnston to Davis, Mar. 30, 1862, ch. II, v. 218, Ltrs. and Tel. Sent, Sept. 61–Apr. 62, Johnston's Command, RG 109, NARA; H.C. Burnett to Floyd, Mar. 1, 1862, Floyd papers, DUL; Richardson, ed., *Messages and Papers of the Confederacy,* II, 193–94, 197–99.

42. ALC, "Fort Donelson," 55; Woodward, ed., *Mary Chestnut's Civil War,* 290, 310; Benjamin Bedford letterbook, 150–51, Bedford to T. Binge, Apr. 27, 1862, both Bedford papers, TSLA; Lunsford Yandell to Sally, Apr. 27, 1862, Yandell family papers, FCL; Albert C. Jewell to parents, Mar. 26, 1862, USAMHI.

43. Andrews, "The Confederate Press and Public Morale," 448–49; Wiley, *The Road to Appomattox,* esp. "Curve of Confederate Morale," 34–36; *Nashville Times,* Mar. 7, 8, 1862; Tennessee Delegation to President, CSA, Mar. 8, 1862;

French diary, Feb. 22, 1862, both TSLA; *ORA,* 1, VII, 257–58; Gonzales, "Henry Stuart Foote," 386–87.

44. *ORA,* ibid., 254–61, 921–22.

45. Ibid., 259–60.

46. Cf. ibid., with Connelly, *Army of the Heartland,* 137–48; Eaton, *Jefferson Davis,* 150; Horn, *Army of Tennessee,* ch. VII; *Confederate Veteran* (Feb. 1926), 62–63; *Richmond Examiner,* Mar. 11, 1862.

CHAPTER 13

1. Simon, *Grant Papers,* IV, 287; Catton, *Grant Moves South,* 182.

2. Simon, ibid., 313, concerning the head cold; Pitkin, ed., *Grant the Soldier,* 34–35, concerning the cigars.

3. *Nashville Times,* Mar. 5, 1862; Hoppin, *Life of Foote,* 23–35.

4. *ORA,* 1, VII, 422–23; Beach, *Along the Warioto,* 201–4.

5. Beach, ibid., 204, 206; Hubert, *Fiftieth Illinois,* 80–81; Simon, *Grant Papers,* IV, 249–50, 261–62, 266.

6. Wallace, *W.H.L. Wallace,* 171; Wilkie, *Pen and Powder,* 135.

7. Wilkie, ibid.; Smart, *A Radical View,* I, 111–14.

8. Simon, *Grant Papers,* IV, 245–46, 264, 278–79, 286–89; Young, *What a Boy Saw in the Army,* 84–89; Wallace, *W.H.L. Wallace,* 173.

9. *Chicago Tribune,* Mar. 4, 1862; F.P. Gray to Grant, Mar. 3, 1862, v. 4, and Special Order 3, Oglesby's brigade, Feb. 26, 1862, v. 9, both Oglesby papers, ISH.

10. Simon, *Grant Papers,* IV, 243n, 265–66, 268–70n, 290–91n; James Drish to wife, Feb. 21, 1862, ISH; Robert J. Price to father, Mar. 28, 1862, IHSL; *Nashville Times,* Mar. 12, 1862; John Riggin to W.W. Leland, Feb. 25, 1862 (2), Ltrs. Sent 1861–62, Cairo District, RG 393, NARA.

11. Simon, *Grant Papers,* IV, 306, and 245, 250, 252–53, 256, 259, 282, 301, 302–4, 312–13, 333–34n, 340–41, 353, 371–72, for Grant's activities at this time; Drish to wife, ibid.; Special Orders 4, Smith's Division, Feb. 17, v. 7, and General Orders 11, Oglesby's brigade, Feb. 17, both Oglesby papers, ibid.; Price to father, Mar. 28, 1862, IHSL; Will Kennedy to father, Mar. 15, 1862, Kennedy papers, DUL; Hubert, *Fiftieth Illinois,* 81.

12. Grant, *Personal Memoirs,* I, 327; *ORA,* 1, VII, 679–83; X, pt. 2, 3; Simon, *Grant Papers,* IV, 295n–96n, 306.

13. *ORA,* 1, X, pt. 2, 4–5; VII, 674–77.

14. Ibid., 1, X, pt. 2, 13–15, 21, 22, 26–27, 30, 32, 42, 45; Simon, *Grant Papers,* IV, 444.

15. Simon, ibid., 78–83n; Grant, *Personal Memoirs,* I, 325, 328–29; Cramer, *Ulysses S. Grant; Conversations and Unpublished Letters,* 184–92; Plum, *The Military Telegraph,* I, 173–76; H. Rumford to Halleck, W.H. Hewitt to Halleck, both Feb. 18; Cullum to Halleck, Feb. 21; G.H. Smith to Halleck, T.A. Scott to Hal-

leck, all Mar. 1; G.H. Smith to Halleck, J.C. Sullivan to Halleck, both Mar. 6; Grant to Halleck, G.H. Smith to Halleck, both Mar. 16, all 1862, all Tel. Recd., Nov. 61–Mar. 62; and Halleck to Stager, Feb. 26, Mar. 1; Halleck to J.S.S. Wilson, Feb. 28, Mar. 2, all 1862, all Tel. Sent, Nov. 61–Jul. 63, all Cairo District, RG 393, NARA.

16. Morsberger, *Lew Wallace*, 79–80; Simon, *Grant Papers*, V, 63, 68–70, 141n; W.S. Hillyer to Wallace, Mar. 1, 1862, Ltrs. Sent, 1861–62, Cairo District, ibid.; McClernand to Lincoln, Feb. 27, 1862, v. 197, Lincoln papers, LC.

17. Simon, ibid., V, 52–53, 78–83, 136–37, 141n, 184, 249; Wallace, *W.H.L. Wallace*, 169–70, 175–76; Hicken, *Illinois in the Civil War*, 44–45.

18. C.B. Tompkins to wife, Mar. 2, 6, 1862; DUL; Robert J. Price to father, Mar. 28, 1862, IHSL; James F. Drish to wife, Mar. 3, 5, 1862, ISH; Castel, ed., "The War Album of Henry Dwight," 32.

19. Sylvester C. Bishop to mother, Mar. 3, 10, 1862, J.N. Kidwell to mother, Mar. 16, 1862, both IHSL; Jacob Lauman to wife, Feb. 17, Mar. 1, 2, 3, 8, 14, all 1862, all CHS; Dugan, *History of Hurlburt's Division*, 98.

20. George S. Durfee to uncle, Mar. 13, 1862, Illinois Historical Survey, UIL; William K. Tebbets to sister, Mar. 2, 1862, ISH; Charles Peck to brother, Mar. 22, 1862, courtesy, R.K. Haerle, Indianapolis; Rerick, *Forty-Fourth Indiana*, 227–28; Moore, *Civil War in Song and Story*, 292–95, esp. 292.

21. Lewis, "Deaths at Clarksville," 65.

22. John H. Brinton, "Account of the Campaign of the Army of the Tennessee," in U.S. Surgeon General, *Medical and Surgical History*, I, pt. 1, 26–27.

23. Ibid., 27–28, 34–35.

24. Ibid., 28–29; W.S. Elliott to Halleck, Feb. 25, 1862, Ltrs. Recd. 1861–67, Box 2, 1862, RG 393, NARA.

25. Halleck to C.H. Eldridge, Feb. 19, 1862, Tel. Sent, Nov. 61–Jul. 62, ibid.; Stampp, *Indiana Politics During the Civil War*, 123–25; Newberry, *Sanitary Commission in the Valley of the Mississippi*, ch. II, esp. 31–33; William Quentin Maxwell, *Lincoln's Fifth Wheel*, 119–20, 128; Marjorie Barstow Greenbie, *Lincoln's Daughters of Mercy*, 114–21.

26. George R. Lee, "Soldiers Experiences," n.d., Lee papers, USAMHI; Churchill, "Wounded at Fort Donelson," I, 162; E.C. Alft, "VI–'A Taste of the Fight,'" *Elgin* (Ill.) *Courier-News*, Feb. 15, 1962; Newcomb, *Personal Reminiscences*, ch. 2.

27. Stanley, ed., *Stanley Autobiography*, 211; for general accounts of prison camps holding Henry-Donelson internees, see: Praus, *Confederate Soldiers and Sailors — Camp Butler*, 1–2; Knauss, *Story of Camp Chase*; Froman, *Rebels on Lake Erie*; Barbiere, *Scraps from the Prison Table*; Lewis and Mewha, *History of Prisoner of War Utilization*, 27–31.

28. A representative sampling of POW sentiment can be gleaned from George Wiley Adams and W. Joseph Bingham for Camp Chase; William H. Farmer and James J. Hallums (Land Between the Lakes collection), for Camp Butler; A.G. Alexander (G.W. Dillon collection), all TSLA; also *Nashville Times*,

Mar. 7, 1862; Knauss, ibid., ch. 3, 193; Military Order, Indiana Command-ery, *Camp Morton*, 12–13; *Sandusky Register,* Apr. 11, 1862.

29. Morton, *Artillery of Forrest's Cavalry,* 39; Adams to wife, Apr. 7, 1862, TSLA; Guy prison journal, VHS.

30. Vesey, "Camp Douglas in 1862," 255; Montgomery, "Daring Deeds of a Con-federate Soldier," 11; Editor, *Confederate Veteran,* "Prisoners of War at Camp Douglas," 530, "Prisoners on Johnson's Island," 495, "Prisoners at Johnson's Island," 442–43; Knauss, *Camp Chase,* 177; Benjamin F. Bedford to Messrs. A.L. Salewell and Son, Apr. 14; B.F. Bedford to Hugh L. Bedford, Feb. 17; Bedford to Polk, Feb. 28, all 1862, all Bedford letterbook, Box 1, TSLA.

31. M'Clung diary, 12, UTA; Adams to wife, May 31, 1862, TSLA; Bowman and Scroggs, ed., "Diary of a Confederate Soldier," 28; Tunnon, "Col. Richard Owen," 252; U.S. Surgeon General, *Medical and Surgical History,* III, 54; Wins-low and Moore, *Camp Morton,* 312; and Editor, *Confederate Veteran,* "Col. Rich-ard Owen," 202–3, "The Richard Owen Story," 109, "Reasons for Richard Owen Memorial," 324–25; "Booklet About Richard Owen Memorial," 471.

32. Stickles, *Buckner,* ch. XI; Gower and Allen, *Pen and Sword,* ch. XXIII; *Nash-ville Times,* Mar. 3, 4, 10, 11, 12, 27, 28, 1862; various N.F. Cheairs letters and "Experience," ch. II, TSLA.

33. Hylan B. Lyon to Cousin Jim, Mar. 9, 1862, MSUL; Cheairs to daughter, Apr. 22, 1862, TSLA; Gower and Allen, ibid., 644.

34. Beale, *Bates Diary,* 245; Graf and Haskins, *Johnson Papers,* V, 190, 191, 201, 212–13, 255; Stanley, *Autobiography,* 212–13; Brown, *Galvanized Yankees,* 59–60; Vesey, "Camp Douglas in 1862"; Montgomery, "Daring Deeds of a Confederate Soldier," 11.

35. Guy prison journal, VHS; M'Clung diary, 14, UTA; Gower and Allen, *Pen and Sword,* 657–61; Lewis and Mewha, *Prisoner of War Utilization,* 27–29; Mitch-ell, "Exchange of Civil War Prisoners," 341–43; Editor, Southern Histori-cal Society Papers, "Treatment of Prisoners During the War Between the States," 156–57; Terrell, "A Confederate Private at Fort Donelson, 1862," 484.

36. A.G. Alexander to Gentlemen, Aug. 9, 1862; Cheairs to daughter, May 3, 1862; Questionnaire, William B. Fonvielle, Tennessee Civil War Veterans Survey, all TSLA.

CHAPTER 14

1. In addition to the official reports in *ORA,* 1, VII, see Pillow to Hardee, Feb. 20, Hardee to Pillow, Feb. 23; Pillow to Editor, *Memphis Avalanche,* Feb. 27, all 1862, all Box 20, Pillow papers, RG 109, NARA; and H.C. Burnett to Floyd, Mar. 1, 1862, Floyd papers, DUL; *Nashville Times,* Mar. 10, 16, 1862; CSA, House of Representatives, *Report of Special Committee,* 1–2.

2. The course of Pillow's campaign for justice can be followed in *ORA,* ibid., LII, pt. 2, 315; also G.A. Henry to Pillow, May 6, 1862, Pillow papers, ibid.

3. *ORA,* ibid., 316–21; Tilghman to Pillow, Sep. 21; Pillow to Earl Van Dorn, Oct. 15, both 1862, both Pillow papers, ibid; Hughes, ed. *Liddell's Record,* 59.

4. Bell, "Gideon Pillow; A Personality Profile," 17–19; Connelly, *Autumn of Glory,* 81–83, 109–10.

5. Barnwell, "Gen. John B. Floyd," 141–42.

6. Hughes, "Vindication of John B. Floyd," 278–84; and "John B. Floyd and His Traducers," 216–29.

7. Cheairs to daughter, Apr. 22, May 7, both 1862; H.C. Lockhard entry, May 2, John C. Brown entry, July 20, W.E. Baldwin entry, Apr. 21, all 1862, all Joseph Palmer Confederate Album, all TSLA; Guy prison journal, VHS; Interview with T.C. Greever, Nov. 26, 1983, reflecting views of Greever's kinsman, Lt. John D. Greever, 50th Va. Infantry, FDNMPL; Gower and Allen, *Pen and Sword,* 611, 673.

8. On Johnson-Woodward raid, see Johnson, *Partisan Rangers,* ch. 5; *ORA,* I, XVI, pt. I, 862–70; Beach, *Along the Warioto,* 363; Holmes, *Fifty-Second Ohio,* 81–82; Lyon, *Reminiscences of the Civil War . . . Correspondence of Colonel William P. Lyon,* 62–63, 70–76.

9. On the battle of Dover, see Cooling, "The Battle of Dover," 143–51; Dyer, *"Fightin' Joe" Wheeler,* 90–91; Henry, *"First With the Most" Forrest,* 123; Jordan and Pryor, *Campaigns of Forrest,* 224–26; *ORA,* I, XX, pt. 2, 397–98; XXIII, pt. I, 37–41.

10. Wyeth, *Life of Forrest,* 128–33; Dyer, ibid., 96–97; Lyon, *Reminiscences,* 78–81; George F. Harding to John C. Burns, Feb. 3, 1911 (copy) accompanying Victor M. Harding to author, Jun. 17, 1981, FDNMPL.

11. On Johnsonville, see *ORA,* I, XLII, pt. I, 119–24; Morton, *Artillery of Forrest's Cavalry,* esp. ch. 19; Whitesell, "Military Operations in the Jackson Purchase of Kentucky 1862–1865," 332–38; Dinkins, "Destroying Yankee Gunboats," 341–44; on the Nashville campaign, see Horn, *Army of Tennessee,* chs. 28, 29; Connolly, *Autumn of Glory,* chs. 16, 17; on naval operations for both, see *ORN,* I, XXIV, 582–90; and for impact of this warfare on the Confederacy, see DeBerry, "Confederate Tennessee," 471–73; and Maslowski, *Treason Made Odious,* ch. 8.

12. M'Neilly, "A Roundabout Way Home," 210–12; *Clarksville Chronicle,* July 14, 1865, quoted in Ash, "Postwar Recovery; Montgomery County, 1865–1870," 209; and Henry, *Land Between the Rivers,* 43–57.

13. Biographical data derived from General Service Schools, *Source Book,* ch. 13; on Pillow, see entry in the *National Cyclopaedia,* IX, 279–80.

14. Benjamin F. Bedford letterbook, 153; TSLA; Vandiver, ed., *Gorgas Diary,* 3; Stickles, *Buckner,* 92–93, 324–29; Andrews, "Confederate Press and Public Morale," 448–49; CSA, Congress, *Facts and Incidents . . . Fort Donelson,* 14.

15. See questionnaires especially for Marion A. Wisenheimer (3d Infantry), J.M. Davis (5th Cavalry), James L. Dismukes (18th Infantry), J.D. Miles (20th Infantry), William McElwee and Charles F. Henley (26th Infantry),

William David Beard (53d Infantry), and James S. Hanna (26th Mississippi Infantry), all Tennessee Civil War Veterans Survey, TSLA.

16. Guy prison journal, VHS; Stiles, "In the Years 1861–1862," 163; Herald, "Shiloh—The First Great Battle," 335; Hughes, "Why Fort Donelson Was Surrendered," 300–3, 317; Vesey, "Why Fort Donelson was Surrendered, 369–70; Barnwell, "Fort Donelson—By Official Record," 16–20; Shephard, "Defending His Book," 47; Hughes, "Facts Not To Be Controverted," 90–91.

17. Melville, *Battle-Pieces and Aspects of the War*, 52; McDonough, *Shiloh*, preface.

18. Carter, *Magnolia Journey*, 142–43; Holmes, *Fifty-Second Ohio*, 93; Sears, ed., *American Heritage Century Collection of Civil War Art*, chs. III, XII, also 359, 361 for examples.

19. Lorenzo Thomas to Halleck, Mar. 28, 1862, Ltrs. Recd. 1861–67, Box 4, Dept. of Missouri, RG 393, NARA; Peterson, "Administrative History—Fort Donelson NMP," 12–14; *Eighty-Third Illinoisan*, May 2, 1865, copy in Joseph Latimer papers, USAMHI.

20. Editor, *Confederate Veteran*, "Memorial Chapel at Fort Donelson," 461; Beach, *Along the Warioto*, 230–33; Peterson, ibid., 15–16; Lee, *Origin and Evolution of the National Military Park Idea*, 40–41.

21. Leech, "Monument at Fort Donelson," 52; Peterson, ibid., 16–29; Cooling, "Fort Donelson National Military Park," 214–17; Henry, *Land Between the Rivers*, 183–91.

22. Editor, *Confederate Veteran*, "Gen. Albert Sidney Johnston, C.S.A," 62–63; Henry, *Forrest*, 47; Rhodes, *Lectures on the American Civil War*, 110; while other representative thinking appears in Jordan and Pryor, *Campaigns of Forrest*, 95; Johnston, *Johnston*, 76; Connelly, *Army of the Heartland*, intro.; Williams, "The Military Leadership of North and South," 42; and Barney, *Flawed Victory*, 15–16.

23. Wiley, *Road to Appomattox*, ii, and chart, "Curve of Confederate Morale," 34–36; Hattaway and Jones, *How the North Won*, esp. ch. 3; and Beringer, et al., *Why the South Lost*, esp. 128, 186, 188.

24. Catton, "Glory Road Began in the West," 235; Reed, *Combined Operations*, ch. 3; Walker, "Command Failure," 335–60; Ambrose, *Halleck*, ch. 3.

25. Wyeth, *Life of Forrest*, 34, 53; ALC, Fort Donelson," 33–62; Goff, *Confederate Supply*, 56–67.

26. Current, *Northernizing the South;* Parish, *American Civil War*, final chapter, "The Enduring Legacy."

27. Henry, *Land Between the Rivers*, 191; Browne, *Bugle-Echoes*, 327, citing original publication of "The Blue and the Gray," in *New York Tribune*, May 30, 1867.

Bibliography

Primary Materials

RECORDS

Confederate States of America, Congress. *Facts and Incidents of the Siege, Defence, and Fall of Fort Donelson, February 1862.* Huntsville, Ala., 1863.

———. House of Representatives. *Report of Special Committee on the Recent Military Disasters at Fort Henry and Donelson and the Evacuation of Nashville.* Richmond, 1862.

Conger, A.L., comp. *Donelson Campaign Sources; Supplementing Vol. VII of the Official Records.* Fort Leavenworth, 1912.

Newberry, J.S. *The Sanitary Commission in the Valley of the Mississippi During the War of the Rebellion.* Doc. 36. Cleveland, 1871.

Praus, Alexis A. *Confederate Soldiers and Sailors Who Died as Prisoners of War at Camp Butler, Illinois, 1862–1865.* Kalamazoo, n.d.

———. *Confederate Soldiers, Sailors and Civilians Who Died as Prisoners of War at Camp Douglas, Chicago, Illinois 1862–1865.* Kalamazoo, n.d.

Richardson, James D., ed. *Messages and Papers of the Confederacy.* 2 vols. Nashville, 1905.

U.S. Army, Corps of Engineers. *Legends of the Operations of the Army of the Cumberland.* Washington, D.C., 1869.

U.S. Army Service Schools. *Donelson Campaign Sources; Supplementing Vol. VII of the Official Records of the War of the Rebellion.* Fort Leavenworth, 1923.

U.S. Bureau of the Census. *Agriculture of the United States in 1860.* Washington, D.C. 1861.

———. *Manufactures of the United States in 1860.* Washington, D.C., 1865.

U.S. Congress, 37th, 3d Session. House of Representatives. Report of Committee 108. *Report of the Joint Committee on the Conduct of the War.* 3 vols. Washington, D.C., 1863.

U.S. Navy Department. *Official Records of the Union and Confederate Navies in the War of the Rebellion.* 30 vols. Washington, D.C., 1894–1927.

U.S. Surgeon General. *The Medical and Surgical History of the War of the Rebellion.* 6 vols. Washington, D.C., 1870–1888.

U.S. War Department. *War of the Rebellion; Official Records of the Union and Confederate Armies.* 129 vols. Washington, D.C., 1880–1901.

U.S. War Department. Quartermaster General's Office. *General Order 33, August 13, 1868; Statement of the Disposition of Some of the Bodies of Deceased Union Soldiers and Prisoners of War Whose Remains Have Been Removed to National Cemeteries in the Southern and Western States.* Washington, D.C., 1868.

COLLECTED WORKS, MEMOIRS, DIARIES, REMINISCENCES

Barber, Lucius. *Army Memoirs.* Chicago, 1894.

Barbiere, Jose. *Scraps from the Prison Tables at Camp Chase and Johnson's Island.* Doylestown, Penn. 1868.

Beale, Howard K., ed. *The Diary of Edward Bates, Washington 1859–1866.* Washington, D.C., 1933.

Brinton, James H. *Personal Memoirs.* New York, 1914.

Browne, Francis F., ed. *Bugle Echoes.* New York, 1886.

Browne, Junius H. *Four Years in Secessia.* Hartford, Conn., 1865.

Cannon, J.P. *Inside Rebeldom: The Daily Life of a Private in the Confederate Army.* Washington, 1900.

Carter, Howell. *A Cavalryman's Reminiscences of the Civil War.* N.p., n.d.

Carter, Joseph C. *Magnolia Journey; A Union Veteran Revisits the Former Confederate States.* University, Ala., 1974.

Chetlain, Augustus L. *Recollections of Seventy Years.* Galena, Ill., 1899.

Clothier, Isaac, comp. *Letters 1853–1868; General William J. Palmer.* Philadelphia, 1906.

Coe, David, ed. *Mine Eyes Have Seen the Glory; Combat Diaries of Union Sergeant Hamlin Alexander Coe.* Rutherford, N.J., 1975.

Coffin, Charles. *Four Years of Fighting.* Boston, 1866.

————. *My Days and Nights on the Battlefield.* Boston, 1865.

Cramer, H.J. *Ulysses S. Grant; Conversations and Unpublished Letters.* Boston, 1865.

Croffut, W.A. *Fifty Years in Camp and Field; The Diary of Major General Ethan Allen Hitchcock, USA.* New York, 1909.

Crummer, Wilbur F. *With Grant at Fort Donelson, Shiloh, and Vicksburg.* Oak Park, Ill., 1915.

Cullum, George W. *Biographical Register of Officers and Graduates of the U.S. Military Academy.* Boston, 1891 edition.

Duncan, Thomas D. *Recollections of Thomas D. Duncan; A Confederate Soldier.* Nashville, 1922.

Dunlap, Leslie W., ed. *"Your Affectionate Husband, J.F. Culver"; Letters Written During the Civil War.* Iowa City, 1978.

Eddy, T.M. *Patriotism of Illinois.* 2 vols. Chicago, 1866.

Gower, Herschel, and Jack Allen, eds. *Pen and Sword, The Life and Journals of Randal W. McGavock.* Nashville, 1959.

Graf, LeRoy P., and Ralph W. Haskins, eds. *Papers of Andrew Johnson.* 1- vols. Knoxville, 1967- .

Grant, Ulysses S. *Personal Memoirs.* 2 vols. New York, 1885.

Greene, Charles S. *Thrilling Stories of the Great Rebellion.* Philadelphia, 1866.

Hughes, Nathaniel C., ed. *Liddell's Record; St. John Richardson Liddell, Brigadier General, CSA Staff Officer and Brigade Commander Army of Tennessee,* Dayton, 1985.

Illinois Military and Naval Departments. *Illinois in the War for the Union.* Springfield, 1887.

Johnson, Adam Rankin [William J. Davis, ed.]. *The Partisan Rangers of the Confederacy.* Louisville, 1904.

Johnson, Robert U., and Clarence C. Buel, eds. *Battles and Leaders of the Civil War.* New York, 1881.

Lindsley, John Berrien, ed. *The Military Annals of Tennessee.* Nashville, 1886.

Logan, Mary. *Reminiscences of a Soldier's Wife; An Autobiography.* New York, 1913.

Lyon, Adelia, comp. *Reminiscences of the Civil War; Correspondence of Colonel William R. Lyon.* San Jose, Calif., 1907.

Lossing, Benson J. *Pictorial History of the Civil War.* 3 vols. Hartford, Conn., 1868.

Melville, Herman. *Battle-Pieces and Aspects of War.* New York, 1886.

Milligan, John D., ed. *From the Fresh-Water Navy, 1861–1864;* The Letters of Acting Master's Mate Henry R. Browne and Acting Ensign Symmes E. Browne. Annapolis, 1970.

Moore, Frank, comp. *The Civil War in Song and Story.* New York, 1889.

———. *The Rebellion Record.* 11 vols. New York, 1862–73.

Newcomb, Mary A. *Four Years of Personal Reminiscences of the War.* Chicago, 1893.

O'Reilly, Miles [Charles G. Halpine]. *Baked Meats of the Funeral; Collection of Essays, Poems, Speeches, Histories, and Banquets.* New York, 1866.

Powers, Elivra J. *Hospital Sketches; Being a War Diary While in Jefferson General Hospital, Jeffersonville, Ind., and others at Nashville Tennessee as a Matron or Visitor.* Boston, 1866.

Rugeley, H.J.H., ed. *Batchelor-Turner Letters 1861–1864;* Written by Two of Terry's Texas Rangers. Austin, 1961.

Russell, William H. *My Diary North and South.* Boston and New York, 1863.

Scarborough, William K., ed. *The Diary of Edmund Ruffin,* 2 vols. Baton Rouge, 1972–76.

Sears, Stephen, ed. *American Heritage Century Collection of Civil War Art.* New York, 1974.

Sherman, William T. *Personal Memoirs.* 2 vols. New York, 1875.

Simon, John Y., ed. *The Papers of Ulysses S. Grant.* 1– vols. Carbondale, Ill., 1967– .

Smart, James G., ed. *A Radical View: The "Agate" Dispatches of Whitelaw Reid, 1861–1865.* 2 vols. Memphis, 1976.

Stanley, Dorothy, ed. *The Autobiography of Sir Henry Morton Stanley.* Boston, 1909.

Stuber, Johann. *Mein Tagebuch über die Erlebnisse im Revolutions-Kriege von 1861 bis 1865.* Cincinnati, 1896.

Thompson, Robert M., and Richard Wainwright, eds. *Confidential Correspondence of Gustavus Vasa Fox, Assistant Secretary of the Navy 1861–1865.* 2 vols. New York, 1920.

Thorne, Mildred, ed. *Civil War Diary of C.F. Boyd; Fifteenth Iowa Infantry 1861–1863.* Millwood, N.Y., 1977.

Tomlinson, Helga W., ed. *"Dear Friends," The Civil War Letters and Diary of Charles Edwin Cort.* N.p., 1962.

Vandiver, Frank E., ed. *The Civil War Diary of General Josiah Gorgas.* University, Ala., 1947.

Victor, Orville J., ed. *Incidents and Anecdotes of the War.* New York, 1862.

Walke, Henry. *Naval Scenes and Reminiscences of the Civil War.* New Haven, 1877.

Wallace, Isabel. *Life and Letters of General W.H.L. Wallace.* Chicago, 1909.

Wallace, Lewis. *An Autobiography.* 2 vols. New York, 1906.

Whittlesey, Charles. *War Memoranda; Cheat Mountain to the Tennessee, 1861–1862.* Cleveland, 1884.

Wilkie, Franc B. *Pen and Powder.* Boston, 1888.

Wilson, LeGrand. *The Confederate Soldier.* Memphis, 1975.

Woodward, C. Vann., ed. *Mary Chestnut's Civil War.* New Haven, 1981.

Young, Jesse Bowman. *What a Boy Saw in the Army; A Story of Sight-Seeing and Adventure in the War for the Union.* New York, 1894.

UNIT HISTORIES

Adair, John M. *Historical Sketch of the Forty-Fifth Illinois Regiment.* Lanark, Ill., 1869.

Ambrose, D. Leib. *History of the Seventh Regiment Illinois Volunteer Infantry.* Springfield, 1868.

Avery, Phineas O. *History of the Fourth Illinois Cavalry Regiment.* Humboldt, Neb., 1903.

Barnard, Henry V. *Tattered Volunteers; Historical Sketch of the Twenty-Seventh Alabama.* Northport Ala., 1965.

Belknap, William W. *History of the Fifteenth Regiment, Iowa Volunteer Infantry.* Keokuk, Iowa, 1887.

Bell, John T. *Tramps and Triumphs of the Second Iowa Infantry.* Omaha, Neb., 1886.

Cluett, William W. *History of the Fifty-Seventh Regiment Illinois Volunteer Infantry.* Princeton, Ill., 1886.

Cope, Alexis. *The Fifteenth Ohio Volunteers and Its Campaigns.* Columbus, 1916.

Davis, William C. *The Orphan Brigade; The Kentucky Confederates Who Couldn't Go Home.* Garden City, N.Y., 1980.

Dugan, James. *History of Hurlburt's Fighting Fourth Division.* Cincinnati, 1863.

Fletcher, Samuel H. *The History of Company A, Second Illinois Cavalry.* Chicago, 1912.

George, Henry. *History of Third, Seventh, Eighth, and Twelfth Kentucky, CSA.* Louisville, 1911.

Giles, L.B. *Terry's Texas Rangers.* N.p., 1911.

Hancock, R.R. *Hancock's Diary; or a History of the Second Tennessee Confederate Cavalry.* Nashville, 1887.

Holmes, James T. *Fifty-Second Ohio Volunteer Infantry; Then and Now.* Columbus, 1898.

Howell, H. Grady. *Going to Meet the Yankees; A History of the "Bloody Sixth" Mississippi Infantry, CSA.* Jackson, 1981.

Hubert, Charles F. *History of the Fiftieth Regiment Illinois Volunteer Infantry.* Kansas City, 1894.

Illinois, Chicago Board of Trade Battery Association. *Historical Sketch of the Chicago Board of Trade Battery, Horse Artillery Illinois Volunteers.* Chicago, 1902.

Illinois, First Artillery, Battery A Association. *First Reunion of Battery A.* Chicago, 1885.

Illinois, Fiftieth Infantry Reunion Association. *Reports of Tenth through Twentieth Annual Reunions, 1896–1906.* N.p., n.d.

Illinois, Fifty-Fifth Infantry, Committee. *The Story of the Fifty-Fifth Regiment Illinois Volunteers.* Clinton, Mass., 1887.

Illinois, Ninety-Second Regimental Association. *Ninety-Second Illinois Volunteers.* Freeport, Ill., 1875.

Iowa, Adjutant Generals Office. *Roster and Record of Iowa Soldiers in the War of the Rebellion, Together with Historical Sketches of Volunteer Organizations 1861–1866.* Des Moines, 1908.

Jones, Thomas B. *Complete History of the Forty-Sixth Regiment Illinois Volunteer Infantry.* Freeport, Ill., 1907.

Kimbell, Charles B. *History of Battery "A" First Illinois Light Artillery Volunteers.* Chicago, 1899.

Morrison, Marion. *A History of the Ninth Regiment Illinois Volunteer Infantry.* Monmouth, Ill., 1864.

Morton, John W. *Artillery of Nathan Bedford Forrest's Cavalry.* Nashville, 1909.

Reed, D.W. *"University Recruits" Company C, Twelfth Iowa Infantry.* Evanston, Ill., 1903.

———. *Campaigns and Battles of the Twelfth Regiment Iowa Veteran Volunteer Infantry.* Evanston, Ill., 1903.

Rerick, John H. *The Forty-Fourth Indiana Volunteer Infantry.* Lagrange, Ind., 1880.

Reynolds, Edwin H. *History of the Henry County Commands.* Jacksonville, 1904.

Smith, Henry I. *History of the Seventh Iowa Veteran Volunteer Infantry.* Mason City, Iowa, 1903.

Smith, John T. *History of the Thirty-First Regiment of Indiana Volunteer Infantry.* Cincinnati, 1900.

Speed, Thomas, R.M. Dudley, and Alfred Pistle. *The Union Regiments of Kentucky.* Louisville, 1897.

Stevenson, Thomas. *History of the Seventy-Eighth Regiment O.V.V.I.* Zanesville, Ohio, 1865.

Stuart, Addison A. *Iowa Colonels and Regiments.* Des Moines, 1865.

Tennessee Civil War Centennial Commission. *Tennesseans in the Civil War: A Military History of Confederate and Union Units with Available Rosters of Personnel.* Nashville, 1964.

Thompson, Edwin Porter. *History of the Orphan Brigade.* Louisville, 1898.

Twombley, V.P. *The Second Iowa Infantry at Fort Donelson, February 15, 1862.* Des Moines, 1901.

U.S. Army Corps of Engineers. *Legends of the Operations of the Army of the Cumberland.* Washington, D.C., 1869.

Vale, Joseph G. *Minty and the Cavalry.* Harrisburg, Penn., 1886.

Van Horn, Thomas B. *History of the Army of the Cumberland.* 3 vols. Cincinnati, 1875.

[Vaughn, Alfred J.]. *Personal Record of the Thirteenth Regiment Tennessee Infantry.* Memphis, 1897.

Walton, Clyde C., ed., with Thaddeus C.S. Brown, Samuel J. Murphy, and William G. Putney. *Behind the Guns: The History of Battery I, Second Regiment, Illinois Light Artillery.* Carbondale, Ill., 1965.

Watkins, Samuel R. *"Co. Aytch" Maury Grays, First Tennessee Regiment, or, a Side Show of the Big Show.* Nashville, 1882.

William, Thomas J. *An Historical Sketch of the Fifty-Sixth Ohio Volunteer Infantry.* Columbus, 1899.

Woodbury, Henry H. *Complete History of the Forty-Sixth Illinois Veteran Volunteer Infantry.* Freeport, Ill., 1866.

MANUSCRIPTS

Library of Congress, Washington, D.C. (LC)
    Andrew Hull Foote Papers
    Roger Hanson Papers
    Abraham Lincoln Papers
    John A. Logan Papers
    Henry H. Lurton Papers
National Archives and Records Administration, Washington, D.C. (NARA)
    Record Group 45: Naval Records Collection of Naval Records and Library
    Record Group 77: Records of Army Corps of Engineers
    Record Group 109: War Dept. Collection of Confederate Records
    Record Group 393: U.S. Army Continental Army Commands
U.S. Army Military History Institute, Carlisle Barracks, Penn. (USAMHI)
    Civil War Miscellaneous Collection
    Confederate Documents, HQ, 1st Div., Western Dept., General Orders, 1861–1862
    Gideon J. Pillow Papers

Civil War Times Illustrated Collection
    George Booth Papers
    Albert Jewell Papers
    George R. Lee Papers
    Joseph Latimer Papers
Alabama Department of Archives and History, Montgomery (ADAH)
    J.P. Cannon Papers
Allegheny College (Peletier Library), Meadville, Penn. (AC)
    George W. Cullum Papers
Chicago Historical Society, Chicago (CHS)
    James Laning Papers
    Jacob Lauman Papers
    George Sawin Papers
    Frederick A. Starring Papers
    Ezra Taylor Papers
Duke University (Perkins Library), Durham, N.C. (DUL)
    Ambler-Brown Papers
    Anonymous Confederate Diary, Gordonsville
    P.G.T. Beauregard Papers
    Eltinge-Lord Family Papers
    John B. Floyd Papers
    Will Kennedy Papers
    Eugene T. Marshall Diary

Munford-Ellis Family Papers
Pope-Carter Papers
M.J. Solomons Papers
C.B. Tompkins Papers
Joseph S. Williams Papers
Filson Club, Louisville, Ky. (FCL)
Yandell Family Papers
Fort Donelson National Military
Park, Dover, Tenn. (FDNMPL)
Spot F. Terrell Journal
Theodore C. Greever Collection
(Private), Alexandria, Va.
John D. Greever
Victor M. Harding Collection
(Private), Milwaukee.
A.C. Harding Miscellaneous
Papers
Rudolf K. Haerle Collection
(Private), Indianapolis.
Charles Peck Papers
Historical Society of Pennsylvania,
Philadelphia (HSP)
Dreer Collection of Confederate
Generals
Gideon J. Pillow Papers
Leonidus Polk Papers
Huntington Library, San Marino,
Calif. (HL)
Simon B. Buckner Papers
Illinois State Historical Library,
Springfield (ISH)
W.A. Bailhache-Mason Brayman
Papers
Jonathan Blair Papers
Daniel Harmon Brush Papers
Simon B. Buckner Papers
George L. Childress Papers
George W. Cullum Papers
James F. Drish Papers
Charles H. Floyd Papers
Ulysses S. Grant Papers
Douglas Haperman Papers
Isham G. Haynie Papers

John A. McClernand Papers
Ira C. Merchant Papers
Thomas F. Miller Papers
W.R. Morrison Papers
Richard Oglesby Papers
Thomas C. Reynolds Papers
Z. Payson Shumway Papers
W.H. Tebbets Papers
W.H.L. Wallace-T. Lyle Dickey
Papers
John S. Wilcox Papers
Indiana Historical Society Library,
Indianapolis (IHSL)
Sylvester C. Bishop Papers
Francis Brainerd Papers
Samuel Coble Papers
John B. Connelly Papers
David A. Fateley Papers
James Frank Papers
John H. Harden Papers
John A. Hoerner Papers
Thomas Johnson Papers
James H. Jones Papers
Robert J. Price Papers
Ross-Kidwell Papers
Joseph H. Vanmeter Papers
Maury County (Tenn.) Historical
Society, Columbia and (Museum of
the Confederacy, Richmond, Va.)
(MC)
James T. Mackey Papers
Mississippi Dept. of Archives and
History, Jackson (MDAH)
Francis Marion Baxter Papers
Missouri Historical Society, St.
Louis (MHS)
Selden Spencer Papers
Murray State University (Forrest
Pogue Library), Murray, Ky. (MSUL)
Hylan B. Lyon Papers
Southern Illinois University Library,
Carbondale (SIU)
Joseph Shipworth Papers

Tennessee State Library and
Archives, Nashville (TSLA)
  George Wiley Adams Papers
  Charles Alley Papers
  Army of Tennessee Papers
  James E. Bailey Papers
  W.A. Bastian Papers
  Benjamin F. Bedford Papers
  David S.M. Bodenhamer Papers
  Nathan Brandon Papers
  W. Joseph Brigham Papers
  John C. Brown Papers
  Robert Franklin Bunting Papers
  Robert Cartmell Papers
  Calvin J. Clack–History of Third
    Tennessee
  Cooper Family Papers
  Mary F. Couch Papers
  Luther H. Cowan Papers
  Thomas Hopkins Deavenport
    Papers
  G.W. Dillon Papers
  William H. Farmer Papers
  V.K. Farris Papers
  William Felts Papers
  Figuers Family Papers
  Virginia French Papers
  Jill Garrett Papers
  Isham G. Harris Papers
  Henry W. Halleck Papers
  Sarah Ann (Bailey) Kennedy
    Papers
  Land Between the Lakes Project
    Papers
  Blanche Lewis Papers
  William Lewis McKay Papers
  Thomas Rawlings Myers Papers
  Joseph B. Palmer Papers
  John M. Porter Papers
  Ross Family Papers
  Veterans (Civil War) Survey
University of Illinois Library,
Champaign (UIL)
  Illinois Historical Survey
    George S. Durfee Papers

University of Michigan Library,
Ann Arbor (UML)
  Charles F. Smith Papers
University of North Carolina
Library, Chapel Hill (UNCL)
  Southern Historical Collection
    Jeremy F. Gilmer Papers
University of Texas Library (Barker
Texas History Center), Austin
(UTA)
  R.L. McClung Papers
University of Virginia Library,
Charlottesville (UVA)
  T.G. Pollock Papers
Virginia Historical Society,
Richmond (VHS)
  John H. Guy Journal
  Robert W. Snead Papers
  Rufus J. Woolwine Papers

NEWSPAPERS

(Batavia, N.Y.) *Spirit of the Times*
Boston Journal
Chicago Daily Tribune
Cincinnati Gazette
Clarksville (Tenn.) *Chronicle*
Elgin (Ill.) *Daily Courier-News*
Frank Leslie's Illustrated Newspaper
Harpers Weekly
Macomb (Ill.) *Journal*
Memphis Appeal
Memphis Avalanche
Missouri Democrat (St. Louis)
Montgomery Advertiser
Nashville Banner
Nashville Evening Bulletin
Nashville Morning Bulletin
Nashville Tennessean
Nashville Times
New York Herald
New York Independent
New York Times
New York Tribune
Richmond Examiner

Sandusky (Ohio) *Register*
Stewart County (Tenn.) *Times*

St. Louis Democrat
West Tennessee Whig (Memphis)

Secondary Materials

BOOKS

Alexander, Augustus W. *Grant as a Soldier.* St. Louis, 1887.

Ambrose, Stephen E. *Halleck: Lincoln's Chief of Staff.* Baton Rouge, 1962.

Baird, Nancy Disher. *David Wendell Yandell; Physician of Old Louisville.* Lexington, 1978.

Baldwin, Leland D. *The Keelboat Age on Western Waters.* Pittsburgh, 1941.

Barney, William L. *Flawed Victory; A New Perspective on the Civil War.* Lanham, Md., 1980.

Barnhardt, John D. *The Impact of the Civil War on Indiana.* Indianapolis, 1962.

Beach, Ursula Smith. *Along the Warioto or A History of Montgomery County, Tennessee.* Clarksville, 1964.

Beringer, Richard, Herman Hattaway, Archer Jones, and William N. Still, Jr. *Why the South Lost the Civil War.* Athens, 1986.

Bettersworth, John K. *Confederate Mississippi; The People and Policies of a Cotton State in Wartime.* Baton Rouge, 1943.

Bill, Alfred Hoyt. *The Beleaguered City.* New York, 1946.

Black, Robert C. *Railroads of the Confederacy.* Chapel Hill, 1952.

Boatner, Mark M. III. *The Civil War Dictionary.* New York, 1959.

Boynton, Charles B. *The History of the Navy During the Rebellion.* 2 vols. New York, 1870.

Brock, William R. *Conflict and Transformation; The United States, 1844–1877.* Baltimore, 1973.

Brown, D. Alexander. *The Galvanized Yankees.* Urbana, Ill., 1963.

Byers, S.H.M. *Iowa in War Times.* Des Moines, 1888.

Canfield, Eugene B. *Civil War Ordnance.* Washington, D.C., 1969.

———. *Notes on Naval Ordnance of the American Civil War.* Washington, D.C., 1960.

Carnahan, James R. *Camp Morton.* Indianapolis, 1892.

Catton, Bruce. *America Goes to War.* Middletown, Conn., 1958.

———. *Grant Moves South.* Boston, 1960.

Clark, Thomas D., and Albert D. Kirwan. *The South Since Appomattox: A Century of Regional Change.* New York, 1967.

Cole, Arthur C. *Centennial History of Illinois, Volume III; The Era of the Civil War, 1848–1870.* Freeport, N.Y., 1971.

Coles, Harry L. *Ohio Forms an Army.* Columbus, 1962.

Connelly, Thomas L. *Army of the Heartland; The Army of Tennessee, 1861–1862.* Baton Rouge, 1967.

———. *Autumn of Glory; The Army of Tennessee, 1862–1865.* Baton Rouge, 1971.

————, and Archer Jones. *The Politics of Command; Factions and Ideas in Confederate Strategy.* Baton Rouge, 1973.

————, and Barbara L. Bellows. *God and General Longstreet; The Lost Cause and the Southern Mind.* Baton Rouge, 1982.

Craven, Avery O. *The Growth of Southern Nationalism, 1848–1861.* Baton Rouge, 1953.

Crozier, Emmet. *Yankee Reporters, 1861–1865.* New York, 1956.

Cummings, Charles M. *Yankee Quaker, Confederate General; The Curious Career of Bushrod Rust Johnson.* Rutherford, N.J., 1971.

Current, Richard N. *Northernizing the South.* Athens, 1983.

Daniel, Larry J. *Cannoneers in Gray; The Field Artillery of the Army of Tennessee, 1861–1865.* University, Ala., 1984.

————, and Riley W. Gunter. *Confederate Cannon Foundries.* Union City, Tenn., 1977.

Davenport, F. Garvin. *Cultural Life in Nashville on the Eve of the Civil War.* Chapel Hill, 1941.

Davis, Darrell Haug. *The Geography of the Jackson Purchase.* Frankfort, Ky., 1923.

Dawson, George Francis. *Life and Services of Gen. John A. Logan as Soldier and Statesman.* Washington, D.C., 1884.

De Jomini, Henri. *The Art of War.* Philadelphia, 1862.

Dew, Charles B. *Ironmaker to the Confederacy; Joseph R. Anderson and the Tredegar Iron Works.* New Haven, 1966.

Dodson, W.C. *Campaigns of Wheeler and His Cavalry.* Atlanta, 1897.

Donald, David, ed. *Why the North Won the Civil War.* Baton Rouge, 1960.

Douglas, Byrd. *Steamboatin' on the Cumberland.* Nashville, 1961.

Durham, Walter T. *Nashville; The Occupied City.* Nashville, 1985.

Dyer, Joseph P. *"Fightin' Joe" Wheeler.* Baton Rouge, 1941.

Eaton, Clement. *Jefferson Davis.* New York, 1977.

Eckenrode, H.J., and Bryan Conrad. *George B. McClellan; The Man Who Saved the Union.* Chapel Hill, 1941.

Eddy, T.M. *Patriotism of Illinois.* Chicago, 1865.

Edwards, William B. *Civil War Guns.* Harrisburg, Penn., 1962.

Faust, Patricia L., ed. *Historical Times Illustrated Encyclopedia of the Civil War.* New York, 1986.

Folmsbee, Stanley J., Robert E. Corlew, and Enoch L. Mitchell. *Tennessee, A Short History.* Knoxville, 1969.

Forman, Jacob Gilbert. *The Western Sanitary Commission; A Sketch.* St. Louis, 1864.

Foulke, William Dudley. *Life of Oliver P. Morton.* Indianapolis, 1899.

Froman, Charles E. *Rebels on Lake Erie.* Columbus, 1965.

Goff, Richard. *Confederate Supply.* Durham, N.C., 1969.

Gosnell, Harpur Allen. *Guns on the Western Waters.* Baton Rouge, 1949.

Greenbie, Marjorie Barstow. *Lincoln's Daughters of Mercy.* New York, 1944.

Hamilton, James. *The Battle of Fort Donelson.* South Brunswick, N.J., 1968.

Hanson, Charles H. *The Plains Rifle.* Harrisburg, Penn., 1960.

Hattaway, Herman, and Archer Jones. *How the North Won; A Military History of the Civil War.* Urbana, Ill., 1983.

Henry, J. Milton. *The Land Between the Rivers.* Paducah, Ky., 1977.

Henry, Robert Selph. *"First with the Most" Forrest.* Indianapolis, 1944.

Hicken, Victor. *Illinois in the Civil War.* Urbana, Ill., 1966.

Hoppin, James Mason. *Life of Andrew Hull Foote.* New York, 1874.

Horn, Stanley F. *Army of Tennessee.* Indianapolis, 1941.

———, comp. and ed. *Tennessee's War 1861–1865;* Described by Participants. Nashville, 1965.

Hubbart, Henry Clyde. *The Older Middle West 1840–1880.* New York, 1936.

Hughes, Nathaniel C. *General William J. Hardee, Old Reliable.* Baton Rouge, 1965.

Hunter, Louis C. *Steamboats on Western Rivers.* Cambridge, Mass., 1949.

Johnson, Robert Erwin. *Rear Admiral John Rodgers 1812–1882.* Annapolis, Md., 1967.

Johnston, William Preston. *The Life of Gen. Albert Sidney Johnston.* New York, 1878.

Jones, James P. *"Black Jack:" John A. Logan and Southern Illinois in the Civil War Era.* Tallahassee, Fla., 1967.

Jordan, Thomas, and J.P. Pryor. *The Campaigns of Lieut. Gen. N.B. Forrest.* New Orleans, 1868.

Kamm, Samuel Richey. *The Civil War Career of Thomas A. Scott.* Philadelphia, 1940.

Killebrew, J.W. *Introduction to the Resources of Tennessee.* Nashville, 1874.

Klein, Maury. *History of the Louisville and Nashville Railroad.* New York, 1972.

Knauss, William. *The Story of Camp Chase.* Nashville and Dallas, 1906.

Kohlmeier, A.L. *The Old Northwest.* Bloomington, Ind., 1938.

Kreidberg, Marvin A., and Merton G. Henry. *History of Military Mobilization in the United States Army, 1775–1945.* Washington, D.C., 1955.

Lee, Ronald F. *The Origin and Evolution of the National Military Park Idea.* Washington, D.C., 1973.

Leslie, J.P. *The Iron Manufacturer's Guide.* New York, 1859.

Lewis, George, and John Mewha. *History of Prisoner of War Utilization by the United States Army, 1776–1945.* Washington, D.C., 1955.

Lewis, Lloyd. *Captain Sam Grant.* Boston, 1950.

Lindsley, John Berrien. *The Military Annals of Tennessee, Confederate.* Nashville, 1886.

Livermore, Thomas L. *Numbers and Losses in the Civil War in America, 1861–1865.* Boston and New York, 1901.

Logan, John A. *The Volunteer Soldier in America.* Chicago and New York, 1881.

Longacre, Edward G. *Mounted Raids of the Civil War.* South Brunswick, N.J., 1975.

Lytle, Andrew. *Bedford Forrest and His Critter Company.* New York, 1931.

McDonough, L.M. *Shiloh — In Hell Before Night.* Knoxville, 1979.

McFeely, William S. *Grant: A Biography.* New York, 1981.

McKee, Irving. *"Ben-Hur" Wallace; The Life of General Lew Wallace.* Berkeley, Calif., 1947.

McWhiney, Grady and Perry D. Jamieson. *Attack and Die; Civil War Military Tactics and the Southern Heritage.* University, Ala., 1982.

Madaus, Howard M., and Robert D. Needham. *The Battle Flags of the Confederate Army of Tennessee.* Milwaukee, 1976.

Maslowski, Peter. *Treason Must Be Made Odious; Military Occupation and Wartime Reconstruction in Nashville, Tennessee, 1862–1865.* Millwood, N.Y., 1978.

Maxwell, William Quentin. *Lincoln's Fifth Wheel; The Political History of the U.S. Sanitary Commission.* New York, 1956.

Merrill, Catherine. *The Story of Indiana in the War for the Union.* 2 vols. Indianapolis, 1866.

Military Order of the Loyal Legion of the United States, Indiana Commandery. *Camp Morton.* Indianapolis, 1902.

Milligan, John D. *Gunboats Down the Mississippi.* Annapolis, Md., 1965.

Mockler, Arthur. *Our Enemies the French.* London, 1976.

Morsberger, Robert E., and Katherine M. *Lew Wallace: Military Romantic.* New York, 1950.

Nevins, Allan. *The War for the Union.* 4 vols. New York, 1959–71.

Nichols, James L. *Confederate Engineers.* Tuscaloosa, Ala., 1957.

Parks, Joseph. *General Leonidus Polk, CSA, The Fighting Bishop.* Baton Rouge, 1962.

Parish, Peter J. *The American Civil War.* New York, 1975.

Pitkin, Thomas M., ed. *Grant; The Soldier.* Washington, 1965.

Plum, William R. *The Military Telegraph During the Civil War.* 2 vols. Chicago, 1882.

Polk, William M. *Leonidas Polk; Bishop and General.* 2 vols. New York, 1915.

Pollard, Edward A. *The First Year of the War.* Richmond, 1862.

Pratt, Fletcher, *Civil War on Western Waters.* New York, 1956.

———. *Stanton, Lincolns Secretary of War.* New York, 1953.

Reed, Rowena. *Combined Operations in the Civil War.* Annapolis, Md., 1978.

Rhodes, James F. *Lectures on the American Civil War.* New York, 1913.

Richardson, Albert D. *Personal History of Ulysses S. Grant.* Hartford, Conn., 1869.

Ridley, Bromfield L. *Battles and Sketches of the Army of Tennessee.* Mexico, Mo., 1906.

Roland, Charles P. *Albert Sidney Johnston, Soldier of Three Republics.* Austin, 1964.

Roman, Alfred D. *The Military Operations of General Beauregard in the War Between the States.* 2 vols. New York, 1883.

Safford, James M. *Geology of Tennessee.* Nashville, 1869.

Seitz, Donald. *Braxton Bragg, General of the Confederacy.* Columbia, S.C., 1924.

Sheppard, Eric William. *Bedford Forrest; The Confederacy's Greatest Cavalryman.* London, 1930.

Sims, Harry H. *Ohio Politics on the Eve of Conflict.* Columbus, 1962.

Smith, Edward. *Incidents Among Shot and Shell.* New York, 1868.

Stampp, Kenneth P. *Indiana Politics During the Civil War.* Bloomington, Ind., 1949.

Stickles, Arndt M. *Simon Bolivar Buckner; Borderland Knight.* Chapel Hill, 1940.

Stivers, Reuben Elmore. *Privateers and Volunteers; The Men and Women of Our Reserve Naval Forces: 1766-1866.* Annapolis, Md., 1975.

Stover, John F. *History of the Illinois Central Railroad.* New York, 1975.

Taylor, George Rogers. *The Transportation Revolution 1815-1860.* New York, 1951.

Thomas, Benjamin P., and Harold M. Hyman. *Stanton: The Life and Times of Lincoln's Secretary of War.* New York, 1962.

Tucker, Louis L. *Cincinnati During the Civil War.* Columbus, 1962.

Vandiver, Frank E. *Ploughshares into Swords; Josiah Gorgas and Confederate Ordnance.* Austin, 1952.

Warner, Ezra T. *Generals in Blue; Lives of the Union Commanders.* Baton Rouge, 1964.

––––––. *Generals in Gray; Lives of the Confederate Commanders.* Baton Rouge, 1959.

Weber, Thomas. *The Northern Railroads in the Civil War, 1861-1865.* New York, 1962.

Whaley, Elizabeth J. *Forgotten Hero: General James B. McPherson.* New York, 1955.

Wiley, Bell I. *The Road to Appomattox.* Memphis, 1956.

Williams, James Harrison. *The Life of John A. Rawlins.* New York, 1914.

Williams, Kenneth P. *Lincoln Finds a General.* 5 vols. New York, 1949-58.

Williams, T. Harry. *P.G.T. Beauregard; Napoleon in Gray.* Baton Rouge, 1954.

Wilson, James Grant. *Biographical Sketches of Illinois Officers Engaged in the War Against the Rebellion of 1861.* Chicago, 1862.

Winslow, Hattie Low, and Joseph R.H. Moore. *Camp Morton 1861-1865; Indianapolis Prison Camp.* Indianapolis, 1940.

Wubben, Hubert H. *Civil War Iowa and the Copperhead Movement.* Ames, Iowa, 1980.

Wyeth, John A. *Life of General Nathan Bedford Forrest.* New York, 1899.

ARTICLES AND ESSAYS

ALC [Arthur L. Conger]. "Fort Donelson," *Military Historian and Economist,* Jan. 1916.

Ambrose, Stephen E. "Fort Donelson; A 'Disastrous' Blow to the South," *Civil War Times Illustrated,* June 1966.

––––––. "The Union Command System and the Donelson Campaign," *Military Affairs,* Spring 1960.

Anderson, Charles W. "After the Fall of Fort Donelson," *Confederate Veteran,* Sept. 1896.

Andrews, J. Cutler. "The Confederate Press and Public Morale," *Journal of Southern History,* Nov. 1966.

Ash, Stephen V. "A Community at War; Montgomery County, 1861-1865," *Tennessee Historical Quarterly,* Spring 1977.

––––––. "Postwar Recovery: Montgomery County, 1865-1870," *Tennessee Historical Quarterly,* Summer 1977.

Bailey, L.J. "Escape from Fort Donelson," *Confederate Veteran,* Feb. 1915.

Baird, Nancy D. "A Kentucky Physician Examines Memphis," *Tennessee Historical Quarterly,* Summer 1978.

————. "There is No Sunday in the Army; Civil War Letters of Lunsford P. Yandell, 1861–62," *Filson Club Quarterly*, July 1979.

Barnwell, Robert W. "Fort Donelson—By Official Record," *Confederate Veteran*, Jan. 1930.

————. "Gen. John B. Floyd," *Confederate Veteran*, Apr. 1931.

Bean, W.G. "The Valley Campaign of 1862 as Revealed in Letters of Sandie Pendleton," *Virginia Magazine of History and Biography*, July 1970.

Bearss, Edwin C. "A Federal Raid up the Tennessee River," *Alabama Review*, Oct. 1964.

————. "The Fall of Fort Henry, Tennessee," *West Tennessee Historical Society Journal*, 1963.

————. "The Ironclads at Fort Donelson," *Register of Kentucky Historical Society*, Jan., Apr., July 1976.

————. "Unconditional Surrender; The Fall of Fort Donelson," *Tennessee Historical Quarterly*, Mar., June 1962.

————, and Howard P. Nash. "Fort Henry," *Civil War Times Illustrated*, Nov. 1965.

Bedford, H.L. "Fight Between the Batteries and Gunboats at Fort Donelson," *Southern Historical Society Papers*, Jan.–Dec. 1885.

Bell, Patricia. "Gideon Pillow: A Personality Profile," *Civil War Times Illustrated*, Oct. 1967.

Bowman, Larry G., and Jack P. Scroggs, eds. "Diary of a Confederate Soldier, *Military Review*, Feb. 1982.

Boyce, Joseph. "The Evacuation of Nashville," *Confederate Veteran*, Feb. 1920.

Bridges, Roger D. "Eyewitness at Fort Henry," *Ulysses S. Grant Association Newsletter*, Apr. 1970.

Bruce, George F. "The Donelson Campaign," Military Historical Society of Massachusetts, *Campaigns in Kentucky and Tennessee, Papers*, VII, Boston, 1908.

Brumbaugh, Thomas B. "A Letter to Fort Donelson," *Manuscripts*, Winter 1984.

Buttenbach, Walter J., and John L. Holcombe. "Coast Defence in the Civil War; Fort Donelson, Tennessee," *Journal of the United States Artillery*, Mar.–Apr. 1913.

————. "Coast Defence in the Civil War; Fort Henry, Tennessee," *Journal of the United States Artillery*, Jan.–Feb. 1913.

Callender, Eliot. "What A Boy Saw on the Mississippi," Military Order of the Loyal Legion of the United States, Illinois Commandery, *Military Essays and Recollections*, I, Chicago, 1891.

Carpenter, Horace. "Plain Living at Johnson's Island," *Century Magazine*, Mar. 1891.

Castel, Albert. "Black Jack Logan," *Civil War Times Illustrated*, Nov. 1976.

Catton, Bruce. "Glory Road Began in the West," *Civil War History*, Sept. 1960.

Churchill, James O. "Wounded at Fort Donelson," Military Order of the Loyal Legion of the United States, Missouri Commandery, *War Papers and Personal Reminiscences*, I, St. Louis, 1892.

Claiborne, Maria Evans. "A Woman's Memories of the Sixties," *Confederate Veteran*, Feb. 1915.

Confederate Veteran, Editor. "Booklet About Richard Owen Memorial," Oct. 1913.

———. "Career of Gen. Gideon J. Pillow," Nov. 1893.

———. "Col. Richard Owen," May 1907.

———. "Confederate Dead Buried in Indiana," Feb. 1914.

———. "Fort Donelson to Camp Morton," Jan. 1897.

———. "Gen. Albert Sidney Johnston, CSA," Feb. 1926.

———. "Gen. G.C. Wharton," July 1906.

———. "Gen. H. B. Lyon," Dec. 1907.

———. "Gen. Lloyd Tilghman," July 1910.

———. "Gen. Simon Bolivar Buckner," Mar. 1914.

———. "Gen. W.B. Wade's Military Achievements," Jan. 1906.

———. "Last Living Lieutenant General; Visit to the Home of Gen. S.B. Buckner," Feb. 1909.

———. "Memorial Chapel at Fort Donelson, Sept. 1897.

———. "Prisoners on Johnson's Island," Nov. 1907.

———. "Prisoners of War at Camp Douglas," Dec. 1918.

———. "Reason for Richard Owen Memorial," July 1913.

———. "Reminiscences of Camp Beauregard," Nov. 1912.

———. "Secession Spirit (1861) in Illinois," Jan. 1901.

Connelly, Thomas L. "The Johnston Mystique," *Civil War Times Illustrated*, Feb. 1967.

Connolly, James A. "Major James A. Connolly's Letters to his Wife, 1862–1865," *Transactions of the Illinois Historical Society*, 1928.

Cook, W.L., "Furnaces and Forges," *Tennessee Historical Magazine*, Oct. 1925.

Cooling, B. Franklin, "Alabamians at Fort Donelson," *Alabama Historical Quarterly*, Fall 1964.

———, ed. "A Virginian at Fort Donelson," *Tennessee Historical Quarterly*, Summer 1968.

———. "Campaigns for Forts Henry and Donelson," *Conflict*, June 20, 1974.

———. "Fort Donelson National Military Park," *Tennessee Historical Quarterly*, Sept. 1964.

———. "Gee's Fifteenth Arkansas Infantry in the Forts Henry and Donelson Campaign," *Arkansas Historical Quarterly*, Winter 1964.

———. "Lew Wallace and Gideon Pillow: Enigmas and Variations on an American Military Theme," *Lincoln Herald*, Summer 1981.

———. "The Attack on Dover, Tenn." *Civil War Times Illustrated*, Aug. 1963.

———. "The Battle of Dover, February 3, 1863," *Tennessee Historical Quarterly*, June 1963.

———. "The First Nebraska Infantry Regiment and the Battle of Fort Donelson," *Nebraska History*, June 1964.

———. "Virginians and West Virginians at Fort Donelson, February 1962," *West Virginia History*, Jan. 1967.

Cooper, James L. "Service With the Twentieth Tennessee Regiment," *Confederate Veteran*, Jan. 1923.

Coulter, E. Merton. "Commercial Intercourse with the Confederacy in the Mississippi Valley, 1861–1865," *Mississippi Valley Historical Review*, Mar. 1919.

————. "Effects of Secession Upon the Commerce of the Mississippi Valley," *Mississippi Valley Historical Review,* Dec. 1916.

Crabb, Alfred Leland. "Twilight of the Nashville Gods," *Tennessee Historical Quarterly,* Dec. 1956.

Crane, James L. "Grant From Galena," *Civil War Times Illustrated,* July 1979.

Crenshaw, Albert B. "Surprises in the Search for the Midwest," *Washington Post,* Oct. 25, 1980.

Davis, J. Lynch. "Confederates at Johnson's Island," *Confederate Veteran,* Sept. 1928.

Dillon, John F. "The Role of Riverine Warfare in the Civil War," *Naval War College Review,* Mar.–Apr. 1973.

Dinkins, James. "Destroying Yankee Gunboats," *Confederate Veteran,* Sept. 1930.

Dodge, Grenville M. "Personal Recollections of General Grant, and His Campaigns in the West," A. Noel Blakeman, ed. *Personal Recollections of the War of the Rebellion* [Military Order of Loyal Legion of the United States, New York Commandery], III, New York, 1907.

Downer, Edward T. "Johnson's Island," *Civil War History,* June 1962.

Dwight, Henry [Albert Castel, ed.]. "War Album," *Civil War Times Illustrated,* Feb., Apr. 1980.

Eads, James B. "Recollections of Foot and the Gun-Boats," *Century Magazine,* Dec. 1884.

Emerson, John W. "Grant's Life in the West," *Midland Monthly,* June 1898.

Engerud, H. "General Grant, Fort Donelson, and 'Old Brains,'" *Filson Club Historical Quarterly,* July 1965.

Feldman, Albert. "The Strange Case of Simon Bolivar Buckner," *Civil War Times Illustrated,* June 1959.

Fisher, Horace N. "Reminiscences of the Raising of the Original 'Old Glory,' over the Capitol at Nashville, Tenn. on February 27, 1862, *Essex Institute Historical Collections,* Jan. 1911.

Frank, John G. "Adolphus Heiman; Architect and Soldier," *Tennessee Historical Quarterly,* 1946.

Fuller, George T. "Camp Beauregard," *Confederate Veteran,* Apr. 1916.

Fultz, W.S. "War Reminiscences: History of Company D, Eleventh Regiment, Iowa Volunteers," *Wilton* (Iowa) *Review,* Nov. 26, 1885.

George, J.H. "Prisoners at Johnson's Island," *Confederate Veteran,* Oct. 1900.

Gonzales, John E. "Henry Stuart Foote; Confederate Congressman in Exile," *Civil War History,* Dec. 1965.

Greenawalt, John G. "A Charge at Fort Donelson, February 15, 1862," Military Order of the Loyal Legion of the United States, District of Columbia Commandery, *War Papers 41,* Washington, D.C., 1902.

————. "The Capture of Fort Henry and Fort Donelson, February 1862," Military Order of the Loyal Legion of the United States, District of Columbia Commandery, *War Papers 87,* Washington, D.C., 1912.

Griffin, Patrick M. "The Famous Tenth Tennessee," *Confederate Veteran,* Dec. 1905.

Hall, Sidney G. III. "Camp Morton: A Model Prison?" *Indiana Military History Journal,* May 1981.

Harding, T. Sherman. "An Unusual Percussion Cap Accoutrement," *North-South Trader,* Nov.-Dec. 1976.

Harrison, Lowell H. "A Confederate View of Southern Kentucky 1861," *Register of Kentucky Historical Society,* July 1972.

———. "Simon Bolivar Buckner: A Profile," *Civil War Times Illustrated,* Feb. 1978.

Hattaway, Herman, and Archer Jones. "Lincoln as Military Strategist," *Civil War History,* Dec. 1980.

Hemstreet, William. "Little Things About Big Generals," in A. Noel Blakeman, ed. *Personal Recollections of the War of the Rebellion* [Military Order of the Loyal Legion of the United States, New York Commandery], III, New York, 1907.

Herald, A.M. (Mrs.). "Shiloh—The First Great Battle," *Confederate Veteran,* Sept. 1928.

Hess, Earl T. "The Mississippi River and Secession, 1861: The Northwestern Response," *Old Northwest,* Summer 1984.

Hesseltine, William B., and Hazel C. Wolf. "The Cleveland Conference of 1861," *Ohio State Archaeological and Historical Quarterly,* 1947.

Hicks, Henry G. "Fort Donelson," Military Order of the Loyal Legion of the United States, Minnesota Commandery, *Glimpses of the Nations Struggle,* 4th series, St. Paul, 1898.

Hinkle, Joseph A. "The Odyssey of Private Hinkle," *Civil War Times Illustrated,* Dec. 1969.

Holloway, W.R. "Treatment of Prisoners at Camp Morton; A Reply to 'Cold Cheer at Camp Morton,'" *Century Magazine,* Sept. 1891.

Hoobler, James A., ed. "The Civil War Diary of Louisa Brown Pearl," *Tennessee Historical Quarterly,* Fall 1979.

Horn, Stanley. "Nashville During the Civil War," *Tennessee Historical Quarterly,* Mar. 1945.

Horrowitz, Murray M. "That Presidential Grub: Lincoln Versus His Generals," *Lincoln Herald,* Winter 1977.

Huffstodt, James T. "One Who Didn't Come Back; The Story of Colonel Garret Nevius," *Lincoln Herald,* Spring 1980.

Hughes, Robert M. "Facts Not to be Controverted," *Confederate Veteran,* Mar. 1931.

———. "John B. Floyd and His Traducers," *Virginia Magazine of History and Biography,* Oct. 1935.

———. "Vindication of John B. Floyd," *William and Mary Historical Magazine,* Oct. 1925.

———. "Why Fort Donelson Was Surrendered; Gen. John B. Floyd and the Fight at Fort Donelson," *Confederate Veteran,* Aug. 1929.

Hunt, George F. "Fort Donelson Campaign," Military Order of the Loyal Legion of the United States, Illinois Commandery, *Military Essays and Recollections,* IV, Chicago, 1907.

Jacobs, Dillard. "Outfitting the Provisional Army of Tennessee; A Report on New Source Materials," *Tennessee Historical Quarterly*, Fall, 1981.

Johnson, Kenneth, ed. "The Early Civil War in Southern Kentucky as Experienced by Confederate Sympathizers," *Register of the Kentucky Historical Society*, Apr. 1970.

Johnson, Robert Erwin. "John Rodgers: The Quintessential Nineteenth Century Naval Officer," in James C. Bradford, ed. *Captains of the Old Steam Navy*. Annapolis, Md., 1986.

Kaiser, Leo M. "In Dusty Files a Coruscation," *Tennessee Historical Quarterly*, Fall 1976.

Kegley, Tracy M. "Bushrod Rust Johnson: Soldier and Teacher," *Tennessee Historical Quarterly*, Sept. 1948.

Keller, Allan. "Commodore Andrew Hull Foote," *Civil War Times Illustrated*, Dec. 1979.

Kentucky State Historical Society Register, ed. "Civil War Letters of Albert Boult Fall, Gunner for the Confederacy," Apr. 1961.

Krick, Robert I. "Salyer of the 50th Virginia," *Lincoln Herald*, Summer 1979.

Larter, Harry. "Terry's Texas Rangers (8th Texas Cavalry) C.S.A., 1864," *Journal of the Military Collectors and Historians*, Mar. 1954.

Leech, Mrs. Herbert N. "Monument at Fort Donelson," *Confederate Veteran*, Feb. 1915.

[Lewis, Blanche]. "Deaths at Clarksville Tenn. in 1861-62," *Confederate Veteran*, Feb. 1901.

Lewis, Samuel E. "The Florence Nightingale of the South," *Confederate Veteran*, Oct. 1908.

Liddell, St. John R. "Liddell's Record of the Civil War," *Southern Bivouac*, Dec. 1885.

Lindsey, G.W. "The Memphis Branch of the Louisville and Nashville Railroad (1850–1871)," *Railway and Locomotive Historical Society Bulletin*, Oct. 1950.

Long, E.B. "Anna Ella Carroll; Exaggerated Heroine," *Civil War Times Illustrated*, July 1975.

———. "The Paducah Affair: Bloodless Action that Altered the War in the Mississippi Valley," *Register of the Kentucky Historical Society*, Oct. 1972.

Longacre, Edward G. "Congressman Becomes General; The Rise of John A. McClernand." *Civil War Times Illustrated*, Nov. 1982.

Lowry, J.T. "A Fort Donelson Prisoner of War," *Confederate Veteran*, July 1910.

McAuley, John T. "Fort Donelson and its Surrender," Military Order of the Loyal Legion of the United States, Illinois Commandery, *Military Essays and Recollections*, I, Chicago, 1891.

McCord, Franklyn. "J.E. Bailey; A Gentleman of Clarksville," *Tennessee Historical Quarterly*, Sept. 1964.

M'Clung, R.L. "Prisoners on Johnson's Island," *Confederate Veteran*, Nov. 1907.

McDonough, James Lee. "The Commander in Chief and Military Operations in Tennessee," *Lincoln Herald*, Summer 1982.

McKinney, Buford. "A Rooster in Camp and in Prison," *Confederate Veteran*, Aug. 1897.

M'Neilly, J.H. "A Roundabout Way Home," *Confederate Veteran*, June 1920.

———. "Early Confederate Days," *Confederate Veteran*, June 1919.

Magazine of American History, ed. "Letters from Colonel Thomas Newsham," Jan. 1886.

Magdeburg, F.H. "Capture of Fort Donelson," *Military Order of the* Loyal Legion of the United States, Wisconsin Commandery, *War Papers*, III, Milwaukee, 1903.

Maihofer, H.J. "The Partnership," *United States Naval Institute Proceedings*, May 1957.

Merrill, James M. "Captain Andrew Hull Foote and the Civil War in Tennessee Waters," *Tennessee Historical Quarterly*, Spring 1971.

———. "Strategy Makers in the Union Navy Department, 1861–1865," *Mid-America*, Jan. 1962.

———. "Union Shipbuilding on Western Rivers During the Civil War," *Smithsonian Journal of History*, Winter 1968–69.

Metcalf, F. "The Illinois Confederate Company," *Confederate Veteran*, May 1908.

Michael, W.H.C. "The Mississippi Flotilla," Military Order of the Loyal Legion of the United States, Nebraska Commandery, *Civil War Sketches and Incidents*, Omaha, 1902.

Milligan, John D. "Andrew Foote: Zealous Reformer, Administrator, Warrior," in James C. Bradford, ed. *Captains of the Old Steam Navy*. Annapolis, Md., 1986.

———. "From Theory to Application; The Emergence of the American Ironclad War Vessel," *Military Affairs*, July 1984.

Mitchell, E.O. "Johnson's Island; Military Prison for Confederate Prisoners," Military Order of the Loyal Legion of the United States, Ohio Commandery, *Sketches of War History, 1861–1865*, V, Cincinnati, 1903.

Mitchell, John Broadus. "Exchange of Civil War Prisoners," *Confederate Veteran*, July 1911.

Montgomery, J.J. "Daring Deeds of a Confederate Soldier," *Confederate Veteran*, Jan. 1899.

Morgan, George H. "Experiences in the Enemy's Lines," *Confederate Veteran*, May 1909.

Morton, M.B. "General Simon Bolivar Buckner Tells the Story of the Fall of Fort Donelson," *Nashville Banner*, Dec. 11, 1909.

Murphy, James B. "A Confederate Soldier's View of Johnson's Island Prison," *Ohio Historical Quarterly*, Spring 1970.

Nashville Banner, Editor. "The Richard Owen Story," *Confederate Veteran*, Mar. 1913.

Newsome, Robert I., "A Kentucky Yankee's Story of Fort Donelson," *Lincoln Herald*, Fall 1985.

Nye, Wilbur. "Jake Donelson, A 'Cocky' Rebel," *Civil War Times Illustrated*, Apr. 1962.

Parker, Theodore R. "Western Pennsylvania and the Naval War on the Inland Waters, 1861–1865," *Pennsylvania History*, July 1949.

Patrick, James. "The Architecture of Adolphus Heiman," *Tennessee Historical Quarterly*, Summer, Fall 1979.

Patterson, G.G.S. "The Yellow Jackets in the Fourth Mississippi," *Confederate Veteran*, Jan. 1917.

Pickett, William D. "The Bursting of the 'Lady Polk,'" *Confederate Veteran*, June 1904.

Pitkin, William A. "Michael K. Lawler's Ordeal with the Eighteenth Illinois," *Journal of Illinois State Historical Society*, Winter 1965.

Porter, Mrs. Albert Sidney. "After Sixty-Five Years," *Confederate Veteran*, Aug. 1929.

Porter, J.D. "Sketch of Gen. B.R. Johnson," *Confederate Veteran*, Jan. 1906.

Priest, J. Percy. "A Fateful Day in the History of the South," *Nashville Tennessean*, Jan. 29, 1939.

Pullar, Walter S. "Abe Lincoln's Brown Water Navy," *Naval War College Review*, Apr. 1969.

Read, C.W. "Reminiscences of the Confederate States Navy," *Southern Historical Society Papers*, May 1876.

Rich, J.W. "The Color Bearer of the Twelfth Iowa Volunteer Infantry," *Iowa Journal of History and Politics*, 1908.

Richmond Times Dispatch, Editor. "Famous War Prisons and Escapes," *Confederate Veteran*, Nov. 1923.

Riddell, Thomas J. "Movements of the Goochland Light Artillery, Captain John H. Guy," *Southern Historical Society Papers*, 1896.

———. "Western Campaign; Movements of the Goochland Light Artillery — Captain John H. Guy — A Virginian's Experience," *Richmond Dispatch*, Feb. 10, 1895.

Riggs, David F. "Sailors of the *U.S.S. Cairo*; Anatomy of a Gunboat Crew," *Civil War History*, Sept. 1982.

Ripley, Peter. "Prelude to Donelson; Grant's January 1862 March into Kentucky," *Register of the Kentucky Historical Society*, Oct. 1970.

Roberts, John C., and Richard H. Webber. "Gunboats in the River War, 1861–1865," *United States Naval Institute Proceedings*, Mar. 1965.

Rogers, Alice Breene. "Those Camp Chase Letters," *Confederate Veteran*, Nov. 1929.

Roland, Charles P. "Albert Sidney Johnston and the Loss of Forts Henry and Donelson," *Journal of Southern History*, Feb. 1957.

Seaton, John. "The Battle of Belmont," Military Order of the Loyal Legion of the United States, Kansas Commandery, *War Talks in Kansas*. Kansas City, 1906.

Sheppard, E.W. "Defending His Book," *Confederate Veteran*, Feb. 1931.

Simon, John Y. "Grant at Belmont," *Military Affairs*, Dec. 1981.

Simplot, Alexander. "General Grant and the Incident at Dover," *Wisconsin Magazine of History*, Winter 1960–61.

Southern Historical Society Papers, ed. "Treatment of Prisoners During the War Between the States," Mar., Apr. 1876.

Spencer, Selden. "Diary Account of Fort Donelson," *Confederate Veteran*, June 1897.

Steuart, R.D. "How Johnny Got His Gun," *Confederate Veteran*, 1924.

Stiles, John C., comp. "In the Years 1861–1862," *Confederate Veteran*, Apr. 1917.

Stonesifer, Roy P. "Gideon J. Pillow; A Study in Egotism," *Tennessee Historical Quarterly*, Winter 1966.

Sutton, Robert M. "The Illinois Central: Thoroughfare For Freedom," *Civil War History*, Sept. 1961.

Tate, Callis. "Story of Clarksville Tobacco," *Clarksville Leaf-Chronicle*, Aug. 31, 1933.

Taylor, John M. "The Career of Carleton Coffin," *Civil War Times Illustrated*, Sept. 1982.

T.D.J. "Fort Donelson," *Southern Historical Society Papers*, Jan. 1891.

Temple, Wayne C., ed. "Fort Donelson in October 1862," *Lincoln Herald*, Summer 1967.

Terrell, Spot F. [Conyers Reed, ed.], "A Confederate Private at Fort Donelson, 1862," *American Historical Review*, Apr. 1926.

Tillman, J.D. "Col. Tillman Pays Tribute to Gen. Bushrod R. Johnson," *Confederate Veteran*, Jan. 1906.

Treichel, James A. "Lew Wallace at Fort Donelson," *Indiana Magazine of History*, Mar. 1963.

Tunno, M.R. "Col. Richard Owen," *Confederate Veteran*, June 1907.

Vesey, M.L. "Camp Douglas in 1862," *Confederate Veteran*, Aug. 1930.

———. "Why Fort Donelson was Surrendered," *Confederate Veteran*, Oct. 1929.

"W" [Robert W. Wolley]. "General Albert Sidney Johnston," *Southern Bivouac*, Oct. 1886.

Wagner, A.L. "Hasty Intrenchments in the War of Secession," *Journal of the Military Service Institution of the United States*, Feb. 1898.

Walke, Henry A. "Operations of the Western Flotilla," *Century Magazine*, Dec. 1884.

Walker, Peter Franklin. "Building a Tennessee Army; Autumn, 1861," *Tennessee Historical Quarterly*, June 1957.

———. "Command Failure; The Fall of Forts Henry and Donelson," *Tennessee Historical Quarterly*, Dec. 1957.

———. "Holding the Tennessee Line: Winter, 1861–62," *Tennessee Historical Quarterly*, Sept. 1957.

Webster, Rowe. "Respite from Hard Service," *Confederate Veteran*, Sept 1908.

Wegner, Dana. "Commodore William D. Porter," *Civil War Times Illustrated*, July 1972.

Weller, J.C. "Nathan Beford Forrest: An Analysis of Untutored Military Genius," *Tennessee Historical Quarterly*, Sept. 1959.

Whitesell, Hunter. "Military and Naval Activity Between Cairo and Columbus," *Register of the Kentucky Historical Society*, Apr. 1965.

———. "Military Operations in the Jackson Purchase of Kentucky, 1862–1865," *Register of the Kentucky Historical Society*, Apr., July, Oct., 1965.

Whitsett, W.H. "A Year with Forrest," *Confederate Veteran*, Aug. 1917.

Williams, Kenneth P. "The Tennesee River Campaign and Anna Ella Carroll," *Indiana Magazine of History*, Sept. 1950.

Williams, T. Harry. "The Military Leadership of North and South," in David Donald, ed. *Why the North Won the Civil War*. New York, 1962.

Williams, W. "A Reminiscence of Clarksville, Tenn.," *Confederate Veteran*, May 1914.

Wilson, James Grant. "Types and Traditions of the Old Army, II. General Henry Halleck, A Memoir," *Journal of the United Service Institution*, May–June 1905.

UNPUBLISHED THESES AND DISSERTATIONS

Carter, Aleen. "The Civil War Papers of John Bell Hamilton and Thomas Hamilton Williams, " MA thesis, Jacksonville (Ala.) State Univ., 1971.

De Berry, John. "Confederate Tennessee," Ph.D diss. Univ. of Kentucky, 1967.

Short, Opha Mason. "General John B. Floyd in the Civil War," MA thesis, West Virginia Univ., 1947.

Stonesifer, Roy P. "The Forts Henry-Heiman and Fort Donelson Campaigns; A Study of Confederate Command," Ph.D. diss., Pennsylvania State Univ., 1965.

Theissen, Lee Scott. "The Public Career of General Lew Wallace, 1845–1905," Ph.D diss., Univ. of Arizona, 1973.

UNPUBLISHED NATIONAL PARK SERVICE STUDIES — FORT DONELSON NMP FILES

Bearss, Edwin C. "The Battle of Dover," Feb. 1960.

———. "The Dover Hotel, Historic Structures Report, Pt. 1," Dec. 1959.

———. "The Fighting on February 13 —The Assault on Maney's Battery," Aug. 1959.

———. "Fort Donelson Water Batteries, Historic Structures Report, Pt. 2," Jan. 1968.

———. "The Fortifications at Fort Donelson," May 1959.

———. "General Smith's Attack on the Rebel Right," Dec. 1959.

———. "Gunboat Operations at Forts Henry and Donelson," May 1959.

———. "On to Donelson," Aug. 1959.

———, and Russell Jones. "Dover Hotel; Historic Structures Report," June 1972.

Luckett, W.W. "Inscriptions on Union Tablets on the Battlefield," Dec. 1934.

Peterson, Gloria. "Administrative History, Fort Donelson National Military Park, Dover, Tennessee," June 1968.

Philadelphia WSC. "Background Information, The Fort Donelson River Batteries," Dec. 1966.

Riggins, Van L. "A History of Fort Donelson National Military Park," 1957.

Shedd, Charles E. "Museum Prospectus for Fort Donelson National Military Park, Tennessee," 1957.

Index

Forts Henry and Donelson was designed by Dariel Mayer,
composed by Lithocraft, Inc., printed by Thomson-Shore, Inc.,
and bound by John H. Dekker & Sons. The book was set in
Compugraphic Baskerville and printed on 60-lb. Glatfelter.